"Lacan famously sinne of the fundamental concepts of psychoague that every human drive is effectively at 'return to Freud', the drive has now beconholars and researchers in the humanities and social sciences, the of the drive has often coincided with a lack of critical reflection on its status and function in the human mind. In this superb collection of essays, the authors truly advance our knowledge and understanding of the drive, both by teasing out lingering inconsistencies in its conceptualisation and by reaching out beyond its conventional figurations in psychoanalysis. Enlightening and exhilarating, this book puts the drive back in the driving seat and invites its readership to be driven by its drift. Whoever takes on the challenge may not feel safe, but will undoubtedly emerge from the experience with a renewed sense of vitality."

**Dany Nobus**, *psychoanalyst, Brunel University London, UK*

"This collection of powerful, thought-provoking essays—adroitly brought together by Dan Collins and Eve Watson—sheds considerable light on the concept of the drive in psychoanalysis in all its thorny complexity. Leading us at times almost to the point of feeling that Freud's accounts of it are so confused and/or self-contradictory that we might wish to jettison it altogether, the subtle explorations of facets of the drive included here convince us, in the end, of its continued usefulness in psychoanalytic practice, as regards activities as fundamental as breathing, speaking, looking, eating, and defecating. The case studies provided in the later chapters beautifully illustrate the continued clinical relevance of distinguishing between drive and desire. *À lire sans modération!*"

**Bruce Fink**, *Lacanian psychoanalyst*

"This book is a delight. Robust critical intelligences are brought to bear on what has been so often a dry and uninviting topic. Lacan himself has described the problematic form, bristling with questions which characterized the introduction and subsequent elaborations of the drive by Freud and Freudians. Here, however, instead of pious iterations of canonical statements by both Freud and Lacan, these are pulverized, to be on some occasions set aside, on others broken open to reveal new directions for psychoanalytic thinking. These directions are wide-ranging, challenging, and in no way conducive to any kind of summative orthodoxy. Also welcome is the fact that throughout this weighty volume, abstract discussion is balanced by chapters that evoke the immediacy and concreteness of the experiences through which the drives become uniquely encoded for each human subject. Readable and invigorating, this book will be of particular insight to psychoanalysts in search of innovative thinking."

**Olga Cox Cameron**, *psychoanalyst, Dublin*

"Lacan was never very fond of the concept, which is why we urgently needed this book with its wonderful collection of essays that explore the many Lacanian transformations of Freud's drive theory."

**Stijn Vanheule**, *psychoanalyst, Ghent University, Belgium*

# Critical Essays on the Drive

This thorough text provides a complete overview of the drive in Lacanian psychoanalysis.

Divided into four key areas, the book considers clinical, theoretical, historical, and cultural aspects of the drive, with editorial headnotes throughout. The introduction to the collection provides a comprehensive overview of the theory and history of the drive as a concept and is followed by discussion of clinical cases. *Critical Essays on the Drive* then assesses theoretical aspects, with chapters by world-leading Lacanian scholars. The final parts of the book explore the history of drive theory and its impact on art and culture, debunking the notion that the drive is a dormant or defunct concept and considering its applications by artists, academics, and cultural theorists.

*Critical Essays on the Drive* will be essential reading for psychoanalysts, psychologists, psychotherapists, and psychiatrists in practice and in training. It will also be of great interest to academics and scholars of psychoanalytic and Lacanian theory, critical theory, and cultural theory.

**Dan Collins** is the Education and Program Director for Lacan Toronto and the founding member of Affiliated Psychoanalytic Workgroups. He lives and teaches in Buffalo, NY, USA.

**Eve Watson** is a psychoanalyst, clinical supervisor, and academic based in Dublin, Ireland.

# The Lines of the Symbolic in Psychoanalysis Series
Series Editor: Ian Parker
*Manchester Psychoanalytic Matrix*

Psychoanalytic clinical and theoretical work is always embedded in specific linguistic and cultural contexts and carries their traces, traces which this series attends to in its focus on multiple contradictory and antagonistic 'lines of the Symbolic'. This series takes its cue from Lacan's psychoanalytic work on three registers of human experience, the Symbolic, the Imaginary and the Real, and employs this distinctive understanding of cultural, communication and embodiment to link with other traditions of cultural, clinical and theoretical practice beyond the Lacanian symbolic universe. The Lines of the Symbolic in Psychoanalysis Series provides a reflexive reworking of theoretical and practical issues, translating psychoanalytic writing from different contexts, grounding that work in the specific histories and politics that provide the conditions of possibility for its descriptions and interventions to function. The series makes connections between different cultural and disciplinary sites in which psychoanalysis operates, questioning the idea that there could be one single correct reading and application of Lacan. Its authors trace their own path, their own line through the Symbolic, situating psychoanalysis in relation to debates which intersect with Lacanian work, explicating it, extending it and challenging it.

**Lacan and Capitalist Discourse**
Neoliberalism and Ideology
*Jorge Alemán*

**Philosophy After Lacan**
Politics, Science, and Art
*Edited by Alireza Taheri, Chris Vanderwees, and Reza Naderi*

**Critical Essays on the Drive**
Lacanian Theory and Practice
*Edited by Dan Collins and Eve Watson*

For more information about the series, please visit: www.routledge.com/The-Lines-of-the-Symbolic-in-Psychoanalysis-Series/book-series/KARNLOS

# Critical Essays on the Drive

Lacanian Theory and Practice

Edited by Dan Collins
and Eve Watson

LONDON AND NEW YORK

Designed cover image: © Rolf Flor, Picabia, Mon Amour.

First published 2024
by Routledge
4 Park Square, Milton Park, Abingdon, Oxon OX14 4RN

and by Routledge
605 Third Avenue, New York, NY 10158

*Routledge is an imprint of the Taylor & Francis Group, an informa business*

© 2024 selection and editorial matter, Dan Collins and Eve Watson; individual chapters, the contributors

The right of Dan Collins and Eve Watson to be identified as the authors of the editorial material, and of the authors for their individual chapters, has been asserted in accordance with sections 77 and 78 of the Copyright, Designs and Patents Act 1988.

All rights reserved. No part of this book may be reprinted or reproduced or utilised in any form or by any electronic, mechanical, or other means, now known or hereafter invented, including photocopying and recording, or in any information storage or retrieval system, without permission in writing from the publishers.

*Trademark notice*: Product or corporate names may be trademarks or registered trademarks, and are used only for identification and explanation without intent to infringe.

*British Library Cataloguing-in-Publication Data*
A catalogue record for this book is available from the British Library

ISBN: 978-1-032-29250-2 (hbk)
ISBN: 978-1-032-29249-6 (pbk)
ISBN: 978-1-003-30064-9 (ebk)

DOI: 10.4324/9781003300649

Typeset in Times New Roman
by Apex CoVantage, LLC

# Contents

| | |
|---|---:|
| List of Contributors | x |
| Series Preface | xiv |
| Preface | xvi |
| Acknowledgments | xvii |
| A Note on Translation | xix |

**1  Introduction: Debunking the Drive**    1
DAN COLLINS

## PART I
## The History of the Drive    41

**2  On the Very German-ness of Freud's *Trieb***    43
ROLF FLOR

**3  Freud's Third Step: On *Beyond the Pleasure Principle***    53
MARCO ANTONIO COUTINHO JORGE

**4  Freud's *Beyond the Pleasure Principle* and the Death Drive: A Concise Overview**    67
CHRIS VANDERWEES

**5  Ex-Pulsion: On the History of Lay Analysis and Gay Analysts in the United States**    77
ONA NIERENBERG

**6  The Nameless Drive**    90
ALAIN VANIER

## PART II
## The Theory of the Drive — 97

7 Problems With Drive Theory — 99
DARIAN LEADER

8 The Drive as Speech — 116
DAN COLLINS

9 *La Vie en Rose*: On the Drive, Between Life and Death — 129
PAOLA MIELI

10 Agitations and Cuts of Our Dark Ally — 140
HILDA FERNANDEZ-ALVAREZ

11 The Skin as the Source of the Dermic Drive: Modes of Dermic Punctuation in the Containment of Meaning — 153
LEON S. BRENNER

12 The Respiratory Drive: Psychoanalysis's Ground Zero — 165
JAMIESON WEBSTER AND PATRICIA GHEROVICI

13 And Yet It Moves — 177
BICE BENVENUTO

14 The Look and the Drive — 187
DAN COLLINS

15 The Voice and Its Drive — 198
EVE WATSON

16 On Self-Relating Negativity: The Lacanian Death Drive — 208
DEREK HOOK

## PART III
## The Drive in the Clinic, Culture, and Art — 217

17 Beyond the Breach: Drive in the Case of a Traumatic Neurosis — 219
KRISTEN HENNESSY

18 **Where the Image Falls: The Drive of the Living Body in Analysis**   229
KATE BRIGGS

19 **The Liminal and the (Oral) Drive: Neurotic Tensions and Neo-Liberal Recuperations**   238
CAROL OWENS AND STEPHANIE SWALES

20 **The Drive as Montage: Freud, Lacan, Moths, and Poetry**   247
ANNIE G. ROGERS

*Index*   *258*

# Contributors

**Bice Benvenuto** is a psychoanalyst practicing in London, a founding member of the Centre for Freudian Analysis and Research, the Director of *Associazione Dolto* in Rome, and a founder of the Maison Verte-UK in London. For many years she has been a visiting professor at the New School of Social Research (NY) and Florida Atlantic University and has lectured extensively in the UK and abroad on psychoanalysis, feminine sexuality, child analysis, and literature. She is the author of *Concerning the Rites of Psychoanalysis* (Polity); co-author of *The Works of Jacques Lacan: An Introduction* (FAB); and a contributor to several books, including *The Klein-Lacan Dialogues* (Rebus), the introduction to the work of F. Dolto in *Theory and Practice of Child Psychoanalysis* (Karnac), and *Further Notes on the Child* (Karnac), which was nominated for the Gradiva 2018 International Prize, among many other books and articles on psychoanalysis and literature.

**Leon S. Brenner** is a philosopher and psychoanalytic counsellor from Berlin. His work focuses on subjectivity theory and the understanding of the relationship between culture and psychopathology. His book, *The Autistic Subject: On the Threshold of Language*, was published with the Palgrave Lacan Series in 2020. Among his extensive international academic speaking and various publications, Brenner has made numerous appearances in interviews and video publications online. He is a founder of Lacanian Affinities Berlin and Unconscious Berlin and is currently a research fellow at the International Psychoanalytic University Berlin and Ruhr-University Bochum.

**Kate Briggs** is a psychoanalyst practicing in Melbourne and the Mornington Peninsula, Australia. She is a PACFA accredited supervisor, mental health practitioner and clinical registrant and the Vice President of the Lacan Circle of Australia. Kate is Chair of the Professional Standards Committee and a board member of PACFA, deputy Convenor of the Australian College of Counselling and Psychotherapy Educators (ACCAPE), and a member of the Psychotherapy Working Party and leadership group for the College of Aboriginal and Torres Straight Islander Healing Practices (CATSIHP). She has published on sublimation and symptom formation and contributed to *Notes on the Child: A Collection* *of Essays on Contemporary Lacanian Child and Adolescent Clinical Practice.* Her essays on contemporary art have appeared in catalogues and books such as *Radical Revisionism: An Anthology of Writings on Australian Art.*

**Dan Collins** lives and works in Buffalo, NY. He is the Education and Program Director of Lacan Toronto, a guest member of the Toronto Psychoanalytic Society, and an overseas member of the Association for Psychoanalysis and Psychotherapy (APPI) in Ireland. Dan writes, lectures, and publishes extensively on psychoanalysis. He also translates psychoanalytic texts, and he gives an annual seminar at Lacan Toronto.

**Hilda Fernandez-Alvarez** works as a Lacanian psychoanalyst in private practice in Vancouver, Canada. She has vast clinical experience in public and private settings in Mexico and Canada. She has a master's degree in clinical psychology from Universidad Nacional Autonoma de Mexico (UNAM) and a master's degree in literature from the University of British Columbia (UBC). She completed a PhD on the discursive spaces of trauma and healing within a mental health institution. She co-founded Lacan Salon in 2007 and currently serves as its clinical director. She has published various articles on psychotherapy and psychoanalysis.

**Rolf Flor** is a psychoanalyst in private practice. He is also Clinical Director for the Eliot Center in Lynn, where he oversees the training, education, and supervision programs. He has published in numerous journals and edited collections. He has taught at schools in the United States and Germany, most recently clinical practice at Boston College and Lacanian theory at the Massachusetts Institute of Psychoanalysis.

**Patricia Gherovici** is a psychoanalyst and analytic supervisor. She is Co-founder and Director of the Philadelphia Lacan Group and Associate Faculty, Psychoanalytic Studies Minor, University of Pennsylvania (PSYS); an honorary member at IPTAR, the Institute for Psychoanalytic Training and Research in New York City; and a founding member of Das Unbehagen. Her books include *The Puerto Rican Syndrome* (Other Press, 2003), winner of the Gradiva Award and the Boyer Prize; *Please Select Your Gender: From the Invention of Hysteria to the Democratizing of Transgenderism* (Routledge, 2010); and *Transgender Psychoanalysis: A Lacanian Perspective on Sexual Difference* (Routledge, 2017). She has published three edited volumes (with Manya Steinkoler): *Psychoanalysis, Gender, and Sexualities: From Feminism to Trans* (Cambridge University Press, 2022); *Lacan on Madness: Madness, Yes You Can't* (Routledge: 2015); and *Lacan, Psychoanalysis and Comedy* (Cambridge University Press: 2016), and a collection (with Chris Christian) titled *Psychoanalysis in the Barrios: Race, Class, and the Unconscious* (Routledge, 2019).

**Kristen Hennessy** is a psychologist in private practice in rural Pennsylvania where she specializes in the treatment of children and adolescents in the "system."

Her presentations include Lacanian clinical work with children and adolescents with histories of abuse, psychoanalysis and intellectual disability, traumatized masculinities, and the intersections of psychoanalysis and qualitative research. In addition to her work in the USA, she has experience developing and running psychoanalytically informed seminars for orphanage caregivers in Kenya.

**Derek Hook** is an associate professor of psychology and a clinical supervisor at Duquesne University, Pittsburgh, USA, and an extraordinary professor of psychology at the University of Pretoria, South Africa.

**Marco Antonio Coutinho Jorge** is a psychiatrist, psychoanalyst, and director of Corpo Freudiano in Rio de Janeiro. He is also Professor at the University of the State of Rio de Janeiro, member of the Société Internationale d'Histoire de la Psychiatrie et de la Psychanalyse, and author of many books on the foundations of psychoanalysis.

**Darian Leader** is a psychoanalyst working in London and a member of the Centre for Freudian Analysis and Research (CFAR). A major contributor to the field of psychoanalysis, his books include *What Is Madness?*, *The New Black*, *Strictly Bipolar*, *Hands*, *Why Can't We Sleep?*, and *Jouissance*. He has also regularly contributed articles on psychoanalysis to *The Guardian*.

**Paola Mieli** is a psychoanalyst practicing in New York City. She is the President of Après-Coup Psychoanalytic Association (New York), a member of Le Cercle Freudien (Paris), Espace Analytique (Paris), the European Federation of Psychoanalysis (Strasbourg), and an associate researcher at the Centre de Recherches en Psychanalyse, Médicine et Société at the University of Paris VII–Diderot. She is the author of numerous essays on psychoanalysis and on culture, including the book *Figures of Space: Subject, Body, Place* (Agincourt Press, 2017).

**Ona Nierenberg** is a psychoanalyst in New York City, a former senior psychologist and director of HIV Psychological Services at Bellevue Hospital, and clinical instructor in the Department of Psychiatry at NYU Langone Medical Center. She is a member and faculty member of Après-Coup; an overseas member of APPI, Dublin; and an honorary member of Lacan Toronto.

**Carol Owens** works in private practice in Dublin. Her book *Lacanian Psychoanalysis with Babies, Children, and Adolescents* (co-edited with Stephanie Farrelly Quinn) was published in 2017 (Karnac/Routledge) and nominated for the Gradiva award. She has given seminars and talks on her work with at national and international psychoanalytic events. Her most recent book is *Psychoanalysing Ambivalence with Freud and Lacan: On and Off the Couch* (with Stephanie Swales), published in 2020 (Routledge). She is the series editor for *Studying Lacan's Seminars* at Routledge.

**Annie G. Rogers** is Professor Emerita of Psychoanalysis and Clinical Psychology at Hampshire College and has a private practice in Amherst, Massachusetts. She is a supervising and teaching analyst at the Lacanian School of Psychoanalysis in San

Francisco and Vice-President of its board. She is a printmaker and member of Zea Mays Printmaking in Florence, Massachusetts. Formerly a Fulbright Fellow at Trinity College, Dublin, Ireland; Radcliffe and Murray Fellow at Harvard University; Whiting Fellow at Hampshire College; and Erikson Scholar at Austen Riggs, Dr. Rogers is the author of *A Shining Affliction: A Story of Harm and Healing in Psychotherapy* (1995); *The Unsayable: The Hidden Language of Trauma* (2005); and *Incandescent Alphabets: Psychosis and the Enigma of Language* (2016).

**Stephanie Swales** is an assistant professor of psychology at the University of Dallas, USA, a practicing psychoanalyst, a licensed clinical psychologist, and a clinical supervisor located in Dallas, Texas. Her books include *Psychoanalyzing Ambivalence*, co-authored with Carol Owens, and *Perversion: A Lacanian Psychoanalytic Approach to the Subject* (Routledge, 2012). She is the founder of the Dallas/Fort Worth area Lacan Study Group, and serves on the executive boards of the Dallas Postgraduate Program in Psychoanalytic Psychotherapy as well as the Dallas Society for Psychoanalytic Psychology.

**Chris Vanderwees** is a psychoanalyst, registered psychotherapist, and clinical supervisor in Toronto, Canada. His books are *Psychoanalysis and the New Rhetoric: Freud, Burke, Lacan, and Philosophy's Other Scenes*, co-authored with Daniel Adleman (Routledge, 2023), and *Psychoanalysis, Politics, Oppression and Resistance* (Routledge, 2022), co-edited with Kristen Hennessy.

**Alain Vanier** is a psychoanalyst and psychiatrist and an emeritus professor at the Université Paris VII Diderot. He is a vice-president of Espace Analytique and an Après-Coup Psychoanalytic Association faculty member. In English translation, the Other Press has published his monograph *Lacan*.

**Eve Watson** is a psychoanalytic practitioner and lectures on psychoanalysis in undergraduate and postgraduate programs in Dublin, Ireland. She has published several dozen articles and book chapters on psychoanalysis, sexuality, culture, and film. She co-edited the book *Clinical Encounters in Sexuality: Psychoanalytic Practice and Queer Theory* (Punctum, 2017) with Noreen Giffney. She is the editor of *Lacunae, the International Journal for Lacanian Psychoanalysis*, and is course director of (FLi) the Freud Lacan Institute (www.freudlacaninstitute.com). In 2022, she was the Erickson Scholar-in-Residence at the Austen Riggs Centre, Stockbridge, Massachusetts. She is working on edited book collections on Freud's major case studies and James Joyce's writing.

**Jamieson Webster** is a psychoanalyst in private practice in New York City and a cultural commentator, and she has written for *Artforum*, *Apology*, *Cabinet*, *The Guardian*, *Playboy*, *Spike*, and the *New York Times*. She is the author of several books, including *Disorganisation and Sex* (Divided, 2022), *Conversion Disorder: Listening to the Body in Psychoanalysis* (2018), and *The Life and Death of Psychoanalysis* (2011). She also co-wrote, with Simon Critchely, *Stay, Illusion! The Hamlet Doctrine* (2013). She teaches at the New School and supervises doctoral students in clinical psychology at the City University of New York.

# Series Preface

Were that the story of the "drive" could be threaded into a seamless narrative, and that we could be clear what Freud and Lacan made of it. Psychoanalysis would thereby nestle comfortably among the other psy professions and give psychotherapists a moral tale they could tell about what was essentially inside us pushing us along, give psychologists a warrant for their supposed discovery of an underlying motive force for each and every behavior they log in their observations of human behavior, and give psychiatrists a way of linking mind and body all the better to provide remedial medical care of the body that would heal the mind. The "drive" and psychoanalysis itself are, however, otherwise.

What we need, what Lacan argued for, and what this book provides is an approach to the drive that, instead, treats it as a convenient fiction, what Freud himself described as a series of "mythical entities" that may help ground theoretical reflection and clinical practice. And, while thus grounding it, psychoanalytic theorists and clinicians also need to pull away that ground and "deconstruct" what the drive seems to offer us as a unifying force. The drive does not unify at all, and so each contributor to this wide-ranging thoughtful exploration of the drive in Freud's and Lacan's work attends to discontinuity. Discontinuity is at the heart of the drive, and speaks of an irresolvable rift between bodily needs and mental representation.

Indeed, that discontinuity, that rift between body and mind is also a gap between registers of human action, between the real and the symbolic. The phenomenon of the drive—what is presented to us in culture, including often in pervasive misleading popular cultures of psychoanalysis—invites a proliferation of origin stories and teleological narratives about where we have come from and where we are going, whether as a species, in phylogenetic ideological accounts, or as individuals, in ontogenetic fantasies. Some of the conceptual speculations Freud engaged in as he tried to explain in everyday language—always an unavoidable and misleading medium to be sure—did borrow the motif of "ontogeny recapitulating phylogeny", and employed that motif to tell us what was real about the drive. Then we would know what this life was that we are leading and what the significance was of every drive also being a death drive, as if that could be discovered and told to us as good or bad news.

Each of the chapters in this book traces a path around the drive, just as the drive itself traces a path around its object, but does so in order to open up questions about clinical work and social analysis, about the different ways we might speculate about what the role of the real and the symbolic are in our lives. And each chapter also, in very different and necessarily contradictory ways, deconstructs the speculative impulse that discussions of the drive invite; they explore and undo the imaginary lure of speculation as such, the temptation to fill in the gaps with an alluring image of what the drive really is for us.

Psychoanalytic clinical and theoretical work circulates through multiple intersecting antagonistic symbolic universes. This series opens connections between different cultural sites in which Lacanian work has developed in distinctive ways, in forms of work that question the idea that there could be single correct reading and application. The Lines of the Symbolic in Psychoanalysis series provides a reflexive reworking of psychoanalysis that transmits Lacanian writing from around the world, steering a course between the temptations of a metalanguage and imaginary reduction, between the claim to provide a god's eye view of psychoanalysis and the idea that psychoanalysis must everywhere be the same. And the elaboration of psychoanalysis in the symbolic here grounds its theory and practice in the history and politics of the work in a variety of interventions that touch the real.

Ian Parker<br>
Manchester Psychoanalytic Matrix

# Preface

The inspiration for this collection emerged from a conference dedicated to the drive organized by the U.S.-based Lacanian psychoanalytic collective, Affiliated Psychoanalytic Workgroups (APW), in June 2019, in Dublin, Ireland. The quality and vision of the papers presented at the conference focused attention on the necessity of considering anew the drive in light of contemporary Freudian Lacanian psychoanalysis and recent socio-cultural developments. Subsequently a number of research seminars and activities were devised to support research and scholarship for a new collection dedicated to the drive.

In 2021 Dan Collins, education director of Lacan Toronto, ran a teaching seminar dedicated to the drive under the title of *The Discontinuous Drive*. This twelve-lecture series contributed to his introductory chapter, "Introduction: Debunking the Drive." In addition, three of the collection's chapters, "The Voice and Its Drive" (Watson), "The Drive as Speech" (Collins), and "The Look and the Drive" (Collins), were delivered as research presentations to the Psychiatry and Psychology Fellows at the Austen Riggs Centre, Stockbridge, Massachusetts. These three lectures, which went on to constitute three of the collections' chapters, were part of a six-lecture research series in April-June 2022 organised by Eve Watson, the 2022 Erikson Scholar-in-Residence, under the title "The Drive in Psychoanalytic Theory and Practice: Inexorable to Normativization."

In inviting leading psychoanalytic practitioners and thinkers of Freud and Lacan to contribute to this collection, we aim to offer incisive analyses of this uniquely psychoanalytic concept which has been, in our estimation, significantly under-theorized. We think this collection goes towards rectifying this in offering historical, theoretical, clinical, and applied analyses of the role and function of the drive in current psychoanalytic thinking and practice. The twenty chapters in the collection are organized into three sections: The History of the Drive, The Theory of the Drive, and The Drive in the Clinic, Art and Culture. The chapters—varyingly incisive, critical, clinical, and creative—subject the drive to rigorous readings that consider the breadth and implications of Freud's and Lacan's conceptualizations of the drive and its various effects.

Dan Collins and Eve Watson

# Acknowledgments

We extend our grateful appreciation to Susannah Frearson, our editor at Routledge, for her steadfast support of the collection, and to Ian Parker, the series editor of the Routledge Lines in the Symbolic Series within which this volume sits. Ian has been far more than an esteemed colleague and is an important supporter of new and emerging work in the psychoanalytic field, and we owe much to his unfettered encouragement and support.

This collection grew from a conference on the drive organized by Affiliated Psychoanalytic Workgroups (APW) in June 2019 in Dublin. Our thanks to the other conference presenters—Marco Antonio Coutinho Jorge, Francine Danniau, Josh Finkelstein, Hilda Fernandez, Rolf Flor, Christine Gormley, Russell Grigg, Judith Hamilton, Kristen Hennessy, Mike Holohan, Liz Monahan, Raphael Montague, Marlene ffrench Mullen, Gerry Moore, Pauline O'Callaghan, John O'Donoghue, Carol Owens, Stephanie Swales, Kevin Murphy, Gerry Sullivan, Chris Vanderwees, Marie Walshe, and Genevieve Watters—for their excellent papers, which were filled with questions, provocations, critical discussion, and scrupulous analysis. The work was inspiring and deepened our commitment to developing the theme of the drive by inviting those who presented and others to contribute to a volume that would scrupulously explore the drive, develop it as much as possible, and reassert it as a fundamental concept in psychoanalysis praxis.

Special thanks to the Lacan Toronto group and the group's founder Judith Hamilton for supporting a series of twelve teaching seminars given by Dan Collins, facilitating a rigorous reconsideration of Freud's and Lacan's thinking on the drive in dialogue with colleagues and invited guests.

The Austen Riggs Centre in Stockbridge, Massachusetts, is one of the leading psychiatric hospitals in the USA and is a centre of excellence in research in the psychoanalytic field. The Erikson Institute at Austen Riggs (AR) sponsors the Erikson Scholar-in-Residence program. Very special thanks go to Jane Tillman, the Evelyn Stefansson Nef director of the Erikson Institute for Education, Research, and Advocacy, and to Jennifer Stevens, director of training at AR, for their support and enthusiasm for a series of six teaching seminars on the drive with the psychiatry and psychology fellows from April to June 2022 in which Dan and Eve presented their work and scholarship on the drive.

Colleagues in the Association for Psychoanalysis and Psychotherapy in Ireland (APPI), the Freud Lacan institute (FLi), and the editorial board of the journal *Lacunae* provided important support and collegiality, and a few deserve a special mention: Martin Daly, Olga Cox Cameron, Claire Hawkes, Emmet Mallon, Ivan Molloy, Pauline O'Callaghan, Peter O'Connell, Harriet Parsons, Helena Texier, Marie Walshe, and Rob Weatherill. As the editor of *Lacunae, the International Journal for Lacanian Psychoanalysis*, Eve has been inspired by the work of the contributors over the years. Thanks to Darian Leader for mentioning this collection in his book, *Jouissance* (2021). Noreen Giffney's ethic of alliance and collaboration which underpinned the editing partnership with Eve in the book *Clinical Encounters in Sexuality: Psychoanalytic Practice and Queer Theory* (Punctum, 2017) was inspiring. The unfailing and extraordinary support of Deirdre Kiely is deeply appreciated.

To the contributors to this collection, whom we acknowledge as being its very core and *Ziel* and without whom the collection would not have been possible, our abiding and grateful thanks, as well as our esteem and admiration. The eighteen contributors—Bice Benvenuto, Leon S. Brenner, Kate Briggs, Marco Antonio Coutinho Jorge, Hilda Fernandez-Alvarez, Rolf Flor, Patricia Gherovici, Kristen Hennessy, Derek Hook, Darian Leader, Paola Mieli, Ona Nierenberg, Carol Owens, Annie G. Rogers, Stephanie Swales, Chris Vanderwees, Alain Vanier, and Jamieson Webster—are among the top Freudian Lacanian analysts and thinkers in the field today, and the breadth, scope, and depth of their extraordinary scholarship, rigor, and commitment throughout the collection inspired us to keep going on the collection's journey and see it through.

The joy of collaboration is an abiding principle, and it has been ours. Its fruits are borne in the collection. We hope *Critical Essays on the Drive: Lacanian Theory and Practice* provokes further work on this fundamental theme.

Dan Collins and Eve Watson

# A Note on Translation

In the Standard Edition of Sigmund Freud's works, James Strachey famously translated Freud's German word *Trieb* into English as "instinct" rather than "drive." "Instinct" is now generally regarded as a mistranslation. In this collection, wherever it appears in quotations from the Standard Edition or other texts, we have replaced *instinct* with the word *drive* in brackets.

Chapter 1

# Introduction
## Debunking the Drive

*Dan Collins*

---

*In this comprehensive introduction, Dan Collins provides important context for exploring and assessing Freud's and Lacan's conceptualizations of the drive. Crucial in distinguishing psychoanalytic praxis, the drive has not been given the place of prominence it deserves within the field. Freud's development of the drive was a radical intervention into the dominant scientific discourses of the day and his dissatisfaction with this theory and his various revisions are, Collins argues, vital to any consideration of what Lacan later details as the drive's role and effects in the subject's subjectification to speech and language. A thoughtful and careful reader of both Freud and Lacan, Collins evaluates the differences between Freud's and Lacan's drive conceptualizations and demonstrates how Lacan builds upon and rectifies Freud's drive dualism, and importantly shows how Lacan needed and built upon Freud's work to do this. This lengthy introduction is divided into four discrete but interconnected sections which work through in dialectical fashion the various developments and revisions of Freud's thinking, Lacan's elaboration of the drive as a fundamental concept, showcasing the inter-relatedness of Freudian and Lacanian drive theory.*

## 1

The psychoanalytic concept of the drive is difficult to study and to understand. We often most thoroughly grasp difficult concepts through the history of their development, but the history of the drive has not been continuous, and it remains opaque. The Greek Stoics had a theory of drive, which they called *horme*—usually translated as "impulse," sometimes as "drive." Then, during the long Christian period, the drive disappeared as emphasis shifted to the contest of desire and will. Drive only reemerged in the modern age with the German idealists, Fichte especially, who used Freud's term *Trieb* for the concept, but we can't really say that Fichte's philosophical *Trieb* was the forerunner of Freud's psychoanalytic concept. Some would try to forge a continuous history by gathering a collection of synonyms—*horme*, urge, need, impulse, instinct, tendency, desire, will—and claiming that they all, more or less, describe the same inner motivation that we call drive. But what's the good of a collection of names when we don't know the thing that they all identify? It's as pointless as saying that "The Morning Star" and "The Evening Star" are the same thing when the whole night has been cloudy.

DOI: 10.4324/9781003300649-1

If we wish to advance the psychoanalytic theory of the drive as offering the most promise for understanding, we will have to justify it. What does the psychoanalytic theory have going for it? Well, for one thing, Freud. No one has ever offered a more complete account of drive. But even in his theory there are problems. Freud provided not one but at least two—some would say three—theories of the drive. Those who claim three theories would identify them as the early libido theory found in the *Three Essays* of 1905, a revised theory in "[Drives] and Their Vicissitudes" of 1915, and the late theory of Eros and Thanatos that was inaugurated in *Beyond the Pleasure Principle* in 1920. Those who claim only two theories subsume the early libido theory under the 1915 model and see "Drives and Their Vicissitudes" as its culmination. Whether it's three theories or two, Freud gave us a lot to work with, but it can't be said that much has been accomplished with the drive in psychoanalysis since Freud. Only Jacques Lacan took seriously Freud's drive theory and developed it.

Freud's and Lacan's difficult work on the drive, though, has had to contend with the naïve conception of the drive as a biologically determined motivational force. We must overcome that naïve conception if we are to understand the drive psychoanalytically. Freud strove mightily to overcome the common conception even though his biologistic rhetoric often seems to support it, and many orthodox psychoanalysts simply have accepted the naïve account, relying on Freud's biologism to support their views. Witness a typical definition taken from Charles Brenner's *An Elementary Textbook of Psychoanalysis*:

> A drive, then, is a genically determined, psychic constituent which, when operative, produces a state of psychic excitation or, as we often say, of tension. This excitation or tension impels the individual to activity, which is also genically determined in a general way, but which can be considerably altered by individual experience. This activity should lead to something which we can call either a cessation of excitation or tension, or gratification.
>
> (1973, 17)

If we allow for Brenner's outdated use of the term *genic* to mean genetic, what we have here is a comfortably Darwinian picture of drives as adaptations that prompt the individual to act on predetermined instincts. The drive is vaguely described here as a genetically determined mental "constituent," though it is hard to see how genes determine the mind. It produces a state of mental tension, though how it does this is this taken for granted, and impels the individual to "activity" in order to reduce that tension. We might say, "Ah! So even though the drive is genetically determined, it's not quite instinct because the drive manifests itself in the vast variety of individual human behaviors." But no. Brenner claims that the behaviors that reduce drive tension are also genetically determined although he allows that they "can be considerably altered by individual experience."

It should be noted that what's missing from Brenner's account is any mention of mental representation. If we add the theory of representation, though, Brenner's description corresponds well enough to the naïve theory: we have bodily needs, those needs are represented in the mind, and they impel the individual to act in order to satisfy need. Most Freudians and many Lacanians would say that the naïve theory comes close enough to the truth. Freud's own biologistic rhetoric recommends it. What undermines this simple theory, though, it the discontinuity that separates bodily needs and mental representations. In Lacanian terms, this discontinuity opens as a chasm between the real and the symbolic.

The concept and theory of the drive is, in fact, shot through with discontinuities. Historically, the drive has appeared only occasionally in human thought—so much so that we can't be sure that we're speaking of the same concept in different historical epochs. Drive is discontinuous with instinct, though many would be hard pressed to say exactly how. Bodily need, as we just noted, is discontinuous with mental drive. The psychologistic drive is discontinuous with the psychoanalytic drive, psychologists generally being content, as Freud noted, to posit a drive for every observed behavior. The Freudian theory of the drive is discontinuous with itself, Freud having produced two, or three, distinct drive theories. And the Lacanian drive is distinct from the Freudian, Lacan as usual taking pains to remain faithful to the text of Freud while largely rewriting his drive theory. Finally, there's a break in the continuity of Lacan's own drive theory. For the first eleven years of his Seminar, he returns to the drive again and again. This development reaches its crescendo in Seminar 11, *The Four Fundamental Concepts of Psychoanalysis* (1964). After that, Lacan largely falls silent on the drive.

To understand the psychoanalytic theory of the drive, and to promote it as the drive theory that is most coherent and consistent, what's required is a skeptical, debunking reading of the original texts of psychoanalysis on the drive. We need to push hard on psychoanalytic drive theory to find its weak points and to overcome the vestiges of biological determinism. We also need to read carefully those passages in which Lacan himself debunks Freud.

## Discontinuities

We are left then to attempt to define what lies behind the term *drive*, which remains empty until we have filled it with content. Freud rejects out of hand the attempts of psychology to define the drive:

> People assume as many and as various [drives] as they happen to need at the moment—a self-assertive [drive], and imitative [drive], a [drive] of play, a gregarious [drive] and many like them. People take them up, as it were, make each of them do its particular job, and then drop them again. We have always been moved by a suspicion that behind all these little *ad hoc* [drives] there lay concealed something serious and powerful which we should like to approach cautiously.
>
> (1933, 95)

The objection to psychology's approach to the problem of the drive is that it is circular. Psychologists observe a behavior and assume that behind that behavior there lies a drive that accounts for the behavior. Why do children play? We posit a "play drive" or a "drive to play." The drive accounts for the play, and the play gives evidence of the drive. Such an "theory" of drives might be called atomistic. The drive that accounts for the behavior is not susceptible to further division or explanation. It just is. Freud's answer is that instead of investigating a number of "little *ad hoc*" drives, we should investigate drive.

What we've said so far emphasizes the drive's role in motivation. Drives seem to motivate behavior, and in that sense, they are the *cause* of behavior. Be that as it may, the idea of drive as motivation causes some problems. Lacan noted the difficulty in reference to the concept of the unconscious, but the same applies to the drive:

> It is certainly not enough to say that the unconscious is a dynamic concept, since this would be to substitute the most common kind of mystery for a particular mystery—in general, force is used to designate a locus of opacity. It is to the function of cause that I will refer today.
>
> . . . Some of you at least will remain unsatisfied if I simply point out that in his *An attempt to introduce the concept of negative quantities into philosophy*, we can see how closely Kant comes to understanding that gap that the function of cause has always presented to any conceptual apprehension. In that essay, it is more or less stated that cause is a concept that, in the last resort, is unanalysable. . . .
>
> I will go so far as to remark that the problem of cause has always been an embarrassment to philosophers. . . .
>
> Cause is to be distinguished from that which is determinate in the chain, in other words the *law*. . . .
>
> Whenever we speak of cause . . . there is always something anti-conceptual, something indefinite. . . . In short, there is cause only in something that doesn't work.
>
> (1964, 21–22)

Lacan's reasoning is subtle here, but it's easily summarized. When we see a stone fall to the ground, for example, we don't ask for a cause. Rather, we see the uninterrupted functioning of the law of gravity. From the moment it is dropped to the moment that it hits the ground, we see the stone follow a smoothly functioning law. Only if the stone were not to fall and were to hover in the air would we ask for a cause.

When it comes to human actions and behaviors, the situation is more complicated. There's an enduring uncertainty as to whether the drive should be considered, in Lacan's terms, a cause or a law. But Freud's initial tendency is clear. His scientific desire to ground the drive concept empirically and theoretically lead him to posit the drive as law, eventually reducing it to the law of the "reflex arc" (Freud

1915a, 118). Stimulus impinging on the interior of the organism leads to action to discharge stimulus outward. Upon this model he attempts, step by step—in other words continuously—to build his theory of the drive.

This leads to a question: Is the drive a continuity? This question has different meanings at different levels. At the subjective level, is the drive as biological reflex arc really continuous with the properly psychoanalytic drive? Is the psychoanalytic drive the result of just a number of complications that are overlaid on and applied to the reflex arc? The implication would be that humans are simply more complex systems than falling stones.

But what of another continuity, the presumed biological continuity between our physical needs and our mental representations of those needs? Freud wants to ground the drive in this way, even ignoring great discontinuities to do so. In his work, he repeatedly invokes the image of an amoeba or single-celled organism as his starting point for explanations of the drive and then slowly builds up—continuously—to the psychoanalytic drive. But the introduction of representation into this development is a great discontinuity that should cause us to be skeptical.

Lacan, for his part, seems everywhere to emphasize discontinuity. Regarding the history of the drive, Lacan seems to take it for granted that Freud's contribution was inaugural. And as usual, he presents his own ideas as a faithful representation of Freud's. But Lacan rejects a simple continuity between the biological and the mental as early as Seminar 4:

> Matter, this primitive *Stoff*, is so intriguing for the medical mind that people think they are actually saying something when they mindlessly assert that we, like all other doctors, posit and organic reality as the basis of everything that is brought to bear in analysis.
>
> (1956–1957, 25)

What follows is the famous (for Lacanians) image of the hydroelectric power station:

> It's a little as though someone in charge of a hydroelectric power station on a wide river, the Rhine for instance, in an attempt to get you to understand what goes on in the machine, were to start going on about the time when the landscape was still untouched, when the Rhine flowed freely, and so on. However, it is the machine that is the source of the accumulation of energy, in this case electrical energy, which can thereafter be distributed and made available to consumers. . . . Saying that the energy was already there in a virtual state in the flow of the river doesn't get us anywhere. Strictly speaking, it means nothing, because energy only starts to concern us in this instance from the moment it begins to accumulate, and it only accumulates from the moment that machines are set running in a certain way. Yes, they are kept going by a sort of permanent

propulsion that comes from the river's flow, but referring to this flow as though it were the primal organisation of this energy is an idea that can only occur to someone who is utterly foolish.

(Lacan 1956–1957, 25–26)

There may be biological energy, but to understand that biological energy as continuous with the machinery of mental representations is, to use Lacan's word, foolish.

The theory of the drive, then, is shot through with discontinuities that pose a challenge to the naïve understanding. To achieve a psychoanalytic understanding of the drive, we must not attempt to resolve these discontinuities but rather explore and elucidate them.

## 2

### *A Skeptical Reading of "Drives and Their Vicissitudes" . . .*

"[Drives] and Their Vicissitudes" (1915) is rightly regarded as the cornerstone of Freud's drive theory, or at least the summation of his early drive theory before the appearance of the revised drive theory of *Beyond the Pleasure Principle* (1920). We accept it as doctrine. But in truth, few texts of Freud are more susceptible to a skeptical reading. The essay is a dense jumble of ideas with many unsignaled shifts in organization and categorization. In contrast to its reputation for being definitive, the work also seems rather tentative and incomplete. Even at the end of a sympathetic reading, we feel that we're on shaky ground. At the end of a skeptical reading, we might feel that we're no closer to a definitive theory of the drive but rather have more questions than answers.

We should begin our reading with Strachey's editorial preface to the drive essay in the Standard Edition. Strachey's reputation has been badly damaged by the fact that in this very essay, and throughout his translations of Freud, he translated the German word *Trieb* as "instinct." Strachey's mistranslation of *Trieb* is rightly criticized, but his editorial work throughout the Standard Edition is excellent, and in this preface, he engages in a skeptical reading of his own.

After defending his use of *instinct* rather than *drive*, Strachey immediately notes that "There is . . . an ambiguity in Freud's use of the term '*Trieb*'" (Freud 1915a, 111). His complaint is that drive is first defined as "the psychical representative of stimuli originating within the organism and reaching the mind" (Freud 1915a, 112) but that Freud isn't consistent in this usage. Strachey points to a series of passages in which "[drive] is no longer regarded as being the psychical representative of somatic impulses but rather as itself being something non-psychical" (Freud 1915a, 113). For example, one passage quoted by Strachey comes from "The Unconscious": "[A drive] can never become an object of consciousness—only the idea [*Vorstellung*] that represents the [drive] can" (Freud 1915a, 112). This sentence highlights the problem that Strachey indicates. Is the drive the representative, or is it what gets represented?

Strachey is right to raise the question. Freud's definitive definition of drive is that drives are mental representations, psychical entities representing bodily urges, but Freud often lapses into referring to those urges themselves as drives. This problem of vocabulary throws into relief the problem posed by our guiding question: is there a continuity between the somatic and the mental, or are the mental representations that we call drives and the bodily urges that give rise to them radically discontinuous, of two completely different orders? Strachey ultimately backs away from this question and suggests that the problem may be merely verbal and have more to do with "the ambiguity of the concept itself" (Freud 1915a, 113). I would insist upon the intractability of this problem, though, and say that drives can't be both real bodily urges and symbolic mental representations.

To turn to the essay itself, Freud begins by saying that he will approach the drive from a number of different angles. The first of these approaches to the drive is that of physiology, and here he reduces the drive to "stimulus" and the response of the subject to "the pattern of the reflex arc, according to which a stimulus applied to living tissue . . . *from* the outside is discharged by action *to* the outside" (Freud 1915a, 118). Freud says that a drive is like a stimulus in that we can conceive of it as a stimulus applied to the mind. We run into an immediate problem here in that the mind is not a physical entity. If we said instead that the drive is a stimulus to the brain, there would indeed be little distinction between drive and stimulus, but Freud, a neurologist, surprisingly allows for a great confusion to arise between the concepts of mind and brain in his work. When it suits him, the mind is continuous with the brain; at other times, it's discontinuous. Here, though, Freud seems to take the difference into account:

> [W]e are immediately set on our guard against *equating* [drive] and mental stimulus. There are obviously other stimuli to the mind besides those of a [drive] kind, stimuli which behave far more like physiological ones. For example, when a strong light falls on the eye, it is not a [a drive] stimulus; it *is* one, however, when a dryness of the mucous membrane of the pharynx or an irritation of the mucous membrane of the stomach makes itself felt.
>
> (1915a, 118)

This passage is meant to be clarifying, but it only highlights our problem of continuity. A bright light shined on the eye causes a physiological reaction—blinking or a contraction of the iris. This is a reflex, but with some imprecision, Freud calls the bright light a "stimulus to the mind." His contrasting example is a dryness in the throat or an irritation in the stomach, which would lead to thirst and hunger, respectively. These are not just stimuli but drives. The distinction seems to be that the dryness or irritation would have to be represented in the mind *as* hunger and *as* thirst before any action could be taken to relieve them. Thus representation of bodily stimuli in the mind represents an interruption, a break, a discontinuity in the functioning of the reflex arc.

Freud highlights that stimuli act with a single impact, while drives are a "constant" force (1915a, 118–119), and this point has led to much confusion. Freud could mean that a bright light shined in the eye is momentary, while a bodily need is continuous. But the distinction that he means to draw, apparently, is that muscular action can react to an external stimulus immediately, while a bodily need persists. It is a "constant" force (1915a, 118). Exactly how it is that drives persist as a constant force will have to wait for further explication, but what Freud seems to mean is that flight "is of no avail" (1915a, 119). One cannot flee from an internal stimulus.

This point is confirmed when Freud next refers to the task of the nervous system, that of "*mastering stimuli*" (1915a, 120). Drive stimuli present a problem that external stimuli don't: for external stimuli, flight is always an option, while for drive stimuli, it isn't. Freud says that internal stimuli "make far higher demands on the nervous system and cause it to undertake involved and interconnected activities by which the external world is changed as to afford satisfaction of the internal source of stimulation" (Freud 1915a, 120). For Freud, the point here is, I think, that the nervous system must take on a greater and greater complexity to master internal stimuli. And we may think that this settles the question of the "constant force." Internal stimuli are unlike external stimuli in that they remain a constant force *until* they are satisfied. But that understanding would just mean that the reflex arc is more complicated than we at first thought, and the satisfaction of the drive would be just a more complex version of the reflex arc. The reflex arc and the satisfaction of the drive, then, would still be continuous. But no. That's not Freud's point. He says that in order to master internal stimuli, "Above all, they [the internal stimuli] oblige the nervous system to renounce its ideal intention of keeping off stimuli, for they maintain an incessant and unavoidable afflux of stimulation" (Freud 1915a, 120). A constant force, then, really is a constant force, and we must ask what kind of constant force is maintained even after it is satisfied. To add another layer of complexity, we must take notice of the fact that Freud, in this passage, refers to the "nervous system." Thus, he is again creating confusion between mind and brain. In short, his language about a "constant force" and the distinction between internal and external stimuli seems to draw a sharp division between mind and brain. One cannot flee from specifically *mental* stimuli. But then, his language about the "nervous system" having the task of "mastering stimuli" seems to collapse that distinction.

Freud next turns to a biological consideration of the drive. In this section of the essay, Freud elaborates on the famous four elements of the drive. He says, as we've already noted, that the drive

> appears to us as a concept on the frontier between the mental and the somatic, as the psychical representative of the stimuli originating from within the organism and reaching the mind, as a measure of the demand made upon the mind for work in consequence of its connection with the body.
>
> (Freud 1915a, 121–122)

Here, clearly, the drive is a mental representative of a demand. But that raises a question: how is this account biological? Again, if Freud is speaking very imprecisely, and he means that the drive is the representative of bodily needs in the nervous system or the brain, then everything would be part of one system and the distinction between drive and need would collapse. The drive would truly represent just a new level of complexity in the reflex arc. If he means, though, that bodily needs are represented in the mind, as he says, then it's hard to see how he claims to be giving a biological account.

For example, the pressure (*Drang*) of the drive is *not* described as a heightening of physical tension. Instead, Freud says that it is the drive's "amount of force or the measure of the demand for work which it represents" (1915a, 122). The terms "amount" and "measure" are indicators of Freud's scientific leanings and his nineteenth-century belief that everything could be measured, at least potentially. But the term *demand*—which Freud uses repeatedly throughout his writings on the drive—can only sound like a linguistic reference to a term that isn't susceptible to measurement. How big is "demand"? Freud may be using the term more loosely: if one hasn't had any water in three hours one has a certain amount of thirst, a certain bodily demand, but if one hasn't had any water in three days, the demand is much greater. Still, Freud made clear in just the preceding paragraph that the drive is a "demand made upon the mind." It's difficult to see how a reference to the mind is included in a biological analysis.

The aim (*Ziel*) of the drive, Freud says, is satisfaction in "every instance" (1915a, 122), but he adds that "although the ultimate aim of each [drive] remains unchangeable, there may yet be different paths leading to the same ultimate aim" (1915a, 122). Again, we ask how a biological account could admit of different paths. Biological processes are fixed. Only in language, by the process of metaphor, could paths be substitutable for one another.

The object [*Objekt*] of the drive, Freud says, "is the thing in regard to which or through which the [drive] is able to achieve its aim. It is what is most variable about [a drive] and is not originally connected with it" (1915a, 122). Once again, from a biological standpoint, this is absurd. In the animal world, objects are fixed. Animals eat food that is within their food chain. They mate with animals who are in their species according to mating patterns that are fixed. Only in language can one metonymically shift or displace one's interest onto another object. Only in language can one replace the object in a subject-verb-object sentence with a synonym—or even an antonym.

As we've been going through this list, I've been casting doubt on Freud's characterization of the list as "biological." But when we arrive at the fourth element of the drive, the source [*Quelle*], we should be on solid ground. Certainly the organic source of the drive must be the most biological thing about it. But even in his definition of source, Freud complicates the matter. The source of the drive, he says, is "the somatic process which occurs in an organ or part of the body and whose stimulus is represented in mental life by [a drive]" (1915a, 123). In spite of the apparent clarity of Freud's language here, a doubt creeps in: is the source of the drive the organ stimulus, or is it the mental representation of that stimulus? In psychoanalysis, we are far more familiar with the assumption that the source is the mental representation. To put it bluntly, if someone is behaving in an anal manner, we don't assume that their anus is acting up.

This observation leads to another. In psychoanalysis, we're accustomed to listing the organs that serve as the source of drives: they are oral, anal, and genital organs, but Freud makes no such restriction, even in the realm of sexual drives. He says that the sexual drives "are numerous [and] emanate from a great variety of organic sources" (Freud 1915a, 125). This raises a question: if the sexual drives can arise from any body part in a search for organ-pleasure, then how do drives become specifically sexual *except* through mental representation? Freud seems to allude to this question in the same paragraph that I've just quoted: "Although [drives] are wholly determined by their origin in a somatic source, in mental life we know them only by their aims" (1915a, 123). Even though he says that drives are "wholly determined" by their source—whatever that means—Freud suggests that ultimately, the source of a drive doesn't matter. He wonders what may account for the different qualities of drives and posits that "the [drives] are all qualitatively alike" (Freud 1915a, 123) and are only *quantitatively* different. He then suggests that "What distinguishes from one another the mental effects produced by the various [drives] may be traced to the difference in their sources" (Freud 1915a, 123). This would indeed be a biological distinction between drives, but not, as he has just made clear, qualitatively. The difference in the qualities of the drives can only come about in mental representation. The energy of the drive at any bodily drive source is qualitatively the same and only quantitatively different. In a surprising passage from the *Three Essays*, Freud even suggests to the reader that we should "drop the figurative expression that we have so long adopted in speaking of 'sources' of sexual excitation" (1905, 205). In the end, then, the very idea of the "source" of the drive may be a metaphor, just a figure of speech. As Freud says, "we know them only by their aims." This is a striking admission on Freud's part that the source of the drive, supposedly its most bodily, organic component, is merely a figurative expression.

We've gotten about halfway through the task of debunking the essay "Drives and Their Vicissitudes." We have been trying to push hard against the essay to see where its arguments give way or even break down. Our assumption is that Freud's own approach to the drive was mired in a nineteenth-century scientism and a belief that the properly psychoanalytic drive could be made continuous with bodily needs.

We have yet to consider the third of the three approaches that Freud takes up to consider the drive, the approach "from the direction of consciousness," which Freud doesn't take up because it involves "insuperable difficulties" (1915a, 125). Freud says, "Since a study of [the life of the drive] from the direction of consciousness presents almost insuperable difficulties, the principal source of our knowledge remains the psycho-analytic investigation of mental disturbances" (1915a, 125). Thus, the first two approaches to the drive are the physiological and biological, and the third is the psychoanalytic.

We've already seen a number of lists in the essay, and in the second half, lists proliferate. Freud's method of analysis here is rather clumsy since his lists—as we've seen—don't always correspond with each other or develop a unified conception of the drive. The first list that we encounter in the second half of the essay is a list of the various vicissitudes that a drive can undergo:

Reversal into its opposite.
Turning around upon the subject's own self.
Repression.
Sublimation.

(Freud 1915a, 126)

Freud tells us immediately that he won't address sublimation in this essay, and sublimation is presumed to be the topic of one of the "lost" metapsychological essays—we actually don't know if Freud ever wrote it. Repression will be the topic of the next of the metapsychological papers, and so it too isn't addressed here. That leaves two vicissitudes of a drive, namely reversal into its opposite and turning around upon the subject's own self.

There are two points to make here. First, Freud tells us that "we may . . . regard these vicissitudes as modes of *defence* against the [drives]" (1915a, 127). We can rightly ask whether this language is precise enough. Are vicissitudes a defense against the drive, or are they a response to defense? Of the vicissitudes that are listed, repression seems to be most obviously a defense against the drive, but the others may strike us as the path that a drive takes once it has encountered resistance, in other words, as a renewed effort to seek satisfaction. Broadly speaking, then, vicissitudes are ways for the drive to continue to seek satisfaction *in spite of* defense. And even repression may be considered such a path if it is considered as a way for the drive to persist in an active form in the unconscious.

Second, we may ask if this list is meant to represent a *complete* list of the vicissitudes of the drive. It is clear that Freud himself doesn't think so. For example, in his paper on repression, we come across the following passage:

In our discussion so far we have dealt with the repression of a [drive's] representative, and by the latter we have understood an idea or group of ideas which is cathected with a definite quota of psychical energy (libido or interest) coming from a [drive]. Clinical observation now obliges us to divide up what we have hitherto regarded as a single entity; for it shows us that besides the idea, some other element representing the [drive] has to be taken into account, and that this other element undergoes vicissitudes of repression which may be quite different from those undergone by the idea. For this other element of the psychical representative the term *quota of affect* has been generally adopted. It corresponds to the [drive] in so far as the latter has become detached from the idea and finds expression, proportionate to its quantity, in processes which are sensed as affects. From this point on, in describing a case of repression, we shall have to follow up separately what, as the result of repression, becomes of the idea, and what becomes of the [drive] energy linked to it.

... The *quantitative* factor of the [drive's] representative has three possible vicissitudes, as we can see from a cursory survey of the observations made by psycho-analysis: either the [drive] is altogether suppressed, so that no trace of it is found, or it appears as an affect which is in some way or other qualitatively coloured, or it is changed into anxiety. The two latter possibilities set us the task of taking into account, as a further vicissitude [of the drive], the *transformation* into *affects*, and especially into *anxiety*, of the psychical energies of [drives].

(Freud 1915b, 152–153)

To the list of vicissitudes, Freud seems willing to add suppression, transformation into affect, and transformation into anxiety. And with this list he draws a sharp distinction between vicissitudes of the *mental representatives* of the drive and vicissitudes of the *energy* related to the drive.

In any case, Freud tells us that in "Drives and Their Vicissitudes," he will deal with only two of the vicissitudes of the drive, reversal into its opposite and turning around on the subject's own self. Immediately, though, lists begin to proliferate again: "reversal of a [drive] into its opposite resolves on close examination into two different processes: a change from activity to passivity, and a reversal of its content" (Freud 1915a, 127). Things immediately become complicated. Freud tells us on this same page that "Reversal of *content* is found in the single instance of transformation of love into hate." But later in the essay, we'll find that this "single instance" divides into a list of three different kinds of reversal of content. Further, we'll find that the reversal of a drive from active to passive also involves a change of object: the subject him- or herself becomes the object. Thus in this form, the reversal of a drive, one vicissitude, "converge[s] and coincide[s]" (Freud 1915a, 127) with another, the turning around upon the subject's self. The list collapses.

To give examples of the process of the change from activity to passivity, Freud chooses two pairs of opposites, sadism/masochism and scopophilia/exhibitionism. Freud represents the process of reversal in sadism/masochism in three stages:

(a) Sadism consists in the exercise of violence or power upon some other person as object.
(b) This object is given up and replaced by the subject's self. With the turning round upon the self the change from an active to a passive [drive] aim is also effected.
(c) An extraneous person is once more sought as object; this person, in consequence of the alteration which has taken place in the [drive's] aim, has to take over the role of the subject.

(1915a, 127)

Strachey notes in a footnote that it's odd to find the "extraneous person" referred to as the "subject," But by "subject," Freud seems to mean here not the individual whose drives are undergoing vicissitudes but rather "agent" or "active party." We should note that the transformation is grammatical.

For the pair scopophilia/exhibitionism, Freud gives a similar set of transformations:

> (a) Looking as an *activity* directed towards an extraneous object. (b) Giving up of the object and turning of the scopophilic drive towards a part of the subject's own body; with this, transformation to passivity and setting up of a new aim—that of being looked at. (c) Introduction of a new subject to whom one displays oneself in order to be looked at by him.
>
> (1915a, 129)

The parallel between sadism/masochism and scopophilia/exhibitionism seems absolute, but Freud adds a complication. In scopophilia/exhibitionism, there's an auto-erotic phase prior to phase (a): "For the beginning of its activity the scopophilic [drive] is auto-erotic: it has indeed an object, but that object is part of the subject's own body" (1915a, 130). This early phase of the scopophilic [drive] gives rise to two equivalent states of phase (a), which lead to active scopophilia or to exhibitionism. Freud illustrates this with a diagram:

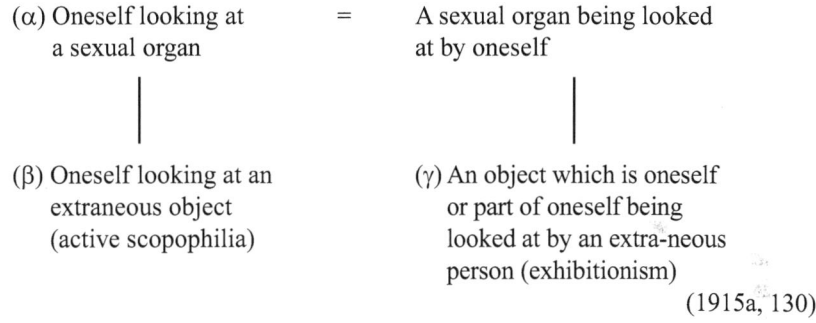

(α) Oneself looking at      =      A sexual organ being looked
    a sexual organ                 at by oneself

(β) Oneself looking at an          (γ) An object which is oneself
    extraneous object                  or part of oneself being
    (active scopophilia)               looked at by an extra-neous
                                       person (exhibitionism)

(1915a, 130)

What's of note here is the comment that Freud makes on the preliminary stage of scopophilia/exhibitionism that exists prior to (a):

> A preliminary stage of this kind is absent in sadism, which from the outset is directed upon an extraneous object, although it might not be altogether unreasonable to construct such a stage out of the child's efforts to gain control over his own limbs.
>
> (1915a, 130)

What Freud postulates here is a possible early stage of sadism in which a motor action of mastery is exerted by the child to gain control over its body. This stage coincides with the early stage of scopophilia, the drive to look.

Freud next turns to the second form of the reversal of a drive into its opposite; first there was the change from activity to passivity, and now he wants to consider the change in content. Freud had promised us that out of the four vicissitudes of the drive that he lists, he would consider two, the reversal of a drive into its opposite and the turning around on the subject's own self, but the analysis of the reversal of a drive into its opposite turned out to involve the change from activity to passivity, which is really the turning around upon the subject. Thus the vicissitude of turning around upon the subject is subsumed under the reversal into the opposite, and so it could be said that in this essay on "Drives and Their Vicissitudes," Freud really only considers one vicissitude—admittedly with all its subsections and dependents.

In considering the change in content, which is the second of the two forms of a reversal of a drive into its opposite, Freud again notes that it "is observed in a single instance only—the transformation of *love* into *hate*" (1915a, 133). But immediately, Freud allows that this transformation subdivides into a list of three:

> Loving admits not merely of one, but of three opposites. In addition to the antithesis 'loving-hating', there is the other of 'loving-being loved'; and, in addition to these, loving and hating taken together are the opposite of the condition of unconcern or indifference.
>
> (1915a, 133)

I would refer to these three opposites as semantic, grammatical, and logical. Hate is the opposite of love in terms of its semantic content: hate is the antonym of love. "Loving and being loved" is a grammatical distinction between the active and the passive forms of the verb. And loving as opposed to indifference is a logical distinction between love and not-love.

But Freud does not adopt this tripartite distinction of semantic, grammatical, and logical opposition. Instead, he schematizes these oppositions on the three great polarities that govern mental life: "Subject (ego)-Object (external world), Pleasure-unpleasure, and Active-Passive" (Freud 1915a, 133). By adopting these three polarities instead of semantic, grammatical, and logical opposition as his guide, we can say that Freud is choosing to consider the drives as real rather than as symbolic. We could ask Freud Lacan's question from Seminar 11, "*have you ever, for a single moment, the feeling that you are handling the clay of instinct?*" (1964, 126). Freud is adopting, we can say, an ontological view. Apparently, he *does* believe that he is handling the clay of instinct.

The first indication of this is that the opposition of loving/indifference allows the subject to distinguish between ego and the external world. In the original autoerotic state of the subject, it has no need of the external world and is indifferent to it. In short, the external world does not exist. But the drives of self-preservation require the subject to seek objects of need. Thus the distinction between internal and external is established. Next, those objects that provide pleasure are taken into the ego by introjection and those that are unpleasurable are expelled by a process of projection (Freud 1915a, 136). Freud summarizes:

> At the very beginning, it seems, the external world, objects, and what is hated are identical. If later on an object turns out to be a source of pleasure, it is loved,

but it is also incorporated into the ego; so that for the purified pleasure-ego once again objects coincide with what is extraneous and hated.

Now, however, we may note that just as the pair of opposites love—indifference reflects the polarity ego—external world, so the second antithesis love-hate reproduces the polarity pleasure-unpleasure, which is linked to the first polarity.

(1915a, 136)

It is because the subject "has" drives that he or she establishes the external world and moves beyond a state of indifferent solipsism. Then, because some of the objects in that world bring pleasure and others don't, the subject loves some and hates others. We can say, then, that it is the drive that creates the external world and the objects in it as real. The establishment of the external world by the necessity of the drive is the first metaphysics. The distinction between loved and hated objects is the first ethics. The third antithesis of loving-being loved Freud summarizes quickly. He says that it corresponds to the polarity of activity/passivity, which amounts to the subject recognizing that it is also an object in the world. This is the first politics.

The final pages of this essay, which are taken up with these arguments, include far-reaching speculations that link to everything else in the essay, but we should remember that in a text that announces four vicissitudes of the drive, we are only looking at one, the reversal of the drive into its opposite, and only in one of its forms, the reversal of content, which, Freud claims, appears only under one type, the reversal of love into hate. A summary of Freud's conclusions can be presented in a chart:

| Polarity of Mental Life | Reversal of Content |
| --- | --- |
| Subject/Object (= ego/external world) | love/indifference |
| Pleasure/Unpleasure | loving/hating |
| Active/Passive | loving/being loved |

Freud concludes the essay as follows:

We may sum up by saying that the essential feature in the vicissitudes undergone by [drives] lies in *the subjection of the [drive] impulses to the influences of the three great polarities that dominate mental life*. Of these three polarities we might describe that of activity-passivity as the *biological*, that of ego-external world as the *real*, and finally that of pleasure-unpleasure as the *economic* polarity.

(1915a, 140)

Freud's final list, in this essay of lists, is a strange one. It is difficult to see how biology, the real, and the economics of drive energy form any kind of coherent list at all. The three items seem radically heterogeneous and discontinuous. And yet Freud takes this list to be the summation of his theory of the drive in 1915. An attempt at clarity is required. And, as I suggested, we'll have to return to the unexploited thread of the essay, namely that all the examples that Freud offers in giving his account of the drive that rely, though he doesn't seem to notice it, on linguistics.

## . . . and of *Beyond the Pleasure Principle*

We've been adopting a skeptical reading of Freud, as we've been attempting to see how well his drive theory holds up to close scrutiny. In doing so, we're only following Freud himself, who admits that the theory of the drive is the most uncertain part of psychoanalysis. Nowhere is Freud's own skepticism more on display than in *Beyond the Pleasure Principle* (1920). The book is shot through with doubts and uncertainties.

Freud's aim in this work is to confront a basic problem. He announces in his first sentence that "In the theory of psychoanalysis we have no hesitation in assuming that the course taken by mental events is automatically regulated by the pleasure principle" (1920, 7). This is true. The theory of psychoanalysis had been built up on the idea of mental conflict and the corresponding idea that the mind is regulated by a mechanism of reducing mental conflict. This idea was the cornerstone of psychoanalytic theory, and we have no way today of experiencing how shocking it must have been in 1920 to learn that Freud had just published a book suggesting that there was something "beyond" that theory.

According to the theory, "unpleasure corresponds to an *increase* in the quantity of excitation and pleasure to a *diminution*" (Freud 1920, 8). But Freud suggests that the reduction of tension and conflict that corresponds to pleasure may not be as primary as was supposed. He suggests that "there exists in the mind a strong *tendency* towards the pleasure principle, but that that tendency is opposed by certain other forces" (1920, 9). He then asks the question of "what circumstances are able to prevent the pleasure principle from being carried into effect" (1920, 10).

The first answer is not necessarily shocking. The pleasure principle is augmented by the reality principle, which "does not abandon the intention of ultimately obtaining pleasure, but . . . nevertheless demands and carries into effect the postponement of satisfaction . . . and the temporary toleration of unpleasure as a step on the long indirect road to pleasure" (Freud 1920, 10). This much would have been familiar to readers in 1920, for it had long been recognized that the reality principle was really just an extension of the pleasure principle. The second answer is no more shocking that the first. Repression demands that some drives or partial drives are "cut off . . . from the possibility of satisfaction" (Freud 1920, 11). When these drives succeed in "struggling through, by roundabout paths, to a direct or to a substitutive satisfaction" (Freud 1920, 11), that satisfaction, which is a success for the drives, "is felt by the ego as unpleasure" (Freud 1920, 11). This too is familiar.

But in the second chapter, Freud raises a more serious challenge to the pleasure principle: traumatic neurosis, which we would today place under the heading of post-traumatic stress disorder. It is a stubborn fact that in the traumatic neuroses, the sufferer (mentally) relives the trauma over and over again. Freud calls the tendency to repetition "the compulsion to repeat" (Freud 1920, 20). And the reader might be tempted to think that the compulsion to repeat arises only from trauma, either the external trauma of some great accident that the subject was unprepared for (in a traumatic neurosis) or the internal trauma of constant mental bombardment by repressed sexual impulses (in a transference neurosis). In other words, the compulsion to repeat might arise solely in pathogenic processes arising from the attempt to master unruly stimuli (Freud 1920, 16–17). In a traumatic neurosis, an external trauma that had crashed through mental barriers would have to be eventually subdued, leading to a reduction of tension. And in a transference neurosis, the traumatic repressed sexual drives are actually seeking satisfaction and have come in conflict with the ego. They are only experienced as unpleasure because "unpleasure for one system [is] simultaneously satisfaction for the other" (Freud 1920, 20). So it might be that the compulsion to repeat is always a means, albeit a pathogenic one, of eventually obtaining pleasure. But Freud says no: "the compulsion to repeat also recalls from the past experiences which include no possibility of pleasure, and which can never, even long ago, have brought satisfaction even to [drive] impulses which have since been repressed" (1920, 20).

Freud goes on to give a list of such neurotic experiences that "include no possibility of pleasure": "Loss of love," the failure of the child's "sexual researches," the "disappointment" of the child's attachment to "the parent of the opposite sex," "the birth of a new baby," the child's "own attempt to make a baby," the "lessening amount of affection he receives, [and the] increasing demands of education" (1920, 20–21). Freud says that "None of these things can have produced pleasure in the past" (1920, 21), and yet they are constantly repeated and reenacted in new ways.

Lest we still think that the compulsion to repeat is only a neurotic mechanism, Freud goes on to detail how it appears in normal people as well. This list is actually much more convincing. In it we see the patterns of repetition followed by those who lead luckless, unsuccessful lives:

> Thus we have come across people all of whose human relationships have the same outcome: such as the benefactor who is abandoned in anger after a time by each of his *protégés*, however much they may otherwise differ from one another, and who thus seems doomed to taste all the bitterness of ingratitude; or the man whose friendships all end in betrayal by his friend; or the man who time after time in the course of his life raises someone else into a position of great private or public authority and then, after a certain interval, himself upsets that authority and replaces him by a new one; or, again, the lover each of whose love affairs with a woman passes through the same phases and reaches the same conclusion. This 'perpetual recurrence of the same thing' causes us no astonishment when it relates to *active* behaviour on the part of the person concerned and when we can discern in him an essential character-trait which always remains the same and which is compelled to find expression in a repetition of the same experiences. We are much more impressed by cases where the subject appears to have a *passive* experience, over which he has no influence, but in which he meets with a

repetition of the same fatality. There is the case, for instance, of the woman who married three successive husbands each of whom fell ill soon afterwards and had to be nursed by her on their death-beds.

(Freud 1920, 22)

This list is worth quoting at such length for its rhetorical power. By it we're convinced that people lead fated lives, that far from seeking new and varied pleasures, human beings are condemned to repeat their dissatisfactions. Freud draws the conclusion: "there really does exist in the mind a compulsion to repeat which over-rides the pleasure principle" (1920, 22). And so we have arrived at the *beyond* of the pleasure principle.

Would that the essay ended there! Freud has successfully argued that prior to the pleasure principle, there is an earlier function of the mind, to master stimuli. Freud begins the next chapter, Chapter 4, with an admission: "What follows is speculation, often far-fetched speculation" (1920, 24). Here's where, rhetorically at least, the wheels fall off. Everything that we remember as bewildering in *Beyond the Pleasure Principle*—single-celled organisms struggling in a hostile world, Weismann's germ plasm theory, bound and unbound cathexis, Eros and Thanatos—all of it occurs in the final four chapters of the book. But we must follow Freud because we've not yet addressed the fact that in *Beyond the Pleasure Principle* Freud introduces a new theory of the drive.

As we launch into these final chapters, Freud begins to bring back vocabulary, arguments, and problems that are familiar to us from "Drives and Their Vicissitudes." And there are some rectifications. In the "Drives" essay, Freud's first approach there was to assimilate the drive to the reflex arc, and we were dissatisfied with that comparison. Here Freud says that the "violent phenomena of [motor] discharge" that constitute a response to pain "occur in a reflex manner—that is, they follow without the intervention of the mental apparatus" (1920, 30). Any suggestion, then, that the drive is continuous with the functioning of the reflex arc is overthrown, for the drive is a mental phenomenon, and the reflex arc is not. Other passages present new formulations that clarify and shed light on the "Drives" essay. In one, Freud considers how the mind handles drive impulses:

Since all [drive] impulses have the unconscious systems as their point of impact, it is hardly an innovation to say that they obey the primary process. Again it is easy to identify the primary psychical process with Breuer's freely mobile cathexis and the secondary process with changes in his bound or tonic cathexis. If so, it would be the task of the higher strata of the mental apparatus to bind the [drive] excitation reaching the primary process. A failure to effect this binding would provoke a disturbance analogous to a traumatic neurosis; and only after the binding has been accomplished would it be possible for the dominance of the pleasure principle (and of its modification, the reality principle) to proceed unhindered.

(1920, 34–35)

In "Drives and Their Vicissitudes," Freud discusses the pathogenic effects of drives insofar as they are functioning under the pleasure principle. According to this account, he clarifies that drives, as long as they are unbound, are traumatic. Freud also repeats his old definition of drives: "The most abundant sources of . . . internal excitation are what are described as the organism's '[drives]'—the representatives of all the forces originating in the interior of the body and transmitted to the mental apparatus" (1920, 34). We seem to be on solid ground.

But for all that is familiar in *Beyond the Pleasure Principle*, there's much more that is shocking and new. Freud, in italics, gives a new definition of the drive: "*It seems, then, that [a drive] is an urge inherent in organic life to restore an earlier state of things*" (1920, 36). This is the famous "conservatism of the drives," and it's Freud's answer to his own question, "But how is the predicate of being '[of the drive]' related to the compulsion to repeat?" (1920, 36). Freud perhaps too quickly assimilates the restoration of an earlier state, that of inanimate matter, to the compulsion to repeat. What they have in common are that both are attempts at return. Freud admits that "The hypothesis of self-preservative [drives], such as we attribute to all living beings stands in marked opposition to the idea that [the life of the drive] as a whole serves to bring about death" (1920, 39). But he quickly answers his own objection: the drives of self-preservation "are component [drives] whose function is to assure that the organism shall follow its own path to death" (Freud 1920, 39).

We should pause here and consider this function of the organism's "follow[ing] its own path to death." In Freud's rhetoric, there's something primal and almost supernatural about this function. We should try to demythologize it. We might imagine from Freud's description a creature fated to die at some point in the future at a certain time and place. We imagine that the creature's eventual death is "written" in some eternal book. But this is not quite what Freud says; he says the organism must "follow its own path to death." That image is forward looking. It does not provide an image of looking backward from the appointed time of death that the creature must reach. So let us imagine the organism on that path, the path of life. It must avoid all dangers and obstacles. It avoids pain. It avoids conflict. What is this avoidance but advance, advance along the path, to reach an end? Most species are prey for other species, and a successful member of a species avoids all predators and reaches its own end. To put it simply, the path to death is simply life with as little conflict as possible. We are familiar with this pattern in common neurotics who avoid relationships, success, and even satisfaction if it means that they can get through the next day, the next hour. They'd rather fantasize a relationship than risk rejection. They'd rather imagine an argument than risk conflict. They'd rather get one step further down their path than risk an increase in tension. The path to death isn't a path towards some mystical appointment. It's surviving.

So Freud has succeeded in establishing the death drive as the primal or primordial drive. But there's a danger here. Remember, Freud's entire metapsychology arises as an answer to Jung. When psychoanalysis began to consider the narcissistic neuroses, it had to allow that the mechanism at work was the reversion of object-libido, which up to this point was the only kind of libido, back upon the ego itself. In other words, the ego itself can be an object that's invested with libido, and so in addition to object-libido, there is ego-libido. This discovery leads to the collapse of the distinction between ego-drives and sexual-drives, between self-preservation and sexuality. Even Freud had to admit that the self-preservative drives depend on a kind of self-love, ego-libido. This discovery also led Jung to posit that there is only one libido, reduced to psychical energy. Freud, whose whole theory depended on mental conflict, needed to maintain a dualism of the drives, but for many years, every time he tried to argue against Jung, he had to admit that he had no strong counterargument.

How does Freud reestablish dualism? He has to refer to single-celled organisms, germ plasm, literally spermatozoa and ova. Germ cells exist within us but have a life independent of us. Human beings are simply germ cells' way of reproducing more germ cells. They are potentially immortal. This leads Freud to posit another drive beside the death drive:

> The [drives] which watch over the destinies of these elementary organisms that survive the whole individual, which provide them with a safe shelter while they are defenceless against the stimuli of the external world, which bring about their meeting with other germ-cells, and so on—these constitute the group of the sexual [drives]. They are conservative in the same sense as the other [drives] in that they bring back earlier states of living substance; but they are conservative to a higher degree in that they are peculiarly resistant to external influences; and they are conservative too in another sense in that they preserve life itself for a comparatively long period. They are the true life [drives].
>
> (1920, 40)

It must be said that Eros is posited on a less secure footing than Thanatos. Freud appeals to poets and philosophers and speculative biology to support his new theory and eventually asks tentatively, "May we venture to recognize in these two directions taken by the vital processes the activity of our two [drive] impulses, the life [drives] and the death [drives]?" (1920, 49).

Freud now rehearses the old argument. If the self-preservative drives are now the result of a narcissistic investment of Eros (instead of ego-libido as before), hasn't the drive theory collapsed once again into monism? (Freud 1920, 52) But he's able to declare his new theory more successful than the old one because the conflict has shifted:

> Our views have from the very first been *dualistic*, and to-day they are even more definitely dualistic than before—now that we describe the opposition as being not between ego-[drives] and sexual [drives] but between life [drives] and death [drives].
>
> (Freud 1920, 53)

We've completed a sketch of Freud's new theory, and although he claims that it's merely speculative, he of course goes on to adopt it in his subsequent writings on psychoanalysis, and in fact on culture. The death drive plays a major role, for example, in *Civilization and Its Discontents* (1930). There are problems that remain. For example, if the death drive is primordially a drive for each organism to return to a state of inanimate matter, and in its own time, is it necessarily the source of aggressiveness towards others and a destructive drive? Is "to die" necessarily related to "to kill"? No matter the difficulties of the theory, though, Freud seems content that he has finally solved the threat posed by Jung's monism and in fact the problem of his metapsychology.

## 3

### Dialectic

On 12 February 1964, Françoise Dolto asks a question in Lacan's seminar, *The Four Fundamental Concepts of Psychoanalysis*, that amounts to an objection. She says,

> I don't see how, in describing the formation of intelligence up to the age of three or four, one can do without stages. I think that as far as the defence phantasies and the phantasies of the castration veil are concerned, and also the threats of mutilation, one needs to refer to stages.
>
> (Lacan 1964, 64)

Dolto is referring to the oral, anal, phallic, and genital developmental stages. She asks her question subtly, insofar as she refers the stages not to the development of sexuality but the development of intelligence, and she refers not to biology but to mental life. Lacan is not fooled. He answers her as if she had referred to biological stages, which, in fact, she had, no matter how subtly. He says, "The description of the stages, *which go to form the libido*, must not be referred to some natural process of pseudo-maturation, which always remains opaque" (Lacan 1964, 64). Lacan goes on to describe how the stages are organized around the fear of castration:

> The fear of castration is like a thread that perforates all the stages of development. It orients the relations that are anterior to its actual appearance—weaning, toilet training, etc. It crystallizes each of these moments in a dialectic that has as its centre a bad encounter. If the stages are consistent, it is in accordance with their possible registration in terms of bad encounters.
>
> (1964, 64)

Lacan makes it clear that the passage from stage to stage is not biologically determined but rather results from dialectical shifts governed retroactively by the castration complex.

So we have Lacan's argument that the developmental stages that are listed in textbooks as if they were indeed a biological program are in fact dialectical stages. An explanation may be necessary here about the term *dialectic*, for we're not referring to the Platonic dialectic, nor to the use of the word that simply means "scholastic disputation." No, we mean something like the Hegelian dialectic, in which each stage in the encounter brings about changes that lead to the next.

Another point to be made: Lacan refers to the stages "which go to form the libido," and as editor, Jacques-Alain Miller places this phrase in italics in the text. Too easily, we think of the libido as a natural force, as the energy of the sexual drive. But Lacan is making it clear that the libido is *formed*, that it is *constructed*. Thus we can refer not vaguely to some life force but specifically to *my* libido, to *your* libido, and to the history behind each. The libido isn't sexual energy. It is, for each subject, a complex historically determined network.

Freud doesn't emphasize the fact, but he often refers to just how far the adult libido is from the childhood stages of its construction. In his two papers on the anal character, "Character and Anal Erotism" (1908) and "On Transformations of [Drive] As Exemplified in Anal Erotism" (1917), Freud lists three features of the anal character. People who have such a character are "*orderly, parsimonious* and *obstinate*" (Freud 1908a, 169). We may say that they are stubborn, stingy, and neat. The point of these two papers is to show how very far the transformations of the libido may stray from its origins. A child who will grow up to possess an anal character and to be an obsessional neurotic, for example, will eventually be reluctant, as an adult, to spend money or to pick up the check at dinner. At first glance, it's very difficult to see how this stinginess relates to the anus. And it doesn't—at least not directly. The individual libido of the anal subject is governed by a number of inaugural contingent events, transformations, historical accidents, and symbolic equations that take it quite far from the supposed anal source.

I've already highlighted the ambiguity of the source of the drive insofar as Freud refers to it as a kind of fiction, a use of "figurative expression" (1905, 205). Further, any part of the body may be a "source." In the *Three Essays*, Freud says, "The analysis of the perversions and psychoneuroses has shown us that . . . sexual excitation is derived not from the so-called sexual parts alone, but from all the bodily organs" (1905, 217). How is it that we come to think of the drive-sources as localized in a number of erogenous zones? It is because of the dialectic transformation that takes the subject from stage to stage of development that dialectic privileges a number of bodily orifices through which the subject interacts with the Other. The localization of libido in the erogenous zones is already a second stage. It is already a complex development in setting up what can call the network of the libido. If the anal subject doesn't pick up the check at dinner, that failure can be traced back through a long symbolic series to withholding from the Other his or her own precious gift.

That doesn't mean that the anus is the source, that means that long ago, the anus *was* the source. It is only through the twists and turns and transformations of the symbolic order that a refusal of the anal subject to pay for dinner can be traced back to a childhood refusal to produce feces on demand. There is a symbolic distance between the source and the eventual manifestations of the drive.

It must be said that Freud doesn't often refer to this distance. His mind encompasses the network so completely that even in clinical examples he tends to collapse the distance, which is why when he refers blithely to a symbolic equation like "girl = phallus," you're left confused unless you've done a lot of reading in psychoanalysis. In his essay on "The Sexual Theories of Children" (1908b), though, Freud does allude to the distance. In the essay, he runs through a number of childhood sexual theories pertinent to the age of ten or eleven, that is, the approaching end of the latency period. Now, instead of formulating theories, the child begins to receive accurate information about sex, usually from more precocious children. The child finds it difficult to coordinate the new and usually incomplete information with his or her earlier theories, and so the child produces new theories to clear up the inconsistencies. These theories don't have the significance of the earlier ones:

> But the theories which he now produces no longer have the typical and original stamp which was characteristic of the primary theories of early childhood as long as the infantile sexual components could find expression in theories in an uninhibited and unmodified fashion. The child's later intellectual efforts at solving the puzzles of sex have not seemed to me worth collecting, nor can they have much claim to pathogenic significance.
> 
> (Freud 1908b, 224)

Freud thus privileges the original establishment of the network of libido over later additions to it. He even says that later additions don't have much effect pathologically. Obviously, the child's entire life is lived after the fifth year, but all subsequent events seem to be fitted to the matrix of an already established libidinal structure that is, ultimately, linguistic.

## *Demand and Fantasy*

The way in which one passes dialectically from stage to stage is through a series of interactions with the Other that Lacan collects under the name *demand*. This leads us to a consideration of demand in the theory of the drive. The concept is so important that Lacan's inscription of the drive is in fact ($ ◊ D), the split subject in relation to symbolic demand. The subject, Lacan says, "fades" before the demand. To anyone coming to Lacan for the first time, this must seem a strange description of the drive, for according to the naïve theory, we're used to thinking of drive as motivation, as an energy that prompts behavior. In Seminar 9, on *Identification* (1961–1962), Lacan opens the sixth session with a long passage assuring his audience that he hasn't forgotten the thread of his argument:

> The last time I left you on a remark designed to give you the sense that my discourse is not losing its moorings, namely that . . . the paradox of the automatism of repetition is that you see arising a cycle of behaviour inscribable as such in terms of a resolution of tension, therefore of the need-satisfaction couple, and that nevertheless whatever may be the function involved in this cycle, however

carnal you may suppose it to be, it nevertheless remains that what it means qua automatism of repetition is that it is there in order to make emerge, to recall, to make insist something which is nothing other in its essence than a signifier . . . and that it is because something happened at the origin which is the whole system of the trauma, namely that at one time there was produced something which took on from that time the form A. . . . Let us say that the behaviour from then on is expressible as behaviour . . . behaviour masked . . . behind [its] apparent motivations; and you know that in this regard no one will find it difficult to find an apparent reason for it: it is proper to psychology always to make a shadow of motivation appear.

(Lacan 1961–1962, session of 20 December 1961)

"The shadow of motivation"—that's the phrase that Lacan uses to critique the psychological approach. Behind any behavior, psychology posits that there must be some vague and shadowy motivation. We have been able to establish that motivations are not as ill-defined as all that. The libido is not just some vague energy but a signifying network that is established by the subject's history, by a dialectic of demand.

In "The Signification of the Phallus," Lacan says that "Demand itself bears on something other than the satisfaction it calls for" (1958, 579); that is, it goes beyond the mere satisfaction of biological need. He goes on: "demand annuls (*aufhebt*) the particularity of everything that can be granted [in response to demand] by transmuting it into proof of love, and the very satisfactions demand obtains for need are debased (*sich erniedrigt*)" (Lacan 1958, 580). The subject's demands of the Other—for example, the child's demands to the mother—address not just the objects of need. They go beyond that. The named object of the demand, and the satisfaction obtained thereby, are in fact "debased," as Lacan says. There is an excess to demand: beyond the demand for the object of satisfaction, there is a demand for love that "debases" the mere object of need. Consider the child who asks his mother for a sandwich. The named object of the demand answers to a basic need, nutrition. But if the mother should take extra care in preparing it, if she should cut the crusts off the bread in just the way he likes, if she gives him the sandwich lovingly and sits down with him as he eats, she is answering to what there is in the demand beyond the need for nutrition. She is answering to a demand for love. Lacan says, "This is why desire is neither the appetite for satisfaction nor the demand for love, but the difference that results from the subtraction of the first from the second" (1958, 580).

This formula can be written as an equation: $D - n = d$, demand minus need equals desire. Insofar as the demand is a signifier, we are pointing here to an excess, a beyond of the signifying material. What is this remainder that Lacan identifies as the demand beyond the demand, the demand for love? We may think of it by contrasting two different sides of the signified. Every signifier signifies, and thus it points to a signified, yet beyond that signification, there is the excess that the signifier doesn't capture. The signified is a *meaning*, a dictionary definition, a denotation. But to the subject it is also *meaningful*. We encounter these two sides to the signified when we read a poem. The poem is made up of words and grammar that have meaning. Each word has a dictionary definition. But beyond that, the poem is meaningful to us. So we can write another equation: signified − meaning = meaningfulness. Meaningfulness is the remainder, the beyond of the signified's meaning.

These two sides of the signified, meaning and meaningfulness, must be kept in mind. Lacan says that the phallus is "the signifier that is destined to designate meaning effects as a whole" (1958, 579). By "meaning effects as a whole," I think Lacan captures both sides of the signified, meaning and meaningfulness. For the "signification of the phallus" is the first metaphor. When the child enters language, it is under the threat of castration and the paternal metaphor. So the child enters the signifying system, the dead order of language and dictionary definitions, only by giving up, under threat, the jouissance, the meaningfulness, that he had access to before. Harry Stack Sullivan has a fine example:

> The original usage of . . . words . . . is magical, as witness, for example, any of you who have a child who has been promised on a certain birthday a pony. As you listen to the child talk about the pony, you realize perhaps sadly that twenty-five years from now when he talks about ponies, pony will not have a thousandth of the richness of personal meaning that pony has for him now.
> (1953, 19)

Sullivan's "richness" in this passage is what I'm referring to as *meaningfulness*. It is the remainder and the excess of any use of the signifier.

The recognition that demand is a signifier, and that it refers to a signified that both means and is meaningful, allows us to return to the drive, ($ ◊ D), and to take it up in its position in the Lacan's big graph. At the lower level of the graph, we have the subject's encounter with language.

The subject of need, $, addresses its demands to the Other, A, and it must do so in the Other's language. As it does so, the subject encounters the signifying chain, S–S′. Lacan is clear that the signifying chain is here to be conceived as functioning automatically, following the rules of language, of metaphor and metonymy. The

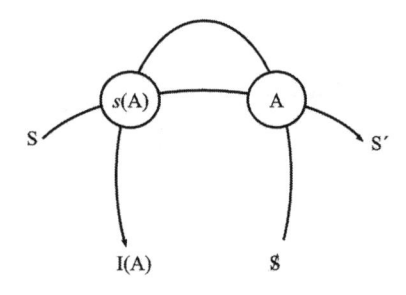

*Figure 1.1*
Source: cf. Lacan 1960, 684

subject intersects that chain in the place of the big Other, conceived both as the synchronic place of the code, "the treasure trove of signifiers" (1960, 693), and as the person who incarnates that code—the mother, the father, authority figures—as being able to grant or deny the subject's demands. The result of this is a signification that is produced, $s(A)$, a signified of the Other, the Other's meaning, and the subject must accept that whatever his or her demand was—and the subject does not initially know because the demand had to be translated into the language of the Other—this is what it ultimately "means." The result is that the subject identifies with the meaning of the Other, with the Other *as* meaning, I(A).

This is the lower level of the graph upon which Lacan then places the upper level.

As Lacan makes clear, the two levels are superimposable. That is, the positions are the same. At the upper level, the drive, ($ \$ \lozenge D$), occupies the same position as the big Other at the lower level. Lacan also refers specifically to the "signifiers constitutive of the upper chain" (1960, 693). The signifying chain at the upper level is labeled "jouissance," J, and we may be tempted to fall back into the old trap of thinking of it as merely the energy of libido or of the subject's lived experience. But as we saw, libido should be conceived of as a "network of libido," as an articulated signifying chain governed by its own laws. The place of the drive, then, ($ \$ \lozenge D$), is to be conceived of exactly as the corresponding place at the lower level, as the place of the code, the treasure trove of the subject's drive signifiers, a "catalog [of] all the neurotic's drives," (1960, 698), as Lacan says.

The code at the lower level is a code of meaning, of the Other's accepted definitions of signifiers that are imposed upon the subject. The lower level of the graph is about the subject's submission to the meaning of the Other. The upper level of the graph, though, starts from the place of the Other, A, and so it involves the submission of the Other to the recalcitrant jouissance of the subject. The big Other, which represents the code, the key to all meaning, addresses itself to the subject and finds that the subject has meanings of his or her own, meanings that escape the meaning of the Other, in other words, meaningfulness. The message at this upper level is the signifier of the barred Other, $S(\bar{A})$. The meanings of the Other are barred. And the endpoint at this level is that the Other is *reduced* to the subjective

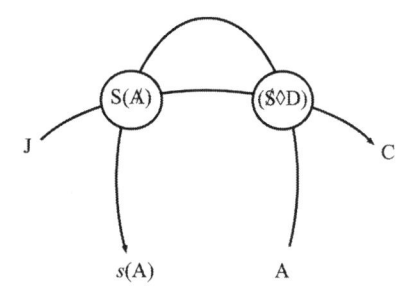

*Figure 1.2*
Source: cf. Lacan 1960, 692

meaning of the subject, $s(A)$. Subjective meanings are inherent in language and always reduce the big Other. Subjective meaning at this level, $s(A)$, is always a kind of castration of the big Other. Thus, while the code at the lower level, A, is a code of meaning, the code at the upper level is a code of subjective meaningfulness, a code of all that escapes the Other's meanings.

We can turn now to the connection between drive and fantasy. When Lacan constructs the big graph in Seminar 5, he uses the example of a joke drawn from Heinrich Heine, a story about that author's character Hirsch-Hyacinth. Hyacinth meets the millionaire Salomon Rothschild, and when he tells the story later, he proudly says, "He treated me in quite a famillionaire manner" (Lacan 1957–1958, 16). This term "famillionaire" is not a word that is indexed in any code. It is not part of the signifying code of the Other. And yet we understand the joke immediately and "get it." A joke is only a joke, Lacan (1957–1958) says, insofar as it is "confirmed" (18), "ratified" (59), and "authenticated" (110) by the Other. So a new usage is incorporated into the Other's treasury of signifiers. Lacan makes it clear that this only happens because of Hirsch-Hyacinth's libidinal investment in Rothschild, who is, Lacan says, "'his' millionaire," his object (Lacan 1957–1958, 17).

Thus, the big Other takes up and gives meaning to this subjective meaningfulness.

At the upper level of the graph, can't we see that the same relationship pertains between the drive, ($ \$ \lozenge D$), and fantasy, ($ \$ \lozenge a$)? The drive is the code at the upper level, and the fantasy is endorsed, ratified, authorized by that code.

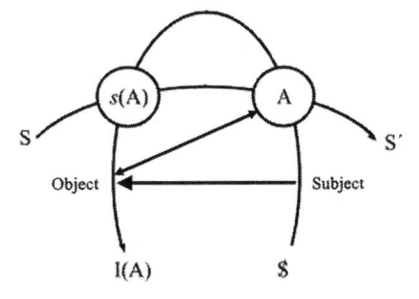

*Figure 1.3*

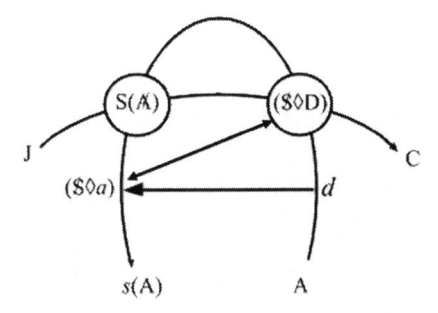

*Figure 1.4*

The subject's desire "arises," to read the graph literally, from the Other, (A). As we have seen, it is the remainder of the demand addressed to the Other. It is a desire beyond the mere signification of the demand. It is desire of the Other and for the Other. But the subject will continue to direct this demand to objects ($a$) in subjective fantasies, which reveal relations of the subject to imagined objects of satisfaction, ($\$ \lozenge a$). Thus for every new fantasy that comes up in the subject's life, demand aims at its object and endorses the fantasy that it will bring satisfaction. Just as the punchline of a joke, or a slip of the tongue, or a pun is endorsed by the code of the Other (A) at the lower level of the graph, any new fantasy is authorized at the upper level by the subjective code of the drive ($\$ \lozenge D$).

The reading we've been doing of Freud's text and Lacan's takes us a long way from any simple psychology of motivations, from the "shadow of motivation," as Lacan calls it. It takes us a long way from the notion of libido as a vague energy that requires discharge and prompts action. It takes us a long way from the naïve notion of drive as a bodily urge or simply an overweening desire. The libido is a signifying system. The drive is its code.

## Representation

In both Freud and Lacan, the drive is a mental representation, the *Vorstellungsrepräsentanz*. We'll have to note once more that Strachey points out the ambiguity of Freud's use of the word *Trieb*. Sometimes Freud uses *Trieb* to mean the mental representation, and sometimes he uses it to mean that which is represented (1915a, 111). In other words, sometimes Freud uses the term *Trieb* to refer to a biological need or urge that is mentally represented by the *Vorstellungsrepräsentanz*, and sometimes the drive is the *Vorstellungsrepräsentanz* itself. Lacan attempts to rectify this state of affairs by asking how mental representations arise at all.

*Vorstellungsrepräsentanz*, as Lacan points out, is made up of two terms. *Vorstellung* is the ordinary German word for "idea." It is made up of the verb which means "to put" or "to place" and the preposition meaning "in front of" or "before" in the spatial sense. Thus the German word for "idea" means a setting up before (one), a placing in front of (one). In philosophical contexts, the word is normally translated as *representation* (although one translator of Kant, Werner S. Pluhar, chooses to translate the word as *presentation*). *Repräsentanz* is a much rarer word that means "representative." So Strachey translates the entire term *Vorstellungsrepräsentnz* as "ideational representative," while Lacan translates it as "representative of the representation."

At stake is what the term *idea* means. Normally in Lacanian psychoanalysis we would say that ideas are imaginary and thoughts are symbolic. Freud seems to tend in this direction, and this is Jean Laplanche's reading of Freud. Freud seems to think that some mental representation, which we would have to class as imaginary, is represented by words symbolically. This fits well with the common understanding of the drive and the naïve reading of Freud's text. Some biological urge is represented in the mind as an image, and it is then represented by signifiers. But

Lacan has argued that the unconscious is structured like a language and that it is made up of signifiers, so he cannot accept this reading. It's not that we can't refer loosely, even in Lacanian psychoanalysis, to ideas and thoughts. Lacan just thinks that when *Vorstellungsrepräsentanz* is used, it's referring to a signifying representation and to a representative of that representation.

Lacan uses this understanding to read Freud's essay "Repression." In this essay, Freud discusses primal repression:

> We have reason to assume that there is a primal repression, a first phase of repression, which consists in the psychical (ideational) representative [(*Vorstellungs-*) *Repräsentanz*] of the [drive] being denied entrance into the conscious. With this a fixation is established; the representative in question persists unaltered from then onwards and the [drive] remains attached to it. . . .
>
> The second stage of repression, repression proper, affects mental derivatives of the repressed representative [*Repräsentanz*], or such trains of thought as, originating elsewhere, have come into associative connection with it. On account of this association, these ideas [*Vorstellungen*] experience the same fate as what was primally repressed. Repression proper, therefore, is actually an after-pressure.
>
> (1915b, 148)

According to the standard reading of Freud's account then, the representative of the drive is repressed. And in a second stage, any ideas associated with it are also repressed. But is this standard reading correct? There's no trouble referring to the repressed *Repräsentanz* as a signifier. But is it really true that in "repression proper," it is only imaginary ideas that are repressed because of their association with the signifier?

Lacan says no, and from our own experience, we'd be inclined to say no, too. It is not images that are repressed. If that were so, we'd have to assume that in a slip of the tongue, for example, an unwelcome *image* occurred to us unconsciously, and then in our speech, our intended signifiers were disturbed because the image that was trying to force its way into consciousness modified the signifying chain (the representations) to produce a slip. Is this what we experience? Or does the elaboration of the slip lead not to images but to more signifiers and to something that the subject didn't want to *say*? Whatever Freud's philosophical thoughts about language might have been—he might well have thought that words represent images—in his reading of slips, he deals only with signifiers.

Lacan discusses *Vorstellungsrepräsentanz* in connection with alienation and separation:

> We can locate this *Vorstellungsrepräsentanz* in our schema of the original mechanisms of alienation in that first signifying coupling that enables us to conceive that the subject appears first in the Other, in so far as the first signifier, the unary signifier, emerges in the field of the Other and represents the subject for another

signifier, which other signifier has the effect of *aphanisis* on the subject. Hence the division of the subject—when the subject appears somewhere as meaning, he is manifested elsewhere as 'fading', as disappearance. . . . The *Vorstellungsrepräsentanz* is the binary signifier.

This signifier constitutes the central point of the *Urverdrängung*.

(1964, 218)

Lacan is quite clear that the original signification of the subject is accomplished by $S_1$, the unary signifier, and the *Vorstellungsrepräsentanz* is the binary signifier, $S_2$. We can see this in the standard diagram of alienation:

The operation of separation consists in depositing this binary signifier at "the initial point, which is that of his lack as such, of the lack of his *aphanisis*" (Lacan 1964, 219). The meaning of the subject becomes the primally repressed *Vorstellungsrepräsentanz* that inaugurates the unconscious. This is the account that Lacan gives of the imposition of the Name-of-the-Father dressed up in new diagrams.

What then of the *Vorstellung* prior to the primal repression? Prior, that is, to its being represented by the *Vorstellungsrepräsentanz*, the binary signifier, $S_2$? The *Vorstellung* would be the Desire of the Mother as it is represented to the subject. Lacan says, "The signifier has to be understood in this way, it is at the opposite pole from signification. Signification, on the other hand, comes into play in the *Vorstellung*" (1964, 220). The wording of this passage may be a bit confusing. Sometimes Lacan uses *signification* to mean simply the signified, and sometimes he uses it to mean the act of signification. What he seems to mean here, though, is that there is an inaugural signification of the subject by $S_1$, the *Vorstellung*, and then that *Vorstellung* is linked to an $S_2$, the *Vorstellungsrepräsentanz*. So we could redraw Lacan's diagram of alienation this way.

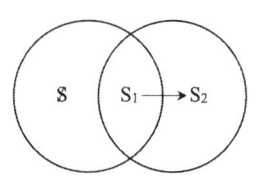

*Figure 1.5*

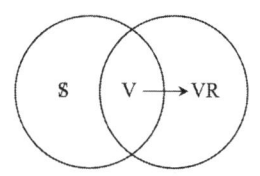

*Figure 1.6*

And the link between the *Vorstellung*, $S_1$, and the *Vorstellungsrepräsentanz*, $S_2$, is complete.

Having gotten this far in our discussion of representation, we can return to the drive. I will put forward the proposition that the drive is entirely a mental construct. All the elements of the drive are mental. But anyone relying on the naïve notion of the drive, which Freud's discourse lends its support to, will ask, "But what about the body? What about the drives originating in the body that are only represented mentally? Surely the needs of our body cross the physical/mental divide."

To this question, I would answer that the body too is mental. The body is wholly imaginary. Lacan repeatedly says as much. He says it, for example, in his MIT lecture in America:

> One can grasp that analysis only ever apprehends the body as what is most imaginary.
>
> A body is reproduced by a form.
>
> A form that is apparent in the fact that this body reproduces, subsists, and functions all on its own.
>
> We don't have the slightest information about the way it functions.
>
> We apprehend it as a form.
>
> We value it, as such, in its appearance.
>
> (Lacan 1975, 31–32)

The idea that we don't have the slightest idea about the way that the body functions separates the biological human organism from the body. Lacan makes the same point in "The Geneva Lecture on the Symptom":

> Man is captivated by the image of his body. This point explains many things, the first of which is the privileged position that this body holds for him. His world, assuming that this word has meaning, his *Umwelt*, what there is around him, he *corpo-reifies it*, he makes it a thing in the image of his body. He does not have the slightest idea, of course, of what happens inside this body. How does a body survive? I don't know whether you are struck by this in any way—when you get scratched, it heals.
>
> (1975, 9)

Freud's big gamble is that he can account for the drives by placing their point of origin in the body. His big mistake was thinking of this body as a biological organism. Lacan says so much directly. In Seminar 11, he says, "Now, is what we are dealing with in the drive essentially organic? . . . Not only do I not think so, but I think that a serious examination of Freud's elaboration of the notion of drive runs counter to it" (Lacan 1964, 162). We are trying to give Freud's elaboration that serious examination—against the naïve reading.

## 4

### Aggression and the Drive

We must return to the question that we have put off—the question of the death drive and its relation to aggression. When he posits the death drive in *Beyond the Pleasure Principle*, Freud is looking for a cause of repetition. Not recognizing a repetition automatism in the functioning of language, Freud literalizes repetition at the biological level: there must be in the organism a drive to return to earlier states of things. He slips perhaps too easily from this idea of "earlier states" to the idea of a return to inorganic matter and so ultimately to the death of the organism. He then supposes that the drives of self-preservation "are component [drives] whose function is to assure that the organism shall follow its own path to death" (Freud 1920, 39). This formulation may seem paradoxical. Self-preservation is about preserving life, but only so that the organism can ultimately achieve death. I've noted that when it's first presented in *Beyond the Pleasure Principle*, the death drive is rather passive. The death drive is not seeking self-destruction. It does not manifest as aggression towards the organism's own self. It only seeks its own path to death.

That path is life. The organism seeks the repetitive satisfaction of need, the reduction of tension so that it may eventually reduce tension to zero. Any obstacles to satisfaction along this path would raise tension, and so the organism wishes to reduce them. On this reading, I place emphasis on the *own* of the organism's own path to death. Obstacles to repetitive satisfaction arise from conflict with the Other, which the organism would try to avoid. This, of course, is a vain hope. The complexity of life involves interaction with the Other—first of all, with the linguistic big Other along paths of which the subject's own drive must travel.

The question I've raised is "Where is aggression in all this?" How does the simple need to die quietly in one's own time become conflated with an aggressive drive? How does the death drive become an aggressive drive in psychoanalytic theory.

I've noted Freud's too-easy slippage from repetition, to a return to earlier states, to a return to inorganic matter, to death. It's this slippage that allows him to posit a death drive as a wish to die. I would argue that he makes a similar slippage from "wish to die" to "wish to destroy." It's in *Civilization and Its Discontents* that this slippage is achieved. There are hints in the text that Freud might have avoided this slippage. In a long footnote to chapter four, which deals mostly with the discontents of sexuality, he says, "Another difficulty arises from the circumstance that there is so often associated with the erotic relationship, over and above its own sadistic components, a quota of plain inclination to aggression" (Freud 1930, 106). What is this "plain inclination to aggression"? There may be, Freud is suggesting, a certain amount of sadism involved in the libido, that is, the supposed "activity" of male sexuality as opposed to the equally supposed "passivity" of female sexuality, but beyond that there is also a "plain" inclination to aggression. Are we to understand *plain* here as meaning uncontaminated by libido? That passage could be understood as arguing for an independent aggressive drive, but there's nothing that links it to the death drive.

There's another hint at the beginning of chapter six. Freud is accounting for the libido as object-directed drive, and he adds,

> One of these object-[drives], the sadistic [drive], stood out from the rest, it is true, in that its aim was so very far from being loving. Moreover it was obviously in some respects attached to the ego-[drives]. It could not hide its close affinity with the [drives] for mastery which have no libidinal purpose.
>
> (1930, 117)

Here, the aggressive drive is given its origin not in a drive towards death but in a drive towards mastery. To imagine such a drive, we may think of masters and authority figures who want to impose their will, but we should also think of the infant who strives to master the objects in his or her world by manipulating them, transforming them, or even destroying them. This account of a drive for mastery is not isolated in Freud's work, and it suggests a separation of the aggressive drive from the death drive.

It's a bit further on in chapter six that Freud accomplishes the slippage that links the death drive to the aggressive drive. He is recapitulating his argument from *Beyond the Pleasure Principle*, and he says the following:

> Starting from speculations on the beginning of life and from biological parallels, I drew the conclusion that, besides the [drive] to preserve living substance and to join it into ever larger units, there must exist another, contrary [drive] seeking to dissolve those units and to bring them back to their primaeval, inorganic state. That is to say, as well as Eros there was [a drive] of death. The phenomena of life could be explained from the concurrent or mutually opposing action of these two [drives]. It was not easy, however, to demonstrate the activities of this supposed death [drive]. The manifestations of Eros were conspicuous and noisy enough. It might be assumed that the death [drive] operated silently within the organism towards its dissolution, but that, of course, was no proof. A more fruitful idea was that a portion of the [drive] is diverted towards the external world and comes to light as [a drive] of aggressiveness and destructiveness . . . in that the organism was destroying some other thing, whether animate or inanimate instead of destroying its own self.
>
> (Freud 1930, 118–119)

Note Freud's language here. He's still being tentative: "Starting from speculations"; "there must exist"; "could be explained"; "It was not easy, however, to demonstrate"; "It might be assumed"; "but that, of course, was no proof"; "A more fruitful idea." Clearly, he's not sure.

The model here is familiar enough. Since Freud's work on narcissism, it had become psychoanalytic doctrine that libido could flow outward to the object or back to the subject. Now Freud assumes the same of the death drive. Its supposed destructive tendency was directed towards the subject's own self, but it could be redirected outward towards others. That, of course, is only if we see the need to follow one's own path to death as a destructive urge. In spite of uncertainties, though, and in spite of tentative language, Freud affirms this understanding of the death drive. It is an urge towards destruction of the self that can be directed outward, just as ego-libido can become object-libido. He says, "In all that follows I adopt the standpoint, therefore, that the inclination to aggression is an original, self-subsisting instinctual disposition in man, and I return to my view that it constitutes the greatest impediment to civilization" (1930, 122).

We must question what is meant by aggression, though. Influenced by *Civilization and Its Discontents*, we are inclined to think that we live in an aggressive world. We are inclined to think that aggression manifests itself in violence towards others. But is all violence that is done to others aggression? We see aggression everywhere. I am only raising the question of whether we should so easily equate the death drive with aggression. Lacan, in 1948, presented "Aggressiveness in Psychoanalysis," in which he seems to give a different account of aggression. Characteristically, he does not contradict Freud, but rather points to the "enigmatic signification" of the "death instinct [sic]" (1948, 82). He calls this enigma an "aporia" and says that "This aporia lies at the heart of the notion of aggressiveness" (Lacan 1948, 82). The paper is divided into five theses. In the first, Lacan says that aggressiveness is "an experience that is subjective in its very constitution" (1948, 83). In his explication of the first thesis, Lacan doesn't even mention aggressiveness but describes the analytic experience, implying that it is the subjective experience in which aggressiveness manifests itself.

In the second thesis, Lacan says that analysis allows us to "experience intentional pressure" (1948, 84). By this, I think he means not "pressure that is intended" but rather "the pressure of intention." He says that "aggressive intention" is manifest in psychoanalysis (Lacan 1948, 84). So there is something like a *Drang* of aggression. This would suggest an aggressive drive. Lacan emphasizes that "aggressiveness is . . . exercised within real constraints" (1948, 85). In other words, we do not act on every aggressive intent. Aggressive intention is carried out upon imagos. Images, Lacan says, "represent the elective vectors of aggressive intentions" (1948, 85).

The third thesis maintains that "The mainsprings of aggressiveness determine the rationale for analytic technique" (Lacan 1948, 86). Aggressive intention can, of course, escalate. The analytic situation is meant to prevent that escalation. How? Through free association: "The rule proposed to the patient in analysis allows him to advance in an intentionality that is blind" (1948, 86). The analyst, meanwhile, "refrains from responding at the level of giving advice or making plans" (1948, 86). Lacan calls this the avoidance of a trap. What would be the trap? It's the trap of replying to intention with intention. The analyst allows him- or herself to bear the brunt of the analysand's aggressive intentions (Lacan 1948, 87) and gives them play in the analysis. Does not all this imply that ordinarily, in everyday life, aggression is intersubjective? If Lacan could say that "Love is always reciprocal," couldn't we say as well that aggression is always reciprocal?

Thesis four states that "Aggressiveness is the tendency correlated with a mode of identification I call narcissistic" (Lacan 1948, 89). Lacan explains that "The aggressive tendency proves to be fundamental in a certain series of significant personality states, namely, the paranoid and the paranoiac psychoses" (1948, 90). This observation does not confine aggression to the psychoses because Lacan is using these personality states as an example that is generalizable. He goes on to talk at length about the mirror stage, in fact recapitulating much of his paper by that title:

> Janet, who so admirably demonstrated the signification of feelings of persecution as phenomenological moments of social behaviors, did not explore their common characteristic, which is precisely that they are constituted by stagnation in on of these moments, similar in strangeness to the faces of actors when a film is suddenly stopped in mid-frame.
> 
> Now, this formal stagnation is akin to the most general structure of human knowledge, which constitutes the ego and objects as having the attributes of permanence, identity, and substance—in short, as entities or "things" that are very different from the gestalts that experience enables us to isolate in the mobility of the field constructed according to the lines of animal desire.
> 
> . . . What I have called paranoiac knowledge is therefore shown to correspond in its more or less archaic forms to certain critical moments that punctuate the history of man's mental genesis.
> 
> (Lacan 1948, 90–91)

The formal stagnation that Lacan refers to implies a world in which the subject and its objects are "frozen"—locked in opposition. He goes on, "There is a sort of structural crossroads here to which we must accommodate our thinking if we are to understand the nature of aggressiveness in man and its relation to the formalism of his ego and objects" (Lacan 1948, 92).

Aggression, then, is to be located in the subject's narcissistic investment in his own ego:

> It is in this erotic relationship, in which the human individual fixates on an image that alienates him from himself, that we find the energy and the form from which the organization of the passions that he will call his ego originates.
> 
> Indeed, this form crystallizes in the subject's inner conflictual tensions, which leads to the awakening of his desire for the object of the other's desire: here the primordial confluence precipitates into aggressive competition.
> 
> (Lacan 1948, 92)

Again, we must note that aggressiveness is intersubjective. We are aggressive only in a state of competition with the other. Note also that Lacan firmly locates aggressiveness in an "erotic relationship" that establishes both the subject's ego and the subject's objects.

The fifth thesis is an ambiguous attempt to tie Lacan's account of aggression to Freud's *Civilization and Its Discontents*: "This notion of aggressiveness as one of the intentional coordinates of the human ego ... allows us to conceive of its role in modern neurosis and in the malaise of civilization" (1948, 98). Note one of Lacan's observations: "The preeminence of aggressiveness in our civilization would already be sufficiently demonstrated by the fact that it is usually confused in everyday morality with the virtue of strength" (1948, 98). In other words, we praise aggressiveness as a virtue of the "strong ego." We should hear in that Lacan's whole critique of ego psychology.

In his "Aggressiveness" essay, then, Lacan gives an account of aggressiveness as structural. It is not an innate, ultimately biological drive. It arises in the formation of the ego and ego's objects and is exercised in what Lacan calls "the triad of other people, ego, and object" (Lacan 1948, 92).

What, then, of *Civilization and Its Discontents*? Freud concludes the work by raising the question of ethics:

> Ethics is thus to be regarded as a therapeutic attempt—as an endeavour to achieve, by means of a command of the super-ego, something which has so far not been achieved by means of any other cultural activities. As we already know, the problem before us is how to get rid of the greatest hindrance to civilization—namely, the constitutional inclination of human beings to be aggressive towards one another.
>
> (1930, 142)

Freud is not very hopeful for this "therapeutic attempt." He even considers, briefly, the idea of a cultural psychoanalysis. If all of culture is neurotic, could it be treated by psychoanalysis? His answer is no. We are all within culture, so he asks who there would be "to impose therapy on the group?" (Freud 1930, 144).

The most surprising revelation of this argument, then, is that the aggressive drive is not primary but secondary, formed within the structure of the subject's narcissistic investment of libido in his own ego. Must we abandon, then, Freud's dualism, which he struggled so hard to maintain, and take the Jungian position that there is only libido? No. Prior to libidinal investment there was auto-erotism, so sexual drives and aggressive drives are both secondary formations brought about by the intervention of the Other. Humans may have a "constitutional inclination" to be aggressive, but that inclination is to be understood as constitutional in that it arises structurally in human interaction and is not to be attributed to the death drive, which seeks only a peaceful end.

### *The Drive and Peace*

The naïve conception of the drive holds that the drive is grounded in the simple satisfaction of bodily need, and its mental elaboration is just a more complex version of the reflex arc. Yet the naïve conception also holds, somehow, that there is a primordial aggressive drive. Freud's death drive, which has caused endless theoretical problems for psychoanalysis, is nonetheless thoroughly embedded in cultural consciousness. We can assume that our ready acceptance of the death drive follows the same pattern as the multiple drives that psychologists posit: we observe aggression; therefore there must be an aggressive drive.

But we've seen that it's not at all clear that an aggressive, destructive drive is aligned with the death drive, which is first described as the tendency of an organism to follow its own path to death. To die is not to kill. We've also seen that in spite of the fact that he pays due deference to Freud's *Civilization and Its Discontents*, Lacan attributes aggressiveness to a narcissistic investment of libido in the ego.

What more subtle, more psychoanalytic conception of the drive, then, should we hold? Reading the *Écrits*, we come across, in the essay "The Freudian Thing," one of those aphoristic statements for which Lacan is so well known:

> I am asking where the peace that ensues in recognizing an unconscious tendency comes from if the latter is not truer than what restrained it in the conflict.
>
> (1955, 338)

The first thing to note here is that "tendency" was a term that Lacan used at this time to translate Freud's term *Trieb*. "An unconscious tendency," then, is a drive. Lacan's question, more fully stated, asks, "Where does that peace that follows the recognition of the unconscious drive come from unless it's the case that the drive is more true than the repression that restrained it in the mental conflict?"

There are several points to make about this startling question. First is that the drive is being described as true and repression, in some sense, as false or deceptive. Second, Lacan's question implies the work of the clinic, where the unconscious drive is recognized. Third, repression and the drive are the two sides of a mental conflict. A drive, seeking satisfaction, is "restrained" by repression and must seek satisfaction through alternate paths. These paths are often symptomatic, and the eventual "satisfaction" of the drive, along different paths and in spite of conflict, is experienced as unpleasure by the ego. Fourth, peace, in this gnomic statement, is a criterion for truth. And finally, perhaps most strikingly, the drive, once recognized and unrestrained, leads not to conflict but to peace.

How different this is from the naïve conception, which imagines that an unrestrained drive would lead to personal and cultural chaos. Lacan's conception is different: an unrestrained drive leads to peace. It's one of the great mysteries of *Civilization and Its Discontents* that Freud so readily fell into the argument that civilization is founded on the renunciation of the drive. He might just as easily have argued that love, home, and family—usually assumed to be cornerstones of civilization—are built upon satisfactions of the drive. It's true that not every unrestrained satisfaction of the drive would lead to peace, but neither is every unrestrained satisfaction of the drive aggression. And if we read Lacan's question carefully, he doesn't quite say that the drive should always be satisfied, only that it should be recognized and freed from restraint. To give some credit to Freud's argument, it's true that mental conflict arises from a cultural condemnation of certain drives. This was his argument in "'Civilized' Sexual Morality and Modern Nervous Illness," published in 1908. But this is, in fact, exactly what Lacan says, too: restraint of the drive leads to mental conflict. Lacan only adds the corollary, that recognition of the drive leads to peace.

In 1964, Lacan returns to this argument and adds to it when he claims, at the end of Seminar 11, that "living the drive" would be the criterion for a successful analysis (1964, 273). (The passage is somewhat obscured in the current English translation.) About the drive, we've been told a lie, that it represents our basest urges and that its satisfaction would lead to chaos. Lacanian psychoanalysis allows us to see that the recognition of the drive and even the pleasure of its humble satisfactions lead instead to peace. If Lacan largely falls silent on the drive after 1964, perhaps it's because he felt that he had said the last word.

## References

Brenner, Charles. 1973. *An Elementary Textbook of Psychoanalysis*, revised edition. New York: Anchor Books, 1974.

Freud, Sigmund. 1905. "Three Essays on the Theory of Sexuality." In *Standard Edition of the Complete Psychological Works of Sigmund Freud*. Vol. 7. Translated by James Strachey, 123–245. New York: Norton, 1953.

———. 1908a. "Character and Anal Erotism." In *Standard Edition of the Complete Psychological Works of Sigmund Freud*. Vol. 9. Translated by James Strachey, 167–176. New York: Norton, 1959.

———. 1908b. "On the Sexual Theories of Children." In *Standard Edition of the Complete Psychological Works of Sigmund Freud*. Vol. 9. Translated by James Strachey, 205–226. New York: Norton, 1959.

———. 1915a. "[Drives] and Their Vicissitudes." In *Standard Edition of the Complete Psychological Works of Sigmund Freud*. Vol. 14. Translated by James Strachey, 109–139. New York: Norton, 1960.

———. 1915b. "Repression." In *Standard Edition of the Complete Psychological Works of Sigmund Freud*. Vol. 14. Translated by James Strachey, 141–158. New York: Norton, 1960.

———. 1917. "On Transformations of Instinct as Exemplified in Anal Erotism." In *Standard Edition of the Complete Psychological Works of Sigmund Freud*. Vol. 17. Translated by James Strachey, 125–134. New York: Norton, 1955.

———. 1920. "Beyond the Pleasure Principle." In *Standard Edition of the Complete Psychological Works of Sigmund Freud*. Vol. 18. Translated by James Strachey, 1–64. New York: Norton, 1955.

———. 1930. "Civilization and Its Discontents." In *Standard Edition of the Complete Psychological Works of Sigmund Freud*. Vol. 21. Translated by James Strachey, 59–145. New York: Norton, 1961.

———. 1933. "Anxiety and Instinctual Life." In *New Introductory Lectures on Psychoanalysis. Standard Edition of the Complete Psychological Works of Sigmund Freud*. Vol. 22. Translated by James Strachey, 81–111. New York: Norton, 1957.

Lacan, Jacques. 1948. "Aggressiveness in Psychoanalysis." In *Écrits: The First Complete Edition in English*. Translated by Bruce Fink, 82–101. New York: Norton, 2006.

———. 1955. "The Freudian Thing." In *Écrits: The First Complete Edition in English*. Translated by Bruce Fink, 334–363. New York: Norton, 2006.

———. 1956–1957. *The Object Relation: The Seminar of Jacques Lacan*, Book IV. Translated by A. R. Price. Cambridge: Polity Press, 2020.

———. 1957–1958. *The Formations of the Unconscious: The Seminar of Jacques Lacan*, Book V. Edited by Jacques-Alain Miller. Translated by Russell Grigg. Cambridge, UK: Polity, 2017.

———. 1958. "The Signification of the Phallus." In *Écrits: The First Complete Edition in English*. Translated by Bruce Fink, 575–584. New York: Norton, 2006.

———. 1960. "The Subversion of the Subject and the Dialectic of Desire in the Freudian Unconscious." In *Écrits: The First Complete Edition in English*. Translated by Bruce Fink, 671–702. New York: Norton, 2006.

———. 1961–1962. *Identification*. The Seminar of Jacques Lacan, Book 9. Translated by Cormac Gallagher. Translated from Transcripts and Privately Published.

———. 1964. *The Four Fundamental Concepts of Psychoanalysis: The Seminar of Jacques Lacan*, Book XI. Edited by Jacques-Alain Miller. Translated by Alan Sheridan. New York, NY: Norton, 1977.

———. 1975. "MIT Lecture on Topology." In *The Lacanian Review*. Translated by Jack Stone and Russell Grigg, 5 (July 2018): 31–38. Cambridge: Polity.

Sullivan, Harry Stack. 1953. *Conceptions of Modern Psychiatry*. New York: Norton.

Part I

# The History of the Drive

Chapter 2

# On the Very German-ness of Freud's *Trieb*

*Rolf Flor*

---

*The illusion of etymology is that if we trace a word back to its origins, we'll find its "true" meaning. This strategy is of little help with the word* drive. *A little investigation shows that the remote ancestor of the word* drive *has remained consistently opaque ever since the time of the Indo-Europeans, always describing an impulse or push. Rolf Flor, an analyst from Massachusetts, takes a different approach. Through a kind of thick description, he explores what the word* drive *means in Freud's own German. The results are rich. In the course of his exposition, Flor cautions against the ways in which Freud's word* Trieb *can be misunderstood, often, but not solely, because of mistranslation. Part of our difficulty with the term is its inherent German-ness, which includes a tendency for it to form difficult and unheard-of compound words. Implicit throughout Flor's argument is that Lacan was exquisitely sensitive to the resonances of Freud's German—and thus to the subtleties of Freud's concept of the drive.*

---

Lacanians spend a fair amount of time puzzling through some monumental sentences. Consider the following example from the opening paragraphs of "Science and Truth":

> Whoever lends credence to the technique for reading Freud that I had to impose when the task at hand was simply one of synchronically resituating each of his terms, will be able to proceed in reverse chronological order from the *Ichspaltung* (to which death put an end), to the articles on fetishism (1927) and the loss of reality (1924), to observe that the doctrinal revamping known as the second topography introduced the terms *Ich*, *Über-Ich* and even *Es* without certifying them as apparatuses, introducing instead a reworking of analytic experience in accordance with a dialectic best defined as what structuralism has since allowed us to elaborate logically: namely, the subject—the subject caught up in a constituting division.
>
> (Lacan 2006, 727)

I cannot say how this sentence about "the subject caught up in a constituting division" sounds in the original to a French ear—but even with Bruce Fink working his translation magic, it remains a mouthful in English. I can say, though, that for a German ear . . . it's not so bad! Lacan was, after all, thoroughly knowledgeable in German, so perhaps Lacan acquired an affinity for *German-ness*.

Already in just this one long-winded sentence—which suggests with its scope the thoroughness and intensity with which Lacan was focused on Freud's writings, taking a stance as it does on twenty years of Freud's work—one can see that Lacan finds terminological anchoring points in Freud's mother tongue. In fact, we know from his biographer that Lacan was already at home in German during his school years, and a quite rarefied German at that. For example, we know that to his family's dismay, he studied Nietzsche in his adolescence. This was soon followed by Kant and then later Heidegger, whom we know he read closely in the original as well, well enough to feel comfortable translating (Roudinesco 1997).

With its vocabulary, this one sentence from "Science and Truth" reminds us that Lacan not only studied Freud—and that at a time when translations for many of Freud's works were not even yet available in French—but also Hegel, under Kojève, when it was reasonable to expect that members of that seminar might read Hegel's *Phenomenology* in its original, awfully dense German, rather than the poor translations available in French.

"Awful" is a word that has come to mind for others when describing Teutonic sentences. Consider the following from Mark Twain's essay "The Awful German Language."

> An average sentence in a German newspaper is a sublime and impressive curiosity; it occupies a quarter of a column; it contains all the ten parts of speech—not in regular order, but mixed; it is built mainly of compound words constructed by the writer on the spot, and not to be found in any dictionary—six or seven words compacted into one, without joint or seam—that is, without hyphens; it treats of fourteen or fifteen different subjects, each enclosed in a parenthesis of its own, with here and there extra parentheses, which re-enclose three or four of the minor parentheses, making pens with pens; finally, all the parentheses and re-parentheses are massed together between a couple of king-parentheses, one of which is placed in the first line of the majestic sentence and the other in the middle of the last line of it—*after which comes the* VERB, and you find out for the first time what the man has been talking about; and after the verb—merely by way of ornament, as far as I can make out,—the writer shovels in "*haben sind gewesen gehabt haben geworden sein,*" or words to that effect, and the monument is finished.
>
> (Twain 1880, 375–376)

With his own "majestic" sentence, Twain skewers the German language by exemplifying its idiosyncrasies, ironically, of course, but also accurately in most ways. For anyone learning German, this certainly hits home, especially the part about waiting for the German verb complements at the end of the sentence, which you then must sift through laboriously, to tell you what "the man has been talking about."

Personally, when I ponder Lacan's "sublime and impressive curiosities," I can't help but wonder if the time Lacan devoted to closely reading Kant, Hegel, and Heidegger didn't contribute to his own style. I would not go so far as to say this can account for all of Lacan's style. Even translated into German, Lacan's Gongorism—his baroque sentences—maintain their inimitableness. My point is just that readers of Hegel and Heidegger will have developed the *breathing stamina* to have make it through Lacan's prose.

Of course, even if my speculation is true, it wouldn't be a good enough reason to have the "awful" German language foisted on you. However, it just won't do to ignore that Lacan was always returning to Freud's work in the original, always encouraging others to do the same, *and always complaining that translations missed their mark*. It has been reported that Lacan's spoken accent was atrocious, but when I read his seminars, I find abundant evidence that his sensitivity to nuances in the German language was extraordinary. A bit of that sensitivity should, I argue, be taken on by those who would like to closely follow Lacan's writings and of course by those who would like to help us access those arguments in other languages.

Given how much Lacan castigates others for their translations of Freud, one would pray that translators would be especially conscientious of Freud's German and Lacan's use of Freud's German. Lacan emphasizes that responsibility frequently, for example, in the *Four Fundamental Concepts of Psychoanalysis*, at the start of the session from May 13 of 1964, referring to Freud's "*Triebe und Triebschicksale*," or "[Drives] and Their Vicissitudes":

> It was this text that I began to approach the last time, when I was trying to make you feel in what a problematic form, bristling with questions, the introduction of the drive presents itself. I hope that many of you will have been able to refer to this text in the meantime, whether you are able to read it in German, which seems to me eminently desirable, or whether, as second best, you will be able to read it, always more or less improperly translated, in the two other languages of culture, English or French—I certainly give the worst marks to the French translation, but I will not waste time pointing out the veritable falsifications with which it swarms.
>
> (Lacan 1964, 175)

Tragically, in Sheridan's English translation of that very session, the paragraphs that immediately follow contain not only translation mistakes that are sure to mislead the reader but *transcription* errors by the translator of Lacan's quotes in German.

In the opening pages of that session and the previous one, Lacan is reading "*Triebe und Triebschicksale*" (Freud 1915b) very closely, and all of the many German words, phrases, and sentences that he uses are taken directly from Freud's text. Specifically, Lacan is highlighting that if the first half of the essay is about the montage-like structure of the drive, the second half is about how "loving" and its various polarities (loving-hating, loving-being loved, loving-being indifferent) relate to a different set of polarities (subject-object, pleasure-unpleasure, active-passive) that produce the variety of the sexual drives. Freud's first point in this second half of the essay seems to be to raise the very question as to why "loving" in the most generic sense of the word isn't the whole story when it comes to sexuality. Freud says we may try to convince ourselves that the loving subsumes sexuality, but we just can't make much sense of that when we think about actual human experiences. Certainly, it doesn't make sense for anyone with analytic experience. In that context, Freud says that with every attempt to see sexuality as just about loving, one "*kommt aber auch damit nicht zurecht.*" The Standard Edition translates this as "but this idea does not clear up our difficulties" (Freud 1915a, 133). Lacan takes the trouble to quote Freud (1964, 175), perhaps because he wanted to help us find the exact passage in Freud, or perhaps because he just thought Freud's comment was a rather pithy way to highlight that one faces *aporias* when we equate sexuality with some quaint idea of love. But the official French edition of the seminar, which Sheridan dutifully quotes in the English translation without checking the German, has "*Kommt aber auf damit nicht zuher,*" which Sheridan then mistranslates as "*that's not at all how it happens*" (Lacan 1964, 175, emphasis original).

If Freud had ever produced such a nonsensical sequence of German sounding words as "*Kommt aber auf damit nicht zuher,*" that would not be the translation. And *Zuher* is not even a word in German. But in fact Freud never wrote such a thing. He *did* write "*kommt aber auch damit nicht zurecht,*" which is indeed a perfectly understandable, thoroughly German phrase that indeed can be found verbatim in *Triebe und Treibschicksale*, the text that Lacan is reading and the text that he is telling his audience to try, if possible, to read in German. I wish I could say this is the only crazy bit of fake German in Sheridan's translation. Unfortunately, it's not. I also wish I could say the problem is limited to Sheridan's translation of Seminar 11. There are actually far too many examples of misquotes and mistranslations. Take for example a passage from Russell Grigg's translation of Seminar 3:

> As to the others, Mr. Heidegger insists upon the two aspects, *Sten* which would be closer to *stare,* to stand alone, and *Verbahen,* to last, to endure, this sense being nevertheless attached to the source *phusis.* According to Mr. Heidegger, the idea of standing erect, the idea of life and the idea of lasting, enduring, is therefore what an etymological analysis combined with a grammatical analysis yields, and it's out of a kind of reduction or of indetermination cast over these senses as a whole that the notion of being emerges.
> (Lacan 1955–1956, 300–301)

Grigg is not creating the confusion here, because the words are taken from the French edition of Lacan's talk. But sadly, again, regardless of where the problem starts, the words referenced are literally nonsense; neither *Sten* nor *Verbahen* are German words!

*Stehen* and *Verstehen* are German words, and I think the first of these is likely what Lacan was referencing with the word which is transcribed as *Sten*. *Stehen* shows up—in its past participle form: *stand*—in numerous Heideggerian words (so much that I would say they create a kind of family of concepts: *Bestand, Beständig,*

*Ständigkeit, Inständigkeit*, and so on). *Verbahen* on the other hand is a lot harder to make sense of for any German speaker. It is wonderful—as invented German words go—because it *sounds* very German. There are words like *Verharren*, which I guess could sound similar to what appears in the French and the English, and that could mean "endure." But I don't think Lacan meant that word, and it is not a word in Heidegger as far as I can tell. I won't belabor this issue further.

Let me extend however my cautionary note in another direction and point out that this problem extends beyond transcription and translation to commentary as well. Ironically enough, in the recently published *Reading Lacan's Écrits*, there is a commentary by Theo Reeves-Evison "On Freud's '*Trieb*' and the Psychoanalyst's Desire" where he also starts us with a bit of craziness. He is trying to distinguish what he claims is the more active resonances in German of the word *Trieb* from the more passive sense of the word *Instinkt* using the common German expression *Was triebst du da?* Which he translates as "What are you driving at?" (2019, 260)

First of all, the distinction between *Trieb* and *Instinkt* in German is not that one is active and the other is passive, nor is that the difference Lacan insists on. Second, "What are you driving at?" sounds like a request to be more explicit. But, most importantly, *Was triebst du da?* is *not* a German sentence because it conflates two related but distinct words, *Trieb* and *treiben* (note the reversed order of the i and the e). *Trieb* and *treiben* are two different German words that historically come from the same word, having branched apart six or seven hundred years ago. The related word in Old Friesian is *driva* and in Old High German *triben*. There *is* a similar-sounding sentence which is very, very common in German, exactly as common as Reeves-Evison suggests, but it uses the other word, *treiben: Was treibst du da?* The correct translation of this would be "What are you doing?" colloquially understood as "Hey! What are you up to over there?"

This misunderstanding, I will add, does not detract from Theo Reeves-Evison's commentary, which is otherwise quite interesting. But it is an error that Lacan never would have made himself, because he is all too aware of the roots of the word, as he shows clearly in Seminar 7, where, once again, he points us to the historical German-ness of *Trieb*, capturing yet another of the important nuances that makes "instinct" such a terrible translation while simultaneously highlighting the value of the translation "drive" because of the etymological resonances of which Lacan is obviously aware.

> Sublimation, Freud tells us, involves a certain form of satisfaction of the *Triebe*, a word that is improperly translated as "instincts," but that one should translate strictly as "drives" (*pulsions*) or as "drifts" (*dérives*) so as to mark the fact that the *Trieb* is deflected from what he calls its *Ziel*, its aim.
>
> (1959–1960, 110)

Indeed, exactly as Lacan suggests, the shared root of *Trieb* and *trieben* connects drive and drift.

The upshot of these warnings—that translation mistakes can lead us awfully far astray—is raised by Lacan to the level of a core conviction about the reception of Freud's work. A few very important but unfortunate choices, like translating *Trieb* as "instinct," have obscured Freud's actual position. This is one of Lacan's principal explanations for why a "return to Freud" is necessary: quite literally what is needed is a return to the meanings of words used by Freud because, to borrow a term from Lacan, translations have rather obscured the "Freudian thing." Of course, every language seems to put up roadblocks that can make translation extremely challenging. Sooner or later, translation finds it limits. Even Lacan's best translators occasionally throw up their hands, most famously in the case of *jouissance*, from which the French-ness apparently just can't be translated away.

*Trieb*, a concept that Lacan returned to repeatedly throughout his teaching, especially during the first eleven years, almost seems to rise to that level of inscrutability. Whenever Lacan touched the topic of the drive, throughout those years, his recommendations and complaints become a veritable leitmotif. In Seminar 5, he even expresses misgivings about his own translation. Lacan generally translated the German word *Trieb* as *pulsion* in French; however, "to be honest," he says, "that rather obscures the thing" (1957–1958, 453). Perhaps this can explain why, with the penultimate *écrit*, "On Freud's '*Trieb*' and the Psychoanalyst's Desire," Lacan simply elected to leave the word untranslated, which he also did in several of the seminars. In the rest of this chapter, I would like to take up the point that Lacan seems to be making with this title and his frequently expressed misgivings and try to shed at least a little light on the very German-ness of the word *Trieb*.

"*Triebe und Triebschicksale*," written in 1915, is the first of Freud's so-called metapsychological papers. Most will have read it in translation with the title "Instincts and Their Vicissitudes." From the very first word of the title, someone who has read the complete text in German and was sensitive to both the resonances of the German word *Trieb* and the English word *instinct* will have noticed a problem. For one thing, Freud uses both words *Trieb* and *Instinkt*, and he uses them differently. His usage lines up well with the difference between *drive* and *instinct* in English, so Strachey would have done well to preserve the distinction.

The word *Instinkt* shows up about fifty times altogether in the complete works of Freud, and when it does, the context makes it clear that Freud is appealing to biology and the animal kingdom where it is assumed that there are innate behaviors that do not need to be learned and that invariably lead toward certain actions. Interestingly, about a fifth of these occurrences of the word are where Freud is actually pointing out that the predictable uniform response that one would expect from an inborn instinct is not so uniform and is far from predictable. In other words, he uses the word frequently to deny that such fixed action patterns are present. See for example when he dismisses the idea that there is anything instinctive about the incest taboo.

It is worth noting that *Instinkt* as a word is relatively new to the German language. It appears for the first time in the in the work of Wieland and Goethe during the eighteenth century. It belongs to the discourse of the Enlightenment and cosmopolitanism, when foreign language influence became more acceptable to the Germans. It starts its very short German life spelled in the English way with the letter *c* (Wieland and Goethe), from which one can be very sure the word is of foreign extraction, since in German the letter *c* almost never appears unaccompanied by an *h*. Only at the beginning of the nineteenth century is the exotic word Germanized with the letter *k* by more down-to-earth humorists such as Jean Paul.

The notion of instinct that Freud would have in mind was prevalent among persons familiar with Darwin's description—even if not from Darwin himself. It would have already been recognized by many naturalists writing in the eighteenth century: an action which turns out to be adaptive that an animal (especially a young one) may perform without any learning and which we ourselves would require experience to enable us to perform. When performed by an animal, more especially by a very young one, without any experience, and when performed by many individuals in the same way, without their knowing for what purpose it is performed, the action is said to be instinctive.

*Trieb*, on the other hand, reaches much, much further back. The word dates at least to the Middle High German of the twelfth century, where it pushed aside an Old High German word, the very one that is the source of the English word *drift*. *Trieb* appears in uncountable works and contexts, including weather, geography, engineering, and animal husbandry. Its resonances evoke the energy or forces that makes something happen, not at all far from the English word *drive*. Think *snowdrift*, *cattle drive*, *drivetrain*, and *driving a nail*.

In other words, *Instinkt* is something of a Johannes-come-lately, with a very circumscribed meaning, but *Trieb* is ur-German and refers to a far broader set of applications that line up quite well with one of the principal things Freud has to say about the drive. And as it turns out, what Freud seems to want to say about drive is that it conspires by its very nature against our being able simply to come out and say what it is. Allow me to paint this image which I hope it will clarify things a little: Picture if you will snow drifting across some scene. What you are aware of is the snow in a movement that appears to belong to it somehow, but of course, as experience teaches, the "invisible" force moving the snow is the wind. The resulting snow drift is appreciated by observation afterwards as having been produced as the result of something, something one could conceptualize as the drive.

And what we see in Freud's writing is that he is quite conscious that he has little to say about instinct but an enormous amount to say about drive. All of the so-called Papers on Metapsychology are built on the foundation of the drive. And overall, *Trieb* shows up many hundreds of times in the complete works of Freud as a word by itself. But if you add to those hundreds of appearances the number of times *Trieb* shows up as part of a compound noun, the usage of the word increases to over two thousand times. How, you may ask, can that be the case?

From a Germanist point of view, this sounds stranger than it is.

Let me remind you of an issue raised by Twain "in the pens" of one of Twain's own parenthesis previously, namely "compound words *constructed by the writer on the spot.*" It is truly common and more challenging than many of you suspect. The German *Volksmund* ("people-mouth") devilishly enjoys creating hybrid nouns.

At their most basic, German compounds consist of at least two words. Most readers will be familiar with the much beloved *Schadenfreude*. The final element, *Freude*, is the "primary word," *das Grundwort*, and it designates the larger set of words of which the compound noun is a member. The primary word determines the gender and the plural form the compound noun will take. The preceding item, *Schaden*, is called the "determiner," or "determinative element" (*das Bestimmungswort*). It designates the subset of the category that the primary word defines. Thus *die Schadenfreude* is, as we all know, the joy that one might experience while watching someone being hurt.

*Schadenfreude* is of course found in German dictionaries. In fact, *Schadenfreude* has proved itself so useful that it has been borrowed by other languages and shows up in their dictionaries. Nevertheless, Twain is only exaggerating a touch when he adds "and not to be found in any dictionary"; Germans not only create compound nouns liberally, but the German language retains them in an official capacity only occasionally.

There are indeed many, many German compound words that have the lifespan of a mayfly, dying on the very day that they were hatched into adult life. Others exist for a period of time in the spoken language, rarely if ever showing up in print. Finally, some show up for a period of time in spoken and written German but never earn a place in the dictionary.

Here is the point I would like you to take in about Freud's *Trieb*. The vast majority of times that the word appears in Freud's writing, it makes up only one part of a much larger word. Here are some examples taken from the Metapsychology papers: *Triebreize, Triebbedurfnis, Treibbefriedigung, Triebverschraenkung, Triebentwicklung, Triebquellen, Triebqualitaeten, Urtriebe, Destruktionstriebe, Geselligkeitstriebe, Selbsterhaltungstriebe, Sexueltriebe, Erhaltungstriebe*. This list nowhere near exhausts the composites Freud creates and invokes. And *Trieb* shows up both as a primary word and as a determinative element. And perhaps this may make you think that obviously the notion of the drive has reached the point of conceptual maturity where it can be explicated with significant detail. The implication for a German speaker is just as likely to be *the opposite*; actually, Freud is pairing this word with *Trieb* so often in composites *because he is struggling to explain exactly what he is saying*. What determines the drive notion in general that he would like to clarify? What kinds of drives can there be? He is literally tying *Trieb* to so many other concepts in order to help the reader and *perhaps even to clarify the notion for himself!*

An interesting note about these and other compound nouns constructed with *Trieb* is that they fall in all of the possible categories: some are words that Freud could have found in previously existing dictionaries; some are words that Freud made up for these texts and became a part of later dictionaries and/or found applications in writing outside of psychoanalysis; some are words that Freud invented whole cloth and never made it anywhere outside of the psychoanalytic literature. This is evidence of the struggle Freud is having to clarify what he thinks could or should be a concept upon which one could create a scientific psychoanalysis. In the English language translation, *the tentativeness, the insecurity Freud feels for the subject is wiped away*, and a series of *ex cathedra* psychological assertions are made instead. In German, the struggle to clarify *Trieb* remains much apparent in the text.

And obviously for Lacan also, who said—as I quoted it at the very beginning—"I was trying to make you feel in what a problematic form, bristling with questions, the introduction of the drive presents itself."

But if you have read "[Drives] and their Vicissitudes," this could have been had by just reading his opening sentences more carefully.

> We have often heard it maintained that sciences should be built up on clear and sharply defined basic concepts. In actual fact no science, not even the most exact, begins with such definitions. The true beginning of scientific activity consists rather in describing phenomena and then in proceeding to group, classify, and correlate them. Even at the stage of description it is not possible to avoid applying certain abstract ideas to the material in hand, ideas derived from somewhere or other but certainly not from the new observations alone. Such ideas—which will later become the basic concepts of the science—are still more indispensable as the material is further worked over. They must at first necessarily possess some degree of indefiniteness; there can be no question of any clear delimitation of their content. So long as they remain in this condition, we come to an understanding about their meaning by making repeated references to the material of observation from which they appear to have been derived, but upon which, in fact, they have been imposed. Thus, strictly speaking, they are in the nature of conventions—although everything depends on their not being arbitrarily chosen but determined by their having significant relations to the empirical material, relations that we seem to sense before we can clearly recognize and demonstrate them.
>
> (Freud 1915a, 117)

A little further, Freud continues:

> A conventional basic concept [*Grundbegriff*] of this kind, which at the moment is still somewhat obscure but which is indispensable to us in psychology, is that of a [*Trieb*]. Let us try to give content to it by approaching it from different angles.
>
> (1915a, 117–118)

Perhaps one of the biggest losses in the Standard Edition, at least regarding the efforts Freud made with *Trieb* as a *Grundbegriff*, occurs in the opening salvo of the translation into English. Consider again the title: Literally translated, *Triebe und Triebschicksale* becomes not "[Drives] and Their Vicissitudes" but "Drives and Drive-destinies." "Drive-destinies": what a strange word!

Unlike either *Trieb*, or even *instinct*, *Triebschicksale* is very definitely a word that did not exist before 1915 when Freud placed it at the start of his metapsychological papers. It is utterly original. "Vicissitudes," of course, has nothing novel about it other than the strangeness of applying it to the drives. Commonly it is understood to the English ear as a change of circumstances, typically unpleasant. "Destiny," however, is evocative, in German as well as English, in a wholly different direction. I would argue that what it suggests is that one of the ways that drive will be understood is being addressed in the very title. To put it briefly, I would argue that Freud is saying that by their outcomes you will know more about them. One of the most important ways we will know about the drives is what they transform into, namely into further *Grundbegriffe*, repression, displacement, and sublimation, to name just three. It is not the change in fortunes of the drives that will interest Freud for his metapsychology; it is their transformations into further experiences that psychoanalysis finds in its practice.

Lacan throughout his oeuvre will frequently highlight the unerring way in which Freud seemed to find his way forward. But specifically regarding *Trieb*, Lacan recognizes with his exquisite sensitivity to Freud's German that Freud is wrestling with *terra nova*. Especially for thinkers like Freud (and for Lacan, it goes without saying), mere translation will never in the end suffice to grasp the fullness of their theory. With this, Lacan of course also shows that to understand someone is to understand their Other—their mother tongue—with which they are always inescapably in a *pas-de-deux*.

## References

Freud, Sigmund. 1915a. "[Drives] and Their Vicissitudes." In *Standard Edition of the Complete Psychological Works of Sigmund Freud*. Vol. 14. Translated by James Strachey, 109–139. New York: Norton, 1960.

———. 1915b. "Triebe und Treibschicksale." In *Gesammelte Werke Chronologisch Geordnet, Band X, Werke aus den Jahren 1913–1917*, 210–232. London: Imago, 1946.

Lacan, Jacques. 1955–1956. *The Psychoses: The Seminar of Jacques Lacan*, Book III. Edited by Jacques-Alain Miller. Translated by Russell Grigg. New York: Norton, 1993.

———. 1957–1958. *The Formations of the Unconscious: The Seminar of Jacques Lacan*, Book V. Edited by Jacques-Alain Miller. Translated by Russell Grigg. Cambridge: Polity Press, 2017.

———. 1959–1960. *The Ethics of Psychoanalysis: The Seminar of Jacques Lacan*, Book VII. Edited by Jaques Alain Miller. Translated by Dennis Porter. New York: Norton, 1986.

———. 1964. *The Four Fundamental Concepts of Psychoanalysis: The Seminar of Jacques Lacan*, Book XI. Edited by Jacques-Alain Miller. Translated by Alan Sheridan. New York: W.W. Norton, 1977.

———, Jacques. 2006. *Ecrits: The Complete Edition*. Translated by Bruce Fink. New York: W.W. Norton.

Reeves-Evison, Theo. 2019. "On Freud's 'Trieb' and the Psychoanalyst's Desire." In *Reading Lacan's Écrits: From "Signification of the Phallus" to "Metaphor of the Subject."* Edited by Stijn Vanheule, Derek Hook, and Callum Neil, 259–267. New York: Routledge.

Roudinesco, Elizabeth. 1997. *Jacques Lacan*. Translated by Barbara Bray. New York: Columbia University Press.

Twain, Mark. 1880. "A Tramp Abroad." In *A Tramp Abroad, Following the Equator, Other Travels*, 1–421. New York: Library of America, 2010.

Chapter 3

# Freud's Third Step
## On *Beyond the Pleasure Principle*

*Marco Antonio Coutinho Jorge*

---

*Taking* Beyond the Pleasure Principle *as the decisive turning point, Marco Antonio Coutinho Jorge in this chapter ranges over the entire history of the drive concept. With ample textual support, Coutinho Jorge argues that "there is a common thread running through the evolution of Freud's thought" on the drive. Coutinho Jorge notes that "Freud had to travel a long path in therapeutic experience to produce his drive theory," and thus he ties Freud's theoretical development of the drive to the clinic. The historical path, mappable in three steps, runs from the pleasure principle to narcissism to the death drive, and along the way, Coutinho Jorge makes a significant contribution by linking the drive firmly to fantasy.*

---

Psychoanalytic practice underwent a decisive renewal in 1920 when Sigmund Freud introduced the concept of the death drive in his essay *Beyond the Pleasure Principle* (BPP). This renewal is strongly evinced by the weight that Freud accorded drive when he examined the problem of the end of analysis in one of his final texts, "Analysis Terminable and Interminable" (1937). Responding point by point to an earlier article in which Sándor Ferenczi (1929) addressed the topic and approached the issues related to the end of analysis from the perspective of the structural conflict established early on between the ego and drive (the id), Freud could not have been more emphatic when he wrote of the irresistible power of the "quantitative factor in the causation of illness" and the "dominance of the quantitative factor" (1937, 226, 227).

The theoretical and clinical scope of BPP became more apparent as more psychoanalytic experience was amassed and its ideas were put to the test. If we bear in mind that the purpose of psychoanalysis is to restructure the subject's relation to the imperative demand for satisfaction that is inherent to drive, we can better understand that the discoveries presented in BPP have a direct bearing on the foundations of the compulsive, repetitive nature of this demand. After all, repetition—or, to borrow Lacan's orthography, re-petition (1972, 486)—is a quest for satisfaction that can never be attained and therefore is repeated indefinitely. BPP addresses the foundations of this impossible need for satisfaction, which proves to be the most important aspect of the drive concept. The libido—which lacks a defined object (it is wholly variable, says Freud, and wholly indifferent, says

Lacan)—is driven by constant pressure (Freud uses the term *konstante Kraft*), and does not wane much—arises from somatic sources that demand continuous psychic work, and yet "something in the nature of the sexual [drive] itself is unfavorable to the realization of complete satisfaction" (Freud 1912, 188–189). This impossible satisfaction is one of the prime elements of the Lacanian concept of the real.

This particular work by Freud has raised eyebrows ever since its original publication. Most of the reviews released shortly after it came out were not as negative as its author expected; a number placed emphasis on the essay's speculative nature, something to which Freud himself called attention. Wielding his usual ironic wit, Freud wrote these words to his close friend Max Eitingon, on March 27, 1921: "For the *Beyond*, I have been punished enough; it is very popular, brings me masses of letters and encomiums. I must have made something very stupid there" (qtd. in Gay 1988, 403).

As pointed out by Paul-Laurent Assoun (2009, 222), BPP took Freudian metapsychology in a new direction, as patent in Freud's trenchant remark to Lou Andreas-Salomé, in a letter dated April 2, 1919, after the latter had inquired about Freud's as-yet unpublished metapsychology papers:

> What has happened to my *Metapsychology*? In the first place it has not yet been written. The systematic working through of material is not possible for me; the fragmentary nature of my experiences and the sporadic character of my insights do not permit it. But if I still have ten years to live and remain capable of work in this period, do not die of starvation, or meet a violent end, nor am too severely afflicted by the misery of my family or of the world around me—a bit too much to ask—then I promise to make further contributions to it. A first example of this will be found in an essay of mine entitled *Beyond the Pleasure Principle*, concerning which I look forward to a detailed *critical*-synthetic appreciation from you.
>
> (Freud and Salomé 1972, 95)

Freud cautiously presented his theses in BPP, together with certain caveats. While he met with resistance from many analysts, these ideas gradually became an essential part of his understanding of the psychic apparatus: "To begin with it was only tentatively that I put forward the views I have developed here, but in the course of time they have gained such a hold upon me that I can no longer think in any other way" (Freud 1930, 119).

## From the Symbolic to the Real

The movement of Freud's writings from that period speaks eloquently to the journey from the symbolic to the real then taken by Freudian thought. In mid-March 1919, he finished writing "A Child Is Being Beaten" and initiated his BPP project, completing the first draft in May. He then returned to an earlier text, evidently begun in 1913 and eventually released as "The Uncanny" in the fall of 1919. He went back to drafting BPP in March 1920, finalized it in July, and published it in early December of the same year. BPP thus occupies a very precise position along the journey of Freudian theoretical construction: it was written in parallel with two other major essays, expanding the Freudian view of the unconscious and shedding new light on clinical practice, making it possible to address certain previously untouched phenomena.

My hypothesis about the significance of this synchrony lies in the supposition that there is a common thread running through the evolution of Freud's thought, from the symbolic to the real, an evolution enabled by the accumulation of clinical experience within the field of psychoanalysis. In 1919, when Freud took up the question of incestuous fantasy, "The Uncanny" and "A Child Is Being Beaten" represented his final exploration of the unconscious in terms of the repressed—and therefore the symbolic—allowing him to address the real unconscious in BPP. Let us see what we can glean from these two essays by approaching them from the perspective of this observation.

Rarely is much attention given to the fact that Freud situates incestuous fantasies at the epicenter of "The Uncanny" (a highly enigmatic hypertext that can be taken in various directions, such as metapsychology, aesthetic debate, and the study of the antithetical meaning of words) and, further, that he startles the reader with two observations, one regarding the lustfulness inherent to "the phantasy . . . of intrauterine existence" (Freud 1919, 244) and the other assigning the primal home of all human beings to the maternal body.

At the same time, in "A Child Is Being Beaten," Freud lists three distinct phases of the beating-fantasies from childhood memories that arise during adult analysis, the second being incestuous fantasy, which is unconscious and only appears transfigured by well-structured syntactic distortions in the first and third phases of fantasy (Freud 1919). The second phase, in which the father beats the fantasizing child (corresponding to the incestuous scene of unconscious desire) remains secret and hidden, in a latent state, and only comes to light through analytical construction, thus being homologous to the glowing nucleus of the *Unheimliche*—the uncanny.

Both examples demonstrate how the focus of the argument is on incestuous desire—an indestructible desire that, as the actual nucleus of the repressed, magnetically attracts all other desires. We cannot forget that the nucleus of dreams, like all unconscious formations, is made up of a fantasy. In *The Interpretation of Dreams*, for example, Freud had noted that dreams are the realization of a desire, but he did not fail to add that dreams are the realization of a desire that is tied to an unsatisfied infantile desire; in other words, he drew a clear relation between fantasies found in dreams and incestuous fantasies.

In "The Uncanny" and "A Child Is Being Beaten," Freud skillfully leads his reader to see what constitutes the actual nucleus of the repressed. In the case of the *Unheimliche*, or uncanny, what should have remained secret and hidden to the child but eventually came to light is a woman as the object of desire, in the form of the mother. In "A Child Is Being Beaten," it is the paternal figure who, in both the young girl's and young boy's incestuous fantastical representations, takes the child as a sexual object. I would venture the hypothesis that at this crucial juncture in his work, Freud was delving directly into the very nucleus of the repressed—incestuous fantasies—and thus moving quickly toward what is situated beyond fantasy, that is, beyond the pleasure principle, insofar as fantasy represents the persistence of this principle in a close, indissoluble connection with the reality principle. Even more essentially, what is seemingly happening here is the processing of the relationship between incestuous fantasies and primal repression, a relationship that will allow Lacan later to address the structure, place, and role of the fundamental fantasy within the psychic apparatus. We will examine this important theoretical development later.

Following the vital formulations of Claude Lévi-Strauss (1958) regarding the effectiveness of symbols, Lacan introduced into psychoanalysis the unprecedented concept that the unconscious is knowledge. He called this knowledge "symbolic." The unconscious is knowledge constructed around the nonknowledge about the sexual difference; in other words, the symbolic order is a knowledge that orbits around the real nucleus of the unconscious, evinced by the "sexual theories of children" that endeavor to symbolize or lend meaning to the meaningless real of sexual difference. It is precisely this dimension beyond the pleasure principle, from which fantasy protects the subject in its constitution, that Lacan will theorize as the real. "There is no sexual relation," Lacan will state in defining sexual nonknowledge, that is, the absence of any registry of sexual difference within the unconscious.

At this point, it is worth remembering that Lacan elevates the second phase of beating fantasies to the category of "fundamental fantasy" and builds his notion of the end of analysis around this concept. The fundamental fantasy as defined by Lacan "inaugurat[es] the locus in which the subject can be fixated as desire" (1960–1961, 193). This definition derives from his general conception of the direction of analytical treatment and contains within itself the resources needed to lend unconscious fantasy its scope, a matter to which we will return at the end of this text. For now, it suffices to bear in mind Lacan's forceful principle on this topic: "The value of psychoanalysis lies in its working on fantasy" (1967, 366). Let us first address the primary underpinnings of the radical shift that took place in 1920, when, according to Lacan, Freud introduced the "additional notions which were at that time necessary to maintain the principle of the decentering of the subject" (1954–1955, 11).

As pointed out, Freud had to travel a long path in therapeutic experience to produce his drive theory, and it is this path, which he himself called the three steps of psychoanalysis, that we will explore next. In *Civilization and Its Discontents*, Freud refers to his 1920 essay as the third step in the evolution of his drive theory—a decisive step, one that reverberates throughout his work, resignifying the discovery of the unconscious. It is no accident that Lacan begins his seminars guided by the motto "return to Freud" with a reading of BPP. With Lacan, we learn the importance of the number three: If one, alone, fashions no bonds and is part of paranoid solitude, and two reflects the illusional ambitions of plenitude and complementarity, it is only with three that everything begins. "I'll count to three," the mother tells her mischievous child; at the theater, it is the third ringing of the bell that announces the subject's immediate appearance on stage. And so three displays its structural pressure and conclusive power: the logic of unconscious temporality also shows us that the moment of conclusion comes in the third period. Didn't Freud also consider the discovery of the unconscious a narcissistic wound within a series, where it had, after Copernicus and Darwin, "presented humanity with the third of three historic injuries to its megalomania" (Gay 1988, 449)?

## 1905–1911: The Pleasure Principle

Freud's first step lay purely and simply in his discovery of the importance of sexuality in the etiology of neuroses: the neurotic symptom stems from the return of the repressed and is related to the demand for drive satisfaction, which is partially realized through fantasy and spills over into the body as an effect of the compelling demand for direct physical gratification, later conceptualized by Lacan as phallic or sexual jouissance. The first step therefore lay in understanding that the workings of the psychic apparatus are governed by the pleasure principle, identified early on by Freud and expressed through very clamorous manifestations of the sexual drive, which differs radically from animal instinct. As pointed out by Lacan, sexuality is "consubstantial with the dimension of the unconscious" (1964, 146). The sexual drive constitutes the most evident stratum of drive, which, as a constant pressure, is continuously expressed through different forms of indirect satisfaction: fantasy, symptom, and sublimatory activities. The sexual drive is noisy; as aptly indicated by Michel Foucault, the true scandal in Freud's early works on sexuality was that he addressed the topic logically and scientifically. Everybody talked about sexuality, which, Foucault wrote, had been "manifestly and massively inscribed in nineteenth-century medicine and psychiatry" (1977, 79), but Freud was the first to bring it into the conference room, away from locker room jokes.

As laid out in *Three Essays on the Theory of Sexuality* (1905), the discovery of childhood sexuality and the identification of its inherent polymorphous perversion enabled Freud both to recognize that sexuality is not limited to the genitalia and also to situate within partial drives (corresponding to body orifices) the quest for the compelling satisfaction inherent to the sexual drive. In Lacan's thorough exploration of the structure of language and the unconscious, he frames the phases of the libido not as biological stages inscribed in the infant's living organism (the developmentalist interpretation) but rather as the expression of the action of language—of the Other—on the body. Lacan showed that the different phases of the libido resulted from the vital action of language on certain areas of the body, in pace with the child's growth. The oral phase arrives in early life, when the infant's survival is ensured by the maternal Other's painstaking feeding care, and is followed by the anal phase, which initiates the process of education through the learning of sphincter control. Next comes the phallic phase, when childhood masturbation, tied to unconscious incestuous fantasies, becomes the center of attention and repression by the Other.

This identification of the concept of drive as accounting for human sexuality was a decisive first step. With the discovery of polymorphous-perverse childhood sexuality, a bridge was drawn between the normal and the pathological, and the nineteenth-century notion of so-called sexual aberration was revised from a patently depathologizing prism. As I have shown elsewhere (Coutinho Jorge 2010, 29), we should not forget that the concept of drive, which was presented in 1905 in *Three Essays on the Theory of Sexuality*, sprang from a lengthy dialogue between Freud and his friend Wilhelm Fliess, who spent seventeen years, from 1887 to 1904, discussing the notion of bisexuality. The concept of drive emerged as Freud's coherent theoretical answer to the mystery of bisexuality, assigning it a structural status and, concomitantly, depathologizing the phenomenon of homosexuality (Coutinho Jorge 2013).

Not long after publishing *Three Essays*, Freud apparently felt he should convey his findings about sexuality more directly, and so he wrote a short paper that is considered a gem in his work: "My Views on the Part Played by Sexuality in the Aetiology of Neuroses" (1906 [1905]). In laying out the evolution of his thinking about the relation between neurosis and sexuality, he offers a surprising explanation of the big shift that allowed him to discover the importance of unconscious fantasy and attribute what he calls "general neuropathic disposition" (Freud 1906 [1905], 276) to the variegated nature of sexual constitution. He also says he began with the notion of childhood sexual trauma, which led him to the concept of psychosexual infantilism. In short, as the enigmatic nature of sexual difference is unknown and contains a real density that cannot be represented by the symbolic, Freud declares that sexual trauma always happens. Lacan makes reference to this when he speaks of sexuality as bearing "the mark of some hardly natural flaw" (1960, 688) and when he underscores "the notion of trauma as contingency" (1960, 687).

In 1910, in the article "Psychogenic Disturbance of Vision," Freud bases himself on the clinical treatment of hysteria in demonstrating that one organ can be imbued with different drive impulses that subvert its biological function in virtue of erotic components, thus constructing his first drive dualism, which opposes sexual drives to self-preservative drives. As this dualism contrasts drives aimed at perpetuating the species with drives whose goal is to preserve individual members of the species, it did not stand up to subsequent discoveries and proved too tightly linked to the theory of evolution.

## 1914–1917: Narcissism

Freud's second step was the discovery of narcissism, a journey he initiated in 1909 and completed in 1914, one that revolutionized his previous theses by showing that the ego is, like external objects, an object imbued with libido, the sexual energy drive. Moreover, the ego is a reservoir that works to distribute the libido to external objects.

This theoretical step added something essential to the first drive dualism and indicated that the narcissistic dimension is both structural and structuring. Psychoanalytic practice gained unprecedented ground when narcissism was shown to be a decisive—necessary but insufficient—stage in the constitution of the subject; the same was true when it was shown how much narcissism is implicated in the psychotic structure, both positively (paranoia) and negatively (schizophrenia). Last but not least, this step revealed the radical schism between the ego and the subject of the unconscious, which was the greatest object of Lacan's investigations throughout his teaching and constitutive of the foundation of the distinction between real, symbolic, and imaginary psychic registers:

> in order to gain an idea of the function which Freud designated by the word "ego", as indeed to read the whole of the Freudian metapsychology, it is necessary to use this distinction of plans and relations expressed in the terms the symbolic, the imaginary, and the real.
>
> (1954–1955, 36)

The fact is that the first drive dualism was rendered less coherent by Freud's second step, which uncovered a deeper psychic layer: narcissism. Once identified, it was evident that this layer was linked directly to the dimension of sexual drive. The step of narcissism lies at the foundation of Freud's major theoretical and clinical developments related to the opposition between mourning, as a normal processing of object loss, and melancholy (which he called narcissistic neurosis), as a pathological manifestation arising from the inability to engage in this processing. Freud finished writing "Mourning and Melancholia" in 1915—in undeniable synchrony with his essay on narcissism—but released it only in 1917. The essay's temporal positioning halfway between "On Narcissism: An Introduction" and BPP demonstrates in and of itself how this text bridged the discovery of narcissism and the hypothesis of the death drive, quintessentially manifested in melancholy.

## 1920–1924: The Death Drive

The Russian psychoanalyst Sabina Spielrein delivered a paper on "transformation" to the Vienna Psychoanalytic Society on November 29, 1911. In it, she made a brief reference to an article she would publish the following year in which the idea of a destruction drive appeared for the first time in the history of psychoanalysis (Spielrein 1912). Freud initially said he had not understood her paper very well but later remarked that his lack of understanding had been born from resistance: "I remember my own defensive attitude when the idea of an instinct of destruction first emerged in psycho-analytic literature, and how long it took before I became receptive to it" (1930, 120). Spielrein's 1911 talk is especially noteworthy because it anticipates the crux of Freud's essay when she says the death component is contained within the sexual drive itself and that a destructive drive is inherent to this instinct, as an indispensable component of the process of becoming (1912, 184).

Curiously enough, Spielrein never delivered her later publication on the destruction drive to the Society, but during the discussion of a paper presented on March 27, 1912, by Victor Tausk, entitled "Sexuality and the Ego," Freud made a comment that remarkably foreshadowed his later development of ideas on the relation between the death drive and masochism: "Dr. Spielrein was right in stating that the problem of sadomasochism is identical with that of the instinct of destruction" (Nunberg and Federn 1975, 86).

This was in 1912, and Freud had recently released "Formulations on the Two Principles of Mental Functioning" (1911), in which he first drew a theoretically consistent link between the pleasure principle and the reality principle, effectively closing out his study on the importance of fantasy in the psychic apparatus (Coutinho Jorge 2010, 55–59). The ideas expressed in this paper underpin the radical breakthrough introduced by BPP and are what lent the 1920 text its true breadth.

According to the theory that introduced the second drive dualism, which opposed life drives to the death drive, the psychic apparatus has a force that endeavors to reduce internal tensions to zero, or as close to this as possible. This is the most elementary force exerted by the psychic apparatus, the one that governs it most deeply and that, once wholly actuated and with the brakes off, leads to death—hence Freud's designation "death drive." And hence the name of its governing precept, the Nirvana principle, a designation first introduced by British psychoanalyst Barbara Low and then, in view of its precision and simplicity, adopted by Freud to designate what is at play in these processes.

The death drive is located beyond the pleasure principle, since the latter likewise tends to reduce the inner tensions of the psychic apparatus while still reining this tendency in somewhat, keeping it from going too far and holding inner tensions at a relatively constant level—thus preserving life, which also implies a certain level of tension. This is what Freud called the principle of constancy. The pleasure principle is thus governed by the principle of constancy, while its beyond is governed by the Nirvana principle. The former designates the processes at play in life drives—or sexual drives—while the latter designates those at play in the death drive.

When Freud introduced this new dimension of drive in 1920 (renewing the previous one by completing rather than abolishing it), he was propelled by certain clinical findings related to traumatic neuroses, children's play, and transference. These clinical phenomena and his own observations of everyday life forced Freud to rethink his thesis on how the pleasure principle dominates the psychic apparatus. In clinical practice related to traumatic neuroses, for example—where the number of cases had risen significantly following the war, in the form of war neuroses—it was found that patients who had endured extremely distressful lived experiences in combat often saw these episodes return to haunt them later, in the form of nightmares and flashbacks. In the case of children's play, Freud concluded that children simulated maternal presence and absence (particularly absence), based on his observations of a child tossing a cotton reel tied to a string out of sight and then bringing it back in, accompanied by the primitive vocalizations "Oh" and "Ah," which he interpreted as attempts to utter the German words "*Fort!*" and "*Da!*", meaning "Gone!" and "There!" (Freud 1920, 14–17). In the case of transference, Freud noted how the patient's painful childhood experiences repeated themselves later. None of these phenomena obeyed the pleasure principle; furthermore, since the common denominator was the compulsion to repeat, Freud recognized in this rather enigmatic, irrepressible repetition the work of a very powerful, basal drive pressure that ruled the psychic apparatus at its most elementary level, countering the pleasure principle.

In Freud's understanding, the fort/da game represented the localization of a basal psychic operation within an everyday activity that was non-pathological and, more especially, creative. Almost the entire second chapter of BPP deals with the fort/da game, which, notably, follows his examination of traumatic neurosis. Freud himself called attention to the sharp difference between both: "At this point I propose to leave the dark and dismal subject of the traumatic neurosis and pass on to examine the method of working employed by the psychic apparatus in one of its earliest *normal* activities—I mean in children's play" (1920, 14). Lacan put great store in the fort/da game, returning to it countless times throughout his work. He saw in it the inaugural moment of human symbolization, in which the child emerges as the subject among the signifiers, symbolizing the real of the loss of the maternal object: "These are the occultation games which Freud, in a flash of genius, presented to us so that we might see in them that the moment at which desire is humanized is also that at which the child is born into language" (Lacan 1953, 262). As the symbolic comes on scene, the object becomes secondary. The value of the object proves insignificant and fort/da becomes a "point of insemination for a symbolic order that preexists the infantile subject and in accordance with which he has to structure himself" (Lacan 1958, 497). The word kills the thing and becomes the very thing, as the object moves into the plane of language. The order of the real becomes absolutely heterogenous to the symbolic, and the symbolic begins ordering human reality—and in this way, the real becomes psychical reality.

There are in fact two different but interconnected sides to repetition, the clinical finding that enabled Freud to propose the notion of the death drive. In Seminar 11, where Lacan listed repetition as one of the four foundational concepts of psychoanalysis—a development unprecedented in the field—he made a vital distinction between it and transference, with which it was so often blended. In Freud's 1914 essay "Remembering, Repeating, and Working Through," repetition appears in the foreground of treatment, yet tightly bound up with sexual drive, the fantasy framing it, and thus the functioning of the pleasure principle. In 1920, however, in BPP, the repetition compulsion reveals its hidden side as a manifestation of the death drive (the real that cannot be symbolized), from which the sexual drive springs forth. We will see further on that this occurs because the fundamental fantasy is constitutive of the bases of the psychic apparatus.

Many psychoanalysts rejected BPP and felt it should not be included in the body of theory. Some saw Freud's theses about the death drive merely as an effect of the day's political and economic context and therefore deemed the drive a "circumstantial notion" (Roudinesco and Plon 1998, 485). They also believed Freud's thinking had been impacted by the deaths of Anton von Freund; of Victor Tausk, his brilliant disciple who died by suicide in 1919; and particularly of Sophie, his oldest daughter, who passed away on January 25, 1920, causing Freud grave consternation, as expressed in a number of his letters. But Freud had written half of his essay while Sophie was still alive and healthy, although this did not keep Fritz Wittels, Freud's first biographer, from establishing a causal relationship between the theory of the death drive and his daughter's passing, as both Max Schur and Peter Gay would later do as well.

From early on, Ferenczi, considered the great clinician of the Freudian era, offered a series of sharp clinical reflections on the death drive. His article "The Unwelcome Child and His Death-Instinct" (Ferenczi 1929) can be read as establishing a powerful link between Freud's formulations and Lacan's elaborations on the role of the Other (language-unconscious) as constitutive of the subject. Love and desire for the Other are what sustain the child and, by sexualizing him, buffer the primal destructive effects of the death drive. The consequences of introducing the death drive into the theoretical and clinical field were not innocuous. In 1923, in his study *The Ego and the Id*, Freud introduced his second topography of the psychic apparatus (id, ego, and superego) in which he assigned the life and death drives to these new psychic entities. In 1924, in "The Economic Problem of Masochism," he applied the concept to the clinical treatment of neurosis and perversion, thus substantially broadening the reach of masochism by revealing its three forms, spread across different psychic structures: erogenous, feminine (or infantile), and moral masochism.

These steps clearly reflect the further development of psychoanalytic experience, which would eventually bring ever deeper layers of the drive structure to light. We cannot forget that, as Freud saw it, psychoanalytic treatment and the obstacles it encounters ultimately have to do with the destiny of drives. Similarly, Lacan focused his exploration of the end of analysis on the following question: What is the subject's relation to drive at the end of analysis? This question (Lacan suggested analysts devote themselves to answering it) is the corollary of a very precise concept regarding the direction of psychoanalytic treatment: analysis begins with a symptom that, whatever form it takes, causes the patient suffering and prompts him to seek treatment. Two moments are discernible during treatment: one, analysis of the symptom uncovers the underlying unconscious fantasy; two, going through the fantasy removes drive from its surrounding symbolic and imaginary frame, allowing access to the real of the drive, beyond fantasy.

$$\text{Drive} \longleftrightarrow \text{Fantasy} \longleftrightarrow \text{Symptom}$$

Thus, the analytical journey retroactively reveals the journey from drive to fantasy that eventually produced the symptom. There is an inherent logic to this concatenation of drive, fantasy, and symptom, in which fantasy represents the possibility of satisfying a drive (a possibility discarded by reality) and in which the symptom is a manifestation of the quest to achieve satisfaction directly in the body, that is, to achieve the true destiny of drive, jouissance, situated beyond the four psychic vicissitudes identified by Freud.

## All Drives Are the Death Drive

Far from countering all psychoanalytic theory, the hypothesis of the death drive—"constitutive of the fundamental position of the human subject" (Lacan 1953–1954, 172)—extends and deepens Freud's preceding theses in that it reorders the previous set of formulations at an even more radical level.

In Seminar 11, when Lacan says, "the drive, the partial drive, is profoundly a death drive" (1964, 205), he apparently overlooks the arguments Freud used to build his two great drive dualisms over the course of many years, introducing a monism that undercuts Freud's theses. But if we delve further into this seeming contradiction, we will note that Lacan's interpretation of the death drive was quite coherent with the crux of Freud's thinking. In a formulation vital to understanding the true theoretical and clinical scope of the death drive, Lacan said that "the distinction between the life drive and the death drive is true in as much as it manifests two aspects of the drive" (1964, 257).

In writing about the constant, inextricable fusion of the life (sexual) and death drives, Freud reveals their continuity. As stated by Luiz Hanns, "Freud makes vague, rare references to moments when the death drive might evade this fusion" (1991, 150). The clinical effects of occasional defusion, particularly as universally displayed in clinical practice related to separation, demonstrate the disruptive power of the death drive throughout analytical experience, manifested distinctly when the sexual drive exits both the frame of fantasy—the "window onto the real" (Lacan 2003b, 259)—and the limitation of jouissance, made possible by the presence of the object of desire. As trenchantly observed by Eugénie Lemoine-Luccioni (1979, 73), a man, in anguished fear that he might lose the object of his passion, says to a woman, "If you leave me, I'll kill you!" A woman, in a similar situation, says "If you leave me, I'll kill myself!" In these cases, the death drive is clearly aimed in different directions: the object (sadistic) or the ego itself (masochistic).

To understand this intimate, indissoluble relationship between both drives and, more essentially, to understand that both drives are in fact two aspects of one single drive, I suggest a return to Freud's and Lacan's formulations on the prime role that fantasy plays in the psychic apparatus. This will allow us to see how Freud's three steps (the pleasure principle, 1905–1911; narcissism, 1914–1917; and the death drive, 1920–1924) in constructing his drive theory are moments of theoretical construction that do not cancel each other out but, to the contrary—by representing the deepening of theory through clinical experience—reveal the tight interweaving of different layers of drive.

## Fantasy and Death Drive

For a long time, Freud insisted that fantasy occupied a fundamentally central place in the psychic apparatus. From 1906 to 1911, in several short but highly instructive papers, he developed the metapsychology of fantasy and its relationships with the symptom and with drive. These two principles of mental functioning, which appear in the title of the paper (Freud 1911) that closes out the so-called "fantasy cycle" (Coutinho Jorge 2010, 38ff.), reveal the primacy of the pleasure principle in its indissoluble relation to the reality principle. If the former is governed by the quest for satisfaction inherent to drive, the latter puts the brakes on drive and, in circumscribing it to the frame of fantasy, which also begins acting as a powerful source of satisfaction, enshrines the reality principle, allowing the demand for drive satisfaction—and remember that we are talking about sexual drive here—to find an imaginary outlet.

Desire arises when drive is framed by fantasy and when the quest for satisfaction (jouissance) is situated in certain objects. Lacan contends that desire (a defense in relation to jouissance) is always supported by fantasy, whose structuring function both situates jouissance and delays the act. Fantasy thus sexualizes the death drive, lending it an object that, in *objecting to* the radical absence of the object of the drive (*das Ding*, the Thing), situates jouissance and, more importantly, limits it.

Lacan's coherent theorization about the constitution of the subject gives us insight into the operation at play here. As summarized by Jacques-Alain Miller, "the heart of Lacan's teaching is not unilateral stress on the signifier, but rather the relation between primal repression and the fundamental fantasy" (2018, 140). In short, the Name-of-the-Father—the vehicle of the father's structuring "No," since the *Nom-du-Père* finds expression in the *Non-du-Père*—is the agent responsible for the operation that Freud called primal repression, whose effect is to introduce the fundamental fantasy. The Name-of-the-Father says "No" to the unlimited jouissance of the death drive, and, in linking jouissance to language (to the signifier of absence, the phallus), the fundamental fantasy is introduced and jouissance is transformed into phallic jouissance, into sexual jouissance, tied to bodily orifices, which seeks partial satisfaction through the massive incidence received from the Other, from language. The death drive is thus largely redirected toward sexual objects and reconfigures itself as the sexual drive. For this reason, Lacan calls pleasure a "barrier to jouissance (but not the other way around)" (1969, 380).

Tying the fundamental fantasy to the death drive allows us to discern the structuring role that fantasy plays in the psychic apparatus, as "the subject situates himself as determined by the fantasy" (Lacan 1964, 185). It also allows us to isolate the destructive power of the death drive, since, without the establishment of the fundamental fantasy that occurs in psychoses, the death drive can no longer put the brakes on jouissance. Fantasy, which can be defined as the association between the unconscious and drive (i.e., the symbolic and the real) sexualizes the death drive and situates unlimited, deadly jouissance.

Understanding this structure also means recognizing the crucial importance of countless derivatives of fantasy within culture. As Lacan said,

> Every human formation has as its essence, and not by accident, the curbing of jouissance. The Thing appears naked to us—and no longer through these prisms and lenses called religions, philosophy . . . even hedonism, because the pleasure principle is the brake of jouissance.
>
> (Lacan 1967, 364)

In psychoses, the foreclosure of the signifier Name-of-the-Father forestalls primal repression and the subsequent establishment of the fundamental fantasy. Delirium is the attempt to make up for the absence of the fundamental fantasy so that jouissance can be situated in the case of the psychotic subject, which, for this very reason, Lacan (2003a, 221)—using an expression he himself considered paradoxical—called the subject of jouissance, in opposition to the subject of the signifier of neurosis.

When he wrote BPP, Freud had discovered the elements ultimately needed to develop a coherent distinction between neurosis and psychosis. It is no accident that BPP was quickly followed by *The Ego and the Id* and the construction of the second topography in 1923 and by the twin texts "Neurosis and Psychosis" and "The Loss of Reality in Neurosis and Psychosis" in 1924. In the latter two texts

Freud distinguishes neurosis from psychosis, approaching from the ego's relationship to drive (the id and fantasy) and to the external world. Freud concludes that both neurosis and psychosis involve a loss of reality related to the omnipresence of fantasy and delirium in these structures.

In this chapter, I wanted to elaborate with essential Lacanian developments the complex questions raised by the evolution of Freud's construction of drive theory, conceived by himself as three fundamental steps. From sexual drive to death drive, the path crossed by Freud can be significantly associated to the Lacanian route from symbolic to real. And as the place of unconscious fantasy can be situated as the heart of psychic apparatus, the psychoanalytical experience obtains much understanding of its ethical direction.

## Acknowledgments

Translated by Diane Grosklaus Whitty.

"Text originally published in Portuguese with the title "Posfácio: Incidências clínicas: 'O terceiro passo de Freud,'" in *Freud, Sigmund. Além do princípio de prazer*. Belo Horizonte: Autêntica, 2020."

## References

Assoun, Paul-Laurent. 2009. *Dictionnaire des oeuvres psychanalytiques*. Paris: PUF.

Ferenczi, Sándor. 1929. "The Unwelcome Child and his Death-Instinct." In *Final Contributions to the Problems and Methods of Psycho-Analysis*. Edited by Machael Balint. Translated by Eric Mosbacher et al., 102–107. London: Karnac Books, 1994.

Foucault, Michel. 1977. "Le jeu de Michel Foucault." In *Ornicar?* Vol. 10, 62–93.

Freud, Sigmund. 1905. "Three Essays on the Theory of Sexuality." In *Standard Edition of the Complete Psychological Works of Sigmund Freud*. Vol. 7. Translated by James Strachey, 135–230. New York: Norton, 1953.

———. 1906 (1905). "My Views on the Part Played by Sexuality in the Aetiology of the Neuroses (1906 [1905])." In *Standard Edition of the Complete Psychological Works of Sigmund Freud*. Vol. 7. Translated by James Strachey, 271–282. New York: Norton, 1953.

———. 1911. "Formulations on the Two Principles of Mental Functioning." In *Standard Edition of the Complete Psychological Works of Sigmund Freud*. Vol. 12. Translated by James Strachey, 218–226. New York: Norton, 1953.

———. 1912. "On the Universal Tendency to Debasement in the Sphere of Love (Contributions to the Psychology of Love II)." In *Standard Edition of the Complete Psychological Works of Sigmund Freud*. Vol. 11. Translated by James Strachey, 179–190. New York: Norton, 1957.

———. 1919. "The Uncanny." In *Standard Edition of the Complete Psychological Works of Sigmund Freud*. Vol. 17. Translated by James Strachey, 217–252. New York: Norton, 1955.

———. 1920. "Beyond the Pleasure Principle." In *Standard Edition of the Complete Psychological Works of Sigmund Freud*. Vol. 18. Translated by James Strachey, 7–64. New York: Norton, 1955.

———. 1930. "Civilization and Its Discontents." In *Standard Edition of the Complete Psychological Works of Sigmund Freud*. Vol. 21. Translated by James Strachey, 64–145. New York: Norton, 1961.

———. 1937. "Analysis Terminable and Interminable," In *Standard Edition of the Complete Psychological Works of Sigmund Freud*. Vol. 23. Translated by James Strachey, 216–253. New York: Norton, 1964.
Freud, Sigmund and Lou-Andreas Salomé. 1972. *Sigmund Freud and Lou Andreas-Salomé: Letters*. Edited by Ernst Pfeiffer. Translated by William and Elaine Robson-Scott. New York: Norton.
Gay, Peter. 1988. *Freud: A Life for Our Time*. New York: W.W. Norton.
Hanns, Luiz. 1991. *A teoria pulsional na clínica de Freud*. Rio de Janeiro: Imago.
Jorge, Coutinho. 2013. "12 pontuações sobre a bissexualidade." In *As homossexualidades na psicanálise na história de sua despatologização*. Edited by Antonio Quinet and Marco Antonio Coutinho Jorge, 209–214. São Paulo: Segmento Farma.
Lacan, Jacques. 1953. "The Function and Field of Speech and Language in Psychoanalysis." In *Écrits: The First Complete Edition in English*. Translated by Bruce Fink, 197–268. New York: Norton, 2007.
———. 1953–1954. *Freud's Papers on Technique: The Seminar of Jacques Lacan*, Book 1. Edited by Jacques-Alain Miller. Translated by John Forrester. New York: Norton, 1991.
———. 1954–1955. *The Ego in Freud's Theory and in the Technique of Psychoanalysis: The Seminar of Jacques Lacan*, Book II. Edited by Jacques-Alain Miller. Translated by Sylvia Tomaselli. New York: Norton, 1988.
———. 1958. "The Direction of the Treatment and the Principle of its Power," In *Écrits: The First Complete Edition in English*. Translated by Bruce Fink, 489–542. New York: Norton, 2007.
———. 1960. "The Subversion of the Subject and the Dialectic of Desire in the Freudian Unconscious," In *Écrits: The First Complete Edition in English*. Translated by Bruce Fink, 671–702. New York: Norton, 2007.
———. 1960–1961. *Transference: The Seminar of Jacques Lacan*, Book VIII. Edited by Jacques-Alain Miller. Translated by Bruce Fink. Cambridge, UK: Polity Press, 2015.
———. 1964. *The Four Fundamental Concepts of Psychoanalysis: The Seminar of Jacques Lacan*, Book 11. Edited by Jacques-Alain Miller. Translated by Alan Sheridan. New York: Norton, 1977.
———. 1967. "Allocution sur les psychoses de l'enfant." In *Autres Écrits*. Edited by Jacques-Alain Miller, 361–371. Paris: Seuil, 2001.
———. 1969. "L'acte psychanalytique: Compte Rendu du Séminaire 1967–1968." In *Autres Écrits*. Edited by Jacques-Alain Miller, 375–383. Paris: Seuil, 2001.
———. 1972. "L'Étourdit." In *Autres Écrits*. Edited by Jacques-Alain Miller, 449–495. Paris: Seuil, 2001.
———. 2003a. "Apresentação das memórias de um doentes dos nervos," In *Outros escritos*. Rio de Janeiro: Jorge Zahar.
———. 2003b. "Proposição de 9 de outubro de 1967 sobre o psicanalista da Escola," In *Outros escritos*. Rio de Janeiro: Jorge Zahar.
Lemoine-Luccioni, Eugénie. 1979. *Partage des femmes*. Paris: Seuil.
Lévi-Strauss, Claude. 1958. "The Effectiveness of Symbols." In *Structural Anthropology*. Translated by Claire Jacobson and Brook Grundfest Schoepf, 186–205. New York: Basic Books, 1963.
Miller, Jacques-Alain. 2018. *Del síntoma al fantasma. Y retorno*. Buenos Aires: Paidós.
Nunberg, Herman and Ernst Federn, eds. 1975. *Minutes of the Vienna Psychoanalytic Society*, Vol. IV, 1912–1918. New York: International Universities Press.
Roudinesco, Elisabeth, and Michel Plon. 1998. *Dicionário de psicanálise*. Rio de Janeiro: Jorge Zahar.
Spielrein, Sabina. 1912. "Destruction as the Cause of Coming Into Being." *Journal of Analytical Psychology* 39 (1994): 155–186.

Chapter 4

# Freud's *Beyond the Pleasure Principle* and the Death Drive

## A Concise Overview

Chris Vanderwees

*Chris Vanderwees in this paper takes us on an important theoretical and historical journey through the development of the death drive in Freud's* Beyond the Pleasure Principle. *Without falling into the common historical error of linking the invention of the death drive to the death of Freud's daughter Sophie, Vanderwees is nevertheless able to anchor the then-new concept of the death drive in the historical milieu of the First World War. In that atmosphere of oppressive death, it still remains a fact, Vanderwees notes, that one can't represent to oneself one's own death. Personal death is repressed and relegated to fantasy. After covering the historical ground that gave rise to the death drive, Vanderwees is in a position to consider the repressed death drive theoretically, as cause of repetition.*

In this chapter, I attempt to outline the central aspects of Freud's *Beyond the Pleasure Principle*, which is a text that marks an early and significant contribution to thinking about the occurrence and recurrence of psychological phenomena following the subject's exposure to traumatic incidents or environments. In this particular text, Freud wonderfully and haphazardly intermingles theories of psychotherapy, philosophy, biology, physics, sexuality studies, and human behavior in an attempt to theorize what he calls the *Todestrieb* or death drive (Smith 2010, 5). He suggests that life is designated through "ever more complicated *detours*" and "circuitous paths to death," or the "[drive] to return to the inanimate state" (Freud 1920, 38–39). With such a notion, Freud designated a form of repetition compulsion where the subject is propelled toward destructiveness, whether this destructiveness is directed inwardly toward the ego (masochism) or outwardly toward others and the external world (sadism). Freud's introduction of the general hypothesis in *Beyond the Pleasure Principle* that "the aim of all life is death" (38) has always been met with not only great interest, but also skepticism, confusion, and dismissal from even his closest contemporaries. Many theorists simply cast the concept aside as Freud's own projection and expression of his own anxieties about death during wartime. More frequently, however, the death-drive is characterized as an unappealing and cynical concept, one that is apparently superfluous, biologically inaccurate, and supposedly contributes little to psychoanalytic metapsychology (McDougall 1936;

Becker 1973; Dufresne 2000). I will not delve into the various controversies or biological criticisms that are available elsewhere (Colby 1955; Jones 1957), but rather I try to follow several of Freud's detours on the death drive so as to clarify the context and significance of this concept as it emerged his work.

## Freud and the First World War

It is hardly surprising that death would be on Freud's mind while living in Vienna through the First World War. Archduke Franz Ferdinand and his wife, Sophie, Duchess of Hohenberg, were shot dead in Sarajevo, and when Austria declared war on Serbia with German support, other nation states quickly took sides, pursuing pathways of aggression and destruction towards each other. Throughout the war, the Austro-Hungarian military would suffer horrendous casualties, well over a million deaths with more than three million reported wounded. Thousands of refugees fled to Vienna to get away from the violence of war in the northern provinces. Food shortages became a widespread problem. It is estimated that almost half a million Austrian civilians died from starvation, cold, or disease during the war years. The disastrous effects of the war, of course, produced a significant amount of instability and uncertainty for the Freud family. When his daughter, Anna, was stranded in England during the outbreak of hostilities in 1915, Freud had to call upon friend and colleague Ernest Jones to help her get home by way of detours through Gibraltar and Genoa. His sons Martin and Ernst volunteered for military service, while Oliver went to work on engineering projects for the army. Freud's son-in-law, Max Halberstadt (his daughter Sophie's husband), and his nephew Hermann Graf (his sister Rosa's son) also served for the Austrian army during the war where ultimately Max would be wounded in France and Hermann would be killed in action. Many of Freud's followers, including Max Eitingon, Sandor Ferenczi, and Karl Abraham, were also put to work for the military in their capacity as physicians. Otto Rank was forced into the editorship of the official military newspaper in Poland, where he became depressed. Prospective patients were drafted to the military or were more preoccupied with the torments of wartime than their own neuroses, leaving Freud with a desolate practice and substantial financial losses, especially when the Austrian krone collapsed as a currency. "The never-relaxing tension of the war years," sixty-year-old Freud told Ferenczi in 1915, "has an exhausting effect" (qtd. In Gay 1988, 369). Much less time could be devoted to psychoanalytic studies and money was not available for scholarly activities. The Vienna Psychoanalytic Society began to meet more infrequently, international conferences were abandoned, and journal submissions and subscriptions dwindled. Producing such instability, "the war posed," writes biographer Peter Gay, "an acute danger to the very survival of psychoanalysis" (350).

With effects of national conflict still lingering heavily on the Austrian population in the war's aftermath, Freud and his family continued to live through a time of hardships. Despite the new Austrian government's desperate appeals for resources and support from foreign nations, conditions remained rather dire after the war. Gay provides a sketch of the state of affairs in Vienna that the Freud family would have lived under in the war's wake:

> Food ... was no less unpalatable or inadequate, heating materials were no less unobtainable, than they had been during the last two years of the war. The government tightly rationed all necessities; even milk was hard to come by. There were weeks when beef was available only to hospitals and to such public employees as firemen and streetcar conductors. Rice was offered as a substitute for meat, and sauerkraut was supposed to take the place of potatoes. Even those holding ration coupons for soap could not find any in the stores. There was virtually no petroleum or coal to be had, and one stubby half candle was all a household could claim in January 1919.... "Our nutrition is still ... scanty and miserable," Freud wrote in April 1919, really a "starvation diet." ... Freud's letters frankly document the impact of the of the general misery on his own household. He was writing in a "bitterly cold room" and searched in vain for a usable fountain pen.
>
> (1988, 381)

While living in this state of post-war depravation, Freud was further met with the suicide of his student, psychoanalyst Victor Tausk, in July of 1919. Tausk fired a pistol into his temple while wearing a curtain braid around his neck, hanging himself as he fell. Not long after Tausk's death, the important organizer and financial supporter of the psychoanalytic movement, Anton von Freund, died of cancer in January of 1920. The loss of Tausk was followed only five days later by Freud's daughter, Sophie, who succumbed to influenza and pneumonia (complications from contracting the Spanish flu in its final wave). Her death sent a shock through the Freud family, as she was also pregnant with a third child. After this string of traumatic losses, Freud wrote to Jones, "Can you remember a time so full of death as this present one?" (Freud and Jones 1920, 370).

The tumultuous socio-political climate of the First World War had a deep influence on Freud's emerging speculations about the relationship between psychology, biology, and death. Although Freud had already raised the idea of death wishes, especially the child's Oedipal aspiration to murder the father, as early as 1892 in his letters to Fliess, and briefly examined several dreams involving death in his major work, *The Interpretation of Dreams*, perhaps his earliest and most sustained ruminations on the social and psychological effects of confrontations with mortality do not appear until 1915 in "Thoughts for the Times on War and Death."

In this text, Freud claimed that the mass deaths of the war had left the people of Europe deeply disillusioned with the notions of universal humanism, civility, and peace between nations:

> Not only is [this war] more bloody and more destructive than any war of other days, because of the enormously increased perfection of weapons of attack and

defense; it is at least as cruel, as embittered, as implacable as any that has preceded it.... It tramples in blind fury on all that comes in its way, as though there were to be no future and no peace among men after it is over.

(1915a, 278–279)

Freud remarked that the brutality and low morality of nation states during the war produced widespread mental distress, feelings of disorientation, and a sense of helplessness amongst the civilian population: "The individual who is not himself a combatant—and so a cog in the gigantic machine of war—feels bewildered in his orientation, and inhibited in his powers and activities" (275). He claimed that the turbulence and bloodiness of the war had resulted in a greater awareness of individual precariousness and mortality. Although one may formally recognize their own death as inevitable, Freud suggested that, prior to the outbreak of the First World War, individuals were more inclined to treat death as though it did not really exist.

With the war having such an overwhelming effect on the social imaginary, Freud proposed that it had become more difficult to suppress thoughts of death. The war, Freud argued, had disrupted something of the individual's defense mechanisms against death, bringing the end of life to the forefront of individual consciousness:

Death will no longer be denied; we are forced to believe in it. People really die; and no longer one by one, but many, often tens of thousands, in a single day. And death is no longer a chance event. To be sure ... the accumulation of deaths puts an end to the impression of chance.

(291)

Grappling with a heightened sensitivity to life as fragile, vulnerable, and expugnable, Freud began to think more directly about the relationship between life and death, being and nonbeing in "Thoughts for the Times."

Here, Freud's theoretical claims are numerous and appear somewhat dissonant as he worked to outline the symbolic aspects of death from a psychosocial perspective. He argued that a conventional and cultural attitude towards death is simultaneously acknowledged and denied in consciousness. He also presented what might seem to be a discrepancy, in which death appeared to be clearly evident to the individual, but also seemed something that the individual was likely to avoid and could not easily imagine or symbolize in representation:

[W]e were of course prepared to maintain that death was the necessary outcome of life, that everyone owes nature a death and must expect to pay the debt—in short, that death was natural, undeniable and unavoidable. In reality, however, we were accustomed to behave as if it were otherwise. We showed an unmistakable tendency to put death on one side, to eliminate it from life. We tried to hush it up; indeed we even have a saying [in German]: "to think of something as though it were death". That is, as though it were our own death, of course. It is indeed impossible to imagine our own death; and whenever we attempt to do so we can perceive that we are in fact still present as spectators. Hence the psychoanalytic school could venture on the assertion that at bottom no one believes in his own death, or, to put the same thing in another way, that in the unconscious every one of us is convinced of his own immortality.

(289)

Freud raises several ideas, suggesting that death exists in the psyche as self-evident but also suggesting that death is a topic that people generally avoid since any mention of mortality may conjure the individual's own fear of that which cannot be easily imagined without some subjective recoil. Freud also conveys in this paper that individuals cannot actually repress death insofar as one's own death cannot be experienced prior to its occurrence. This idea can be traced to Immanuel Kant's *Anthropology*, where the philosopher argues that

Nobody can experience his own death (since it requires life in order to experience); he can only observe it in others. . . . The thought, I am not, cannot exist at all; because if I am not, then it cannot occur to me that I am not.

(1978, 55–56)

Adrian Johnston (2010) also summarizes this point when he writes that one cannot experience one's own death since "death 'as such,' (that is, the individual's 'own most' death as anticipated from his/her first-person perspective) escapes the powers of mental representation)" (42). The thought of one's own demise might be repressed, but this remains the repression of a fantasy. This imaginary fantasy or wish still leaves the individual in the position of a detached spectator. In 1915, death appears to be both simultaneously absent and present in the psyche for Freud. Despite any theoretical inconsistencies in "Thoughts for the Times," what is clear is that Freud was attempting to grapple with the individual's psychological suffering while living through times of instability, loss, and destruction, questioning what the lasting effects of the war would be on the broader social sensibility towards morality and mortality.

## Freud's **Todestrieb**

In his early work, Freud thought that there was a duality between the self-preservative (ego) drives and the sexual (libidinal or object) drives. Throughout the First World War, Freud began to think about self-preservation and self-love not as oppositional but as actually operating in close relation. In 1915, he attempted to resolve this issue with distinctions between love and hate in "Instincts and their Vicissitudes." It was not until 1920 with *Beyond the Pleasure Principle*, however, that Freud more clearly brought the self-preservative and libidinal forces together under the notion of the life drive. Freud's proposition of the death drive is partially a resolution to the inconsistency within his earlier theory of narcissism. His main contention in *Beyond the Pleasure Principle* appears to be that the fundamental biological inevitability for each organism to return to an inorganic substance may explain destruction or death as a primary motivation for life. He is not only concerned with theorizing a biological principle. Freud directly acknowledges that he has "unwittingly steered [the] course into the harbour of Schopenhauer's philosophy" (Freud 1920, 49–50). One can easily see Schopenhauer's influence on *Beyond the Pleasure Principle* if the German philosopher's words from the 1818 text, *The World as Will and Representation*, are read alongside Freud's ideas. It is also clear that Freud drew his inspiration for *Beyond the Pleasure Principle* from Empedocles, Plato, Schopenhauer, Kant, and also likely from Nietzsche. As an aspiring philosopher, Freud instated the Greek mythological term, *Eros*, as a designation for the life drive. Although Freud never used *Thanatos* as a descriptor for the death drive, followers of psychoanalysis would later employ this term so often that it would become synonymous with the concept.

It is clear that Freud outlined the revised drive theory in binary terms. Responsible for the subject's tendency toward hate, separation, alienation, self-destruction, and disorganization, the death drive exists in opposition to the life drive or *Eros*, the drive that tends towards love, creation, reproduction, organization, unity, and cohesiveness. He is optimistic in his suggestion that, despite the death drive's persistence, the ego has a "strong tendency towards the pleasure principle" (Freud 1920, 9). It is only under certain circumstances or conditions that this tendency will be subverted or structured at odds with the life drive. He provides three key examples in *Beyond the Pleasure Principle*. First, Freud begins with an examination of patients who have experienced trauma and suggests that the nightmares of railroad accident survivors and war veterans have the "characteristic of repeatedly bringing the patient back into the situation of his accident, a situation from which he wakes up in another fright" and, as a result, do not seem to conform to the pleasure principle (13). Death wish dreams as well as dreams of violence or aggression had already raised some questions surrounding the pleasure principle and the notion of dreams as wish fulfillment in the initial work of Freud's early students, Alfred Adler and Wilhelm Stekel[1] and Sabina Spelrein.[2]

Second, Freud suggests that the childhood game of *fort* and *da* ("gone" and "there") appears to be a reenactment of the child's separation from the mother. Observing the play of his grandson, Freud observed that Ernst would play "away" with his toys, throwing them out of sight. Eventually, Freud observes a second variation of the game:

> What he did was to hold the reel by the string and very skillfully throw it over the edge of his curtained cot, so that it disappeared into it. . . . He then pulled the reel out of the cot again by the string and hailed its reappearance with a joyful '*da*' ['there']. This, then, was the complete game—disappearance and return.
>
> (15)

Freud suggests several possible interpretations of the child's play. The boy might have dramatized the mother's absence through the first act of the game, throwing the objects away as a way to express or discharge anger towards the mother that would otherwise have been suppressed. The child's internal anger or distress at the mother's absence becomes displaced or projected onto objects within the child's environment. "The child," writes Freud, "cannot possibly have felt his mother's departure as something agreeable or even indifferent" (15). Freud suggests that the game allows the previously passive child who was separated from the mother to assert an active role in repeating the displeasure of separation. The child repeats a distressing event of the past, performing a destructive impulse, but also seems to derive some pleasure from being able to control the return. In this sense, the game might be understood as the child's attempt at mastery of the original experience whether it was pleasurable or not. With the child's game of his grandson in mind, Freud poses a question to the problem, "How . . . does his repetition of this distressing experience as a game fit in with the pleasure principle?" (15). For Freud, such a game demonstrates the child's repetitious attempt to achieve mastery over the trauma of separation while also expressing aggression towards the mother in her absence.

Thirdly, Freud raises the issue of transference where patients are often "obliged to *repeat* the repressed material as a contemporary experience instead of, as the physician would prefer to see, *remembering* it as something belonging to the past" (1920, 18, emphasis Freud). At this point, Freud begins to think about masochism as "the turning round of the [drive] upon the subject's own ego . . . [which would be] a return to an earlier phase of the [drive's] history, a regression" (54–55). Freud characterizes the death drive in terms of regression and repetition compulsion and then begins to think of its influence on categorizations of masochism and sadism, which partially provided him with a structure for thinking about patients who continue to relive the trauma of past experience in the present. He has in mind those patients who may continually repeat acts of aggression towards themselves or others or those patients who find themselves in destructive situations that uncannily resemble previously terrifying or disastrous relational dynamics and environments. At this stage of Freud's theory, the death drive is thought to have the capacity to override the pleasure principle if the patient's past experience has overwhelmed the protective barriers and boundaries of the ego. The object of the death drive is fleeting, partial, displaced, and divided through the compulsion to repeat, leading the individual to unconsciously seek approximations of the overwhelming past.

## Trauma and the Unbound

How does Freud explain the emergence of the subject's tendency to be overwhelmed with the death drive? Such a drive is the result of extreme distress and psychological trauma, an experience or environment that has not been integrated, processed, or worked through in speech, but to understand this better, it is important to explore his theory of psychological binding. It may be helpful to think through the Freudian theorization of binding as Lacan might have in terms of a poetic knowledge which resists being reduced to biology or understanding and provides something of an overdetermined psychoanalytical metaphor but one that also speaks to the phenomena of clinical experience (Felman 1987). The notion of binding initially appeared in *Studies on Hysteria* (1895) but was further developed through Freud's letters to Wilhelm Fliess. Freud envisioned psychic energy in two different states: "one in which the energy is tonically 'bound' and the other in which it is freely mobile and presses towards discharge" (1915b, 188). Binding has a psychological function in Freudian theory in relation to the origin and function of the ego. Freud imagined an economics of physical and psychical energy whereby the ego is composed of a bound mass of neurons, resulting in a secondary process that is well connected, organized, and able to have a binding effect on other processes. Perhaps most simply put, binding conveys the psychic function of signification, the process whereby the subject constructs meaning from signs composed of signifiers and signifieds. If energy is bound, it is linked to an object. An idea that comes to one's mind and is spoken aloud, for instance, might be understood as the free energy of the primary processes linked to the unconscious, manifesting as a bound and conscious symbolization in the secondary processes. In other words, the drive is bound to a representative for the ego.

Unbound energy correlates with the id and the primary process. If energy is unbound, it can be prone to immediate discharge. What may go beyond the pleasure principle is an excess of this unbound or free energy. The unbound energies within the primary psychical process can produce intense and overwhelming feelings as a result of unsymbolized internal conflict. From this perspective, trauma results from the ego's encounter with too much unbound information that cannot properly be processed, understood, or integrated. During exposure to the traumatic incident or environment, the ego is unable to form enough of a protective shield against an overflow of internally experienced or externally encountered energy. Freud provides the example of an undifferentiated "vesicle," which is harmed from the intensity of an overwhelming experience. As a result, the subject becomes prone to compulsive repeating presumably as an unconscious attempt at binding, discharge. Freud suggests that repetition compulsion may also be understood as an attempt at mastery of the original traumatic scene. While the death drive is composed of unbound energy that moves the subject towards disintegration, the life drive binds energy and creates unity for the ego. Richard Boothby writes that the crucial polarity expressed in *Beyond the Pleasure Principle* is not really "between the organic and the inorganic, between biological life and death, but rather that between the organic and the properly psychological, between the force of unbound instinctual energies and the bound structure of the ego" (83; cf. Boothby 1991, 2001). Ultimately, Freud thought that the function of the psyche was to regulate and bind flows of affective energy and intensity. For Freud, the death drive is non-matter, an energy, and involves entropy as in thermodynamics.

From this perspective, the ego might be understood as a defensive, preservative, and regulatory structure, "establish[ing] a controlled economy of excitations by acting as a kind of sieve or semi-permeable membrane" as it "admits some portion of energies impinging on the psychic apparatus from both inside and outside the organism but screens out other energies, thereby protecting the system from overload" (Boothby 53).

A few years later in 1923, Freud further developed his ideas concerning these two drives in *The Ego and the Id* and remained dedicated to the concept of the death drive throughout the remainder of his life. For Freud, the oppositional dualism of the drives designates a dialectical tension, a reversed interdependence whereby the life drive aims towards creation, order, and integration, while the death drive aims towards destruction, disorder, and disintegration. Seemingly opposed yet entangled, the tension between these mutually constitutive poles is the foundation for much psychoanalytical thinking about psychical conflict as well as related and overlapping divisions and splits in various theories regarding human subjectivity: ego and id, good and bad, love and hate, bound and unbound, conscious and unconscious. Ultimately, Freud attempted to conceptualize the *Todestrieb* as a force of destructive or aggressive energy aimed towards oneself that may also emerge as hostility or violence towards others. For Freud, psychoanalysis must account for the analysand's own experience with death or self-effacement as part of the repetition compulsion, which is what is so crucially being opened up for psychoanalytical and philosophical thinking throughout *Beyond the Pleasure Principle*.

Here, I have provided an overview of the death drive as Freud theorized the concept during his survival of war crises. I have also outlined Freud's shift in thinking from his earlier works to his revisionary attempts to articulate the concept in *Beyond the Pleasure Principle*. For Freud, the death drive is non-matter at the level of the subject's primary processes and the unconscious. It is that which animates the repetition compulsion. With Freud's theory of the death drive, we have an important concept that further destabilizes the notion of the conscious and rational Cartesian subject, but we also have a very early attempt to understand what happens to the subject following traumatic experience. The concept has influenced many psychoanalysts and theorists since Freud, but especially Jacques Lacan, who does the work of tying the death drive to the symbolic realm of language in the psychoanalytic clinic.

## Notes

1 Freud's initial followers Wilhelm Stekel and Alfred Adler were perhaps the first to propose psychoanalytic thoughts on an aggressive drive within a psychoanalytic context as early as 1908.
2 Sabina Spielrein published "Destruction as the Cause of Coming into Being" in 1912, which raised questions about the premise of the Freudian pleasure principle in relation to destructive thoughts, feelings, and behaviors.

## References

Becker, Ernest. 1973. *The Denial of Death*. New York: The Free Press.
Boothby, Richard. 1991. *Death and Desire: Psychoanalytic Theory in Lacan's Return to Freud*. New York: Routledge.
———. 2001. *Freud as Philosopher: Metapsychology after Lacan*. New York: Routledge.
Colby, Kenneth. 1955. *Energy and Structure in Psychoanalysis*. New York: Ronald Press.
Dufresne, Todd. 2000. *Tales from the Freudian Crypt: The Death Drive in Text and Context*. Stanford: Stanford University Press.
Felman, Shoshana. 1987. *Jacques Lacan and the Adventure of Insight: Psychoanalysis in Contemporary Culture*. Cambridge: Harvard University Press.
Freud, Sigmund. 1915a. "Thoughts for the Times on War and Death." 1915. In *Standard Edition of the Complete Psychological Works of Sigmund Freud*. Vol. 14. Translated by James Strachey, 273–300. London: Vintage and Hogarth Press, 2001.
———. 1915b. "The Unconscious." In *Standard Edition of the Complete Psychological Works of Sigmund Freud*. Vol. 14. Translated by James Strachey, 159–215. London: Vintage and Hogarth Press, 2001.
———. 1920. "Beyond the Pleasure Principle." In *The Standard Edition of the Complete Psychological Works of Sigmund Freud*. Vol. 18. Translated by James Strachey, 1–64. London: Vintage and Hogarth Press, 2001.
Freud, Sigmund and Ernest Jones. 1920. "To Ernest Jones." In *The Complete Correspondence of Sigmund Freud and Ernest Jones, 1908–1939*. Edited by R. Andrew Paskauskas, 368–370. Cambridge: Harvard University Press, 1995.
Gay, Peter. 1988. *Freud: A Life for Our Time*. New York: W.W. Norton & Company.
Johnston, Adrian. 2010. "Sextimacy—Freud, Mortality, and a Reconsideration of the Role of Sexuality in Psychoanalysis." In *Sexuality and Psychoanalysis: Philosophical Criticisms*. Edited by Jens Vleminck and Eran Dorfman, 35–62. Leuven: Leuven University Press.
Jones, Ernest. 1957. *Sigmund Freud Life and Work, Volume Three: The Last Phase 1919–1939*. London: Hogarth Press.
Kant, Immanuel. 1978. *Anthropology from a Pragmatic Point of View*. Translated by Victor Lyle Dowdell. Carbondale: Southern Illinois University Press.
McDougall, William. 1936. *Psycho-Analysis and Social Psychology*. London: Metheun.
Smith, Robert Rowland. 2010. *Death-Drive: Freudian Hauntings in Literature and Art*. Edinburgh: Edinburgh University Press.
Spielrein, Sabina. 1912. "Destruction as the Cause of Coming into Being." *Journal of Analytical Psychology* 39 (1994): 155–186.

Chapter 5

# Ex-Pulsion
## On the History of Lay Analysis and Gay Analysts in the United States[1]

*Ona Nierenberg*

*Many have commented on James Strachey's mistranslation of Freud's* Trieb *as "instinct." Ona Nierenberg here suggests that the famous mistranslation is perhaps not a cause but a symptom of misunderstanding—a misunderstanding that did real damage. Nierenberg, a U.S.-based psychoanalyst, takes as her test case the historical exclusion of gay and lay analysts in the United States, and she links it directly to the ego-psychological notion of the drive as instinct. Harking back to Freud's early text* Three Essays on the Theory of Sexuality, *Nierenberg notes that it has always been a basic Freudian assumption that all human sexuality is constitutively "out of sync." With precise historical and theoretical references, Nierenberg's important contribution shows how this basic Freudian insight was lost in American psychoanalysis, but she also shows that Lacan's relentless attacks on the ego-psychologists did little to foster understanding. Nierenberg concludes by emphasizing the importance of bisexuality in psychoanalytic thought, and the importance of a drive independent of biological instinct.*

## Introduction

Often characterized by his supposed pessimism, Freud was perhaps far too optimistic in calling psychoanalysis "the plague" during his one and only visit to the United States of America in 1909. The powerful immunological response that arose here took the form of suppressing psychoanalysis by domesticating it, insisting that it belonged to the land of medicine. While Freud unwaveringly held that psychoanalysis is unequivocally Other to medicine and cannot be mapped on to a medical model of treatment, the Americans made clear that they fundamentally renounced the alterity of the Freudian thing by restricting the practice to medical doctors. Freud came close to expelling the Americans from the International Psychoanalytic Association over this matter, realizing full well that while the question of lay analysis may appear to be about *who* can (or cannot) practice psychoanalysis, it is actually the kernel of truth that reveals *what* psychoanalysis is. For Freud, medicalization was one of the names for the repression of psychoanalysis, a potent force against the radical implications of his discovery. Observing that a medical education is "more or less the opposite of what [one] would need as a preparation for psychoanalysis" (1926, 230), Freud appreciated that limiting the practice of psychoanalysis to physicians was antithetical to his discovery.

Throughout his teaching, Lacan called attention to the profound impact medicalization had on the history of psychoanalysis, highlighting the causes and effects wrought by the intransigent opposition to lay analysis in the United States.

While this history, and the *méconaissance* of the Freudian field it implies, has long been appreciated as one of the roots of Lacan's call for a "Return to Freud," perhaps less considered have been the dire consequences of medicalization for the history of psychoanalysis's relationship to homosexuality, including the barring of homosexuals from analytic training in the United States. It is my belief that the destinies of gay analysts and lay analysis in the United States are joined by a missing link: Freud's concept of the drive in ego psychology. Thus, it is my intention to call attention to the urgency of the drive for the social link, recalling its importance as a—if not *the*—fundamental concept of psychoanalysis by revealing what took place when the drive was driven out. Strachey's famous (infamous?) mistranslation of Freud's word *Trieb* as "instinct" rather than "drive" can be viewed not just as the *cause* but also as the *symptom* of a misunderstanding regarding Freud's most radical concept. Strachey's misreading had a profoundly negative impact on the trajectory of psychoanalysis and most regrettably, damaged many lives in the process.

In this chapter, I will be tracing the series of expulsions, excommunications, exclusions, excisions, and extractions involved in the fate of the Freudian drive and its consequences for gay analysts and lay analysis in America. This will inexorably lead us to an encounter with the perhaps all-too-well-known *bêtes noires* of Lacan. Although place of origin did not exempt anyone from Lacan's criticism, his contemptuousness, sarcasm, and mockery were at their apex when directed towards the ego psychologists whose forced exile from Europe shifted psychoanalysis' "center of gravity" away from the continent to the United States of America (Guido 2015). In my opinion, Lacan's derisiveness and disdain towards the ego psychologists has not served psychoanalysis well and has deafened us to hearing his derision as a specific response that took place within a particular history and context. While exploring this aspect of Lacan's style would be a worthy independent project, I believe it is important to raise here because the malice Lacan directed toward the ego psychologists—holding them in contempt for their reduction of the Freudian drive to a biological instinct as the corollary to promoting the supremacy of the ego—has created an impediment to the transmission of Lacan in the United States, where I live and work. Furthermore, it has functioned as an obstacle to reading the ego psychologists' work for ourselves, supporting an illusion that "everybody already knows" and contributing to a mirage of "common knowledge."

While Lacan's rhetorical displays may seduce readers towards an easy enjoyment of mockery and disdain, I would urge us to recall Freud's observation that the most significant resistances to psychoanalysis are *internal*, meaning not only those resistances that are internal to the psychoanalytic field but also those that each one of us bear by virtue of being subjects. Indeed, as Freud discovered, resistances are a present and constant force, as well as the very spur, of analytic work. Resistances are necessary, and it is necessary to address them. Therefore, my analysis of the trajectory of the Freudian drive in no way implies a lack of regard for ego psychologists, to whom we owe a significant debt, and whose careful readings and misreadings of Freud still have much to teach us about resistances internal to psychoanalysis and how to reckon with them.

## Discrimination?

While the questions I am raising here vis à vis medicalization and the drive may seem to be long-settled distant history, perhaps you will find it as surprising as I did to discover that it was as recently as 1991 that the American Psychoanalytic Association Executive Council passed a "non-discrimination" by-law that excluded sexual orientation from being considered as a factor in the admission of candidates for psychoanalytic training as well as for faculty appointments. Prior to that point, gay and lesbian prospective analysts either hid their same-sex desire or did not apply to institutes of the American Psychoanalytic Association. After all, homosexuality was considered a de facto psychopathology that would expel them from consideration as candidates. In fact, it wasn't until 2002 that the International Psychoanalytic Association caught up to the Americans and passed a similar by-law. Of course, the background to these administrative "correctives" is the fact that until 1973, homosexuality was inscribed in the *Diagnostic and Statistical Manual of Mental Disorders* as a psychiatric diagnosis, a so-called "mental illness." It should not be forgotten that American non-analyst psychiatrists spearheaded the de-classification of homosexuality as a "mental disorder" while the psychoanalysts (as an association) objected to it. In fact, in large part, the politically motivated removal of "homosexuality" as a stand-alone diagnosis was propelled by the desire to distance psychiatry from the virulently anti-homosexual views represented most vociferously by American psychoanalysts Charles Socarides and Irving Bieber, who asserted that homosexuality represents a *necessarily* pathological deviation from the supposed naturally-derived norm of heterosexuality (Bayer 1987, 125).

With respect to "non-discrimination" and psychoanalysis, 1991 was indeed a remarkable year. Strikingly, it was that very same year that the American Psychoanalytic Association also approved a by-law amendment allowing doctoral level psychologists and social workers (who, as non-physicians, would formerly have been considered "lay") to be admitted for psychoanalytic training. Nevertheless, it is difficult to interpret this as a change of heart regarding "discrimination" against non-physicians. The by-law amendment was the result of a legal mandate resulting from a Federal antitrust class action suit alleging restraint of trade and monopoly practices filed in 1985 by the Group for Advancement of Psychotherapy and Psychoanalysis in Psychotherapy (this is often referred to as the GAPPP lawsuit). The suit was not settled until 1989, and its implementation in 1991 by way of passing the by-law amendment ended the long and restrictive policy limiting the training of psychoanalysts solely to psychiatrists (who are also medical doctors) in American

Psychoanalytic Association institutes, a constraint that had been in place since the 1920s. Not quite an admission of "lay" analysts, this by-law amendment was also quite restrictive since it included only those with mental health licenses (psychologists and social workers). It was on the ground of this history of exclusion and physicians' monopoly that a specific psychoanalytic license was created in certain states, for better and worse (see Nierenberg 2007).

It is crucial for us to consider what it means for psychoanalysts to have to pass "non-discrimination" amendments, clauses, and by-laws. The first dictionary definition of *discrimination*, according to Webster's, pertains to "unjust prejudicial treatment of a people." This would leave us with the important question of how such an "unjust prejudice of a people" would come about in a psychoanalytic association. But the second definition of *discrimination*—"the recognition of the difference between one thing and another"—leaves us with even more vital questions. This definition unveils a profound difficulty given that the remedy—non-discrimination (not being able to tell the difference between one thing and another)—is antithetical to occupying the position of psychoanalyst. Here we find the crucial paradox: It is my assertion that "non-discrimination" (not being able to tell the difference) was, in fact, the *cause* of "discrimination" as prejudice, as hatred towards the other. I believe that the exclusion of lay and gay analysts in the history of American psychoanalysis has as its cause the inability to discriminate, to distinguish between the specificity of psychoanalysis and the discourse of biology (scientism), between the psychoanalyst and the doctor, between the human and the animal, and finally, but not lastly, the instinct and the drive.

## The Ceaselessly Stunning Surprise of the Freudian Drive

We can appreciate the importance of discrimination in psychoanalysis by turning to Freud's *Three Essays on the Theory of Sexuality* (*Drei Abhandlungen Zur Sexualtheorie*, also translated as *Three Contributions to the Sexual Theory*), a book that has lost none of its power to astound and astonish. Truly a testament to the disjunction between knowledge and truth, we see that its "truths" to this very day cannot be absorbed into "knowledge," which is why this text is just as ahead of our time as it was of its own. Originally written in 1905, Freud continued to modify the *Three Essays* over the next twenty years, adding footnotes, new terminology, and new introductions, but never revising the book in its entirety, which is one of the elements that make it most precious. It is a palimpsest and a primary psychoanalytic text, since here Freud reveals his unique psychoanalytic conception of sexuality based on the drives (psychosexuality), which has as its foundation the rejection of biological determinism with respect to human sexual desire and object choice, underlining the fundamentally "un-natural" status of sexuality for human subjects.

Here is how Freud begins the *Three Essays*:

> The fact of the existence of sexual needs in human beings and animals is expressed in biology by the assumption of a 'sexual instinct,' on the analogy of the instinct of nutrition, that is, of hunger. . . .
>
> Popular opinion has quite definite ideas about the nature and characteristics of this sexual instinct. It is generally understood to be absent in childhood, to set in at the time of puberty in connection with the process of coming to maturity and to be revealed in manifestations of an irresistible attraction exercised by one sex upon the other; while its aim is presumed to be sexual union. . . . *We have every reason to believe, however, that these views give a very false picture of the true situation. If we look into them more closely we shall find they contain a number of errors, inaccuracies and hasty conclusions.*
>
> (1905, 135, emphasis mine)

What an opening salvo in the guise of understatement—so typical of Freud! It takes him a mere two paragraphs to forge an absolute cut from the hegemony of biology and popular opinion, telling us that psychoanalytic sexuality is to be distinguished from the realm of instinct and that human sexuality is not a biologically innate, fixed pattern of behavior with a pre-established aim and object. The implications of this are far reaching and remain breathtaking. Here Freud reveals the truth of human subjectivity: we are fundamentally "out of sync." Estranged from the possibility of having an "instinct of nutrition," we are destined to always eat too much or too little or to be confused about it. By cleaving human sexuality from the realm of instinct by way of the drives, Freud opens us to a universe of consideration of *how* the human subject in all its singularity and complexity comes into being, without its destiny or its Sovereign Good having been written in advance by God or Nature. Lacan captures it thus: "In man, there is (always) already a crack, a profound perturbation in the regulation of life" (1954–1955, 37). This crack is the opening through which Lacan conceives of the subject, and while it is beyond the scope of this chapter, we can find here in the Freudian drive the derivation of Lacan's fundamental concepts, including the subject, the object *a*, desire, jouissance, even the ends of analysis.

In the *Three Essays*, Freud refuses to accept that sexual desire, sexual object choice, or even sexual identification as a man or women are innate, biologically determined capacities of human subjects. This is the foundation for his announcement that what is considered socially "normal" (i.e., heterosexuality) only *appears* as if it were biologically natural. Famously, Freud said,

> from the point of view of psychoanalysis the exclusive sexual interest felt by men for women is also a problem that needs elucidating and is not a self-evident fact based upon an attraction that is ultimately of a chemical nature.
>
> (1905, 146, fn.)

He insisted many times that homosexuality is not pathological and never wavered from his position that

> Psychoanalytical research is most decidedly opposed to separating off homosexuals from mankind as a group of special character. . . . All human beings are capable of making a homosexual object choice and have in fact made one in their unconscious.
>
> (1905, 145, fn.)

Each time Freud referred to what he called *Instinckt*, it was to reference an innate, motivational force arising from need, which results in a relatively fixed pattern of behavior with a fixed object through which satisfaction can be achieved and is exclusive to non-human animals. While instinct is a purely biological concept, drive is defined as "lying on the frontier between the mental and the physical" (1905, 168). While the instinct is innate, the sexual drive has its origins in the specific prematurity of human beings, with all of its dependency on the Other for survival. This protracted period of human helplessness and its consequences remained a touchstone for Freud throughout his work. As Lacan formulates it, drive is the result of the operation of signification on need; i.e., for humans, there is the necessity that "need" takes a detour through the Other, through demand, ultimately in both directions. This is literally the cause of desire, according to Lacan's famous formula, "desire is neither the appetite for satisfaction, nor the demand for love, but the difference that results from the subtraction of the first from the second, the very phenomenon of their splitting" (1958, 580). From the first, Freud tells us that the drive is a *representation* through which a somatic need makes itself known and produces effects; a physiological stimulus is only available for consideration via its effects in the form of a representation which must be interpreted. Following Freud, Lacan tells us that for the human, need must pass through the defiles of the signifier, and this will make all the difference—the difference between organism and body with its little leftover, the fragile difference between ego and other, and the difference between positions proper to sexuation itself. Importantly, an instinct can be sated, whereas Freud points out that there is something in the nature of the sexual drive which renders it unsatisfiable. Unlike the rhythmic cycles of instinct, drive pressure is constant. As Lacan poetically describes it in Seminar 11, "the drive has no day or night, no spring or autumn, no rise and fall. It is a constant force" (1964a, 165). In contrast to an instinct, always already linked to an object of satisfaction, Freud tells us that the object of the drive is its most contingent, arbitrary, and variable aspect. (Human subjects are most fortunate to have available an entire universe of objects that can never satisfy!) For Freud—and this is what we see every day in the clinic—the object is *always* the lost object; where it is sought it is never found; and where it is found, it is always inadequate. No subject escapes this fate, whether heterosexual or homosexual.

Freud refers to the drives as "our mythology. [Drives] are mythical entities, magnificent in their indefiniteness. In our work we cannot for a moment disregard them, just as we are never sure that we are seeing them clearly" (1933, 95). In his short 1965 paper, "On Freud's 'Trieb' and the Analyst's Desire," Lacan comments on this directly: "The drives are our myths, said Freud. This must not be understood as a reference to the unreal. For it is the real that the drives mythify, as myths usually do" (1964b, 723–724). "Mythification" points to the limits of knowledge as such: the "pre" or "beyond" of language (the real) can only be supposed through language itself. Freud appreciated this, as did Lacan, who described "the natural" as "the field of science in which there is no one who uses a signifier to signify" (1955–1956, 187).

And now that we have placed the drive "there" (albeit in an all-too-brief and schematic manner), let us see what happens when it disappears.

## The Dream of a General Science

Let us begin with one of the foremost names on Lacan's enemy list: Heinz Hartmann, well known as one of the founders of ego psychology. While usually we think of Hartmann in terms of Lacan's critique that he elevated the ego to the dignity of the subject, I will focus specifically on how this relates to the issue of the drive. It is important to keep in mind that Hartmann was absolutely dedicated to psychoanalysis (as he conceived it), as well as being a close and careful reader of Freud's text. He spent most of his life in Vienna before having to flee the Nazis, did a tranche of analysis with Freud himself, and was one of Freud's favorite pupils. Nevertheless, for reasons that we should remain curious about, he was unable to grasp the radicality of Freud's concept of the drive.

Hartmann's foremost desire was to "coordinate" and "synchronize" Freud's psychoanalytic theory in an effort to improve its "coherence" (Schafer 1981, 63, 67). His approach was to organize, edit, and augment Freud's concepts under the umbrella principle of adaptation to the environment as the primary motivation of human existence, finding this completely consistent with Freud's vision of psychoanalysis: "We may not fully appreciate," he wrote, "how fruitful it is that the foundation on which Freud built his theory of neurosis is not 'specifically human' but 'generally biological' so that for us, the differences between animal and man . . . are relative" (Hartmann 1958, 26). This "relative difference" plays out in Hartmann's approach to the drive, which he notably translates as "instinctual drive." From a Freudian perspective, this semantic pairing constitutes an oxymoron. Rather than following Freud in emphasizing the gap between human and animal through the cleaving of instinct and drive, Hartmann's instinctual drives are different in *degree*, not in *kind*, from the instincts of "lower" animals. The term *instinctual drive* for Hartmann indicates the existence of biologically determined impulses that the ego (also a biologically determined entity) mediates. Hence, the phylogenetic superiority of human beings over "lower" animals in the chain of being, since the ego offers the human being a greater capacity for plasticity of response and thus increased opportunities for adaptation. (It is worth commenting that this idea is so far from reality, it must represent a wish.)

Relative to his extensive body of work, Hartmann's explicit commentary on sexuality is rather paltry. Furthermore, his remarks on homosexuality are nearly nonexistent. In his 492-page collected works, there is not one index entry for homosexuality, nor is there any discussion of this topic. It is precisely this significant absence that I believe marks Hartmann's importance to the subsequent psychoanalytic theorization of homosexuality. In this, I break from Kenneth Lewes, who authored *The Psychoanalytic Theory of Male Homosexuality*, a classic reference published in 1988 (reissued 2009). Lewes claimed the development of ego psychology was "not crucial" to mapping the psychoanalytic theory of male homosexuality (95), which I think misses a crucial point. In contrast to Hartmann, there is barely a work of Freud's where sexuality is not taken up in one way or another. Freud could not leave his ideas unwritten because not only was the perverse nature of sexuality the bedrock of this theory of human subjectivity, but his ideas could not be left to the reader to intuit because they were (and are) so far removed from any conventional understanding. Hartmann's reliance on a biological bedrock for an explanation of human behavior, his positioning of the ego as the agent of adaptive behavior, is so fully imbued with the idea of the human as animal that he does not need to elaborate a special theory of human sexuality. His thesis of adaptation as the overarching goal and motivation of human life left no room for Freud's elaboration of the irresolvable effects of sexuality through the formation of human subjects. Whereas Freud had to insist at every turn that psychoanalytic sexuality could not be reduced to genitality or reproduction, Hartmann made no such protestations. He relied upon a biologically deterministic perspective, one that presumes the human is always already-there (given by Nature) and that the unfurling of what is immanent produces human beings who have every possibility of adapting to the natural world because they are part of it from birth. It was the hegemony of Hartmann's ego psychology in the late 1950s through the 1960s that led to the incorporation of biological determinism into mainstream psychoanalysis, which had pernicious effects of the sort Lacan had in mind when he wrote, "the equation of drive and instinct stand for the supposition of morals in nature" (1964b, 722).

## The Importance of Bisexuality

Two of the major psychoanalytic theorists of homosexuality-as-psychopathology, Charles Socarides and Irving Bieber, the loudest protesters against the removal of homosexuality-as-diagnosis from the DSM-3, also share a certain structuring absence at the core of their theories of the etiology of homosexuality. The shared foundation of their position that homosexuality is, by definition, pathological, is Sandor Rado's obliteration of Freud's postulate of bisexuality, which relates to the active/passive vicissitudes Freud postulated for the drives.

Beginning with the *Three Essays*, Freud attempted to explain bisexuality anatomically, albeit uneasily (1905, 141–142, 144). However, as his work continued, he relied less and less on physiology, although he found himself in murky water, forced to acknowledge that there was no clear alignment among the biological, psychological, and social meanings of masculinity and femininity (1905, 219–220). After numerous back-and-forths regarding the reversibility of "activity" and "passivity" and the difficulty mapping them on to the terms "masculinity" and "femininity" (for example, the vicissitudes of the drive and the gaze, where what appears to be passive, as in "to be seen" involves the active "making oneself be seen"), Freud said in 1930, "The theory of bisexuality is still surrounded by many obscurities" (106), but he refused to give it up as a concept. In *An Outline of Psychoanalysis*, published posthumously, Freud noted that it is absolutely inadequate to associate activity with masculinity and passivity with femininity, finally concluding that the theory of psychological bisexuality "embarrasses all of our enquiries into the subject and makes them harder to describe" (1940, 188). Nevertheless, embarrassed as he may have been, he never renounced this idea. Based in pseudobiology and tied to conservative conventions, bisexuality is nevertheless one of the most subversive notions in psychoanalytic sexuality. Why? Because bisexuality precluded the biologically deterministic notion that the choice of sexual object is determined by biological sex and formed the basis for Freud's universalization of both positive and negative Oedipal configurations. Bisexuality means that neither homosexuals nor heterosexuals—in fact, neither men nor women—are born, but that they are "made." It is thanks to bisexuality that Freud could say,

> The claim made by homosexuals or inverts to being exceptions collapses when we learn that homosexual impulses are invariably discovered in every single neurotic. . . . Those who call themselves homosexuals are only the conscious and manifest inverts, whose number is nothing compared to that to the *latent* homosexuals.
> (1916–1917, 307–308)

In 1940, the year after Freud's death, Sandor Rado published "A Critical Examination of the Concept of Bisexuality" in the journal *Psychosomatic Medicine*. Rado, a Hungarian émigré to the United States in the 1930s, is a fascinating and polarizing figure in the history of psychoanalysis. He was the analyst of Heinz Hartmann, onetime education director of the New York Psychoanalytic Institute, champion of merging psychoanalysis and medical science, and the founding director of the first psychoanalytic institute to be based at a medical school (Psychoanalytic Clinic for Training and Research at the College of Physicians and Surgeons of Columbia University, founded In 1945) (Davidman 1964, 21). He was a very powerful figure when the power of psychoanalysis was at its apex. Though Rado liked to stress the differences between the school of thought he originated called "adaptational psychoanalysis" and the ego psychology of his analysand, he and Hartmann are actually very similar in pursuit of revisionist goals, centering their theories on evolutionary biology. Rado was dedicated to eliminating what he felt were the "mystic elements" from psychoanalysis, meaning those that could not be "proven" (perhaps meaning the entirety of metapsychology!). In his "Critical Examination," Rado published a comprehensive argument against bisexuality, saying that because his careful and comprehensive survey of anatomy showed that "there is no such thing as bisexuality in man or in any other of the higher vertebrates," there could be no such thing as "psychological bisexuality" (1940, 463). He stated that belief in bisexuality was unscientific, belonged to outdated anthropology, and stemmed from the "primeval, emotional needs of animistic man" to deny the biological fact of sexual difference (460). He was unwavering in his position that "the sexes are an outcome of evolutionary differentiation of contrasting yet complementary reproductive systems . . . the view that each individual is *both* male and female . . . has no scientific foundation" (1962, 96). As the result of his evolutionary logic, Rado asserted that "the male-female pattern is not only anatomically outlined, but, through the *marital* order, [it] is also culturally ingrained and perpetuated in every individual since early childhood" (1956, 205). On this ground, Rado condemned homosexuality and, moreover, asserted that homosexuality could be "cured" since the beyond of every instance of same-sex desire was antecedent heterosexuality which analysis could uncover and reinforce. "Every homosexual is a latent heterosexual" wrote analyst Irving Bieber, who also declared that homosexuality was an illness caused by developmental dysfunction and anxiety (Bieber et al. 1962, 220). Thus, Rado's refutation of Freud's core concept of bisexuality, grounded in a belief in a human "heterosexual instinct" inaugurated a momentous shift in psychoanalysis, spawning a decades-long pernicious history of "curing" homosexuality. With the manifest intention of progressing beyond Freud in the name of scientific advancement, Rado managed to arrive at the exact theory of human sexuality that antedates the *Three Essays*: two distinct sexes existing from birth, a biological imperative toward reproductive heterosexuality and against homosexuality, and each a discrete clinical entity. As uncertain a concept as bisexuality was for Freud, he never abandoned it, for it stood for the uncertainty of sexuality for all human subjects, not just a select group. Furthermore, it provided the ground for an account of the distinction between the sexes that is a cultural and subjectifying event, not a biological given (the Oedipus Complex). Without bisexuality as a core concept, psychoanalysts found themselves endorsing the very same religio-scientific prescriptions for "normality" that Freud previously scrutinized, opposed, and undermined.

## To Conclude

In the *Three Essays*, Freud defined the drive as "lying at the frontier between the mental and the physical" (1905, 168), belonging neither to one side or the other. As we have seen, this suspended state proved nearly impossible to sustain following Freud's death. Without this concept that speaks to the "out-of-sync-ness" between the human order and supposed "biological reality," there can be no psychoanalysis. Once the strangeness of the drive was replaced by ego psychology's term "instinctual drive" (a contradiction, in Freudian terms), it opened the way for the return to the idealization/naturalization of reproductive heterosexuality and its complement, the pathologizing of homosexuality.

The concept of the drive with its curious borderline status is the psychoanalytic concept par excellence. Psychoanalysis is born of exile, wanderings from the disciplines with which it shares borders—for example, psychology, philosophy, anthropology, sociology, literature, poetry—while remaining Other to them. Its originality was to bring into being a new realization of being human which marks a rupture from psychiatry and medicine. This break is not a social/historical contingency but rather marks the specificity of the Freudian field (Fuks 2008).

It is what is excluded from these discourses that returns to us via the formations of the unconscious and that Freud first recognized as hysterical symptoms. Freud lays this out very clearly in *The Question of Lay Analysis* (1926), where he finds countless ways to assert that psychoanalysis is not a branch of medicine—and perhaps this should not be surprising from a founder who described the practice he invented as a plague rather than a cure! The reprobate discourse and practices that designated homosexuality a pathology cannot be separated from the effort to provide psychoanalysis with a home in the field of medicine, to suture the cut that constituted its birth. By its very nature, the discourse of medicine could not accommodate the foreignness and indeterminacy of a concept like the drive; the borderline collapsed. Freud believed that medical education, in its relationship to a body of "objective facts" and a discourse premised upon the supposed transparency of knowledge, would function as an obstacle to occupying the place of the psychoanalyst. According to Freud, an analyst must be an analysand in order to be able to question knowledge and its effects, as well as to reckon with its limits. Certainly, the problem is not that there is a difference between the doctor and the psychoanalyst, only that one would take herself for the other. In a very beautiful statement that Freud makes about the non-rapport of psychoanalysis and medicine, he writes that for psychoanalysis "the patients are not like other patients ... the laymen are not really laymen ... and the doctors have not exactly the qualities one has a right to expect of doctors" (1926, 184). Transporting us to a virtual dreamscape, this phrase opens onto an Other scene where appearances are deceptive, language is not transparent, and knowledge cannot be assumed. This marks the strangeness and absolute alterity of psychoanalysis, which Freud insisted "stands or falls with the recognition of the [drives], of the erotogenic zones, and of the extension thus made possible of the concept of a 'sexual function' in contrast to the narrower 'genital function'" (1913, 323).

We can see here that the stakes are not exclusive to the survival of psychoanalysis but extend to the social universe we are a part of. Many, many lives were damaged—and moreover, destroyed—by psychoanalysis's position vis-à-vis homosexuality, which is inseparable from medicalization. This history has not ceased to haunt us. Its effects include contemporary psychoanalytic theories that seek to circumvent the shame of this legacy by thoroughly expelling sexuality from the purview of psychoanalysis. Paradoxically, this provides a non-stop return ticket to the very biological determinism that led to the problem in the first place.

Time and time again, Freud observed the difficulty of those who called themselves psychoanalysts to remain on the side of uncertainty and the unknown. While certainly not sufficient, extra-territoriality is absolutely necessary to affect a break with the mortifications Freud referred to as the "compact majority." As our precious myth of the drive makes evident, psychoanalysis shatters received notions of subjectivity and by definition sexuality, subverting the idolatry of common sense, pseudo-science, and morality. It confronts us with our irretrievable exile from the "natural order of things," destined to seek but never find the "sexual rapport" and all it stands for—and, furthermore, opens us to the fact that this is our good fortune. No amount of anti-discrimination by-laws or amendments can compensate for our efforts to sustain the ethics of psychoanalysis, an ethics that calls for our desire to attain absolute difference—and necessitates all our discrimination.

## Note

1 This essay was originally published in French in its entirety in © Revue *Insistance* n 13 *Sexualité et diversité II*, Éditions érès, 2018. Additionally, several sections previously appeared in "A Hunger for Science: Psychoanalysis and the Gay Gene," in *differences*, vol. 10, no. 1, Copyright 1998, Brown University and *differences: A Journal of Feminist Cultural Studies*. All rights reserved. Reprinted by permission of the publisher and the copyright holder. See www.dukeupress.edu.

## References

Bayer, Ronald. 1987. *Homosexuality and American Psychiatry: The Politics of Diagnosis*. Princeton: Princeton UP.
Bieber, Irving et al. 1962. *Homosexuality: A Psychoanalytic Study of Male Homosexuals*. New York: Basic Books.
Davidman, Howard. 1964. "The Contributions of Sandor Rado to Psychodynamic Science." In *Science and Psychoanalysis*. Vol. 7, 17–38. New York: Grune & Stratton.
Freud, Sigmund. 1905. "Three Essays on the Theory of Sexuality." In *Standard Edition of the Complete Psychological Works of Sigmund Freud*. Vol. 7. Translated by James Strachey, 123–245. New York: Norton, 1953.
———. 1913. "The Disposition to Obsessional Neurosis." In *Standard Edition of the Complete Psychological Works of Sigmund Freud*. Vol. 12. Translated by James Strachey, 313–326. New York: Norton, 1957.
———. 1916–1917. "Introductory Lectures on Psychoanalysis." In *Standard Edition of the Complete Psychological Works of Sigmund Freud*. Vol. 15. Translated by James Strachey, 123–245. New York: Norton, 1963.
———. 1926. "The Question of Lay Analysis." In *Standard Edition of the Complete Psychological Works of Sigmund Freud*. Vol. 20. Translated by James Strachey, 177–258. New York: Norton, 1959.
———. 1930. "Civilization and Its Discontents." In *Standard Edition of the Complete Psychological Works of Sigmund Freud*. Vol. 21. Translated by James Strachey, 64–145. New York: Norton, 1961.
———. 1933. "New Introductory Lectures on Psychoanalysis." In *Standard Edition of the Complete Psychological Works of Sigmund Freud*. Vol. 22. Translated by James Strachey, 3–182. New York: Norton, 1961.
———. 1940. "An Outline of Psychoanalysis." In *Standard Edition of the Complete Psychological Works of Sigmund Freud*. Vol. 2. Translated by James Strachey, 144–207. New York: Norton, 1961.

Fuks, Betty B. 2008. *Sigmund Freud and the Invention of Jewishness*. Translated by Paulo Henriques Britto. New York: Agincourt Press.

Guido, Salvatore F. 2015. *After Freud: The Fateful History of Psychoanalysis in Exile*. Unpublished dissertation.

Hartmann, Heinz. 1958. *Ego Psychology and the Problem of Adaptation*. Translated by David Rapaport. New York: International Universities Press.

Lacan, Jacques. 1954–1955. *The Ego in Freud's Theory and in the Technique of Psychoanalysis: The Seminar of Jacques Lacan*, Book II. Edited by Jacques-Alain Miller. Translated by Sylvana Tomaselli. New York: Norton, 1988.

———. 1955–1956. *The Psychoses: The Seminar of Jacques Lacan*, Book III. Edited by Jacques-Alain Miller. Translated by Russell Grigg. New York: Norton, 1993.

———. 1958. "The Signification of the Phallus." In *Écrits: The First Complete Edition in English*. Translated by Bruce Fink, 575–584. New York: Norton, 2007.

———. 1964a. *The Four Fundamental Concepts of Psychoanalysis: The Seminar of Jacques Lacan*, Book XI. Edited by Jacques-Alain Miller. Translated by Alan Sheridan. New York, NY: Norton, 1977.

———. 1964b. "On Freud's 'Trieb' and the Psychoanalyst's Desire." In *Écrits: The First Complete Edition in English*. Translated by Bruce Fink, 722–725. New York: Norton, 2006.

Lewes, Kenneth. 1988. *The Psychoanalytic Theory of Male Homosexuality*. New York: Simon and Schuster.

Nierenberg, Ona. 2007. "The Lay and the Law: Legislating the 'Impossible Profession.'" *Psychoanalysis, Culture & Society* 12: 65–75.

Rado, Sandor. 1940. "A Critical Examination of the Concept of Bisexuality." *Psychosomatic Medicine* 2 (4): 459–467.

———. 1956. *Psychoanalysis of Behavior*. Vol. 1. New York: Grune and Stratton.

———. 1962. *Psychoanalysis of Behavior*. Vol. 2. New York: Grune and Stratton.

Schafer, Roy. 1981. *A New Language for Psychoanalysis*. New Haven: Yale UP.

## Chapter 6

# The Nameless Drive[1]

*Alain Vanier*

---

*Alain Vanier, a Paris-based psychoanalyst, assesses Freud's late work to explore the specificities of the drive as denatured and nameless, aspects that significantly inform Lacan's drive elaboration. Pleasure and displeasure and pleasure and jouissance interplay in the drive's silent and nameless circuit of repetition captured by Freud in* Beyond the Pleasure Principle *(1920), notably in the fort/da exemplar and in other infantile activities. Vanier delves into the function of the drive as a drive to speak that aims to bridge across the divide to the Other, to support and bear the anguish of the Other's separation and reduce the anxiety-provoking dimension of being consumed by the Other's desire. The death drive, as formulated by Freud, is the ex-nihilo unnameable, the unthinkable, and is what insists beyond the drive in its sexuality and unconscious aspects. Its emanations, as Vanier meticulously lays out, can be found in artistic creations, poetry, and in the mysteries of language.*

---

Since Freud's (1920) *Beyond the Pleasure Principle*, psychoanalysts have taken up the new notion put forward in this text—the death drive—to give it their own signification and particular scope. Some have likened it to mere destruction, others to aggressiveness and have given it as a new name for Evil, even though Freud had said that one drive never exists without another, even in times of war. Others have rejected it, finding no place or need for it in metapsychology, despite Paul Federn giving this nameless drive a proper name, *Thanatos*. While Freud did name the life drives *Eros*, he gave no name to the death drives. What value, if any, is to be attributed to this nameless death drive?

Freud seemed to hesitate in the fifth chapter of *Beyond the Pleasure Principle*, making the inertia of organic life a specificity of each drive, only to immediately insist on a new dualism, that of the life and death drives. As he was completing the text, he wrote a preface for the fourth edition of the *Three Essays on the Theory of Sexuality* (1905) where he referred to the scandal caused by the first edition of the book. This was a scandal thought to be linked to the discovery of the sexuality of children, but it was actually about infantile sexuality, namely the fact that sexuality is infantile from childhood through to adulthood. In 1905, he put forward the term *Trieb* for the first time as a concept by making use of two terms in German to speak of the sexual drive, *Geschlechtstrieb* and *Sexualtrieb*. In the *Three Essays* preface, he mentions Schopenhauer, who had already put forward the *Geschlechtstrieb*, writing there, "it is some time since Arthur Schopenhauer, the philosopher, showed mankind the extent to which their activities are determined by sexual impulses" (Freud 1905, 134). Freud specified that *sexual* is to be taken "in the ordinary sense of the word" and affirmed "how closely the enlarged sexuality of psychoanalysis coincides with the Eros of the divine Plato" (134). Human sexuality is thus profoundly denatured. Indeed, for Schopenhauer the sexual instinct is the primacy of the will to live over the intellect (1844, II, 28), an obscure will to live that is not truly conscious and which aims to reproduce. This will to live therefore lies beyond our finitude; it aims at the transmission of life because there is death. Lacan would find a certain place for this when he asserts that interhuman copulation possesses something transcendent in relation to individual existence and when he says that making love implies satisfying a demand that bears a certain relation to death (Lacan 1964, 176–177). Moreover, is it not curious that at the moment of orgasm we speak of the *petit mort*, the "little death"? For Schopenhauer, the ultimate finality is the transmission of life, the continuation of the species. As for Freud, he came to conceive of a "wider sexuality" detached from genital organs which is distinct from the mere aim of perpetuating life and which Lacan translated as sex is "everywhere it shouldn't be" (1976). There is no mention of the death drive in the version of the preface to the *Three Essays* that is strictly contemporaneous with the drafting of *Beyond the Pleasure Principle*. What to make of this?

Should we follow Lacan in calling into question the dualism that Freud was so adamant about, in his assertion in the 1960s that the "life drive and death drive are two aspects of the drive" and "every drive is virtually a death drive" (1960, 719), against Jean Laplanche's more recent assertions that the death drive refers back to a "dichotomy that is inherent to the sexual drive" (1999, 129)? I propose that a single name suffices to designate the drive: *Eros*. But if *Eros* is not Schopenhauer's sexual drive and it is no longer directly tied to the preservation of the species, can one still think of the death drive as a strict tendency to return to the inanimate, to the inorganic, comparable for the subject with preprogrammed cellular death, to a suicide of the living in favor of a death that gives rise to creation (Ameisen 2003)?

I will not go into all the qualities that Freud attributes to the drive, but in conferring upon it a *constant thrust*, it is radically distinguished from any finality of survival. What then can lead a subject to repeat beyond the pleasure principle, to return to the scene of a horrifying event, to insist on the painful absence of the mother, to ruminate the experience of feeding in merycism (symptomatic regurgitation) to the point of putting one's life in danger, or to allow some painful symptom to persist which nevertheless yields a certain satisfaction? This is what leads Lacan to say that what is at stake in the life and death drives in what he termed "jouissance": pleasure and displeasure, pleasure and beyond.

This is what is going on in the game of the child who throws the cotton reel as far as he can, then winds it back in, punctuating the to-and-fro with sounds that Freud identifies as *fort* and *da*, a pair of opposites that are a matter of mastering, to use Freud's word, the painful absence of the mother (Freud 1920, 14–17). Why then does the mother's return give rise to a pleasure that is markedly diminished, with the game continuing after her return? In repetition, beyond the satisfaction that it produces, there is a fundamental failure that doesn't allow the child, once language has done its work (fort/da), to refind the totality of what this language was treating in order to make the departure of the primordial Other bearable. Now what has been lost and cannot be recovered is what motivates any drive, incessantly, even beyond the limits of the living.

The drive is not autoerotic, properly speaking, as it turns to the outside; it is the trace, the active remainder of these first encounters with the Other in which the subject will constitute himself, inside and outside, the Other as alterity, the return of something irreducible that insists in the subject to try to refind in the Other the thing that was lost and to bring it back into one's own field. These losses are linked to the separation from the first Other, and this is operative only through speech, though a "reality of nomination," according to Lacan (1955). For life and death do not go without saying. We have some idea of them only because we are beings of speech. Likewise for otherness: it is because we have been named that we have been able to become an individual in the mirror image, in spite of the neoteny of our species. The word is the death of the thing. Lacan said that all human things are alive only on account of first having been killed, then brought to life by the symbol. From this perspective, the death drive bears a paradoxical relation to the language of which it is a consequence. For it is speech that brings about this separation from the Other in opening up the following insistent question that has no answer: "what am I for you?" "what am I for this first Other?" We constitute our symptoms and organize our lives to fill the void left by this question with no answer. For the Other does not know what I am for him. It was not so long ago that mothers could still be heard calling their child *ma crotte* (my turd) or *mes yeux* (my eyes), which is doubtless an indication of what is in play.

This enigma of the desire of the Other is always anxiety provoking. Children's fantasies of being devoured or children's tales on this theme indicate the anguishing dimension of the question "might I be an object that could satisfy the Other, which he could enjoy?" This anxiety-provoking separation, which is regularly neutralized by each one of us, bears a close relation to the death drive. It is never to be found alone, says Freud, but we ought to add there is one exception. Freud locates this exception in melancholia, the example of "a pure culture of the death [drive]" (1923, 53), an effect of the superego's rage. The superego is the residue of the first relation to language in which each spoken word from the Other appears as a command linked to the very first experiences but also to those demands from the Other that are experienced as imperatives.

In this way, the death drive indicates the ultimate end of any drive as something that language has not been able to deal with, a remainder which literally cannot be thought and which cannot be found again but the subject will never stop searching for. That which cannot be thought is the remainder of the first traumas that are the subject's foundation. Therefore, the death drive is there precisely because death is, by definition, unthinkable. It is because of this founding link to language which also makes the drive knowable only through its effects that Lacan rejected Freud's naming of the drive as a "myth." Lacan preferred to call it "fiction" because of the importance Bentham gave to language in his *Theory of Fictions* (Ogden 1932), a status of fiction that he also gave to truth.

The silence of the death drive refers back to what speech is not able to speak of and has been left in silence. Perhaps this is also why it has remained nameless. In this respect, Lacan spoke of *innominé* (1964–1965, session of 20 January 1965). Was this a slip of Lacan's tongue, or was it intentional, a remainder of his medical studies, or a deliberate will to link the drive to the biological? Today *innominé* is only used in anatomy: one speaks of an "innominate artery" or an "innominate line," and it is a leftover from the time when medicine was taught in Latin: *innominatus*.

We shall say *unnamed*. The unnamed drive, the nameless drive in as much as it aims at something that language cannot reach, is the founding loss that is tightly bound to our entry into language. To this come objects which are substitutes for the originary relation to the Other in which the subject finds once again what they have lost or found in their relation with the Other. These objects bring some satisfaction in conformity with the pleasure principle but which is confirmed each time is the sense that "this isn't it." This is what gives rise to movement which is what repeats, and at the same time, is what aims beyond. In this way, the first words heard from the Other are experienced as a sonorous continuum, and what is lost is prosody, that of "motherese" and all the sensations and experiences that can accompany it. Children maintain these intonations for a long while in the particularities of "babyish" which their schooling will iron out.

This is what insists in each aim of the drive and is why there is both sexuality in the unconscious as well as death, not as finitude, properly speaking, but as the *ex-nihilo* based on speech's creative function which is an innominate, unnamed part which one attempts tirelessly to come back to. Thus, Lacan says, "life is no longer the set of forces that resist against death, as Bichat put it, but the set of forces in which death would be the guiderail of life" (1966–1967, session of 15 February 1967). We seek out in the future what we have lost in the past. In other words, "life aspires to death" to the point where the organism has been turned into a body by the mediation of the Other which this constitution separates us from. The drive is therefore not to be understood as the translation of an instinct but refers to the specific drive modes proper to each of us that have been inscribed via a trace that has been left somewhere.

This unnamable and inarticulable is precisely what art works on and has been remarkably indicated by logicians such as Quine (1950). Artistic production is one of the few destinies of the drive that questions what gives rise to it. The artist shows this unnamable, circumscribes it, and paradoxically plugs it up, having indicated it. This is captured by Proust, himself dying, in *Remembrance of Things Past*, in the character of the elderly writer, Bergotte, who, upon catching sight of an elusive patch of yellow wall, a small swathe of color that is abstract and almost asignificant (*"petit pan de mur jaune"*) in Vermeer's *View of Delft*, promptly fell ill and died (Proust 1927).

In poetic terms, this is what Novalis magnificently wrote as touching on something essential in our relationship to speech that we always overlook: "It's quite a peculiar thing about speaking and writing; a proper conversation is a mere word game. One can but marvel at the ridiculous error that people make in thinking they speak about things" (1798, 145). He writes further of "the musical soul of language," and of the fact that "No one realizes the very particularity of language: that it is only concerned with itself" (Novalis 1798, 145), commenting ironically on those who want to speak knowingly without having ears and seek to define poetry clearly as saying something idiotic from which all poetry is excluded. But is a poem for all that the effect of a poet's will? What is a poet's inspiration? What is this *Sprachtrieb*, this drive to speak? Is it not, as Novalis says, the "distinctive sign of language, of the efficacy of language in me," adding "what if my will had nowise wanted what I had to say?" Novalis adds that what poetry literally works over and makes appear is the "mystery" of language. Poetry and the chanted word restore for an instant something of the beyond of words which words support and is why verse "pays back the fault of tongues" (Mallarmé 1945). The poet is sensitive to this gap and to what ceaselessly misses it. What then of the fleeting moments of intense emotion one feels on reading a poem and in listening to a piece of music? It is right there and is no sooner grasped than it's already gone and lost. Isn't this, as Benjamin wrote, the figure of a pure manifest present, "a present that is not a passage but which keeps itself immobile on the threshold of time" (1968, 254)?

So there remains time as a trace of this lost object that is glimpsed, a pure present that the artist knows how to play with. This ungraspable instant is the manifestation of the necessarily lost object. This is the same object necessarily lost in the abyss of the present, the pure present of this time-object which we are always far from, and this plunges us into the time that signifies to us our mortal condition. This is the work of clinical treatment, as attested to by certain formations of the unconscious and the decisive effects of surprise that punctuate it. The death drive is a nameless drive because it indicates what naming has left out and it haunts language. It is everything at stake in an analytic treatment: to circumscribe it and to rework it.

## Note

1 A version of this text was originally given at a colloquium on *Beyond the Pleasure Principle* organized by *Psychanalyse en Extension* in Paris, November 14–15, 2020.

## References

Ameisen, Jean-Claude. 2003. *La sculpture du vivant, Le suicide cellulaire ou la mort créatrice*. Paris: Seuil.

Benjamin, Walter. 1968. "Theses on the Philosophy of History." In *Illuminations*. Edited by Hannah Ardent. London: Pimlico, 1999.

Freud, Sigmund. 1905. "Three Essays on the Theory of Sexuality." In *Standard Edition of the Complete Psychological Works of Sigmund Freud*. Vol. 7. Translated by James Strachey, 123–245. New York: Norton, 1953.

———. 1920. "Beyond the Pleasure Principle." In *Standard Edition of the Complete Psychological Works of Sigmund Freud*. Vol. 18. Translated by James Strachey, 7–64. New York: Norton, 1953.

———. 1923. "The Ego and the Id." In *Standard Edition of the Complete Psychological Works of Sigmund Freud*. Vol. 19. Translated by James Strachey, 7–64. New York: Norton, 1953.

Lacan, Jacques. 1955. "Notes en allemand préparatoires à la conférence sur la Chose freudienne." In *Ornicar?* Vol. 42. Translated by Geneviève Morel & Franz Kaltenbeck, 1987.

———. 1960. "Position of the Unconscious." In *Écrits: The First Complete Edition in English*. Translated by Bruce Fink, 703–721. New York: Norton.

———. 1964. *The Four Fundamental Concepts of Psychoanalysis: The Seminar of Jacques Lacan*, Book XI. Edited by Jacques-Alain Miller. Translated by Alan Sheridan. New York, NY: Norton, 1977.

———. 1964–1965. *Problèmes cruciaux pour la Psychanalyse : Le Séminaire de Jacques Lacan*, Book XII. Unpublished.

———. 1966–1967. *La Logique du Fantasme Psychanalyse : Le Séminaire de Jacques Lacan*, Book XIV. Unpublished.

———. 1975. "Réponse de Jacques Lacan à une question de Marcel Ritter." *Lettres de l'EFP* 18: 7–12, 1976.

Laplanche, Jean. 1999. *Essays on Otherness*. London: Routledge.

Mallarmé, Stephane H. 1897. *Crise de vers*. Paris: La Pléiade, Gallimard. 1945.

Novalis. 1798. "Soliloquy." In *Theory as Practice: A Critical Anthology of Early German Romantic Writings*. Edited by Jochen Schulte-Sasse et al. Translated by Jochen Schulte-Sasse et al. Minneapolis: University of Minnesota Press, 1997.

Ogden, Charles Kay. 1932. *Bentham's Theory of Fictions*. London: Kegan Paul, Trench, & Trubner.

Proust, Marcel. 1927. *Remembrance of Things Past*. New York: Modern Library, 2003.

Quine, Willard. 1950. *Methods of Logic*. Cambridge, MA: Harvard University Press, 1982.

Schopenhauer, Arthur. 1844. *The World as Will and Representation*.

# Part II

# The Theory of the Drive

Chapter 7

# Problems With Drive Theory

*Darian Leader*

*London-based psychoanalyst Darian Leader draws from a wealth of psychoanalytic literature to critically assess drive theory and evaluate conceptual difficulties that have continued since Freud, to which translation problems have added. Critical of Lacanian expositions which draw unquestioningly from Lacan's eleventh seminar, Leader proposes that drive theory would benefit from incorporating elaborations in the wider psychoanalytic field, and in other fields. Ethology studies, for example, show activities that characterise the drives' "excess" and their plasticity, so important to psychoanalytic conceptions of drive. Dissecting and expanding upon the four characteristics of the drive outlined by Freud in "Drives and their Vicissitudes"—source, aim, object, pressure—Leader adds to each a Lacanian emphasis on the role of the Other in drive circuits at a grammatically complex modal level. Multiple drives can be seeking satisfaction at once and this "intermodality" is important in considering drives' repetition and their plasticity in seeking release in several sense modalities at once. Lacan's reading of the Freudian drive as operating in the gaps in signifying structure and the body is rigorously reconsidered by drawing from the work of Marie-Christine Laznik and Marie Couvert to leave the reader with a series of questions about Lacanian drive theory.*

Although Freud famously called drive theory a "mythology" of psychoanalysis and drives "mythical entities," today the drive's conceptual legitimacy seems largely uncontested. The drives are part of the analytic canon and, in Lacanian circles, form one of the four fundamental concepts of psychoanalysis together with transference, repetition, and the unconscious. It is claimed that Lacan differentiated drives from instincts, that he de-biologized the drive, showed the drive's dependency on language, and even introduced the new category of invocatory drive. Drive and desire are routinely opposed as alternate structures, and the experience of the drive "beyond" the fundamental fantasy is often taken to be the ultimate rung on the ladder of ascent in a Lacanian analysis.

Expositions here tend to follow an identical format: drive is distinguished from instinct, Freud's four drive components are enumerated—the push, the source, the object, and the aim—and then Lacan's pronouncements about the drive from Seminar 11 are repeated. In this chapter, I hope to encourage a questioning of some aspects of this approach and to offer some contextualization. In general, accounts of Lacanian theory or clinical orientation are based on abstractions, pitching Lacan against fictitious ego psychologists or advocates of extreme positions on such questions as the handling of transference or the end of analysis. With the drives, our theory is equally dehistoricized, and, as we shall see, significant developments of drive theory in the 1940s and 1950s can help us to situate what remain conceptual problems today.

Let's follow the now-obligatory format and start with the question of drive versus instinct. It is well known that Freud employs the term *Trieb* rather than *Instinkt* and that the latter is only used sparingly in five of his works (Nagera 1970). English translations have tended to blur the distinction, yet the difference between a drive and an instinct was commonplace in discussions from the 1920s onwards in Vienna, Berlin, and the United States (von Hattingberg 1920; Isham 1954). Hartmann, Kris, and Loewenstein repeatedly reminded their readers between 1945 and 1949 that the two concepts should be sharply separated and that the notion of instinct had come to "contaminate" that of drive (Hartmann et al. 1946, 1949, 1953). This was not a disagreement between biology and psychoanalysis—as the term "biology" had a rather different meaning then than today—but between theories of how interaction with one's caregivers and environment could shape bodily responses and processes.

Biologists, indeed, had by this time come to recognize the role of social factors in what might have seemed to be innate and immutable reflex mechanisms, and the notion of "instinct" was often taken to include intersubjective processes (Kaufman 1960). Richard Sterba could write in 1942 that "The term 'instinct' should be reserved for the instinctive reactions of animals, these innately given responses to specific stimuli coming from their surroundings," in contrast to drives, which are "characterized by their plasticity" and "transformability," yet in fact the animal responses being studied at that time were shown to be both transformable and non-specific (Sterba 1942, vi). It was precisely this transformable and non-specific nature of instincts that had puzzled ethologists and which would lead to the research on motivation and behavior that, in turn, would feed back into psychoanalysis.

The relation of drives to instincts had become a central theme in ethology, and many careful studies challenged simplistic models of inherited instinct as an endogenous and invariant pattern of behavior (Thorpe 1954). Both Tinbergen and Lorenz would modify their views on instinct, and their work attracted the attention of analysts, including Lacan, who were especially interested in the concept of "displacement activities," whereby unexpected behavior would interrupt predicted response patterns (Lacan 1953, 11–13). In the middle of a fight, for example, a herring gull might suddenly pluck at nesting material, just as a cock might turn away from combat to peck at the ground. Courtship rituals might be broken off in similar ways, with the bird starting to forage or behave as if another aim has supplanted its initial concerns.

These strange out-of-context acts were assumed to index situations of conflicting motivation, or of a lack of external stimuli required for the release of the consummatory act. So when something blocked the discharge of one instinct through its own motor pattern, it would find an outlet using the pattern of another instinct, yet the evidence from ethology suggested that this could also happen when the necessary stimuli were indeed present. This model had a short-lived success as an explanation for neurotic symptoms—revolving around conflicting motivations—and was also applied to anxiety and to the theory of libidinal phases (Schur 1958; Weigert 1956). A review of the ethological work here was the subject of a panel at the Copenhagen Congress in 1959, and it was significant for much of the work on drives during the 1950s.

Initially termed "sparking over" acts, the odd behavior sequences noticed by the ethologists became known as "displacement activities" and opened up a number of questions about the drive. In the classic Freudian model, drives had been taken to follow a pattern of energy discharge, where an energy specific to each drive would be released by an appropriate stimulus. Yet the work from ethology seemed to undermine this discharge model, since so-called "terminating stimuli" such as sight of the mother or termination of nest building would interrupt the activity in question, suggesting a cybernetic model rather than a quantitative, energetic one (Hinde 1956; Kaufman 1960). In other words, a sign perceived in the Other would prompt the change in behavior rather than a release of energy.

Yet this ethological model would itself swiftly be modified, as it was pointed out that birds may continue to construct their nests compulsively long after they have technically been completed, just as chicks may still emit distress calls after their mother has returned. Lorenz would argue that it is a mistake to see the initial activities as direct expressions of a single drive, so that a behavior that seems to serve nutrition is not necessarily caused by hunger, just as hunting behavior will not necessarily be terminated by a catch of prey. The drive, he says, "can be driven," so that there is a fundamental disparity between the register of need and the excess of the drive, which always seeks "more" (Lorenz 1963, 76).

This "excess," described carefully by David Levy in animal behavior, was used to explain drive functioning more generally (1928). The "over-production" was linked by analysts and ethologists to the oral situation, and Spitz pointed out how infants whose milk was too easily sucked from the bottle had an excess of sucking movements even after they had rejected the teat, which they would then expend on substitute objects (1963). For Harry Stack Sullivan, the energy to be transformed in the oral zone will be greater than the energy required for the satisfaction of need, generating both a further need to suck and other related actions. So "there is a zonal need to suck . . . which is quite supplementary, you might say, to the general need for food," and this excess applied to all the other erogenous zones, renamed "zones of interaction" to emphasize their creation via interaction with the caregivers (Sullivan 1953, 126). In this model, when Kentucky Fried Chicken uses as its tag line "Finger-licking good," this would refer less to the wish to suck the delicious batter from one's greasy fingers than to the "extra" sucking necessitated by the too-rapid consumption of the fried meal.

This perspective could also shed light on the plasticity of drives that had so struck Freud. The ethological work indicated that sucking was emancipated from any link to the breast and could move to other body parts and processes, from smoking to fantasies of anal or vaginal sucking, to the mechanical activity of pumps and siphons, or indeed the very concept of a vacuum (Ostow 1957). Although one might see in some of this research a return of the energy discharge model, its real import lay perhaps in its questioning of the link of surface behavior with drive objects, as what Lorenz and others had shown is how the search for food or sex or combat may be deceptive and can never simply reflect a single instrumental drive but, rather, a confluence or conflict of different drive vectors or components.

As Mortimer Ostow pointed out, after reviewing the ethological research, "It is impossible to define an instinct uniquely in terms of any group of behavior patterns" (1957, 305). And indeed, the work of Lorenz, Tinbergen, and others had ultimately challenged the very concept of a hunger drive and of a sex drive, with their conclusion that there were no unitary drives in biological processes. This should make us pause before facile contrasts of analytic drive theory with the supposed biology of instincts and encourage us to return to the unpacking of the drive into composite elements, as Freud attempted in his 1915 essay.

\* \* \* \*

Freud has famously broken the drive down into four components in "[Drives] and Their Vicissitudes," and these invariably feature in Lacanian expositions of drive theory. First up is the *Drang*, translated as "force," "push," "pressure," or "impetus," the characteristic of which is its constancy. Unlike an external stimulus which can be avoided, fled from, or dealt with by a single expedient action, drive pressure comes from within, and hence such evasive action is not possible. Since "it impinges not from without but from within the organism, no flight can avail against it" (Freud 1915a, 118). Freud emphasizes this point several times, so that the constancy of internal pressure is seen as central to the very definition of the drive.

Commentaries often formulate this motif in terms of the place of satisfaction. An instinct, such as hunger or thirst, we are told, can be satisfied and is thus discontinuous, whereas the drive's force never stops. But one might observe here that the thing that never really stops is our repetition of this cliché, despite the fact that all of the clinical evidence indicates that the drive, precisely, waxes and wanes, and it is not a constant force. This lack of constancy applies both to a specific time in a person's life, to changes of circumstance or situation (see studies of love, sleep, or solitary confinement, for example) and to periodizations such as adolescence or menopause. Analysts with post-adolescent children might have noticed this, as their fridges are miraculously no longer empty, but even the most cursory review of clinical data confirms this.

Freud, indeed, points out in the contemporary paper on repression that a drive may be "inactive," that is, "only very slightly cathected with mental energy" (Freud 1915b, 151). It is simply not the case that the oral, scopic, anal, or invocatory drives, to name the most well known, operate 24/7, although we can certainly say in an expressionist way that they may broadly guide a person's life. We might wonder whether we mean the drive or the fantasy here, but the real question is whether, if we recognize the non-constancy of a drive, this just means that other drives take over or admix so that there is in fact a latent constancy at play that moves from one drive dimension to another.

Freud, after all, gives drive tension a very privileged place in terms of this sort of plasticity: as originating from within, drive stimuli "make far higher demands on the nervous system and cause it to undertake involved and interconnected activities by which the external world is changed as to afford satisfaction," leading to "the high level of development" of the nervous system itself (1915a, 120). Should we understand these "interconnected activities" as involving a "spread" of the drive across sensory modalities, action schemas, and cognitive functions, and, if so, what remains of the specificity of the drive?

We should also note here that the pressure of the drive is equated by Freud and by many of his students with a motor factor. This has proven difficult to reconcile with subsequent theorizations and belies the notion of a constant force, as the bodily pressure that human beings experience may oscillate to a remarkable degree. When, on the other hand, we encounter a subject who is beset by a terrible internal tension they are desperate to alleviate via motor activity, we have no reticence in simply ascribing this to the drive, despite the fact that the vicissitudes constitutive of the drive may be absent. So, on this question of the motor factor, we want to eat our cake and have it, too.

Lacan says in his commentary on Freud in *The Four Fundamental Concepts* that the drives cannot be regulated by movement (1964a, 165), but is this, in fact, correct? There are certainly states of agitation that seem resistant to motor treatments, and, in some cases, this can have tragic consequences, as the person may be forced to harm or even kill themselves to escape the unbearable sensations. But there are many tension states that, on the contrary, do respond to the motor factor, and this is surely one of the main reasons for the ubiquity of human exercise and sport. Is everyone who goes to the gym or runs under the misapprehension that tension states are not in some way regulated by their activity? Words of course do it too, as Freud (1895) argued in the Project for a Scientific Psychology, and the different effects of speaking and moving, together with their moments of failure, invite further study.

The second Freudian component of the drive is the source, invariably identified with one of the body's apertures that possesses a rim-like structure. This is often equated with the erotogenic zones, but Freud also comments that the partial drives "appear in a sense independently of erotogenic zones" (1905, 192), although in the context, it is possible that Freud means "genital" by "erotogenic." The source of the drive is a hole in the body, we sometimes hear, yet once again this is a lazy romantic formulation. Let us first note that Freud links the source to both bodily zones and processes, which may not in any way be reducible to zones. Such processes may be, strictly speaking, internal to the body, and we might infer that the importance given to surface edges in fact results from parental attention to these areas, which, of course, are necessary for drive functioning. As Hartmann, Kris, Loewenstein, Sullivan, and many others insisted, it is the social priming of the body that activates the drives.

The source, for Freud, is where the stimulus is felt, where tension is experienced, and, as the later analysts would point out, refers to how this is met, responded to, and initiated by the parents. As a zone in the body, skin at certain points becomes converted into mucous membrane, establishing erotogenic zones due to the abundant presence of anastomoses. To speak of a rim is helpful in some instances and not in others, especially when we remember that edges can be produced by interaction and are not purely an anatomical property. In one case, an analysand linked a zone on his body that he repeatedly sought stimulation for to the fact this was the one point of his body where his mother's caresses stopped as she was putting him to bed as a child. The mother's touch thus created an edge, and he craved body contact at—and beyond—that precise point.

It is also worth observing here that a parent's own drive activity may be linked to a particular source yet selects a different surface area—perhaps with no rim-like structure—in his or her child. An analysand who had himself experienced an overzealous anal education, with the premium set on having a clean bottom, turned his attention to making sure that his daughter always had an impeccably clean and scrubbed face and then, as she got older, insisted that she herself carry out these operations. As she took up the parental injunction, should we speak of an anal drive or, on the contrary, simply of a superegoic imperative?

Lacan's 1958 description of the drive as expressing "the dependence of the subject in relation to a certain signifier" (1957–1958, 454) would imply the former (i.e. the drive), as would the 1975 description of the drive as "*l'echo dans le corps du fait qu'il y a un dire*" (Lacan 1975–1976, 17), "the echo in the body of a fact of saying." The emphasis is supposedly less on an internal excitation than speech coming from the Other, but one is absolutely linked to the other here, and although it is a nice poetic formulation, it is hardly a serious theory of the drive. Clinically, one might argue that the drive is just as much an echo in the body of the fact there is a *dit* rather than a *dire*, as the previous example suggests.

The third dimension of the drive, the object, is described by Freud as the most variable of the components, consisting of whatever allows drive satisfaction to proceed. This could be a part of the body or something extraneous. Freud notes the same object may serve the satisfaction of several different drives "simultaneously," a fact that again is curiously overlooked in contemporary accounts. Post-Freudians such as Erikson and Sterba had often pointed out how oral retention, for example, may represent an anal process, just as anal retention may index an oral one. Lacanians like the idea of the stain when discussing the scopic drive, with a link to the anal object implied, but should we posit that one object is serving two drives here, or, perhaps, complicate our model of drive functioning?

In our Lacanian reading, we tend to distinguish the place of the object from actual objects that may occupy this empty space: the object is a hole, and different things may go into this place. For some, this means that there is an oral hole, an anal hole, a scopic hole, and an invocatory hole, each with their own topologies. For others, there is just a basic structural hole with oral, anal, scopic, and invocatory inflexions. So far so good, but we should then be cautious when we describe drive as some particular fixation to an object. An infant who remains riveted to the breast may be showing precisely the failure of drive functioning, and, as we shall see, it is perhaps plasticity itself that characterizes the drive, in the way that it can abstract from its objects.

Erikson's distinction between zones and modes of the drive is helpful here. The zone corresponds more or less to the somatic source, the points at which Freud had shown "the tragedies and comedies that center in the apertures of the body," whereas the mode involves signifying batteries generated through these interactions (Erikson 1963, 60). A zone may be linked to a variety of modes so that the mouth, for example, may be taken up in incorporative (jaws and gums), eliminative (spitting up and out), or intrusive (moving into, penetrating) activities. An oral mode could thus apply to the musculature, to the eyes, the mouth, or hearing, and, indeed, a single mode could dominate multiple zones, just as a particular zone could be used to dramatize a specific mode, such as retaining or eliminating.

This dynamic creates a more complex grammar of the drive, with two forms of libidinal inertia. A zonal fixation might mean that the subject stays glued to an oral pleasure, whereas a modal fixation means that a particular verb, or binary, say, "to obtain" or "to obtain and to reject," will structure bodily zones, behaviors, and relations with the Other, in what Erikson calls an "estrangement" of modes (1937). Drives thus operate primarily at a modal level, and the signifying battery initially linked to a certain zone may then gravitate from one zone to another, perhaps as a result of experiences of disappointment or frustration, structuring the search for satisfaction in any part of the body.

The isolation of zones that this search might suggest can then be understood, as Fromm observed, as a way of interpreting modal questions. If someone dreams repeatedly of sucking on a breast that gives no milk, rather than implying an early disturbance in feeding, it may simply mean that the breast is being singled out as a way of representing a relation to the Other, using "the language of the body" (Fromm 1965, 318–320). Our idea of the object is thus shaped by our relations with the Other, substantializing signifying relations, and implying that ultimately zonal questions are functions of modal ones rather than vice-versa, as is usually supposed.

This brings us to the fourth component of the drive, the aim, which Freud equates with satisfaction and Lacan with the satisfaction of non-satisfaction. Freud had emphasized the removal of the initial somatic stimulus, a fact that has often led to an erroneous association of satisfaction with some sort of discharge of energy. In this model, the aim of a drive is the removal of its accumulated energy. But, how, it was asked, could drive aims then be differentiated? With Erikson's distinction between zones and modes, the aim of a drive becomes less the discharge of energy than a pattern specific to the modal function in question. Drives are differentiated by their modes rather than by the energy supposedly specific to each zone, as some of the post-Freudians had believed.

* * * *

Although Freud had often linked drive satisfaction with discharge, there is a second model of stimulus removal which is clearly distinct. Freud describes this as the establishment of an additional stimulus at the same point, rather like an itch and a scratch, when we remember the way that each of these terms can be substituted for the other, so that "scratch" can designate the "itch" and vice versa. The need for a repetition of satisfaction, he writes, reveals itself in not one but two ways: by a feeling of tension (*Spannungsgefuhl*), which is unpleasurable, and by a sensation of itching or stimulation (*Juck oder Reizempfindung*), which is centrally conditioned and projected on to the peripheral erotogenic zone. This allows a different formulation of the aim of the drive:

> it consists in replacing the projected sensation of stimulation in the erotogenic zone by an external stimulus which removes the sensation by producing a feeling of satisfaction. This external stimulus will usually consist in some kind of manipulation that is analogous to the sucking.
> (Freud 1905, 184)

So this is hardly a discharge phenomenon but the replacement of one form of stimulation by another, which seems altogether closer to what we learn from both infant research and the clinic. As Freud says, "this strikes us as somewhat strange only because, in order to remove one stimulus, it seems necessary to adduce a second one at the same spot" (1905, 185). Thus a circuit is created of different activities, and one might wonder to what extent the subjectivity of the Other is necessary—or not—in this movement, and, also, what exactly would be "analogous to the sucking"?

The most obvious answer to this latter question is digital manipulation. In Arnold Gesell's bestselling infancy primer, the index entry for "Hands" says "See mouth," reflecting the archaic compact between these parts of the body (Gesell 1952). In the early months of life, the hands seem very much a satellite of orality with oral functions delegated to them such as pressing, pushing, clenching, exploring, and, indeed, sucking. Infant researchers had shown how the musculature of the hands iterates that of the mouth and jaw, as if they were both governed by the same aims. Towards three months, there is a progressive emancipation of the hands from the mouth, and their coordination with vision becomes tighter (Leader 2016). Until then, however, the infant will not necessarily look at what it is holding or try to hold what it is looking at.

Infants, indeed, never just suck. They are always doing something with their hands at the same time: scratching, pulling, tugging, clenching, whether it is a part of their own body or that of the mother or of a piece of blanket or fabric. This is what the pediatrician Lindner called "combinatory movements" in an article that Freud cites from 1879, and what later researchers termed "accessory movements" (Lindner 1934). Babies cannot feed only with their mouths. The hands have to be used too, and hence the way that many bottle-feeding devices used to have attachments to keep the infant's hands busy at the same time. Fingers may stroke, claw, or cup the breast or bottle, just as they find their way to the mouth itself during feeding. Yet even when a finger or thumb is being sucked, the other hand may search for something to hold. Freud evoked a "grasping drive" (*Grieftrieb*) here, which combines the infant's sucking with a tugging activity on a part of oneself or of the mother. This could be the mother's hand, ear lobe, or, famously, the little bit of rag or cloth that Winnicott called the "transitional object."

Why this necessity for a simultaneity of actions? And just as an infant can suck the nipple and tug at the hair at the same time, so an adult may have to smoke while writing, pick their nails while listening, snack while watching TV. . . . We could think also of Dora, sucking her thumb while at the same time tugging on her brother's ear, and all the other omnipresent cultural practices of simultaneous hand activity. At the start of the pandemic, health authorities around the world advised people not to touch their faces to reduce the risk of COVID infection, a tall order given the fact that, as they reminded us, human beings tend to touch this part of the body around 2000 times per day. Now, if this involuntary and compulsive self-touching isn't a manifestation of the drive, then what is? But, if so, which drive is at play?

Perhaps it is the very simultaneity of corporeal practices that indicates that the drive is operating, the fact that, precisely, it is not confined to one single bodily register. As we munch and snack while watching TV, it is thus less a question of choosing between the oral and the scopic than of indexing the drive to the very ambiguity of this question, to the fact that we are doing one thing AND another (Leader 2016). As Spitz (1963) pointed out many years ago, although the infant at the breast is often given as the model of the oral drive, a lot more is going on than sucking, and it was once widely believed that the object of the oral drive is not the breast but communication itself. As Lacanians, our own conception of the oral drive as the circuit "to suck—to be sucked—to make oneself sucked" is also inadequate, leaving aside all the other bodily practices that occur at the same time. And yet there is no good reason to exclude these activities, which, as we are arguing, are perhaps what allow us to speak of drive functioning in the first place.

This intermodality is a key characteristic of the drive, although we could put it another way and say that the drive is just our name for intermodality. The implication would be that when human interest and activity seems confined to a single zonal vector, we are in fact not in the realm of the drive. As Freud writes in the *New Introductory Lectures*, "the sexual [drives] are noticeable to us for their plasticity, their capacity for altering their aims, their replaceability, which admits of one drive satisfaction being replaced by another, and their readiness for being deferred" (1933, 97). But what exactly is this "replaceability" and what is at stake in drive plasticity?

Sometimes we see the same modal function operating across different sense modalities or body parts—for example, hand and mouth opening or clenching—but sometimes there seems to be no common denominator, for example, picking the nails while reading. It might be worth distinguishing two currents here: in the first, well documented by Piaget, the same abstract schema colonizes multiple bodily activities, while in the second, different schemas are operating, perhaps along the lines suggested by Freud in the second model from the *Three Essays*, which involves an adjunct stimulation. In terms of satisfaction, it is possible that the second activity functions as a respondent or even antagonist of the first, to inscribe and thus create a structure, a problem I have discussed elsewhere (Leader 2021).

\* \* \* \*

If we turn now in more detail to Lacan's perspective on the drive, we find a number of problems. Earlier in the 1950s, his approach had been more or less to equate the drive with the imposition of the signifier and the dependence on the Other's demand. The drive would be born of the encounter between the needs of the organism and the responses, interests, and preoccupations of the Other—as the American analysts had described—although Lacan's model appears more sophisticated with its emphasis on the structure of speech. But in Seminar 11 there is a shift in emphasis.

First, we note the surprising eschewing of language structure. This is surely the only point in Lacan's work where, rather than pursuing a linguistic reference in Freud, he chooses to contest it. Earlier in 1951, François Rostand had argued in his pioneering book about language and the unconscious that the movements of the drive were linked to the acquisition of the relevant grammatical forms, yet Lacan claims now that Freud's notion of a "grammar" of the drive is inaccurate as what is at stake is in fact a "reversion," a back-and-forth movement (Rostand 1951; Lacan 1964a, 178). Indeed, the apparent binaries of voyeurism-exhibitionism and sadism-masochism are only there in Freud because of this mistaken emphasis on grammar (Lacan 1964a, 178). The drive circles a hole, and its circuit is less linked to grammar than to "signifying reversion."

Through a reading of "[Drives] and Their Vicissitudes," Lacan puts a special emphasis on the third time of the drive which he qualifies as a *se faire*, a "making oneself" (1964a, 195–196). In terms of the classical drive series, this would give "to make oneself sucked/shitted/seen/heard," and this third time is rendered possible by the emergence of a "new subject," an expression taken from Freud's paper which references a pole of the subject's identification as the drive moves from active to passive and reflexive modes. Taking the example of the scopic drive, Freud had postulated the following sequence: looking as an archaic activity directed at part of oneself; looking as an activity towards an external object; giving up of this object and turning to look at part of one's own body, with the aim now of being looked at; introduction of a "new subject" to whom one displays oneself to be looked at by this other (1915a, 129).

In Lacan's reading of Freud, the "new subject" is understood less as a pole of identification than as an Other which the drive aims at, seeking to generate a response. Note how this is rather different from the earlier model, ($ ◊ D), in that it focuses less on the impingement of the Other's signifiers on the subject than on the subject's active search for something in that Other. It aims to make something respond in the Other. We can remember here how Freud stressed that these transformations were never mutually exclusive: they would function side by side, so an active aim would continue to operate alongside a passive one, allowing earlier vicissitudes to co-exist with later ones.

And now we have Lacan's central hypothesis about drive functioning: the drive operates a correspondence between gaps in signifying structure and gaps in the body:

> It is in so far as something in the apparatus of the body is structured in the same way, it is because of the topological unity of the gaps in play, that the drive assumes its role in the functioning of the unconscious.
>
> (1964a, 181)

The living being is "called to subjectivity," yet petrified in the signifier, generating a lack through signifying dependence which in turn takes up a prior, real lack: the lack here is real in that "it relates to something real, namely, that the living being, by being subject to sex, has fallen under the blow of individual death" (Lacan 1964a, 205).

In the field of sexuality, we thus search less for our complement than for a lost part of ourselves, due to the fact of being a sexed living being and therefore no longer immortal. The signifying impasses linked to the question of what the Other wants generate the subject's bringing this previous lack into play, superimposing the one on the other. And hence the definition of the drives as the activity "wherein the subject seeks an object to take the place of the loss of life he has sustained due to the fact that he is sexed" (Lacan 1964b, 720).

So the drive consists in the activity of putting the object into play, to recover and restore to oneself the archaic loss linked to sexed reproduction and this is imagined to lie on the side of the Other. The link here of sex and death tends to be left out of Lacanian expositions—perhaps it seems embarrassing—and the drive's aim is usually just explained as the effort to recuperate jouissance drained from the body. As sex gives an image of what we are separated from, it is then no surprise that it might generate the idea that there is some sort of sexual instinct or drive, in the sense of one that aims at copulation.

We can make three points here. First, isn't it clear that Lacan is actually moving towards replacing the concept of the drive with the dialectic of alienation and separation? The way the latter is formulated in the paper the "Position of the Unconscious"—where the drive is the subject's activity of putting the object in place, "to restore to himself his earliest loss" (1964b, 720)—leaves little doubt that this is exactly the process that he was describing as "drive" in Seminar 11 (1964a, 239–240). The subject searches for an object to take the place of the loss of life that he has encountered due to being sexed. The fact that the concept of separation more or less vanishes in Lacan after this date, and that the drive hardly features, suggests that the redrafting was not satisfactory or, more likely, that his attention just moved on to other things.

Second, when we examine the behaviors that are commonly described as illustrations of drive functioning, we find the effort to reach the Other—as described by Lacan—and to make the Other respond. But to get the lost part of oneself due to sexed reproduction seems hardly parsimonious. Someone who constantly goes to the fridge in search of something—they don't know what—is seeking a stimulation, something from the Other to respond to their tension state, but is this a lost part of themselves? Well perhaps, but the emphasis might be more on the void created by the non-response from the Other than on the object, although the object could also be defined as simply whatever it is that is appealed to in this void, or, of course, as the void itself.

Third, it is bizarre that this strange idea of the object's link to reproduction has not raised more eyebrows in our Lacanian circles as it implies that the signification of sexed reproduction is established as a condition of drive functioning. But can an infant or young child really be said to grasp anything about sex and death, let alone the link between them? Of course, this connection may be absolutely present for the parent, as we often see in the symptomology of parenthood, and will certainly be crucial later in childhood, but either we then accept that drives do not operate until this happens—maybe around the third and fourth year—or, if we think that drives function in the first couple of years, we have to question Lacan's conceptualization.

On the latter question, the work of Marie-Christine Laznik and her colleagues is of great value. This complex and evolving research needs to be studied closely, but let's summarize and then offer a few comments. She distills from Seminar 11 the three times of the drive: first, the baby is active, sucking the breast, taken as the object of satisfaction; second, a part of its own body is taken as object, in a reflexive activity such as thumb sucking; third, the child makes itself an object for the Other, so finds satisfaction now in satisfying the Other. Laznik's argument here is that this third time is only made possible by a point of "jouissance" in the Other, which introduces a kind of "active passivity" seen in the many moments when an infant can playfully make itself eaten, looked at, and so on (Laznik 2000a, 2000b, 2000c, 2006).

The "new subject" that Freud had referred to and that Lacan had taken up is identified with the place of the Other at this third stage: the infant actively makes itself an object for this new subject, which is also actively generated. This formulation then opens up a number of conceptual and clinical pathways. First, in mapping out the consequences of a failure of time three, which she links to autism, the implication is that early intervention which focuses on this element may decisively change what may appear to be a bleak prognosis (Laznik 2005). If the mother can learn to delight in her child, this time three may usher in the "making oneself" necessary to activate the drive in its tiered form. Laznik's film studies offer convincing evidence of this process.

Second, if Freud's vicissitudes of the drive are taken as constitutive of the drive rather than contingent, problems at each successive stage can be identified and used to explain clinical material and, by implication, suggest therapeutic approaches. Significantly, Laznik does not count times one and two as indicative of the establishment of the drive, but only subsequent to the activity of time three, a conclusion that echoes the work of Spitz and the earlier researchers. In her development of Laznik's work, Marie Couvert sets out the three times of all of the main drive candidates—and adds a tactile drive—with clinical examples of the kind of problems and difficulties that can beset each of them (2021).

In a nice historical irony, the framework here turns out to be Anna Freudian, in that infancy is seen as a passage from relating to an object of satisfaction to making oneself an object of satisfaction, as the wish to be gratifying overrides the wish for gratification, a process that Anna Freud situates around the five- to six-month mark. The use of the term "jouissance" seems unnecessary here, as the mother's delight is not fused with pain, nor a hybrid, disturbing phenomenon, and surely resonates with what American infant researchers simply described as the mother's mutual enjoyment in playing with her child (Klein 1972). The importance of this was stressed years ago by infant researchers, and the absence of this enjoyment in the autistic child's mother, but it takes a more rigorous form in Laznik's work, linked to the process of drive construction. The activation presupposes a capacity for make-believe in the mother as Winnicott and others had suggested.

If the key to drive functioning lies in the mother's delight in some aspect of her baby, the latter's active efforts to access this, and the creation of a space for make-believe, this might appear to then constitute a phase of the so-called phallic trajectory. In the classic model, the infant seeks to be the phallus for the mother, a pursuit that will take a variety of forms and undergo a set of transformations. In drive terms, this is the effort to make oneself something for her, although it is uncertain as to whether all of the drives have parity here. This is essentially Lichtenstein's 1957 theory of the drive, which he likens to a mathematical function of the identity principle, the identity in question being that of phallic instrumentality for the mother (Lichtenstein 1957, 249).

One might also wonder whether the developments studied by Laznik constitute the birth of the drive or, in a more general sense, object relations as such. For a mother to show delight in her child and for a child to try to generate this suggest, after all, the establishment of processes that allow these dynamics to take place, the most obvious example of which is the creation of the "new subject." But there is a question as to whether the emphasis should be on the "new" or on the "subject": do we mean here a new subject or just a subject as such? In other words, is this time of drive construction simply that of localizing subjectivity in the Other—or of recognizing that one has created this—which is what non-Lacanians call object relations.

If this is correct, then we have a problem in our use of the term "drive," as it is so often invoked to refer to some apparently repetitive autoerotic activity that makes no appeal to a sign from the Other. Of course, exhibitionism does require this, voyeurism sometimes but not always, the anal drive most obviously when it revolves around the engineering of praise or blame, the invocatory drive via a sign of listening in some instances. But the sign of delight in the Other that Laznik sees as a condition of drive activation is hardly ubiquitous. Perhaps it just needs to happen early on and should be seen as a developmental signature rather than a constituent as such.

\* \* \* \*

Let's conclude with some questions about the drive and our use of the term. First, how should we conceptualize the "and" of the drive? I would guess that without an intermodality, drives would not function. A minimum of two activities at once seems to be the rule here, but what relation do the two forms of stimulation, friction, or satisfaction have? Lacan's argument that one drive can never engender another drive does not seem evidenced, and clashes with what we can learn from research into infancy and childhood, where we see one drive activity operating or initiated at the point that another is blocked (Wolff 1987).

Second, we might pause before parsing the times of the drive into three neat stages. A baby surely has the experience of being the object of speech, of the look, of touch, of the breast or the bottle, and so it is difficult to suppose a first, active time. Activity itself may often be a defense against these early experiences of helplessness and being rendered passive. Time two is also problematic, as it is well known that apparently passive phenomenon such as thumb sucking may be active repetitions of the experiences of being handled. Hence the conclusion of all the serious studies of autoerotism, from Karin Stephen to Ernst Kris to Marie-Christine Laznik, that the Other is present in the body here (Kris 1951; Laznik 2000b; Stephen 1933).

A thumb that is being sucked may be an index of the Other, as well as the actual mouth that is doing the sucking, or indeed, any tension state in the body. When Lacan discusses the image of the mouth kissing itself or of the "*bouche fléchée*," a "mouth in the form of an arrow," to represent the structure of autoerotism, this does not mean that the mouth is necessarily solely that of the subject (1964a, 179). And just as these archaic localizations and inscriptions of the Other do not seem to obey an either/or logic, so we could note that for Freud, the different times of the drive were not mutually exclusive but could be coterminous, with a passive and an active aim operating simultaneously. This ambiguity is indexed in the way that expositions of the oral drive will situate time two as either "to be sucked" or "to suck oneself," an inconsistency that itself opens up a number of questions about sexuality and humor.

Third, there is a risk of losing sight of the notion of defense here. We often hear it said that desire is itself a defense against the drive, defined as any sort of overwhelming psychical or bodily tension, but Freud had been careful to characterize the vicissitudes of the drive as the result of obstacles and frustrations, and he equated them with "modes of defense against the drive." Thus, the turn from activity to passivity may occur when an active aim has been blocked, just as anxiety, for example, may indicate a reversion from passive to active, or guilt from active to reflexive. Now this means that there is no natural circuit of the drive, but in our Lacanian model we identify the drive, precisely, with its vicissitudes. Clinically, when someone tries to "make themselves" seen or shitted, for example, isn't this always as a response to some problem at another level? The "making oneself" emerges, then, as a defense or solution, but never as just part of a simple circuit-like process.

Fourth, we tend to equate the drive with its object. Despite our sophisticated distinctions between the empty place that the drive revolves around and the place-holders that may seem to fill it, the placeholders are usually taken to identify the drive. If someone eats a lot or has elaborate toilet rituals, we have little hesitation in invoking the oral or anal drive, despite the caution here that our own theories prescribe and that the work of the ethologists had suggested. We would do well to remember Erikson's separation of zones and modes to clarify such practices, where a mode can govern any bodily site or process. It would surely be more accurate to see the mass buying of toilet paper during the COVID-19 pandemic, which was linked in the media to the anal drive, as embodying an oral concern: that of supplies running out.

Finally, if the key to drive functioning lies in the point of "jouissance" produced in the mother, why is it so rare to see examples of this after childhood? People might even try their best to avoid this, and, certainly with men, they may try to satisfy or destroy women, but much less to delight them. Scenarios which echo the early scenes of delight charted by Laznik are rather rare, after all, in adult life. Likewise, if the "making oneself" can be a moment of joy between baby and mother, establishing the drive circuit, why is joy so absent from drive manifestations? Making oneself seen, eaten, shitted or heard are more often fused with terror, misery, and shame, and some satisfaction of course. Is this due to an absence of phallicization, as the drive is distanced from demand, or should we rethink here what we really mean by "drive"?

## References

Couvert, Marie. 2021. *The Baby and the Drive*. London: Routledge.
Erikson, Erik. 1937. "Configurations in Play: Clinical Notes." *Psychoanalytic Quarterly* 6: 139–214.
———. 1963. *Childhood and Society*, 2nd edition. New York: Norton.
Freud, Sigmund. 1895. "Project for a Scientific Psychology." In *Standard Edition of the Complete Psychological Works of Sigmund Freud*. Vol. 1. Translated by James Strachey, 281–397. New York: Norton, 1953.
———. 1905. "Three Essays on the Theory of Sexuality." In *Standard Edition of the Complete Psychological Works of Sigmund Freud*. Vol. 7. Translated by James Strachey, 123–245. New York: Norton, 1953.
———. 1915a. "[Drives] and Their Vicissitudes." In *Standard Edition of the Complete Psychological Works of Sigmund Freud*. Vol. 14. Translated by James Strachey, 111–140. New York: Norton, 1957.
———. 1915b. "Repression." In *Standard Edition of the Complete Psychological Works of Sigmund Freud*. Vol. 14. Translated by James Strachey, 146–158. New York: Norton, 1957.

———. 1933. "New Introductory Lectures on Psychoanalysis." In *Standard Edition of the Complete Psychological Works of Sigmund Freud*. Vol. 22. Translated by James Strachey, 3–182. New York: Norton, 1964.
Fromm, Eric. 1965. *Escape from Freedom*, 2nd edition. New York: Avon.
Gesell, Arnold. 1952. *Infant Development*. London: Hamish Hamilton.
Hartmann, Heinz, Ernst Kris, and Rudolph Loewenstein. 1946. "Comments on the Formation of Psychic Structure." *The Psychoanalytic Study of the Child* 2 (1): 11–38.
———. 1949. "Notes on the Theory of Aggression." *The Psychoanalytic Study of the Child* 3 (1): 9–36.
———. 1953. "The Function of Theory in Psychoanalysis." In *Drives, Affects, Behavior*. Edited by Rudolph Loewenstein. New York: IUP.
Hinde, R.A. 1956. "Ethological Models and the Concept of 'Drive.'" *British Journal for the Philosophy of Science* 6: 321–331.
Isham, Chapman. 1954. "Emotion, Instinct and Pain-Pleasure." *Psychoanalytic Review* 41: 99–113.
Kaufman, Charles. 1960. "Some Theoretical Implications from Animal Behaviour Studies for the Psychoanalytic Concepts of Instinct, Energy and Drive." *The International Journal of Psycho-Analysis* 41: 318–326.
Klein, George. 1972. "The Vital Pleasures." *Psychoanalysis and Contemporary Science* 1: 181–205.
Kris, Ernst. 1951. "Some Comments and Observations on Early Autoerotic Activities." *The Psychoanalytic Study of the Child* 6: 95–116.
Lacan, Jacques. 1953. "The Symbolic, the Imaginary and the Real." In *On the Names of the Father*. Translated by Bruce Fink, 1–52. Cambridge: Polity, 2013.
———. 1957–1958. *The Formations of the Unconscious: The Seminar of Jacques Lacan, Book V*. Edited by Jacques-Alain Miller. Translated by Russell Grigg. Cambridge: Polity, 2017.
———. 1964a. *The Four Fundamental Concepts of Psychoanalysis: The Seminar of Jacques Lacan, Book XI*. Edited by Jacques-Alain Miller. Translated by Alan Sheridan. New York, NY: Norton, 1977.
———. 1964b. "The Position of the Unconscious." In *Écrits: The First Complete Edition in English*. Translated by Bruce Fink. New York: Norton, 2006.
———. 1975–1976. *Le Sinthome: Livre 23*. Edited by Jacques-Alain Miller. Paris: Seuil, 2005.
Laznik, Marie-Christine. 2000a. "La voix comme premier objet de la pulsion orale." *Psychanalyse et Enfance* 28: 101–117.
———. 2000b. "La theorie lacanienne de la pulsion permettrait de faire avancer la recherche sur l'autisme." *La Celibataire* 67–78.
———. 2000c. "Des psychanalystes qui travaillent en sante publique." *Le Bulletin Freudien* 34: 89–108.
———. 2005. "Traitement conjoint mere-bebe chez un bebe de 3 mois, presentant des clignotants de risque d'autisme." In *Aspects cliniques et pratiques de la prevention de l'autisme*. Edited by Graciela Crespin, 105–112. Paris: L'Harmattan.
———. 2006. "Godente ma non troppo—le minimum de jouissance de l'Autre necessaire a la constitution du sujet." *Cahiers de l'Association lacanienne internationale* 13–27.
Leader, Darian. 2016. *Hands*. London: Hamish Hamilton.
———. 2021. *Jouissance*. Cambridge: Polity.
Levy, David. 1928. "Fingersucking and Accessory Movements." *American Journal of Psychiatry* 7: 881–918.
Lichtenstein, Heinz. 1957. "Identity and Sexuality." *Journal of the American Psychoanalytic Association* 9 (1961): 179–260.
Lindner, S. 1934. "Das Saugen an den Fingern, Lippen etc bei den Kindern." *Zeitschrift für psychoanalytische Padagogik* 8: 117–138.

Lorenz, Konrad. 1963. *On Aggression*. London: Methuen, 1967.
Nagera, Humberto, ed. 1970. *Basic Psychoanalytic Concepts on the Theory of Instincts*. Vol. 3. London: Hampstead Clinic Library.
Ostow, Mortimer. 1957. "The Erotic Instincts." *International Journal of Psycho-Analysis* 38: 305–324.
Rostand, Francois. 1951. *Grammaire et Affectivité*. Paris: Vrin.
Schur, Max. 1958. "The Ego and Id in Anxiety." *The Psychoanalytic Study of the Child* 13: 190–220.
Spitz, Rene. 1963. "Ontogenesis: The Proleptic Function of Emotion." In *Expression of the Emotions in Man*. Edited by Peter Knapp, 36–60. New York: IUP.
Stephen, Karin. 1933. *Psychoanalysis and Medicine*. Cambridge: Cambridge University Press.
Sterba, Richard. 1942. *Introduction to the Psychoanalytic Theory of the Libido*. New York: Nervous and Mental Disease Monographs.
Sullivan, Harry Stack. 1953. *The Interpersonal Theory of Psychiatry*. New York: Norton.
Thorpe, W. H. 1954. "Some Concepts of Ethology." *Nature* 101–105.
von Hattingberg, Hans. 1920. "Trieb und Instinkt. Ein definitorischer Versuch." *Zeitschrift fur angewandte Psychologie* 17: 226–258.
Weigert, Edith. 1956. "Human Ego Functions in the Light of Animal Behavior." *Psychiatry* 19 (4): 325–332.
Wolff, Peter. 1987. *The Development of Behavioral States and the Expression of Emotions in Early Infancy*. Chicago: University of Chicago Press.

# Chapter 8

# The Drive as Speech

## Dan Collins

*Dan Collins explores the evolution of Freud's drive theory in his key texts on the drive ("[Drives] and their Vicissitudes,"* Beyond the Pleasure Principle, Civilization and Its Discontents) *as crucially distinguishing a psychoanalytic theory of the drive but also as effecting a discontinuous theory that has supported naïve biologistic and psychologistic readings of the drive. Freud's problematic explication of the drive was rooted in his commitment to dualism based on mental conflict, and to establishing an ontological status to the drive. In referring to the drive using terms of representation and substitution, Collins poses that Freud "relied upon linguistics without realising it," a problematic later identified and rectified by Lacan. Lacan's return to Freudian drive theory sets out the drive as linguistic, as repetition in language, and drive-libido as a signifying network that is organised by formative demand-led interactions with the Other. Essential reading for all serious students of drive theory, this chapter meticulously plots out the significance of Freudian drive-theory, provides a fresh approach to distinguishing aggressivity from the drive, and gives the drive a key role in clinical practice and in group relations.*

The title gives away the thesis: the drive is speech. This is a proposition that's at odds with our intuitive conception of the drive. Our everyday, naïve notion of drives is that they are unknown, unseen, unspoken forces that impel action. From there, we assume that there are specific drives that lead to specific urges and actions. Since we're usually more concerned with our overt actions than their covert motivations, we only question the drives when our actions surprise us, when we can't account for them. And since we can't account for behaviors that take us by surprise, we're happy enough to attribute our impulsive actions to *natural* drives. We're happy enough to create a sharp divide between our rational and our irrational acts, or rather between our rational acts and their irrational—or at least non-rational and presumably biological—motives. This naïve conception is powerful. Even many in the psychoanalytic community may take it as their default position.

What we can call the standard psychoanalytic theory of the drive, though, is more nuanced. In psychoanalysis, drives are mental representations of bodily needs. To take the simplest example, there are biological sexual needs that get represented in the mind as sexual drives. The endpoint of these drives is obtaining sexual satisfaction. But this standard account also raises questions. How do biological urges "get represented"? And which biological urges? The body has lots of biological processes that work in silence and never give rise to mental representation. For example, our immune system fights an infection, and this gives rise to symptoms and to a mental awareness that we are sick. There are outward signs of illness and even changes in behavior, but no one would say that there's an "immune drive." So how is the selection of what gets represented as drive made? Which biological processes are susceptible to becoming drives and which are not? Finally, what is the nature of the mental representation of the drives? Clearly, the representation isn't direct. For example, when we are sexually aroused, we don't have a *thought* that hormonal levels or blood flow to the sexual organs are increased. Nor is the representation imagistic. We don't necessarily picture objects that would bring us satisfaction. This is especially true of those actions and behaviors that surprise us. They may have no conscious mental representation at all. The proof is that we're surprised. A supposed lack of mental representation may be even more characteristic of habitual actions that aren't accompanied by any conscious thought. And I haven't even mentioned repressed drives or unconscious representations, both of which considerably complicate the question of representation.

All of these considerations render the standard psychoanalytic theory of the drive counterintuitive and obscure. We should note, though, that there's no theory to compete with it. Skinnerian behaviorism, for example, doesn't take up the question of motivation. A rat is simply conditioned to press a bar according to a learned schedule of reinforcement. The motivation of the rat is literally the black box of the problem. Maslow's hierarchy of needs as a theory of motivation is likewise simply posited. One just climbs up the pyramid. And a biological or neurological theory of motivation must forgo any subjective agency whatsoever. You are depressed simply because you lack sufficient quantities of serotonin to prevent you from being depressed. The Yerkes-Dodson law, meanwhile, assumes an optimal level of arousal for a task, a level of drive tension necessary for performance, without questioning the drive itself. And the late nineteenth-century theory of motivation and action depends upon the model of the reflex arc. In other words, it's a mechanism. William James (1892) is brilliant at teasing out all the complexities of the reflex arc, but he's also insistent that the reflex arc obeys natural laws. In other words, there's no problem at all: ultimately, it's only a matter obeying physical laws.

Given the history of the drive concept, Lacan is right to draw a sharp break between previous conceptions of the drive and Freud's. He's right to say that "this notion is absolutely new in Freud" (Lacan 1964b, 161). But because Freud was trained in nineteenth-century science and because he adopts its rhetoric, he cannot resist explaining the drive in terms of a biological force. And because Lacan is a faithful reader of Freud, he can't resist following Freud's argument even as he critiques it—or at least its scientific rhetoric—at every turn. Lacan says that when we deal with the drive, "There seems to be . . . a reference to some ultimate given, something archaic, primal. Such a recourse, which my teaching invites you to renounce, . . . seems inevitable" (1964b, 162). Lacan does not want to define the drive as an obscure and opaque force. He says that force "in general . . . is used to designate a locus of opacity" (Lacan 1964b, 21). And so Lacan must perform something of a high-wire act. He must read Freud's text faithfully while insisting that Freud doesn't really mean what Freud seems to say. Ultimately, he's right.

Seminar 11, *The Four Fundamental Concepts of Psychoanalysis*, provides Lacan's most sustained reading of the Freudian drive. But in spite of its inviting title, this seminar on the *fundamentals* of psychoanalysis is not a basic work. It's not an introduction. It's the culmination of years of Lacan's nuanced and rigorous reading of Freud, and its exploration of Freud's drive theory is complex.

Chapter 13 of the seminar is called "The Deconstruction of the Drive," though possibly a better translations would be "The Dismantling of the Drive" or "The Dissection of the Drive." In this chapter, Lacan announces his program right away. He asks directly the question that I've been alluding to: "Now, is what we are dealing with in the drive essentially organic? Is it . . . some manifestation of inertia in the organic life?" (Lacan 1964b, 162). And he answers, "Not only do I not think so, but I think that a serious examination of Freud's elaboration of the notion of drive runs counter to [this notion]" (Lacan 1964b, 162).

Lacan lists the four elements of the drive that Freud gives in the essay "Drives and Their Vicissitudes." In the Standard Edition of Freud, these are given as pressure, source, object, and aim (Freud 1915, 122–123). This list is familiar to all psychoanalysts. Lacan says, "such a list may seem quite a natural one. My purpose is to prove to you . . . that it is not as natural as all that" (1964b, 162). Again, I must anticipate my argument and say that we're trying to establish that the drive is speech. This proposition is nothing that Lacan ever states himself but one that Jacques-Alain Miller, his son-in-law and literary executor, derives from Lacan's text. Miller argues that Lacan's whole argument on the drive points towards this proposition. So Lacan's first step is to *denaturalize* the drive, to take it out of the murky realm of biological urges and to place it in the domain of language. And he begins with the four elements.

What James Strachey translates in the Standard Edition as the *pressure* of the drive, Lacan calls in French *la poussée*, and Lacan's translator Alan Sheridan translates this as *thrust*. Luckily that's the only difficulty of translation that we have to overcome in this list of four elements. So what does Lacan say about this thrust of the drive? He notes that it cannot be a biological function because "a biological function . . . always has a rhythm" (Lacan 1964b, 165). In spite of Freud's own rhetoric, Lacan is arguing that Freud is trying to distance himself from the model of the reflex arc which suggests that a stimulus, an increase in tension, is always discharged. Thus the model of the reflex arc is one of rising and falling tension while the thrust or pressure of the drive, just as Freud indicates, is a constant (Freud 1915, 118). Lacan is right that Freud is trying to draw a distinction. When Freud introduces the pressure of the drive, he says "We have now obtained the material necessary for distinguishing between [drive] stimuli and other (physiological) stimuli that operate on the mind" (1915, 118).

Next Lacan takes up the aim of the drive. He quotes Freud as saying that the satisfaction of the drive is reaching one's aim (Freud 1915, 122; Lacan 1964b, 165). But then Lacan brings up the objection that Freud himself brings up in "Drives and Their Vicissitudes": "sublimation is . . . satisfaction of the drive [even though] it is *zielgehemmt*, inhibited as to its aim—it does not attain it. Sublimation is nonetheless satisfaction of the drive, without repression" (Lacan 1964b, 165). Lacan argues that Freud's whole purpose is "to put into question what is meant by satisfaction" (1964b, 166). The nature of sublimation again violates the natural law of a rising and falling biological tension. The pressure of the drive does not fall with satisfaction, and the satisfaction cannot be a natural, biological one if its aim can be diverted.

In a mercifully lucid passage, Lacan draws the clinical implications of this argument, from this questioning of satisfaction:

> It is clear that those with whom we deal, the patients, are not satisfied, as one says, with what they are. And yet, we know that everything they are, everything they experience, even their symptoms, involves satisfaction. . . . They are not content with their state, but all the same, being in a state that gives so little content[ment], they are content. The whole question boils down to the following—*what* is contented here?
>
> On the whole, and as a first approximation, I would say that to which they give satisfaction by the ways of displeasure is nevertheless—and this is commonly accepted—the law of pleasure. Let us say that, for this sort of satisfaction, they give themselves too much trouble. Up to a point, it is this *too much trouble* that is the sole justification of our intervention.
>
> (1964b, 166)

What Lacan provides in this passage is a very simple definition of the psychoanalytic symptom: it is a satisfaction for which one gives oneself too much trouble. And this simple definition serves his larger purpose of complicating the question of satisfaction and removing it from the realm of a biological reduction of tension.

Next Lacan turns to the object of the drive. He paraphrases Freud: "*As far as the object of the drive is concerned, let it be clear that it is, strictly speaking, of no importance. It is a matter of total indifference*" (Lacan 1964b, 168, emphasis Lacan). Freud's own words are these:

> The object [*Objekt*] of [a drive] is the thing in regard to which or through which the [drive] is able to achieve its aim. It is what is most variable about [a drive] and is not originally connected with it but becomes assigned to it only in consequence of being peculiarly fitted to make satisfaction possible.
>
> (1915, 122)

If anything, Freud's passage is stated more forcefully than Lacan's paraphrase. Lacan says that one must never read Freud "without one's ears cocked . . . one really ought to prick up one's ears" (1964b, 168). And so we should note the phrases in Freud's passage that contrast some presumed biological drive with the psychoanalytic drive. The object is "not originally connected with" the drive. In other words, it is not a natural object. The object is "assigned to" the drive. Assigned how, and by what? And it is assigned to the drive because it is "peculiarly fitted to make satisfaction possible." A naïve conception of the drive would assume that the object that is "peculiarly fitted" to the drive is its natural object—for example, the breast is the object of the oral drive. But Freud suggests otherwise, and Lacan takes up just this example. He says that after reading Freud's passage, "the breast, in its function as object, is to be revised in its entirety" (Lacan 1964b, 168).

Lacan concludes his consideration of the object with a passage that is famous among Lacanians. He says that regarding the object "The best formula seems to me to be the following—that *la pulsion en fait le tour*" (Lacan 1964b, 168). And he says that he means *le tour* in both senses in French: a *turn* or a tour around something and also a *trick*. In his translation of Seminar 11, Sheridan leaves *la pulsion en fait le tour* in French and only provides a footnote in which he suggests "the drive moves around the object" and "the drive tricks the object" (Lacan 1964b, 168). It's difficult to get both these senses into English, but Sheridan might have translated "the drive gets around the object" or, even better, "the object is taken in by the drive." Two points are being made here. First, the aim of the drive isn't to reach the object. The aim of the drive is satisfaction. So the object isn't really a target. Rather the drive encircles the object, encloses it in the path it takes to satisfaction. Second, there's a sense of evasion and even deception here. The drive is taking in a gullible object for its own purposes. The breast is the breast, of course, and it's the object of the oral drive, but so is a stick of chewing gum or a cigarette. The aim of the oral drive isn't the breast but, Lacan assures us, "the pleasure of the mouth" (Lacan 1964b, 167).

Finally, Lacan takes up the source of the drive, the fourth element. He teases us by saying, "If we wished at all costs to introduce vital regulation"—that is, *biological* regulation—"into the function of the drive, one would certainly say that examining the source is the right way to go about it" (Lacan 1964b, 168). Lacan is suggesting that if anyone wants to find a biological justification of the drive, one would have recourse to the erogenous zones, which Lacan calls "rimlike structure[s]" (Lacan 1964b, 169). The erogenous zones would seem to justify an argument for specific biological drives. But Lacan complicates the question. If we're really talking about the biology of an oral drive, "Why does one speak of the mouth and not of the oesophagus, or the stomach? They participate just as much in the oral function" (Lacan 1964b, 169). In other words, the drive is not constructed along the lines of continuous biological functions. Rather, the drive isolates certain structures, like the mouth and the anus. To see what Lacan is getting at here, we could invoke the old example of a hysterical conversion symptom like a glove paralysis. The paralysis doesn't correspond to any set of damaged nerves or muscles in the hand. It corresponds to the word "hand." A function is isolated that is not at all a biological or anatomical function. Even if we take an example of a drive in its nascent state, for example, the infant sucking at the breast, we've already passed beyond simple biological function. I'm aware of studies that have been done that have measured the amount of muscular work that an infant has to do to suck milk from a breast, and it's enormous. It's not an easy task. Already the pleasure of the mouth is a pleasure for which the infant goes to too much trouble. And the object is already substitutable. The infant will also suck a thumb or a pacifier or the edge of a blanket.

Having completed his survey of the four elements of the drive, Lacan takes a sudden turn. He refers to the drive as a *montage* (Lacan 1964b, 169). In his translation, Sheridan leaves this word in French, which doesn't help us much. *Montage* in French has a range of meanings. It can mean an assembly or assemblage, or a set-up, or an apparatus. In electronics, it can refer to the way in which the wiring of a device is set up, literally how the wires are "mounted" within the device. In film, *montage* is the French word for editing, literally how the shots of a film are pasted together. When Lacan says that the drive is a *montage*, he's at great pains to clarify that he doesn't mean any kind of natural or artificially natural apparatus that might be borrowed from Gestalt theory. A hen in a farmyard will run away if it sees "a cardboard outline of a falcon" (Lacan 1964b, 169), but Lacan says definitively, "I am not speaking of this sort of *montage*" (Lacan 1964b, 169).

Instead, Lacan tells us that he means *montage* in the sense of "a surrealist collage" (1964b, 169). And he says, "If we bring together the paradoxes that we just defined at the level of the [thrust], at that of the object, at that of the aim of the drive" (Lacan 1964b, 169)—we should stop here and wonder why he mentions just three of the Freudian elements of the drive. It's because the *montage* is taken up in his discussion of the fourth element, and we're meant to understand that the paste up of these elements in a surrealist collage is meant to represent the source. Lacan says that

> If we bring together the paradoxes [of the four elements] . . . the resulting image would show the working of a dynamo connected up to a gas-tap, a peacock's feather emerges, and tickles the belly of a pretty woman, who is just lying there looking beautiful.
>
> (1964b, 169)

You may try to make sense of this surrealist image if you like. Is the dynamo the thrust, are the gas-tap and the feather the aim, is the woman the object, and is the tickling the satisfaction? It's tempting to try to make sense of this absurd image, but Lacan says that

> the thing begins to become interesting from this very fact, that the drive defines, according to Freud, all the forms of which one may reverse such a mechanism. This does not mean that one turns the dynamo upside-down—one unrolls its wires, it is they that become the peacock's feather, the gas-tap goes into the lady's mouth, and the bird's rump emerges in the middle.
>
> (1964b, 169)

In other words, Freud's "vicissitudes" of the drive imply that the montage can be reassembled in seemingly random—and not natural—ways.

Remarkably, as he often does at the most Lacanian moments of his Seminar, Lacan attributes the entire argument to Freud. Lacan is referring to the second half of Freud's essay "Drives and Their Vicissitudes." So far, he's covered the first half quite thoroughly. Regarding the second half, he tells his audience, "Read this text of Freud's between now and next time and you will see that he constantly jumps, without transition, between the most heterogeneous images" (Lacan 1964b, 170). In other words, Freud is responsible for the *montage*. At least, in Lacan's reading, Freud performs a kind of montage in the second half of his essay and Lacan merely, innocently, as it were, presents us with an absurd montage to illustrate the point.

But what does this elaborate image have to do with the drive? Freud says that he's going to consider, in the second half of his essay, the vicissitudes of the drive. He tells us that one, repression, will be considered in a separate essay, and he says that he doesn't intend to consider sublimation at all. That leaves two: "the reversal [of the drive] into its opposite" and "the turning round [of the drive] on the subject's own self" (Freud 1915, 126). And Lacan says, "All of this occurs only by means of grammatical references" (1964b, 170). Finally, we have what Lacan, in his faithfulness to Freud's text, has been withholding from us: a reference to language. The vicissitudes of the drive are grammatical. The ultimate source of the drive is language, through which subject can become object, verbs can be negated, and active can become passive. Lacan's reading is a powerful one. If Freud made rhetorical concessions to the vocabulary of nineteenth-century science in laying out the elements of the drive in the first half of the essay, what he really wanted was to get to the second half, a consideration of the grammar of the drive.

In the next lecture of Seminar 11, chapter 14, "The Partial Drive and Its Circuit," Lacan says that he wants to continue where he left off last time, and we may expect that he will immediately take up the grammar of the drive, but the direction that he initially takes may surprise us. He says that he was led to consider the drive "after positing that the transference is what manifests in experience the enacting of the reality of the unconscious, in so far as that reality is sexuality" (Lacan 1964b, 174). He goes on to ask, "Does love represent the summit, the culminating point, the indisputable factor that makes sexuality present for us in the here and now of the transference?" (Lacan 1964b, 174). This question may seem to come out of nowhere, and within the confines of this argument, we don't have time to trace Lacan's development of the concept of transference in Seminar 11, but we can see to what use Lacan puts this question. First, he answers it: "Freud says quite specifically that love can in no way be regarded as the representative of what he puts in question in the term *die ganze Sexualstrebung*" (Lacan 1964b, 175). This last term Strachey translates as "the whole sexual current" (Freud 1915, 133). Lacan's reading of Freud is close and correct. Both he and Freud are at pains to stress that the drives are partial drives. They do not represent the whole current of sexuality, or rather they only partially represent it, and they are not assimilable to love, which is identified with the "whole sexual current."

What's of interest to us is the way in which Lacan discusses these partial drives. Lacan refers to what he calls the "two extremes of the analytic experience" (1964b, 176). First there is the signifier. The function of signifiers in the unconscious is the result of a synchronic structure (Lacan 1964b, 176). And at the other extreme, there is interpretation, which Lacan describes as diachronic. What's important about these terms for us is that they are borrowed from linguistics. In fact, they are borrowed from the linguist who had the most influence on Lacan, Ferdinand de Saussure. Synchronic linguistics refers to language taken as a whole at any given moment in time, to the functioning of the language system, or to the very structure of language. Diachronic linguistics refers to the functioning of language over time, whether that's taken to refer to the historical development of an entire language or simply the unfolding of a sentence. A third term that Lacan introduces is *retroaction*, a translation of Freud's *Nachträglichkeit*. Lacan says, "The legibility of sex in the interpretation of the unconscious mechanisms is always retroactive" (1964b, 176). Linguistically speaking, retroaction means that we only understand the meaning of a sentence once we get to the end of it. We can illustrate what Lacan means by retroaction in psychoanalytic interpretation with the most mundane of examples. Let's say there is an analysand who complains of obsessively chewing gum or smoking. After lengthy sessions of free association, the analyst may arrive at the interpretation that the analysand has an oral fixation because he or she resents the mother for weaning. That's a very banal example, but it serves to show what Lacan means when he says that sexuality in unconscious mechanisms is always "read back" into the analysand's history. An oral fixation manifested in chewing gum or smoking is not to be interpreted as a manifestation of the entire sexual current of the subject (*die ganze Sexualstrebung*) but only as the synchronic grammar of a partial drive endlessly displacing itself diachronically.

Lacan draws a conclusion from this argument: all subjects "deal only with that part of sexuality that passes into the networks of the constitution of the subject, into the networks of the signifier" (1964b, 177). And he adds, "sexuality is realized only through the operation of the drives in so far as they are partial drives" (Lacan 1964b, 177). Thus, he argues, "Freud now introduces us to the drive"—and Lacan is still reading the second half of the "Drives" essay—"using at every moment the resources of . . . language, and not hesitating to base himself on something that belongs only to certain linguistic systems, the three voices, active, passive and reflexive" (1964b, 177). We know from our reading of Freud's text that Freud wants to discuss the two vicissitudes of the drive's reversal into its opposite and of the turning around the drive upon the subject's own self. We also know that Freud accomplishes this study of the two vicissitudes by exploration of the two pairs voyeurism-exhibitionism and sadism-masochism. And Lacan is right. Freud explores these phenomena grammatically, through the means of the structure of the verbs *seeing/being seen* and *torturing/being tortured*.

At this point, we've come quite far, and we've firmly established the linguistic structure of the drive. But we still have a way to go to get to our conclusion, that the drive is speech. This is the conclusion that Jacques-Alain Miller reaches in his talk that was published under that title. It's a session from his 1995–1996 seminar, some fifteen years after Lacan's death. It took some time to arrive at this insight, but Miller proceeds in the same way that Lacan did. He reads Lacan closely in the same way that Lacan read Freud closely.

Miller plunges right into his argument. He picks up where we left off with Lacan. If the sexual drives are only ever partial drives, then they give no access to the other subject as a whole. In classical psychoanalysis, this supposed access to another subject was called "mature genital sexuality," and it was taken as a criterion of the cure. One's analysis was assumed to be over when one could relate to another person not as a part object but as a whole person. For Lacanian psychoanalysis, this "mature genital sexuality" is a myth. Miller doesn't hesitate to relate this insight to another one from much later in Lacan's career: "There is no sexual relation" (1996, 16). There is no relation to the whole other subject because there is no whole sexual drive, only partial drives. Miller, repeating what Lacan said in Seminar 20, goes so far as to say that insofar as it is sexual enjoyment, phallic jouissance is a solitary jouissance, a masturbatory jouissance, the "jouissance of the idiot" (Miller 1996, 20; Lacan 1972–1973, 81).

In a striking formulation, Miller goes on to say that with this insight, Lacan "abandons the Freudian language of the drives. From the Freudian drive he extracts *jouissance*" (1996, 23). This is, in fact, true. After Seminar 11, the drive is mentioned less and less in Lacan's work, and jouissance takes its place. Miller's assertion is somewhat shocking, though. Lacan abandons Freud's drive? How could this be so?

Miller says that Lacan arrives at this point because he himself reformulated Freud's drive in terms of demand: "he abandons [Freud's language of the drive] because he, Lacan, elaborated the drive as a demand" (1996, 23). Some unpacking is required here. Lacan's formulaic notation of the drive is the subject in relation to the demand, written as ($ ◊ D). For Lacan, this is what it means to say that the drives are the mental representation of bodily needs. Whatever those bodily needs may be—and we don't know what they are before the demand—we must express them in the language of the Other, the language of our parents first of all. The infant's first cry to the mother is a demand. And as we become immersed in language, we express our needs as demand. But this is not an unproblematic detour of a biological need through language. First of all, we can say that our needs are *alienated* in the language of the Other, essentially a foreign language. The needs of the body do not correspond to their representations. And we've already seen that our demands can be displaced. Instead of the breast we demand chewing gum or cigarettes. Further, in the demand, we always ask for something more than the satisfaction of a simple biological need. We demand jouissance.

In his big graph, developed in Seminars 5 and 6, Lacan indicates the language of the Other in the place of the code. That's a linguistic term that Lacan ultimately rejects because there is not a one-to-one correspondence between speech and meaning. But in a rough-and-ready fashion, we can say that when one speaks, one appeals to the code of the Other to make oneself understood. The important thing to note about Lacan's big graph is that it has two levels, the lower level of the statement, that is, "what is said," and the upper level of enunciation, that is "the saying." We could call these "what we say" and "the urge to say it." In the same position that Lacan places the code, represented by A, at the lower level, he places drive, ($ ◊ D), at the upper level. This means that the drive is itself a code. It encodes our urge to speak. And in case you think we are getting too far from Freudian theory, we can refer to Freud's essay "The Dynamics of Transference," in which he says that each subject has "a specific method of his own in his conduct of his erotic life" (1912, 99). He compares each subject's particular mode of jouissance to stereotype plates that repeat the same pattern over and over again. The drive is like that. It's our code of enjoyment, and all of our demands are submitted to that code. To refer to this code, Miller does not hesitate to use the term "drive signifiers" (1996, 25).

Miller says that the crucial question of the big graph is "Who speaks?" (1996, 24). If we are using the language of the Other, is it truly we who are speaking? Or is it the Other? And then again at the upper level of the graph, are we the source of the enunciation, of the speaking? Or is it the drive that speaks? Miller's answer is that when we do not know who is speaking, "It speaks" (1996, 24). This may not be very meaningful in English, but in French, it's a phrase that Lacan used often, *Ça parle*, "it speaks." To make sense of this, what we need to know is that the word *Ça* is the French translation for Freud's *Es*, the id. There is a speaking that goes on without us, that is always going on, and it's the speech of the drive.

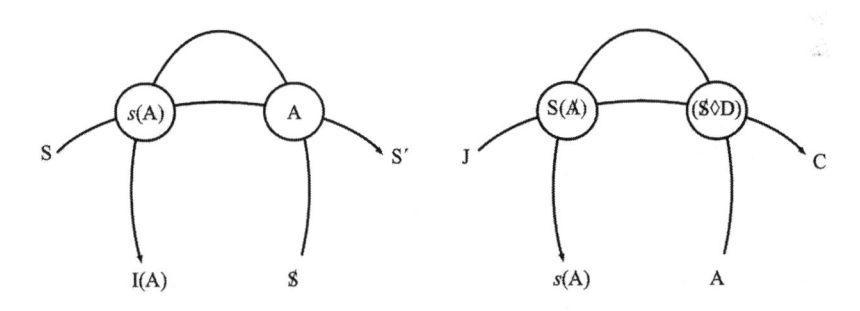

*Figure 8.1* The lower and upper levels of Lacan's big graph side by side.

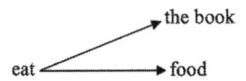

*Figure 8.2* "Eat the book" as an example of sublimation.

$$d \xrightarrow{(\$ \Diamond D)} \$$$

*Figure 8.3* The drive separation the subject and desire.

$$d \xrightarrow{(\$ \Diamond D)} (\$ \Diamond a)$$

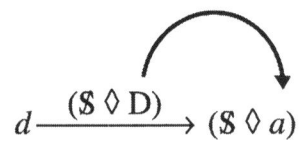

*Figure 8.4* Demand for an object.

So the drive is speech. But what are some ways in which we can understand that? I'll point to some Lacanian references. First, from Seminar 7, Lacan makes use of a biblical passage from the book of Revelation, chapter 10, verses 8–11. The same image appears in Ezekiel. It's the image of "eating the book" (Lacan 1959–1960, 322) as a metaphorical way to express receiving the prophetic call. The angel gives John a scroll and tells him to eat it. We don't have to go too far into the biblical imagery because Lacan is using it only illustratively. There is an object of eating, and that's food. But the aim of the drive to eat can be diverted to the book.

And for Lacan that change in aim is a kind of sublimation that follows the paths of language, the paths of speech. Thus all speech is a sublimation of the drive, a diversion of the drive along paths laid down by chains of signifiers.

The next reference point is from the *Écrits*. In a difficult passage from his essay "Freud's 'Trieb' and the Psychoanalyst's Desire," Lacan says, "the drive divides the subject and desire, the latter sustaining itself only by the relation it misrecognizes between this division and an object that causes it. Such is the structure of fantasy" (1964a, 724). How are we to read this? How does the drive effect a separation between the subject and desire?

There are two separations here. First, there's the separation between the subject, $, and desire, $d$. Very simply put, this separation occurs because, according to the Lacanian maxim, desire is the Other's desire. Desire is on the side of the Other. The other separation that we encounter, though, is the subject's separation from the object of satisfaction, object $a$. This could be summed up in the formula for fantasy: ($ $\Diamond$ $a$). In the passage just quoted, Lacan says that the desiring subject misrecognizes the separation from the Other's desire as its separation from the object. How does this misrecognition come about?

The subject doesn't realize that because desire is the Other's, he or she will *always* be separated from it. Because the he or she misrecognizes this separation as the separation from the object of satisfaction, the subject keeps chasing after objects in a vain hunt for the elusive satisfaction that would presumably come from attaining them. Of course, that satisfaction is never attained from the object, so we keep seeking something else.

How does this chase come about? How does the subject misrecognize the one separation for the other? And how does the drive effect this misrecognition? The formula for the drive is ($ ◊ D), the subject in relation to demand. And demand is always demand *for*, demand for *something*. So the drive makes us imagine that it's in the object, in the *something*, that we'll find satisfaction.

It's because the drive is speech, in the form of a demand *for* something namable, that we think we'll find satisfaction in the object. This is how we misrecognize our separation from desire as a separation from the object.

Finally, in a passage from Seminar 14, Lacan says, "it's when demand shuts up that the drive begins" (1966–1967, session of 12 April 1967). We can align this with the comment that we just made on the demand for the object. We chase after namable objects because we think they will bring satisfaction, but there's always a remainder of desire, from which we always remain separated. But there is also the drive as that "other speech," the "It speaks." It's when our constant demands for satisfaction are quieted that we can truly live the drive, the drive of the "It speaks." This observation has clinical implications as well. In the same passage from Seminar 14, Lacan draws a distinction between silence and shutting up. Silence is mere silence. Shutting up is the suppression of speech. And this is the analyst's position. The analyst isn't merely passively silent. The analyst knows how to shut up—in order to let the analysand's drive speak.

To conclude, I'd say that we've gone quite far into Lacanian theory, but there's a way to simplify the notion that the drive is speech. It's the earliest insight of psychoanalysis. When Freud first got patients to free associate, it was because he hoped that the way to understand their neurosis was to get them to speak. He understood that the drive could be expressed in two ways, through speech or through symptomatic acting out.

The wager of psychoanalysis is that if an analyst gets someone to lie on the couch and to free associate, the analysand's drive will be expressed in speech rather than in acting out. For the neurotic, this is the great unknown of the symptomatic acting out of drives, that they are themselves a kind of speech. The goal is to get the analysand to speak for the drive, and to seek satisfaction in another way, one that won't be too much trouble.

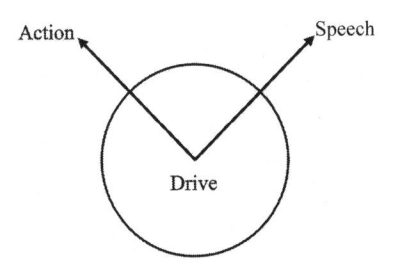

*Figure 8.5* Two outcomes for the drive.

## References

Freud, Sigmund. 1912. "The Dynamics of Transference." In *Standard Edition of the Complete Psychological Works of Sigmund Freud*. Vol. 12. Translated by James Strachey, 99–108. New York: Norton, 1958.

———. 1915. "[Drives] and Their Vicissitudes." In *Standard Edition of the Complete Psychological Works of Sigmund Freud*. Vol. 14. Translated by James Strachey, 109–139. New York: Norton, 1960.

James, William. 1892. *Psychology, The Briefer Course*. New York: Dover, 2001.

Lacan, Jacques. 1959–1960. *The Ethics of Psychoanalysis: The Seminar of Jacques Lacan*, Book VII. Edited by Jacques-Alain Miller. Translated by Dennis Porter. New York: Norton, 1992.

———. 1964a. "On Freud's 'Trieb' and the Psychoanalyst's Desire." In *Écrits: The First Complete Edition in English*. Translated by Bruce Fink, 722–725. New York: Norton, 2006.

———. 1964b. *The Four Fundamental Concepts of Psychoanalysis: The Seminar of Jacques Lacan*, Book XI. Edited by Jacques-Alain Miller. Translated by Alan Sheridan. New York, NY: Norton, 1977.

———. 1966–1967. *The Logic of Fantasy: The Seminar of Jacques Lacan*, Book XIV. Translated by Cormac Gallagher. www.lacaninireland.com/web/wp-content/uploads/2010/06/14-Logic-of-Phantasy-Complete.pdf.

———. 1972–1973. *On Feminine Sexuality, the Limits of Love and Knowledge, Encore: The Seminar of Jacques Lacan*, Book XX. Edited by Jacques-Alain Miller. Translated by Bruce Fink. New York: Norton, 1998.

Miller, Jacques-Alain. 1996. "The Drive is Speech." *Umbr(a): A Journal of the Unconscious* 1 (1997): 15–33.

Chapter 9

# *La Vie en Rose*
## On the Drive, Between Life and Death

*Paola Mieli*

---

*New-York-based psychoanalyst Paola Mieli begins her essay by highlighting the COVID-19 pandemic, saying that "What we thought concerned a far-away elsewhere was in fact all around us." Could there be a better description of the drive, that internal "elsewhere" that we discover everywhere? Mieli skillfully negotiates the terms that Lacan used throughout his career to circumnavigate and delineate the drive: libido, jouissance, speech, lalangue, body, Other. What makes Mieli's essay stand out, though, is her emphasis on love, and her connection of love to the drive. Psychoanalysis is born, Mieli observes, by abandoning the hypnotic fascination of love and reconfiguring love as transference. Far from diminishing love, psychoanalysis allows for it by creating a distance, Mieli says, between the ideal love object and the object of the drive. The drive, no longer deceived by the demand for the ideal, is then free to follow new paths, along which "the signification of a love without limits emerge" (Lacan).*

---

The COVID-19 pandemic confronted us with a disruptive real, with disease, danger, death, and a future on hold. In certain countries, the situation was greatly aggravated by government policies, discrimination regarding care, biopolitical manipulations. And the attacks on democracy of the past few years have intensified the anxiety engendered by the disease's propagation. As we celebrated the centennials of *Beyond the Pleasure Principle* (1920) and *Group Psychology and the Analysis of the Ego* (1921), we were well placed to understand Freud's thinking. We still are.

At first, we were struck by a feeling of incredulity. What we thought concerned a far-away elsewhere was in fact all around us. We were right in the middle of it. This first stage blindsided us. It was a moment of surprise that suspended the daily routine and turned into angst. The situation's persistence launched a period of understanding, a period of disillusion and repositioning of the fantasmatic frame through which we approach the world. This very painful period for many of us who lost friends or family members, for those who were gravely ill, for those who lost their jobs, for those who found themselves isolated—was also a period of reflection that brought up the choices we made and those we needed to make, the present we were managing, and the future.

As far as the virus is concerned, we may be approaching the time to conclude. But for many people, on the individual level, this situation has already turned into a need to conclude, to make a decision and act—the act being, as we know, a punctuation that opens a new perspective in our life.

## On the Drive, Far From the Biological

Rereading *Beyond the Pleasure Principle*, one is struck by the fact that here Freud situates the drive at the very center of the living. The accent shifts from the drive as a limit concept between the somatic and the psychic, as he formulated it just a few years earlier. At that time, the drive was "the psychic representative of the stimuli originating inside the body and reaching the psyche" and "the measure of the operations required of the psychic sphere by virtue of its connection to the bodily sphere" (1915a, 214). In 1920, the drive is the foundation of the living, without, however, removing from the drive its quality of limit. "The drive," concludes Freud,

> appears to be a thrust, innate to the living organism, aiming to re-establish an earlier state which this living being had to abandon under the influence of perturbing forces coming from the outside; it seems a kind of organic elasticity or, if you will, the manifestation of the inertia characteristic of organic life.
>
> (1920a, 38)

All the drives prove to be conservative, which manifests their most intimate character as acquired "historically," to use Freud's term, and they tend to restore a preceding state. Yet, in this attempt to reestablish an earlier state, their enable life to unfold and express itself.

Thus, the drive is centered around life and death. In his representation of an initial mythical state of the tendentially inert elementary organism, Freud puts forth the hypothesis that the phenomena of organic development must be attributed to the influence of external factors. "The exterior" presents as a real radical other, whose traumatic impact involves a form of violence; by provoking a change, it entails an inscription that ceaselessly insists. The encounter with an unassimilable real is at the same time an engine of life and opportunity, in repetition, for the drive's inertia. Thus, the paradox of life takes shape. With extreme energy, the living organism resists events and dangers, for example, "that could help it more rapidly attain its life goal"; "the organism," Freud says, "wishes to die only in its own fashion" (1920b, 39). The *organism*, he says. But he does not stop there. He dares to go further. In 1927, he states it is possible that "death as such may not be a biological necessity. Maybe we die because we want to die" (Viereck 1927). This maintains and revives the nature of the drive as concept at the limit between psychic and somatic.

Is the organic register what is involved in the drive beyond the pleasure principle, wonders Lacan? He promptly answers that he doesn't think so. Freud tells us that the drive is a *Grundbegriff*—a fundamental concept. In this context, he uses the term *Konvention* which Lacan translates as "fiction" in the sense that Jeremy Bentham attributes to this term. By fictitious entity "is here meant to be designated," according to Bentham, "one of those sorts of objects which, in every language, must for the purpose of discourse be spoken of as existing" (1997, 87). The fictitious, Lacan stresses, "is not in essence that which is deceiving, but strictly speaking what we call the symbolic" (1959–1960, 22). The drive articulates in the symbolic register the impact of the real on the living. Moreover, we can only approach the world through the signifier. The things of the world are staged according to the laws of the signifier and this scene is the reality where the *parlêtre* (speaking-being) lives and experiences the world, where the things of the world are designated.

If "the unconscious is the effect of speech on the subject" (Lacan 1964a, 137), if it is the way in which the subject has been permeated by language, the reality of the unconscious "is sexual reality" (1964a, 138). According to Lacan, this truth is unbearable by virtue of the fact that the division of the sexes, inasmuch as it reigns over most living beings by ensuring the maintenance of a species, condemns the individual to transitory being. A link is thus established between sex and death. This link gives the division of the sexes an inescapable and, perhaps, unbearable quality, inscribed on the horizon of the encounter between body and language.

The division of the sexes, a point of reference in the biological register, constitutes the terrain on which society has based a distribution of functions "in a play of alternations" in family and social structures. The play of alternations makes Lacan wonder: "The integration of this combinatory into sexual reality raises the question of whether it is not in this way that the signifier came into the world" (1964b, 150–151). It is a hypothesis, of course, but one which highlights that, if this had actually taken place, it would have followed a logical montage that by definition departs from the biological. In the place of the Other, the signifier emerges. But this relation to the Other, Lacan stresses, does not bring about "sexed polarity":

> [Not] the relation between masculine to feminine, but the relation between the living subject to what he loses by having to pass, for his reproduction, through the sexual cycle. In this way I explain the essential affinity of every drive with the zone of death and reconcile the two sides of the drive—which, at one and the same time, makes present sexuality in the unconscious and represents, in its essence, death.
>
> (1964b, 199)

Thus, the division of the sexes only remains on the horizon of the signifying combinations invented by the *parlêtre* to contend with his or her singular and transitory destiny—far from any polarity of the sexes. The echo of the division of the sexes resonates in the unconscious knotting of sex and death. The biological, sexual cycle is bound to the signifier and can only be approached through the signifying combinatory, which makes it the occasion for a multiplicity of signifying articulations and singular productions, occasions of deviations from any so-called norm, the manifestation of a life being, in and of itself, a deviation.

The drive, this "montage" through which sexuality participates in psychic life, is not "natural": its pressure is a constant force (which forbids any assimilation of the drive to a biological function), its source is an edge, its object is indifferent, and its goal is the satisfaction that it derives from its own trajectory in a loop. Sublimation "reveals the particular character of the *Trieb*" in as much as it is not an instinct (1959–1960, 133). In sublimation, the drive finds its satisfaction without repression, inhibited as to the goal: inhibited as to the goal but not as to the aim, the aim being the trajectory through which it finds its satisfaction. This is the opposite of the idea of the realization of some biological function, of something of the order of a *ganze Sexualstrebung*, the goal being missed, by definition, given the very nature of the drive which is only ever partial.

Lacan proposes translating *Trieb* by *dérive* ("drift," which is close to the word "drive"); topologically, the approach to a hole is accomplished by moving around it, just like the drive does in its own approach to the missing object: the cause of desire. Drift is also the echo of death, of the entropic side of the drive. Except, says Lacan, "there is only progress when marked by death" which Freud stresses with "*trieber*, this death . . . to make a *Trieb* of it" (1975–1976, 125). Organic death, the biological, is going to *trieb*—a drift that remains woven into the mesh of the signifying montage.

The libido—life—unfolds in this manner, following always singular variants. This engenders all kinds of subjective manifestations and solutions, including, as Freud points out, the choice of our own death and that of our own sexuation.

And now, by *triebing*, so to speak, death remains extimate to the *parlêtre*. Which is precisely why the encounter with the unassimilable real can be both the engine of an entropic, jouissant repetition, and an opportunity for life.

## On Drive Objects and Love

At the border between psychic and somatic, on the edge between knowledge and jouissance, the drive expresses "the conjunction of logic and corporality" (1968–1969, 229). It is "*un écho dans le corps du fait qu'il y a un dire*" (1975–1976, 17), "an echo in the body of the fact there is an uttering."

In the exchange of early nurturing, the encounter between speech and body incarnates jouissance, shapes an unconscious knowledge, and provokes all kinds of affects that go well beyond what the speaking being is able to express. The "body of the symbolic," as Lacan calls it ("which should be understood as no metaphor" (1970, 409)) is metabolized in the organic, shaping the subjective body. It is in the encounter of speech with the body that living substance is subjectivized, that the body materializes in a signifying way; that it is humanized. The body's manifestation is always marked by speech; the symptom is always the renewed expression of the encounter between body and language. The logic of jouissance is tied to the way it inhabits language. Coming from the Other, the *lalangue*, in which the newborn floats, carries the traces of the Other's jouissance; embodied, it conveys fragments of jouissance between generations. And the pleasure in the use of language, the everyday blah-blah-blah, is rooted in the jouissance that circulated between the subject and the Other.

Lacan terms the libido "life drive," drive of immortal, irrepressible, indestructible life. He adds that the libido "is precisely what is subtracted from the living being by virtue of the fact that it is subject to the cycle of sexed reproduction. And it is of this that all the forms of the object *a* that can be enumerated are the representatives, the equivalents" (1964a, 180; 1964b, 198). The objects *a* are its figures. While desire is the engine of the apparatus, the object, Freud repeats, must be found again, since it is constituted as lost—which manifests its real, inaccessible quality. Above all, the object appears as what is lacking, a lack of jouissance that takes the place of cause. "We observe desire and from this observation, we induce the cause as objectified" (1975–1976, 36). The object *a* can take the shape of different episodic substances, according to the relation of the newborn to the caretaker, to the primordial Other. It is structured by a cut, as much in relation to the cuts of the body that border outside and inside as to the signifying cut. In the contact between the caretaker and the child, the partial drives mark the edges of the body. Breast, stool, gaze, voice are four forms of the drive object, objects that are separable from the subject's body since they can be situated between the mother and child, neither on one side nor the other, always on the other side of the border that separates them. The object *a* designates the structural lack at the heart of the subject, that lack that subjective identification seeks to veil.

In the operations of alienation and separation, the object *a* is at the center of the logical combinations between subject and Other; however, between the object *a* as cause and the drive objects, there is no symmetry. The *plus-de-jouir* object, in the episodic substances of the drive objects, comes to supplement the lack. The vital movement is thus stretched between cause and goal, between a structural "less" and a "more" which is, by definition, unsatisfying. While the object *a* is the inscription of a loss, of a subtraction of life, it is at the same time representative of the libido, of the life force. In the framing of the fantasm, through which one approaches the world scene, this object connects to the subject to support desire, thus also giving a frame to the drive.

In his metapsychology (1915a), concerning one of the vicissitudes of the drive—its transformation into its opposite—Freud introduces love into the field of the drive. But he immediately adds that love, as well as hate, does not tolerate being fit into the description of partial drives. Freud returns here to the genealogy of the psychic apparatus from the starting point of love, defined as the relation of the ego with its sources of pleasure. On the basis of the three polarities that dominate psychic life, 1. subject (ego)/object (outside world), 2. pleasure/displeasure, 3. active/passive, he follows the logical passages that go from primary autoeroticism (where "the ego is invested by its own drives and partially capable of satisfying them on itself" and where the *Ich-Subjekt* coincides with the enjoyable) to the pleasure ego

(*Lust Ich*) in its pure state, where "the external world is divided into a pleasurable portion that the ego has incorporated into itself, and a remainder which is extraneous to it." Moreover, the *Lust-Ich* "has extracted from his own ego an element that it projects onto the external world and that it experiences as hostile" (Freud 1915a, 228). Between *Real-Ich* and *Lust-Ich*, the objects of the partial drives gain the upper hand in the psychic scene: they come to the fore as an effect of the needs being taking care of. The original narcissistic condition could not "evolve," Freud notes, "if each living being did not go through a period during which he is helpless and needs care, during which his pressing needs are satisfied thanks to a response coming from the exterior" (1915a, 227). For Lacan, while primary autoeroticism shows that "there would be no emergence of objects if there were not good objects for me" (1964a, 174), and love is rooted in primary narcissism (as Freud had so meticulously shown in his "On Narcissism: An Introduction" (1914)), it's the dialectic of primary drives activated by the relationship of the subject to the Other which libidinizes the subject and articulates the psychic apparatus. At the time of his "Project for a Scientific Psychology" (1895), Freud had already outlined an archeology of the relation to the object: the *Hilflosigkeit*, the original state of distress of the newborn, who requires external help to survive, establishes the qualities of the primordial object, as well as the dialectic between *Mensch* and *Fremde*, between fellow and stranger. The first *Nebenmensch* becomes such because she or he offers an object of satisfaction, but this object is split from the outset as a result of conveying at once the first hostile object.

As Lacan stresses, this absolute Other, *Das Ding*, is an "excluded interior" (1958–1959, 122). It ties what is most intimate for the subject to a radical exteriority.

In "[Drives] and their Vicissitudes," Freud establishes three oppositions:

1. autoeroticism/indifference to the outside world.
2. pleasure ego/outside world unpleasure.
3. love/hate.

He specifies that it is only with the object's appearance on the level of primary narcissism that the dimension of hatred develops. The antithetical couple love/indifference reflects the polarity "ego/outside world," just as the antithesis love/hate reproduces the polarity pleasure/unpleasure.

Freud also establishes a dissymmetry between love and hate, saying that hate is more ancient than love, because it is associated with the primordial rejection of the outside world effected by the ego. This echoes what he develops in "Negation" (1925). The original *Bejahung*, the affirmation through which the pleasure ego decides the thing's quality by introducing it into itself or excluding it outside of itself, represents the mythic moment of a primordial symbolization, of an original inscription constitutive of the psychic scene and of the real as what is primordially excluded from it. The first act, the inaugural *Bejahung*, mythically institutes the psychic scene and the field of reality that affect the subject, its relation with the world, with the external reality that concerns him or her; simultaneously, it institutes what is completely excluded from this field and which demarcates it, the non-symbolized and non-symbolizable that is the real (Lacan 1953–1954, 234). As Lacan says in his "Response to Hyppolite,"

> this is how we must understand 'Einbeziehung ins Ich,' taking into the subject, and 'Ausstossung aus dem Ich,' expelling from the subject. The latter constitutes the real insofar as it is the domain of that which subsists outside of symbolization.
>
> (1953–1954, 324)

By the very fact of being excluded, the non-symbolizable remains tied, extimate, to the apparatus, a hole of the real in the symbolic.

In 1915, speaking about the irrepresentability of subjective death, Freud stresses that "our belief in death has no corresponding drive" (1915b, 350). The belief in death is not the same thing as the death drive. Freud maintains that taking our own death into account is only possible in the face of the death of our beloved, and he develops the theme of affective ambivalence as the basis for the development of thought, moral laws, and society. The very possibility of being affected by death goes through love and ambivalence, through the loss of the beloved, and through the work of mourning.

Love is called into question. Love, as passion, is situated between the symbolic and the imaginary, while providing an edge to the abyss of the real. Love both veils and aims at the ungraspable real in the Other that inhabits us.

## Love's Punctuations

Falling in love, its unexpected character and ephemeral nature, makes one reflect on the times of love, as well as what love can teach us about subjective time. While she is deep in mourning for her husband taken by a sudden incurable disease, a woman falls in love with a man she meets by chance. And there are other cases just like hers. Falling in love comes to the rescue of life, rekindles the fantasm, and gives desire a frame.

In *Massenpsychologie*, Freud further elaborates his definition of the libido as "energy of the drives relating to everything that can be summarized by the word love" (1921, 98–99) which, according to him, coincides with Plato's Eros and the love beyond all things celebrated by the apostle Paul in his "Letter to the Corinthians." Among the cases of love, Freud analyzes falling in love—or better, enamoration (*Verliebtheit*)—which involves both a sexual overvaluation of the object and its idealization; here, "a remarkable quantity of narcissistic ego spills onto the object," adding, "The object is loved by virtue of the perfections we have sighted for the ego, and that now, through this indirect route, we wish to procure in order to satisfy our narcissism" (1921, 124). The object stands in the place of the ego ideal.

At the moment of the crush, of the lighting strike, "*la vie est en rose*," as in the song. The ego is very present, it is audible. And if endless nights of love bring about great happiness and cares and sorrows vanish, it's because a vital impulsion takes command and feeds the feeling of a (re)discovered completeness. It is a time of bliss, of pure happiness. The problem with this jouissant completeness is its "Stormy Weather" side, and in fact as the song goes, one doesn't know why the sun is not in the sky when the lover goes away. This shows the extent to which the separation from the beloved is a separation from oneself.

Freud points out that the duration of the sexual appetite goes hand in hand with the appeasement of satisfaction and that it is rather the drives inhibited in their aim that produce the most durable ties, both those that are addressed to our partner and those that solidify friendship and the social bonds. For a physical bond to last "it must from the outset be associated to strictly tender components, that is to say, inhibited in their aims" (1921, 108). But tenderness, as Freud stresses, is an integral part of the libido's vicissitudes, of their genealogy.

Because of its dazzling completeness, enamoration masks the discordance that sets it in motion. There is a dissymmetry between lover and beloved (*erastes* and *eromenos*), between the one who thinks s/he has found in the beloved all the attributes s/he is seeking and the one who finds him or herself invested with love, narcissistically exalted. The problem with love is that what is lacking for the one is not really something the other possesses, as Lacan (1960–1961) points out in his seminar *Transference*. Thus unfolds another temporal aspect of love: the time to understand. What we expected turns out to be different from what we thought we had found. Besides, isn't expecting a form of knowing, of filling the new with the hope of the past, of loving something we already loved?

The discordance that provokes the amorous encounter opens the path to the unbeknownst. The feeling of completeness dissipates; what keeps missing keeps insisting. So, if we don't drop it, love can turn into a progressive exploration of the discordance that binds us to the other. From the demand for love, we move thereby to the signification of love, which marks a new phase. In the *Symposium*, Diotima says that love is *poiesis*, the passage to creation; *poiesis* is the moment of *ecstasis* when something passes from one state to another. It is no longer a question of having (of possessing, of completing) but of a letting difference be, letting the singularity of the living be, and welcoming transformation.

The notion of transformation requires a clarification. According to Aristotle, change (*métabolé*) goes from one thing to another (*ek tinos eis ti*), which marks the passage of time. Here, movement is thought of as a before and an after, a point of departure and a point of arrival, as François Julien (2001) stresses. There would therefore be a goal to movement (*telos*) and a substance (*hupokeimenon*) that underlies change, a substrate that remains the same in the transformation. Such a concept of time, woven into Western thought, associates the substrate of accidents to the logic of predicative forms, according to a tradition in which the act of saying something and the form in which one says it are inseparable. But linguistic form is first and foremost the "condition for the accomplishment of thought," as Benveniste puts it with finesse (1966, 64), showing, among other things, how the Aristotelian attributes of being coincide with the predicative forms of the Greek language.

The conception of change as the movement between a before and an after, so inherent to our way of thinking, turns the passage between the before and the after into a kind of fatality, a being for death, as Heidegger says. I was young and I am no longer young. I am the same and I am no longer the same. Yet, "ageing has already always started" (Julien 2001, 72), and going from youth to old age, as Julien notes, is not going from hot to cold, from one state to another. It is a global continuous process of which we are the expression in the present. We are process, we are present, change being at the same time the opposite of continuation and its condition.

Rememoration always takes place in action, as Freud stresses, and memory unfolds forward, to the rhythm of a production that invests what has preceded it with effects of meaning. Past and future are always dimensions of the present. It is the lesson of love in the transference, of that "narrative that would itself be the place of the encounter that the narrative is about" (1958–1959, 572). An ethic, a subjective transformation, results from it. By designating the act of creating, of causing existence, the word "formation" (from the Greek *morphe* and the Latin *forma*) refers at the same time to the articulation of a process and its outcome, the results of which can never be anticipated. While, in the transference, love—the appeal to the subject supposed to know—calls into question a knowledge already there, the words that guide the analysand's task and the analyst's act, paint in the present an unprecedented narrative. The field of knowledge thus deployed is construction in action, is the production of a new knowledge.

To love and to believe you are loved—to put the object in the place of the ideal and shine for it, feeding your own narcissism—is the key to the fascination, to that bewitchment that renders, according to Freud (1921), the hypnotic relation identical to a mass psychology, where the ego ideal blends into, is superimposed on, the object of the drive. Psychoanalysis is born precisely by abandoning hypnosis and this confusion. If transference is a form of love—since we love the one who is supposed to know—it can also fuel the scene from where one thinks is loved and admired, as in the case of suggestion, or love of the Master, but also of the identification to the analyst. However, as Freud states, the transference is instrument and obstacle (1912). It is destined to its own dissolution, specifically to the fall of the subject supposed to know. In the analytical act, the attribution of knowledge to the Other punctuates the repeated encounter with the structural incommensurability between truth and knowledge and goes in the direction of the destitution of the One, of the whole, towards the not-all, towards the desire for absolute difference. As Lacan stresses, the analytical operation is constituted in the maintenance, in the distance, in the differentiation, between the ideal and the object of the drive. It's a distance that reboots the paths of the drive and opens the path to all kinds of *savoir faire*. "Only there can the signification of a love without limits emerge, because it is outside the boundaries of the law, where only it can live" (Lacan 1964a, 247).

In the last lines of his "Thoughts for Times on War and Death" (1915b), Freud tells us that to "tolerate life" is the primary duty of the living being. And he adds that it might be time to modify the old saying: "*Si vis pacem, para bellum*" ("If you want to preserve peace, prepare for war") by "*Si vis vitam, para mortem*" ("If you want to tolerate life, be ready to accept death"). But this readiness for death must not be understood as a predisposition for pessimism and depression, as Freud reiterates in the interview granted to Viereck (1927). On the contrary, it is rather the *Bejahung*, the affirmation, of our nature as *parlêtre*, of our aliveness that includes death and, in the unconscious knot of sex and death, includes our predisposition to life. It is also a predisposition to love, which supplements a sexual relationship that doesn't cease not being written.

Federico Fellini's words come to mind. During an interview shortly before his death, he spoke about meeting Giulietta Masina. He tells that during his life he had the amazing luck of truly extraordinary encounters. But he adds that he had a merit, a great merit, of having been able to recognize these encounters and act accordingly (Pettigrew 2002). This is not necessarily the case for everyone. Such is an ethic for life: to be ready to recognize what does not come along twice in the waters of the river of the present.

## References

Bentham, Jeremy. 1997. *De l'Ontologie et Autres Textes sur les Fictions*. Paris: Le Seuil.
Benveniste, Émile. 1966. *Problèmes de Linguistique Générale I*. Paris: Editions Gallimard.
Freud, Sigmund. 1895. "Project for a Scientific Psychology." In *Standard Edition of the Complete Psychological Works of Sigmund Freud*. Vol. 1. Translated by James Strachey, 281–397. New York: Norton, 1953.
———. 1912. "The Dynamics of Transference". In *Standard Edition of the Complete Psychological Works of Sigmund Freud*. Vol. 12. Translated by James Strachey, 97–108. New York: Norton, 1958.
———. 1914. "On Narcissism: An Introduction." In *Standard Edition of the Complete Psychological Works of Sigmund Freud*. Vol. 14. Translated by James Strachey, 73–104. New York: Norton, 1953.
———. 1915a. "Triebe und Triebschicksale." In *Gesammelte Werke*. Vol. X. Frankfurt am Main: S. Fischer Verlag, 1991.
———. 1915b. "Zeitgemässes über Krieg und Tod." In *Gesammelte Werke*. Vol. X. Frankfort: S. Fisher Verlag, 1991.
———. 1920a. *Jenseits des Lustprinzips. Gesammelte Werke*. Vol. XIII. Frankfurt am Main: S. Fischer Verlag, 1987.
———. 1920b. "Beyond the Pleasure Principle." In *Standard Edition of the Complete Psychological Works of Sigmund Freud*. Vol. 18. Translated by James Strachey, 3–64. New York: Norton, 1955.
———. 1921. *Massenpsychologie und Ich-Analyse. Gesammelte Werke*. Vol. XIII. Frankfort: S. Fisher Verlag, 1987.
———. 1925. "Negation." In *Standard Edition of the Complete Psychological Works of Sigmund Freud*. Vol. 19. Translated by James Strachey, 233–240. New York: Norton, 1953.
Julien, François. 2001. *Du Temps. Elément d'une Philosophie du Vivre*. Paris: Bernard Grasset.
Lacan, Jacques. 1953–1954. "Response to Jean Hyppolite's Commentary on Freud's 'Verneinung.'" In *Écrits: The First Complete Edition in English*. Translated by Bruce Fink, 318–333. New York: Norton, 2006.
———. 1958–1959. *Le Désir et son Interpretation, Le Séminaire, Livre* VI. Paris: Editions du Seuil, 2013.
———. 1959–1960. *L'Éthique de la Psychanalyse, Le Séminaire, Livre* VII. Paris: Editions du Seuil, 1986.

———. 1960–1961. *Le Transfert, Le Séminaire, Livre VII*. Paris: Editions du Seuil.
———. 1964a. *Les Quatre Concepts Fondamentaux de la Psychanalyse, Le Séminaire, Livre XI*. Paris: Editions du Seuil, 1973.
———. 1964b. *The Four Fundamental Concepts of Psychoanalysis: The Seminar of Jacques Lacan*, Book XI. Edited by Jacques-Alain Miller. Translated by Alan Sheridan. New York, NY: Norton, 1977.
———. 1968–1969. *D'un Autre à l'autre, Le Séminaire*, Livre XVI. Paris: Editions du Seuil, 2006.
———. 1975–1976. *Le sinthome, Le Séminaire, Livre* XXIII. Paris: Editions du Seuil, 2005.
———. 1970. "Radiophonie." In *Autres Ecrits*, 403–447. Paris: Seuil.
Pettigrew, D. 2002. *Fellini: I'm a Born Liar*. Documentary Film written and directed by Damian Pettigrew filmed in 1991 and 1992. Released in 2002, France.
Viereck, G. S. 1927. "An Interview with Freud." La Psychanalyse au Luxembourg. Société Psychanalytique du Luxembourg. Accessed 15 June 2023. www.psychanalyse.lu/articles/FreudInterview.pdf.

# Chapter 10

# Agitations and Cuts of Our Dark Ally

*Hilda Fernandez-Alvarez*

*Hilda Fernandez-Alvarez is an analyst of great clinical and theoretical acumen. In this essay, she takes as her text an interview that Freud gave in 1926. In the interview, Freud considers life and death. If there is a death drive, why then do we not all choose suicide? Ultimately, it is because the life drive is stronger, at least for a time. Could we, then, vanquish death? No, Freud says, because death has an ally within us, the drive. The question that Fernandez-Alvarez asks is not idle, for she has worked intensively with suicidal subjects. The drive, through repetition, both leads towards death, the end of repetition, and promotes life, repetition's continuance. What we are left with is the subject's stubborn wish to die in his or her own way and own time, what amounts to the endurance of life—life that takes a stand against death with the complicity of its "dark ally," the death drive. That endurance has a name: jouissance.*

No mortal has come nearer to explaining the secret of human conduct than Freud.
—G. S. Viereck

### Introduction

Walking around his Viennese garden in 1926, an unpretentious Sigmund Freud gives a beautiful yet not so well known interview to G.S. Viereck, entitled in Portuguese and in Spanish "The Value of Life" (Viereck 1927). George Sylvester Viereck was a German-American poet with strong ties to Nazism. Neil M. Johnson states that Viereck "in the 1920s he wrote articles reflecting sympathy for Hitler and Ludendorff on the one hand and displaying deep respect for Shaw, Freud, and Einstein on the other" (1968, 31). Indeed, after Freud, Viereck went to interview Hitler. Sharing in the interview his insights on the ephemerality of life, the ubiquity of death, and the arduousness of human existence, Freud offers us a generous gift of love, giving precisely what he did not have just then: time, ideals, or fear. This interview could also be an aesthetic act whose beauty resides in letting the other receive his assertion of castration without implicating himself in a masochistic debasement.

What Freud offered in this interview, and indeed in the wide breadth of his work, is not, however, exclusively a gift of aesthetic and amorous nature but a lesson on psychoanalysis since the transmission of knowledge about castration is one of the foundations of the psychoanalytic act. When analysis affords the subject an epistemic acknowledgement of castration, possibilities unfasten for an analysand who opens to the act of desiring, thus restricting the insistence of deadening enjoyment, which is an effect of the drive. In the interview, Freud depicts the drive as a dark ally:

> Mankind does not choose suicide, because the law of its being abhors the direct route to its goal. . . . In every normal being, the life-wish is strong enough to counterbalance the death-wish, albeit in the end the death-wish proves stronger. We may entertain the fanciful suggestion that Death comes to us by our own volition. It is possible that we could vanquish Death, except for his *ally in our bosom*.
>
> (Viereck, 3, my emphasis)

The ally in question, our most intimate frenemy, is always obscure and silent, undercover, and intensely powerful. This ally splits our subjectivity into one part that wants us to live and another that seeks our death. Death, as is known well in psychoanalysis, refers not only to the final cessation of the living organism but also to the intrinsic death in repetitive compulsion that arrests life, seizes desire, coagulates meaning, and shatters subjectivities and dreams.

The manifestations of the dark drive are significantly challenging, both in the clinic and in the socio-political realms, and while both are linked in an extimate way, for what is mostly intimate for the subject is found in the exterior of social discourse, the method of analysis is always in parallax: while we focus on the social, we necessarily blur the subject (Žižek 2006). In this chapter, I discuss some possible agitators and cuts of the drive with a focus on the scale of the subject, and I do so by approaching the following underlying question, inspired by Freud's interview with Viereck: considering the inherent catastrophe of every subjectivity, why do we decide *not* to take our own life? I have worked on the phenomenon of suicide elsewhere, and here I aim to elucidate what saves the subject from suicide, which in psychoanalysis is understood as the absolute satisfaction of the death drive.

To advance my questions I organize my premises in three sections: 1) drive as a form that loops around a void, constituted by the lost object cause of desire; 2) drive's agitators constituted by the temporality of repetition and the spaces of Freud's *Unbehagen* that trigger the urge of the drive; and 3) drive's cut, which refers to the interventions that allow the emergence of the subject of unconscious desire.

## The Form of the Death Drive Constitutes Its Resistance

> Death is the mate of Love. Together they rule the world. This is the message of my book, *Beyond the Pleasure Principle*.
>
> Sigmund Freud

Let's start from the basics. In "[Drives] and Their Vicissitudes" (1915), Freud defines *Trieb* as "the frontier between the mental and the somatic, as the psychical representative of the stimuli originating from within the organism and reaching the mind" (1915, 121–122). Freud further analyzed this liminal concept from diverse angles:

1. Thrust (*Drang*) is the constant pressing tendency to discharge internal excitations (Freud 1915, 122), which prevents, Lacan adds, "any assimilation of the drive to a biological function, which always has a rhythm" (1964, 165).
2. Source (*Quelle*) refers to "the somatic process which occurs in an organ or part of the body and whose stimulus is represented in mental life by [a drive]" (Freud 1915, 123).
3. Object (*Objekt*) is the most variable aspect of the drive and thus "of no importance" (Lacan 1964, 168) because this object is indeed a loss, the object *a*, cause of desire.
4. Aim (*Ziel*) is directed at "satisfaction, which can only be obtained by removing the state of stimulation at the source" (Freud 1915, 122). Lacan, however, asserts that the aim of the drive consists not so much in the acquiring the object but rather in "*la pulsion en fait le tour*" or the drive as touring/tricking the object (1964, 168).

The drive thus explained constitutes the form that Lacan proposed in the previous model: a force entering through a hole (erotogenic orifice) and circulating around object *a*. At various points in his work, Lacan conjures up topologies that organize psychical spaces through an absence or hole, most specifically through topologies such as the Moebius strip and the cross-cap. For the subject, such a hole constitutes the traumatic real—death, sex, otherness—which requires a heuristic strategy that involves symbolic and imaginary means, such as the fundamental fantasy. Marco Antonio Coutinho Jorge, paraphrasing Lacan, reminds us that fantasy is a "window onto the real" (2010, 240) locating the fantasy between the unconscious (transference) and the drive (repetition) and rendering it as the creation of reality principle, a neurotic mechanism that is equivalent to the function of delusion for the psychotic.

For Lacan the drive is a myth, a fiction, a montage, and a *Grundbegriff* or fundamental concept, and for Freud there are two classes of drive: the erotic drive and the death drive. The latter is aligned with libido, or the sexual force of life, while the other tends to the Nirvana principle, which seeks the return to a complete stasis (Freud 1924, 160). But Lacan redirects this apparent polarity towards an "essential affinity of every drive with the zone of death . . . [that] makes present sexuality in the unconscious and represents, in its essence, death" (1964, 199). Freud's initial division of the drive into two types poses a challenge of how to defuse one from the other: "The erotic instincts and the death instincts would be present in living beings in regular mixtures or fusions; but 'defusions' would also be liable to occur" (1923, 258–259).

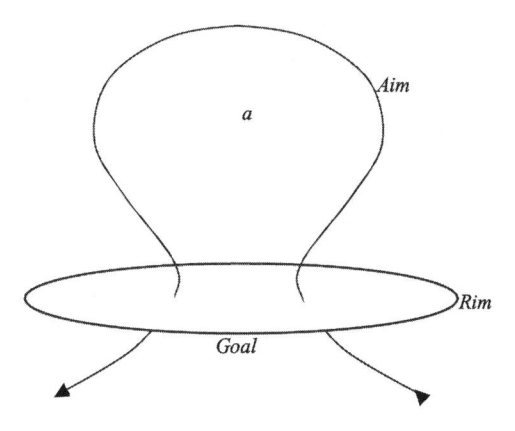

*Figure 10.1* Lacan's topology of the drive.
Source: Lacan 1964, 178

Before sorting out possible defusions we must remember that the drive's repeated trajectory around the lost object to satisfy its very circuit is never a matter of the individual alone. Lacan's visual model of the drive assumes that the hole of object *a* circulates in discourse, among others, and such a hole, albeit absent of meaning, is constituted through the language of the Other. Such discourse, an effect of culture, tradition, and lineage, opens the subject to the process of jouissance by eliciting an early learned musicality—a rhythm of lalangue—based on a psychosomatic partiture of silences and letters. The drive is in principle a real structure towards which language gravitates and gets caught up in a loop that paradoxically organizes the symbolic. The structural topology of the drive constitutes indeed its resistance, as when Lacan explained resistance to the analytic treatment, either by the analysand's ego or the analyst himself, he concludes that "after the reduction of the resistances, there is a residue which may be what is essential" (1953–1954, 121). This is the principle of repetition, a force that drags the subject into a certain compulsive repetition and which defines the drive's form. With its immoderate and unfathomable qualities of the unspeakable, the drive insists in the subject, who (re)turns to the following vicissitudes: 1) repression, as the core of the symptom and inhibitions; 2) displacement of activity, such as switching passivity to activity or masochism to sadism; and 3) sublimation, the favored path where the object is elevated to the dignity of the Thing (Freud 1915, 126–133). These vicissitudes of the drive are related to its points of agitation and cuts, to which we turn now.

## Agitations of the Drive

> I detest my mechanical jaw, because the struggle with the mechanism consumes so much precious strength. Yet I prefer a mechanical jaw to no jaw at all.
> —Sigmund Freud

An agitator is defined as someone who urges others to protest or rebel, a troublemaker, rabble-rouser, or an incendiary. The primary agitation of the drive is a matter of an internal process of sexual excitation that surpasses "certain quantitative limits," Freud asserts, and that "it may well be that nothing of considerable importance can occur in the organism without contributing some component to the excitation of the sexual [drive]" (1905, 205). By the topology of its form, the drive is always an agitation that leads to jouissance, and the subject responds to it with their unconscious know-how, allowing them to partially metabolize the impact of the drive. Sometimes drive agitations lead to opportunities for enjoyment, on the bright side of pleasure and life, but when the drive overflows and the dark ally takes over the subject's capacity to respond, the destructive morbid enjoyment congeals, halting the analysis with the repetition of endless suffering manifested in somatizations of all kinds, unbearable affect, inability of finding one's emotional bearings, or overwhelming tensions that can't be discharged. In this chapter, the agitation of the drive refers to the clinical challenges in which a subject is unable to activate a *savoir-faire*, or know-how to preserve the drive within limits, which prevents the subject's engagement with life. Pondering the conditions that might agitate the drive or cut its insistence is useful to better understand the direction of treatment at the scale of the subject and the complexities of discourse in the social.

We learn with Freud that what makes a drive pleasurable or destructively enjoyed is influenced by the increase or decrease of a quantitative tension, yet the decisive aspect is not a matter of libidinal economy but rather depends "on some characteristic of it which we can only describe as a qualitative one" (1924, 160). This quality *is* language, which is the inherited code of the Other that shaped the drive's form in the first place. In *Beyond the Pleasure Principle*, Freud observed the phenomena of repetition as a possible entry to the enigmatic "qualitative" property of the drive. Through the canonical example of the fort/da game, Freud discovered something about (dis)pleasure and repetition: The "good little boy" of eighteen months old did not cry when his mother left but instead hid his toys under the crib and played a game, throwing and pulling a cotton reel while using phonemes ("o-o-o-o"/"da") that represented words for absence and return (fort/da). (Freud 1920, 14). This repetition, accompanied by the boy's demonstrations, was observed by Freud as a joyful repetition. Yet by reflecting on other phenomena, Freud discovered stronger primitive forces that opposed the principle of constancy, homeostasis, and the pleasure principle, fort/da. Traumatic neurosis, the phenomenon of transference, or fate neurosis showed tougher forces operating within the subject to compulsively repeat actions despite well-known unpleasant consequences, paradoxically generating another kind of suffering pleasure "that can't be experienced as such" (Freud 1920, 11). Such displeasure emerges from processes of repression and inhibition of the drive, which oblige the subject "to repeat the repressed material as a contemporary experience instead of . . . remembering" (Freud 1920, 18). We constantly repeat because we can't remember the words that shape such insistence or because there are no words for it.

I am not always enthused at finding neurophysiological support for the unconscious, as such "discoveries" easily lead to reductionism. However, to elucidate a possible "defusing" of the drive and to understand how a drive gains destructivity, the work of Magistretti and Ansermet, a neuroscientist and a Lacanian psychoanalyst, respectively, might be useful. These authors claim that conscious somatic states "S" (introception, coming from the source of the drive) are associated with representation "R" (language) and that "the reestablishment of homeostasis will be constrained by the content of the representation R and therefore engage an action related to it" (Magistretti and Ansermet 2016, 140). In other words, to calm the insistence of the drive, the subject requires a representational gimmick, always linguistic in nature, that can be a word, a gesture, or an action to discharge the excess of the drive and gain some homeostasis. The anatomic seat of the drive, according to these authors, is the insular cortex, a part of the cerebral cortex whose functions include sensory processing, affect representation (feelings and emotions), autonomical and motor control, and decision-making, as well as bodily and self-awareness, among others. In that way, the drive constitutes a neurobiological and subjective site of contestation where functions such as representations of the drive (*Vorstellung*) and rerepresentation (*Vorstellungsrepräsentanz*) are key to resolving the drive's excess so the subject can unconsciously decide how to act at the insistence of the drive (Magistretti and Ansermet 2016, 140).

Thus, it is the repeated absence of language, either by the lack of signifiers ("unbound" drive with no representation) or by the absence of a signified (lack of meaning with no rerepresentation), that turns the drive deadly. Not having representations to signify the effects of the drive is a common occurrence for the speaking subject because the death drive as an entropic derivation of the sexual drive generates jouissance, which is the production of "what shouldn't be" but that simultaneously "could never fail" (Lacan 1972–1973, 59). Inaccessible to rational knowledge, jouissance is sanctioned via the superego's injunction: "Enjoy!" Because jouissance is divorced from knowledge, the speaking being manages the drive's disruption through symptomatic arrangements, inhibitions, or acts of diverse sorts. Yet there are what Fink calls "jouissance crises," "in which the analysand's former ways of enjoying himself (whether in an explicitly sexual manner or otherwise) have broken down, and he comes to analysis asking the analyst to help him restore them to their former efficacy" (Fink 2007, 91). When drive agitation surpasses a certain threshold of psychic stimulation, the increase of tension is unbearable and unhinges suffering, which can be thought as the topology of the drive accelerated and overstretched. Let's now proceed to the discussion of the temporal and spatial agitations of the drive.

The drive agitates in the temporality of repetition itself, a fact that Lacan elaborated upon in Seminar 11 through the Aristotelian categories of repetition: *tuché* and *automaton*. As an effect of *Wiederholen*, repetition, a force drags the subject into a certain repetitive path and makes coded marks on the surface of the speaking body. I argue that the drive agitates mostly with *tuché*, the unpredictable chance that appears always as a surprise and reveals a letter (the minimal mark of language in the real that insists meaninglessly), while *automaton*, the programmed repetition of signifiers, is the constitutive support of the signifying chain, and thus it calms the agitation.

When the drive agitates the subject with trauma or through repeated haphazard events, *tuché* evinces the uncanny as much as the appearance of a letter through the ever-failed (mis)encounter with the real (Lacan 1964, 55). The puzzling letter requires a subject to take agency of it to transform it into a signifier, which indeed does have meaning, for it represents the subject for another signifier within a signifying chain (Fernandez-Alvarez 2021).

*Automaton*, on the other hand, designates the necessary repetition of the phallus as signifier of lack that supports the signifying chain and manifests in the insistent flow of speech seeking "explications" and rendering associations for the symptoms. *Automaton* is a *familiar* repetition of the same content, with different words, and often appeases the subject because it allows the drive to run its course; hence the analyst intervenes to disrupt the stabilized jouissance. However, when the drive finds no words, it gains deadly power by reloading *automaton* and thus words in themselves agitate the subject's suffering, reducing the plasticity of language and restricting the space for polyphony.

Now, let's map some agitations of our dark ally in the social space by looking into what Freud identified as the three sources of discontent, *Unbehagen*:

> We are threatened with suffering from three directions: from our own body, which is doomed to decay and dissolution and which cannot even do without pain and anxiety as warning signals; from the external world, which may rage against us with overwhelming and merciless forces of destruction; and finally, from our relations to other men. The suffering which comes from this last source is perhaps more painful to us than any other.
>
> (1930, 77)

Our first approach suggests that drive agitates in the rim-like structures of the body and erotogenic orifices by default. Locating the space of agitation in these somatic areas might lead us to an omnipresent agitation as those erotogenic zones participate in the exchanges between the internal and external worlds. Moreover, given the amboceptor quality of our exchanges with others, those somatic areas are already discursively implicated in the subject's very pleasure and discontent by the mediation of the Other. Nonetheless, for the purpose of finding a minimal structural approach to the drive agitations, we can focus on the body through the three Lacanian registers.

In the imaginary, the body is agitated through the ideal ego, a phallic aspiration of a certain self-image that nonetheless is always in lack. In its dark modality, the subject is agitated through the ideal ego with envy, unworthiness, disorientation, or wounded narcissism that paralyzes action in the social and transference in the clinic. One example is that of an analysand whose obsessional symptom of dissatisfaction peaks when he compares himself to a big Other who includes him as an ideal; his attempts to let go are yet to no avail, as he fears losing his very being alongside the ideal image. Or another analysand with psychosis who appears to have a blurry body image unless it is supplemented by another body who can provide a material model to imitate. When in one session I covered my body with a blanket, his physical agitation was evident.

Signifiers harness a representational element of the drive and consequently have an appeasing effect; however, the symbolic register can also agitate the drive in the body when the words are perceived as imposed by an Other, such as in the case of medical diagnoses, assessments of competency, or an unrequited offer to confess how oneself is perceived. For example, an analysand in the mental health team was diagnosed with bipolar disorder and the diagnosis, *qua signifier*, agitated the drive in his body, because it was seen as the cause of the loss of his maniac grandiosity which he could no longer afford. The new name given to him by the psychiatrist, instead of assuaging the excessive thrust of the drive, agitated it even more despite the amount of medication given.

The drive agitates also in the real materiality of the body, such as through illnesses, hormones, stress, or psychosomatic symptoms, which fail to turn the letter into a signifier and remain in the body as implicit memory or somatic marker without any signifier or signified. This constitutes the return of the real within the body, as in the case of an analysand who suffers from a violent and debilitating psychosomatic arrest, a chronic infection that flares up very easily. She has not yet found an act to harness such drive. Somatically, then, the drive and its consequent lawless jouissance insist, instead of being remembered, persist instead of being recreated.

The reality principle or "the influence of the external world" (Freud 1924, 167) might also agitate the subject by the pressures exerted by the environment. The subject facing duress or unbearable sensorial stimulation gets tired or irritated and gives ground for the unnamed to flourish, making the subject overwhelmed with affect that turns into crisis, paralyzing stasis, or toxicity. Freud claimed that the drive can go outwards or inwards, so either we discharge it out of the organism or turn it inwards. If we turn the drive inwards, we implode with a self-loathing of sorts; if turned outwards, my fellow other is to be hated. Such insistence of the drive, a form of (self-)destruction, becomes charged with libido as the speaking being appears to enjoy what harms him too: "Instincts tolerate one another"—erotogenic, masochism—pleasure in pain, moral masochism as unconscious guilt (Freud 1924, 161). Darian Leader renders this in the following way: "the body pleasure zones are transformed by frustrations into displeasure zones, fusing hate and love, and stimulation of them will be 'resented as an insult and dreaded as a danger, as well as welcomed'" (2021, 15–16).

Finally, a third source of drive agitation might occur through our interaction with others, and as Freud reminds us, this is the most painful of all sources. I approach this agitation through the castration complex, which Lacan recuperates from Freud's conservative anatomical frame—castration anxiety for boys, penis envy for girls—and the Oedipal myth to recast it through the phallic signifier, which mainly signifies lack. The castration complex involves the confluence of various functions: frustration, castration, and privation. Based on the unconscious formation of the phallus, Lacan classifies these functions as follows: "*castration* is a symbolic action—*frustration* is an imaginary term, and *privation* is a real term. I also indicated their relations to objects" (1958–1959, 348).

Frustration, "which is imaginary in nature, is always related to a real possession or term" (Lacan 1958–1959, 348), could be instantiated when a social worker mandates a hoarder to give away a great deal of their belongings; such an intervention might consequently produce the horror of emptiness in the hoarder because although the objects being lost are real, what is experienced as lacking are not the material objects but what the subject imagines such a loss to signify. Castration, as Lacan sees it, is a symbolic loss of an imaginary phallic object such as when a hysteric subject discovers he has been cheated by a lover he boastfully assumed to be at his feet or the obsessional who can't accomplish a fixed routine because of other people's refusal to give in to her obsessional stubbornness. Privation is the real lack of a symbolic term, as in the example of an analysand who didn't stop hallucinating persecutory figures for a full month, protesting elements of her trauma that emerged in a dream. Here, the earnest hallucination revealed a lack of a symbolic term that prevented knotting the experience to put this issue to rest. The epitome of privation, however, is found in discourse via the *bare life* of social inequalities; when people are unable to afford basic services, such as housing, food, or daycare, the real lack of basic goods affects the symbolic status of life as *bios*, "the form or way of living proper to an individual or a group" (Agamben 1998, 1).

## Cutting the Drive

> I do not rebel against the universal order. After all.
>
> Sigmund Freud

For fourteen years I worked in a clinic with people who wanted to kill themselves or had the fantasy of being taken by a fatal disaster. In the first few sessions, I would often ask what had kept them alive so far, and this question was often received with puzzlement, annoyance, and sometimes a confession of how difficult it was to answer. The reason for wishing death was clear for the analysands: life had become unbearable. Yet the mysteries of why they were still alive appeared often apodictic and relational: "because it is what we humans do," "there is always some hope," or "I don't want my loved ones to suffer." Many others, after finding their bearings in speech, talked about how many things they indeed love in life but how the agitated drive—financial debts, romantic separations, illnesses, accumulated stress, or socioeconomic insecurities—had them imprisoned, burning in jouissance. Such incendiarism requires a cut or a punctuation because each of the drive agitations simultaneously offers an opportunity to cut it.

The cut in psychoanalysis refers to the analyst's intervention that engenders structural bending, separations, punctuations, interruptions, or transformations. It is in this polysemic sense that cutting the drive is to be understood here. The interruption of the drive's loop allows a possibility to redirection of the drive, or, as Lacan says: "it is at the level of the drive that the state of satisfaction is to be rectified" (1964, 166).

In psychoanalysis, cutting the drive involves an analytic intervention that sheds light—just like cutting a diamond, so that the light is reflected in the gem—to transform and channel the power of the death drive into desirous subjectivities. The analyst aims to cut the insistence of the repeated drive through interventions that go from the management of demand within transference, the variable-length session, or an attentive listening to polyphony and equivocations that might harness logical contingencies for the subject's ethic and erotic desire to emerge and counterattack the death drive.

Regarding the management of demand within transference, we ought to remember that the speaking being demands by the very fact of speaking and searching for recognition. Frustrating demand within the treatment is vital. As Lacan puts it, "not, as people say, to frustrate the subject, but in order to allow the signifiers with which the latter's frustration is bound up to reappear" (1958, 516). Frustrating the demand means, at core, that the analyst does not respond as a subject, mirroring language in its communicative mooring, but rather preserves the inquiry posed by the insistence of demand to safeguard desire.

Desire, as the source of life, emerges in the clinic as an effect of the said and heard but also as an effect of what has been written or rewritten in the analysands' desire. Or the erotic recuperation of the drive, can be brought about when the drive is cut by polyphonies or equivocations. For example, a middle-aged analysand struggling with substance use identified himself as a "waste." At a certain point in his analysis, he hears this signifier for the first time in a new negative form: "not wasted [no longer drunk], no more wasted time." The analyst counts on their way of listening to the equivocation of language, as in this example, so that a possibility of (re)inscription—a new writing of the necessary—might emerge, showing the polyvalence of the signifier's truth, which the subject must occupy with a new signification that represents them for another, in this case a possible "no." An auspicious intervention, whose effects are always unknown to the analytic partners, can perhaps lead to a partial inscription of a traumatic residue to write something of that which can't, but must, be written somehow (Fernandez-Alvarez 2020). There are situations in which even death can inscribe, for example, to mark the end of a form of deadly jouissance for a lineage or for a tradition.

To cut the drive's insistence, the analyst listens to the subjective split between the latent (enunciation) and manifest (statement) contents of speech, as Lacan expressed that desire "as such raises for man the question of his subjective elision, $, with regard to any and every possible object" (1958–1959, 116). Transference actualizes the literality of the subject's sayings and contrasts them with a signified content that insists in their lineage. By opening the question of this linguistic split, the subject might emerge to take a place in their *response ability* of the unconscious drive.

To cut the drive, the analyst also can cut the session at an unexpected moment, either to stop the flooding of a repeated empty speech, to punctuate a phrase that requires a full stop in the signifying chain, to intervene in act to set a limit, or to allow a loss to materialize. With the scansions, so often producing affective effects, the analyst cuts the metric pattern of *automaton*, enabling perhaps a relief in the deadly insistence of sameness, bringing into transference aspects of vital investigation in a subject's life.

Cutting the death drive aims towards a subjective emergence, epitomized by the ethical assumption of unconscious desire. The desire of the speaking subject is always the desire of the Other (Lacan 1964, 235), and while "desire and reality are related in a seamless texture" (Lacan 1966–1967, session of 16 November 1966) via the fantasy, desire in essence relates to lack. As Lacan explains, this lack is the lack of being properly speaking. It isn't the lack of this or that but lack of being whereby the being exists (1964).

If drive endures when we are alive, desire—the emergence of the ethical subject—resists because it is paradoxical in many accounts: 1) because being different from want, it can't be fully satisfied, or else we are complete, which is the state of death; 2) because while desire is always alienated—it emerges in the place of the Other—the subject must renounce the place of being the object for the Other and in that process pay a price, including the risk of being unloved; 3) because when acting on desire the subject only appears as an effect, the result of having to own something of their alienated desire, even in the unknown consequences; 4) because desire must be articulated symbolically, yet it is inarticulable as its cause is the object *a*; and 5) because while desire is the force of life, the fidelity to whether or not I have acted in conformity with a desire that is *in me more than me* (Lacan 1964) can only be answered in a status of the "last judgement," (Lacan 1959–1960, 294). Even if death is inextricable from life, desire is a life antidote against the destructiveness of the death drive, and the shortest effect of the drive's cut is the return of pleasure principle, "the watchman over our life rather than merely over our mental life" (Freud 1924, 159) Even, as a poet of despair knew well, we are all "deep in a hell each moment of which is a miracle" (Cioran 1969, 120). And vice versa.

## Conclusion

I still prefer existence to extinction.

Sigmund Freud

Let's return to our initial question: Considering drive as a perpetual force and desire as a path of frustration, why do we cling to the desire to live life? Freud gives us the best guidelines: "What we are left with is the fact that the organism wishes to die *only* in its own fashion" (1920, 39, my emphasis). In that way, choosing life is identical to choosing jouissance. We choose to live life the way it comes to us, either in its pleasure principle or in its morbid martyrdom, and the question that truly matters, then, is: what qualitative life for our bodies of jouissance do we desire then?

At least psychoanalysis never closes the door to a new truth.

Sigmund Freud

## References

Agamben, Giorgio. 1998. *Homo Sacer: Sovereign Power and Bare Life*. Translated by Daniel Heller-Roazen. Stanford, CA: Stanford University Press.

Cioran, E. M. 1969. *The New Gods*. Translated by Richard Howard. Chicago: University of Chicago Press, 2013.

Coutinho Jorge, Marcus Antonio. 2010. *Fundamentos da psicanalise: De Freud a Lacan. Volume 2: A clínica da fantasia*. Rio de Janeiro: Zahar.

Fernandez-Alvarez, Hilda. 2020. "So, you want a Master? Psychoanalytic Reflections on the Intellectual's Responsibility in Light of Traumatic Repetition." In *Spectres of Fascism*. Edited by Samir Gandesha. London: Pluto Press.

———. 2021. "Aokigahara Forest: An Aesthetic Space of Residual Surplus." In *Lacan and the Environment*. Edited by Clint Burnham and Paul Kingsbury. New York: Palgrave.

Fink, Bruce. 2007. *Fundamentals of Lacanian Technique: A Lacanian Approach for Practitioners*. New York: Norton.

Freud, Sigmund. 1905. "Three Essays on the Theory of Sexuality." In *Standard Edition of the Complete Psychological Works of Sigmund Freud*. Vol. 7. Translated by James Strachey, 123–246. New York: Norton, 1953.

———. 1915. "[Drives] and Their Vicissitudes." In *Standard Edition of the Complete Psychological Works of Sigmund Freud*. Vol. 14. Translated by James Strachey, 109–139. New York: Norton, 1960.

———. 1920. "Beyond the Pleasure Principle." In *Standard Edition of the Complete Psychological Works of Sigmund Freud*. Vol. 18. Translated by James Strachey, 7–64. New York: Norton, 1955.

———. 1923. "Two Encyclopaedia Articles." In *Standard Edition of the Complete Psychological Works of Sigmund Freud*. Vol. 18. Translated by James Strachey, 233–260. New York: Norton, 1955.

———. 1924. "The Economic Problem of Masochism." In *Standard Edition of the Complete Psychological Works of Sigmund Freud*. Vol. 19. Translated by James Strachey, 155–170. New York: Norton, 1961.

———. 1930. *Civilization and Its Discontents*. In *Standard Edition of the Complete Psychological Works of Sigmund Freud*. Vol. 21. Translated by James Strachey, 64–146. New York: Norton, 1961.

Johnson, Neil M. 1968. "George Sylvester Viereck: Poet and Propagandist." *Books at Iowa* 9: 22–36. https://doi.org/10.17077/0006-7474.1312.

Lacan, Jacques. 1953–1954. *Freud's Papers on Technique: The Seminar of Jacques Lacan, Book 1*. Edited by Jacques-Alain Miller. Translated by John Forrester. New York: Norton, 1991.

———. 1958. "The Direction of the Treatment and the Principles of Its Power." In *Écrits: The First Complete Edition in English*. Translated by Bruce Fink, 489–542. New York: Norton, 2006.

———. 1958–1959. *Desire and Its Interpretation: The Seminar of Jacques Lacan*, Book VI. Edited by Jacques-Alain Miller. Translated by Bruce Fink. New York: Polity, 2019.

———. 1959–1960. *The Ethics of Psychoanalysis: The Seminar of Jacques Lacan*, Book VII. Edited by Jacques-Alain Miller. Translated by Dennis Porter. New York: Norton, 1992.

———. 1964. *The Four Fundamental Concepts of Psychoanalysis: The Seminar of Jacques Lacan*, Book XI. Edited by Jacques-Alain Miller. Translated by Alan Sheridan. New York: Norton, 1977.

———. 1966–1967. *The Logic of Fantasy: The Seminar of Jacques Lacan*, Book XIV. Translated by Cormac Gallagher. www.lacaninireland.com/web/wp-content/uploads/2010/06/14-Logic-of-Phantasy-Complete.pdf.

———. 1972–1973. *On Feminine Sexuality, the Limits of Love and Knowledge, Encore: The Seminar of Jacques Lacan*, Book XX. Edited by Jacques-Alain Miller. Translated by Bruce Fink. New York: Norton, 1998.

Leader, Darian. 2021. *Jouissance: Sexuality, Suffering and Satisfaction*. Cambridge: Polity.

Magistretti, Pierre, and François Ansermet. 2016. "The Island of Drive: Representations, Somatic States and the Origin of Drive." In *A Neuro-Psychoanalytical Dialogue for Bridging Freud and the Neurosciences*. Edited by Sigrid Weigel and Gerhardt Scharbert, 137–147. Switzerland: Springer.

Viereck, George S. 1927. "An Interview with Freud." La Psychanalyse au Luxembourg. Accessed 15 March 2023. www.psychanalyse.lu/articles/FreudInterview.pdf.

Žižek, S. 2006. *The Parallax View*. Cambridge, MA: MIT Press.

Chapter 11

# The Skin as the Source of the Dermic Drive

Modes of Dermic Punctuation in the Containment of Meaning

*Leon S. Brenner*

---

*In this chapter, Leon Brenner asks us to consider the skin as a site of the drive. Negotiating between Freud's conception of the skin as bodily surface that is the origin of the ego and Lacan's conception of the drive as origin of the subject, Brenner suggests a transposition: What if the skin were an originary surface giving rise to the Lacanian drive? Through a meticulous account of the drive as linguistically grounded, Brenner arrives at the notion of the skin as establishing a relationship between subject and Other. The skin serves not as an orifice but as a point of contact/separation that allows for the punctuation of signifiers. Brenner's thesis, drawing from Lacan's work on the role of language in subjectification and in desubjectification found in psychosis, illustrates well that there's much creative work left to be done in the world of Lacanian theory.*

---

A well-known question among trivia fans is: what is the largest organ in the human body? The answer is the skin: a special kind of organ that covers the surface of the body, providing it with protection, regulation, and sensation. The skin takes shape very early in the development of the fetus, around weeks five through eight, giving it access to sensory experiences that precede the formation of the eyes, ears, and tongue. Skin sensations are among the first sensory representations imprinted on the human psyche, even before the fetus can hear the voice of the mother from inside the womb. This renders the skin itself a significant object of interest in many disciplines, especially psychoanalysis.

The significance of the skin for the understanding of human psychic processes has been acknowledged in the field of psychoanalysis from its very inception. For example, we have, in *The Ego and the Id* (1923), Sigmund Freud's explicit remarks about the role of the surface of the body in the initiation and development of the ego (26). Following Freud, many other psychoanalysts have commented on the indispensable function of the skin for the ego's formation and integration (e.g., Anzieu 1989; Bick 1968; Bion 1962; Meltzer 1994; Ogden 1989; Tustin 1986; Winnicott 1945). Some even suggest that disturbances in the early experience of the skin play a key role in the onset of most psychopathologies.

For Jacques Lacan, the ego is a secondary construct that has a peripheral role in the psychoanalytic treatment. Following Freud's (1900) distinction between "secondary" ideational processes, which concern the integration of the ego, and the "primary" drive processes, which concern the "core of our being" (603), Lacan (2006) puts emphasis on the latter and their effect on the structuration of the subject (347). Drawing from Lacan, this chapter will transpose the psychoanalytic discussion of the skin's psychic function from the arena of *ego construction* to that of Freudian *drive theory* (*Trieblehre*). This aims toward the development of a novel perspective on the skin as a source of a partial drive: the "dermic drive." To that end, the Freudian and Lacanian perspectives of the drive will be delineated and the implications of conceiving of the skin as the *dermic drive* will be developed in structural and linguistic terms.

## The Four Drives

Freud (1915) and Lacan (1964) both distinguish the drive (*Trieb*) as one of the fundamental concepts of psychoanalysis. They do so by distinguishing it from the instinct (*Instinkt*) of the organism. In this sense, Freud (1911) argues that the drive is "a concept on the frontier-line between the somatic and the mental" (74). To this, Lacan (1964) adds that the drive originates exactly at the point of the rupture of the human instinctual organizing function that occurs when the subject enters language. The drive thus becomes a unique byproduct of this collision and embodies the mutual effect the body and language have on each other. For Freud, these effects manifest in the way that libido is invested in localized cathexis sites in the body. In stricter Lacanian terms, these are interpreted as the *cuts* that the *signifier* introduces into the *body* (Lacan 2006, 678), cuts that create the rim-like structures of the erogenous zones from which the drive emerges (Lacan 1964, 168). Freud introduces several drives that correspond to the body's erogenous orifices, the oral and the anal being two of them, which have the breast and the feces as their respective objects. Lacan added the scopic drive, associated with the eyes, and invocatory drive, associated with the ears, with the gaze and the voice as their objects. Each of these drives and their objects play a crucial role in the shaping and constituting of the psyche. This is the way the "fate of the drives" in Freud's psychoanalysis aligns with Lacan's development of the "subject's lines of fate" (2006, 499).

The particular role each drive plays in the constitution of the human psyche is determined, according to Freud, at an early age in a child's life. Freud (1911) argues that at a certain point in its development a drive becomes fixated, that is, it persists in an unaltered state (pp. 62–68). In doing so, drive fixation establishes consistent modes of drive function, modes that determine the ways in which drive stimuli can be mediated in the body and establish the subject's modes of enjoyment and suffering.

Being situated between body and language, the drive's fixation plays a crucial role in the initiation of the subject's relationship with the Other (Brenner 2020, 187). It does so by establishing itself within the field of demand where signifiers attach the drive object to the field of the Other (Dravers 2011). In Seminar 10 (1962–1963), Lacan describes the unique features in the relationship between the subject and the Other established by each drive (291). In this sense, we could say that, in Lacan's teaching, we can identify four distinct modes of the initiation of the subject's relationship to the Other. Through the initiation of these modes, a "series of thresholds starts to bring structure to the world" giving rise to its humanized dimension (Lacan 1956–1957, 239). What I will soon argue is that the skin should be determined as an erogenous zone that functions as a source of a distinct partial drive exactly because it initiates a singular relationship between the subject and the Other, a relationship that cannot be reduced to those initiated by the oral, anal, scopic and invocatory drives.

In support of my argument, I will first provide a rudimentary description of the initiatory effects that the oral and anal drives have on the relationship between the subject and the Other. These will enable me to distinguish the unique initiatory effects I attribute to the dermic drive. In psychoanalytic literature, these relationships are commonly described in reference to infantile psychological experiences that originate in the mouth and anus. As the reader will shortly see, the strength of Lacan's teaching on the drive resides in its focus on the way the drive establishes the set of rules that determine the function of signifiers in the relationship between the subject and the Other, using figurative terms only as an illustration.

Let us begin with the oral drive, which is described by Lacan as circumventing the rim-like structure of the lips. It is initiated in the infant's cry when it is directed to the Other in the demand to be fed. As Freud (1905) states, the oral demand is situated on the side of the subject's bodily need to be fed but concerns the Other's body, particularly the breast. The breast then is considered to initiate a relationship between the subject and the Other insofar as it involves a *disjunction of bodies*, where the breast is an object that is fully located neither on the side of the mother nor the infant (Lacan 2014, 302).

In structural terms, the disjunctive object of the oral drive initiates a spatial splitting in the psyche by demarcating a space for the *pleasurable* distinct from that of the *unpleasurable*. Freud argues that this division is established in relation to the pleasure principle: "'I should like to eat this', or 'I should like to spit it out'. . . . That is to say: 'It shall be inside me' or 'it shall be outside me'" (Freud 1925, 237). In Lacanian terms, we might say that, when viewed in this way, the oral drive initiates the spatial division that enables the attribution of disparate pleasure values to signifiers.

With the anal drive, Lacan situates the demand in the Other. He adds that this demand is "educative" because it entails pedagogical instructions that come from the Other (Lacan 2014, 292). These instructions consist of, on the one hand, the demand to hold the excrement in the body until the right time and, on the other, the demand to produce a "nice feces": a gift offered to the Other in compliance with particular cultural and ritualistic features. The anal drive situates the infant at an intersection, where it can choose to comply with the Other's demand or not. In this sense, the anal drive initiates the entry into the intersubjective domain, where the subject's engagement with the Other's demands come to the fore in a struggle to conform with the particular cultural guidelines for the proper "keeping it in" and "giving it out" (Lacan 2014, 302).

The anal drive divides the subject, as it embodies the gap between the demand of the Other and the object produced as a response to it. This is a different division than the one offered by the oral drive, which establishes a division between "good" and "bad" psychic spaces. The anal drive offers a designation of a space on the side of the subject that complies with the "goods" that the Other demands. In other words, the anal drive affirms a space for privileged signifiers that are identified in the Other's discourse and are provided by the subject to the Other in an inverted form.

To summarize, Lacan argues that each drive initiates a particular relationship between the subject and the Other. In other words, in its initial inscription, each drive is fixated and structures a set of rules that determine the particular function of signifiers in the psyche. The oral drive establishes a spatial division that enables the attribution of disparate pleasure values to signifiers. The anal drive deciphers the signifiers coming from the Other in the production of valuable objects on the side of the subject. I have not discussed the scopic and invocatory drives, which are developed in great length by Lacan. Briefly, I will mention that according to Lacan, the scopic drive determines what signifiers are associated with the desirable imaginary ideal that the subject sees in itself (Lacan 2014, 238, 292, 325). Finally, the invocatory drive establishes the dimension of otherness in one's speech and the space between signifiers that carry the subject's enunciative being (Lacan 2014, 249–250, 277, 292).

## The Dermic Drive

The skin is not an orifice: it does not entail an opening of the inside of the body to the outside. However, one must note that, unlike the mouth and the anus, the eyes and the ears are not literal openings, as they both entail a protective layer, be it the retina or the eardrum. Similarly, the skin is composed of the epidermis, which provides waterproofing and serves as a barrier to infection; the dermis, which cushions the body from stress and strain; and the hypodermis, which contains blood vessels and nerves. It is the latter that provides the infant with its first sensational opening to the world, even before it is born, even before the mouth, the anus, the eyes and the ears develop.

Previous psychoanalysts have primarily engaged with the notion of the skin in terms of its effect on the construction of the ego. In order to better describe the integrating function of the skin, they developed categories such as "primal skin function" (Bick 1968), "boundedness" (Ogden 1989), "separateness" (Tustin 1986), and "containment" (Bion 1970). These psychoanalysts describe early stages of psychic development in terms of boundary formation and psychic containment. When doing so, they describe psychological narratives that have to do with the surface of the body—the skin. However, while their theories sometimes rely on actual sensory experiences that involve skin sensations, they all emphasize at some point that the notion of the skin goes beyond its literal meaning and reflects a level of representation that takes place in the psyche (Bick 1968, 484; 1986, 294; Ogden 1989, 136; Tustin 1972, 105–106). In this sense, while the tactile sensory experience of containment enabled by the skin of the body might serve as the foundation of the experience of psychic integration, it seems that, for Bick, Ogden, Tustin, and Bion, the skin function is not fully reducible to the somatic experience of the outer tissue covering the body. The drama of the skin function also unravels on a level that conditions psychic representations. Accordingly, I suggest that, as a psychoanalytic concept, the skin's *psychic function* would be determined as playing a fundamental role in the initiation of the most primitive psychic boundaries that give rise to the creation of psychic spaces where further psychic functions can materialize. According to this interpretation, I suggest that the skin functions as an erogenous source for the dermic drive. The fixation of this drive instantiates a particular mode of psychic division that is established in the relationship between the subject and the Other. Corresponding with the elaboration of the oral and anal drive presented in the previous section, my hypothesis is that this mode of division establishes the psychic capacity to separate and distinguish between signifiers—to *punctuate* them. In the following section, I will describe several distinct clinical phenomena that exemplify the way the punctuation of signifiers affects the subject's access to exceedingly complex levels of representation as they are expressed in cases of psychosis and autism.

## Modes of Dermic Punctuation

In order to provide a structural and linguistic interpretation of the dermic drive, it is advisable to examine Lacan's understanding of signifiers. According to Lacan (1955–1956), the building blocks of any "natural language"—namely, a language that evolves through use and repetition and is not deliberately engineered—are signifiers (167). Following Saussure (1959), Lacan conceives of a signifier as a phonological element: a basic vocalization like "ba," "du," "ah," and so on. Because they are basic vocalizations, signifiers do not refer to objects and by themselves do not signify anything. When several signifiers are opposed to one another, signification or, in Lacan's terms, the *signified* is produced. Human beings listen to chains of signifiers and, when they perceive oppositions between signifiers, they conceive of the signified. This might be the most crucial characteristic of language according to Saussure (1959): the fact that it does not convey meaning through constant relationships between words and referents in the world but that meaning is solely engendered through the ever-changing relationships between signifiers.

Signifiers are commonly presented in speech in a constant flow without clearly discernible gaps. Accordingly, an important step one takes when learning a new language is to intuitively acquire its laws of punctuation. These laws list the particular phonological patterns that determine when a word or a sentence start and end as well as distinguish between signifiers that oppose each other within words. According to Lacan (1955–1956),

> there are properly symbolic laws of intervals, of suspension, and of resolution, there are suspensions and scansions that mark the structure of every calculation . . . this structure . . . is the very structure, or inertia, of language.
>
> (112)

Punctuation is one important feature of the "symbolic laws" that are initiated in the relationship between the subject and the Other. This feature is distinct from those established by the oral, anal, scopic and invocatory drives, as it precedes the attribution of the value of signifier in the subject and the Other's demand. In the following subsections, I divide them into four categories of punctuation that correspond with four levels of "separation strength" that I have associated with the dermic drive in a previous publication in mathematical terms (Brenner 2022).

## No Punctuation

In the hypothetical state where the psyche is not endowed with any capacity to distinguish between signifiers all forms of psychic representation are impossible to render. This means that not even a single linguistic unit can be distinguished, and in this sense, nothing can be psychically represented. A psyche without access to any mode of psychic division can be said to be completely blank and prior to any form of representation, which is to say, not yet established as a psyche in the strict sense.

## Minimal Punctuation

A minimal mode of psychic division between signifiers endows the psyche with the capacity for rudimentary forms of representation. We might say, in simple terms, that this degree of separation enables signifiers to be distinguished one at a time but not simultaneously. Recall that, according to Lacan, signification is only produced when several signifiers are opposed to one another. Therefore, when two signifiers cannot be distinguished at the same time their relationship does not warrant the creation of the standard form of signification. Lacan (1964) does discuss the creation of rigid linguistic objects that are composed of a single signifier: "holophrases" (237). Holophrases are the result of the solidification of the first dyad of signifiers $S_1$–$S_2$ and its reduction into an autonomous self-referential utterance that entails no interval between signifiers. In this sense, a holophrase is conceived of as a master signifier ($S_1$) that is frozen and has no access to other binary signifiers ($S_2$) (Maleval 2022, 56).

Lacan (1955–1956) discusses the use of holophrases in terms of the disturbances in the "internal structure of language" seen in psychotic speech (250). Particularly, Lacan states that in paranoid psychosis "certain words take on a special emphasis, a density that sometimes manifests itself in the very form of the signifier, giving it this frankly neologistic character" (32). Neologisms in psychosis are, for Lacan (2006), autonomous self-referential utterances that are impossible to contextualize in relation to other signifiers (450). They hold immense libidinal value but are by themselves excluded from the process of signification and thus commonly provoke anxiety. Correspondingly, in the later phases of his delusional development, Daniel Schreber (1955) describes how autonomous utterances such as "nerve-contact" (*Nervenanhange*) and "soul-murder" (*Seelenmord*) were imposed on him from without, interrupting his train of thought and evoking confusion (23–24, 33–35). The use of holophrases in psychosis can be said to result from a retreat from the stronger degrees of separation established by the dermic drive and a reliance on a weaker mode of minimal punctuation.

One of Lacan's (2006) famous dictums states that "a signifier is what represents the subject to another signifier" (694). Because holophrastic utterances do not entail a relationship between two signifiers, we conclude that they are expressed without reference to the subject or, in other words, they entail the erasure of the position of the subject. In terms of clinical material, we can identify such moments where the subject's position is compromised in cases of schizophrenic psychosis and autism.

Many schizophrenic subjects report losing their capacity to feel like a person or that their body is demarcated from the outside world. These subjects are bombarded by senseless drive representatives that seem to erase the position of the subject and monopolize the psyche, reducing it to a space for signifiers that have nothing to do with the subject (Vanheule 2011, 141).

The position of the subject is also radically compromised in autism, especially in particular instances that I have previously called "transitive equations" (Brenner 2021, 960). When resorting to transitive equations, many autistic subjects incorporate themselves in the objects they engage with as though they are one unit. These are moments where the subject is invested in shielded interactions with objects that entail the erasure of the subject's position and the total equation with the position of the object. One might say that, in these moments, the subject *is* the object rather than being *represented* by it.

In summary, we see that a minimal mode of punctuation can enable an initial distinction between signifiers that might, at that point, be arbitrary. Be that as it may, it is implemented by psychotic and autistic subjects in their attempt to construct a boundary that could confront an unbearable real that invades their body. This boundary created by the dermic drive might be "full of holes," as Bick (1968) argues (484), but it can still provide some protective functions through its minimal separation strength.

## Loose Punctuation

A second stronger mode of psychic division between signifiers endows the psyche with the capacity for the signification of complex perceptions and concepts. On this level, a chain of signifiers can be demarcated and distinguished from other chains of signifiers and vice versa. In this sense, the signification of an internal and external space in the psyche and the experiential relationship to objects can be established and expanded using other signifiers. However, what distinguishes this "looser" degree of separation from the third standard degree of separation between signifiers is the fact that in the former any distinction between chains of signifiers always entails an overlap. In other words, we might say that the loose mode of punctuation bestows the psyche with the capacity to distinguish between chains of signifiers but that the resulting signification might include some language disturbances that are rooted in the sliding of the signified under the chain of signifiers.

One example of such language disturbances is commonly referred to as "associative looseness" or "derailment" in cases of psychosis. Both refer to vague and confusing speech, in which the subject will frequently jump from one idea to a seemingly unrelated one without any contextual referent. This feature of psychosis was already recognized by Bleuler (1911) as "loosening of associations," a disordered mode of thinking so severe that associations among ideas become fragmented and disturbed and, as a result, lacking in any logical relationships. Today they are categorized as one type of the positive symptoms of schizophrenia, together with delusions and hallucinations (APA 2013).

Due to its *seemingly* thematically inconsistent nature, associative looseness is said to manifest itself at the level of the signified. While that might be true, from a Lacanian perspective, associative looseness can be determined as a disturbance rooted in the functioning of signifiers in the metonymic process. Lacan's view on metonymy is rooted in the work of Roman Jakobson (1953), who considered metonymy as one of the fundamental processes in meaning-making (61). Particularly, metonymy takes place when one signifier in a chain of signifiers evokes another due to their lexical connection. For example, the sentence "a poet writes books" contains several chains of signifiers—"p-o-e-t," "w-ri-te-s," "b-oo-k-s"—that are thematically related and, in this sense, are limited in their associative scope: a poet is a man who writes; one can write books, papers, pamphlets, and so on. For Lacan, these are connections on the level of the signified, of meaning, rather than the signifier (the sounds composing words). Metonymic speech, therefore, is characterized by the fact that the meaning conveyed by it remains thematically consistent when speech slides on the chain of signifiers without producing any ambiguity in meaning (Vanheule 2011, 52).

Identifying the thematic relationships between chains of signifiers (whole words) in a sentence requires punctuation. For example, the sentence "Let's eat, grandma" would mean something completely different when we lose the comma after the verb: "Let's eat grandma." This is also true in terms of the punctuation of signifiers that are internal to whole words. Without any written correlate, a word can be heard in many different ways, especially when this word is adjacent to other words in a sentence. For example, the sentence "I need fork handles" can also be heard as "I need four candles" depending on the perception of the punctuation of signifiers internal to the words in the sentence. Reconstructing a message from the sounds we hear is an extremely complex task that requires acquaintance with the nuanced punctuations characterizing a particular form of a spoken language.

I argue that the associative looseness identified in psychotic speech is rooted in a loose mode of punctuation, similar but more extensive than the one presented previously. After all, every word is composed of chains of signifiers that are directly related to—or by themselves are made of—other signifiers. When one's capacity for punctuation always entails an overlap between chains of signifiers, the process of meaning-making also becomes disorganized and leans towards the homophony and intertextuality of words. Therefore, I argue that the associative looseness identified in psychotic speech is rooted in disturbances in the punctuation of signifiers in the metonymic process, disturbances that are rooted in the functioning of the dermic drive. However, unlike the psychiatric model that describes associative looseness in terms of a disturbed train of thought that lacks in logical relationship, I suggest describing it as a hypertrophied mode of contextualization within the metonymic process. In this mode, the dispersed punctuation of signifiers deflects the process of meaning-making into alternative but phonetically related thematic threads. Particularly, it draws our attention to the fact that the signifier is not rigidly linked to the signified, causing the latter to slide under the chain of signifiers in an endless deferral of meaning (Lacan 2006, 419).

Another clinical example for the reliance on this mode of punctuation can be found in disturbances of identity, commonly associated with the notion of depersonalization seen in cases of psychosis and autism. Depersonalization disorder is a diagnosis attributed today to individuals who persistently experience feelings of either bodily or cognitive detachment from themselves or their environment (APA 2013). The notion of depersonalization is not explicitly addressed in Freud's work. Several psychoanalysts, like Schilder (1939), began to describe it in terms derived from Freud's theory of narcissism as an effect of the libido's withdrawal of cathexis from the image of the body. Later on, Federn (1947) came to describe it in terms of alteration in drive functioning in the body and its boundaries. Lacan (2006) also addressed the notion of depersonalization in terms of the subject's disinvestments in ego identification (569). However, he did not strictly define it as a psychotic phenomenon but described it as a necessary way-point in the analysis of neurotic subjects, where the subject loses the narcissistic strongholds that support it as an ego (Harari 2004, 178).

In the previous subsection I have described more severe forms of depersonalization in terms of bodily disintegration, catatonia and transitive equations. These phenomena demonstrated the erasure of the position of the subject commonly associated with depersonalization. Relative to the loose mode of punctuation, I suggest defining a "softer" form of depersonalization that involves the blurring of ego boundaries. This form of identity diffusion can be associated with the psychoanalytic notion of "transitivism." Transitivism is a phenomenon that refers to a special form of identification often observed in the behavior of young children. A common example would be when a child hits another child on the left side of their face and then touches the right side of their own face and cries in pain. Lacan (2006) describes transitivism as a confusion between two egos in the process of identification (571). In terms of the loose punctuation of signifiers, I argue that the overlap between chains of signifiers might cause a confusion between one's body image—the ideal ego—and the body image of others (Brenner 2021, 951).

This type of phenomena is expressed more extensively in cases of autism where autistic children attest to an identity diffusion between themselves and others around them. Many autistic children "borrow" particular features from objects and people that surround them and attribute them to themselves. For example, Tustin (1969) describes the case of an autistic child named David, who would "pluck" features from his father and adorn himself with them (27).

**Standard Punctuation**

The strongest mode of punctuation between signifiers enables any two chains of signifiers to be demarcated and distinguished from one another while both are completely disjoint, namely not overlapping in any way. This degree of separation initiated by the dermic drive characterizes the standard punctuation of signifiers described in Lacan's interpretation of Saussure (Lacan 1955–1956, 112). With standard punctuation, every element in the symbolic domain can be fully distinguished from all others. This enables chains of signifiers to give rise to significations that "*contain*" meaning. Here, my linguistic interpretation of the function of the dermic drive moves away from the containment metaphor provided by Bick (1968), Bion (1970) and other Kleinian psychoanalysts. Instead of defining containment in relational terms, I play on the double meaning of the word: 1) I describe it in terms of the capacity of language to produce concepts: *containers* of meaning. 2) I associate it with the psychic capacity to *contain* the incessant sliding of the signified under the chain of signifiers that brings it to a halt and enables the signification of a coherent meaning.

**Conclusion**

Physical and psychological disturbances of the skin have been addressed in the past as a causal factor in the onset of various psychopathologies, particularly ones having to do with ego construction. In this chapter, I have provided a different take on the psychic skin function, as it is presented in psychoanalytic literature. Instead of describing modalities of skin containment in figurative terms, I have proposed a theory of the skin function in structural and linguistic terms. Particularly, I developed a theory of the dermic drive: a particular drive that establishes a specific relationship between the subject and the Other. Like with the other drives, I have described this relationship in terms of the use of signifiers in the spatial demarcation of the psyche. Accordingly, I argued that the dermic drive initiates three degrees of separation that condition the punctuation of signifiers. In doing so, I provided examples from the clinic of psychosis and autism in support of my argument. However, this does not mean that other subjective structures are not affected by alterations in the dermic drive; these effects still need to be studied and developed.

From the implications of the theoretical developments presented in this chapter, I conclude that reliance on stronger degrees of separation between signifiers extends the psychic capacity to encode complex forms of representation. In arguing this, I do not come to endorse a developmental outlook on the dermic drive. In contrast, I believe that a subject can lean on different modes of punctuation in different circumstances and dimensions of psychic life. It seems that, in psychosis, the subject commonly leans on loose punctuation while having access to all other modes of punctuation. In autism there is a stronger foreclosure that prohibits access to the standard mode of punctuation (Brenner 2022). This results in a diminished mode of access to the first two modes of punctuation.

The clinical implications of the theory of the dermic drive remain to be further developed. In passing we might say that, when working with psychotic and autistic subjects, one is also expected to support them in strengthening their access to the different modes of punctuation enabled by the dermic drive. This is to be done by developing their linguistic skills and helping them handle the pain of achieving access to stronger degrees of separation between signifiers. We might say that this entails establishing a supplementary fixation within the dermic drive, where three modes of psychic division correspond to three modes of punctuation in the containment of meaning.

The research presented in this chapter received support from the Gerhard Fichtner Scholarship. The author extends his sincere gratitude for this generous contribution.

## References

American Psychiatric Association. 2013. *DSM 5*. American Journal of Psychiatry, 5th edition. Washington, DC: American Psychiatric Publishing.

Anzieu, Didier. 1989. *The Skin Ego: A Psychoanalytic Approach to the Self*. Translated by Chris Turner. New Haven: Yale UP.

Bick, Esther. 1968. "The Experience of the Skin in Early Object-Relations." *International Journal of Psycho-Analysis* 49: 484–486.

———. 1986. "Further Considerations on the Function of the Skin in Early Object Relations: Findings from Infant Observation Integrated into Child and Adult Analysis." *British Journal of Psychotherapy* 2 (4): 292–299.

Bion, Wilfred R. 1962. *Learning from Experience*. London: Karnac, 1984.

———. 1970. *Attention and Interpretation*. London: Karnac, 1984.

Bleuler, Eugen. 1911. *Dementia Praecox or the Group of Schizophrenias*. Translated by Joseph Zinkin. New York: International Universities Press, 1950.

Brenner, Leon. S. 2020. *The Autistic Subject: On the Threshold of Language*. London: Palgrave Macmillan.

———. 2021. "The Autistic Mirror in the Real: Autism in Lacan's Mirror Stage." *Theory & Psychology* 31 (6).

———. 2022. "Autistic Disturbances in Skin Containment: The Dermic Drive as a Psychoanalytic Concept in the Study of Autism." *Psychoanalytic Psychology* 39 (3): 198–208. https://doi.org/10.1037/pap0000400.

de Saussure, Ferdinand. 1959. *Course in General Linguistics*. Translated by Wade Baskin. New York: Philosophical Library.

Dravers, Philip. 2011. "The Drive as a Fundamental Concept of Psychoanalysis." *Psychoanalytical Notebooks* 23: 117–149.

Federn, Paul. 1947. "Principles of Psychotherapy in Latent Schizophrenia." *American Journal of Psychotherapy* 1 (2): 129–144.

Freud, S. 1900. "The Interpretation of Dreams." In *Standard Edition of the Complete Psychological Works of Sigmund Freud*. Vols. 4 and 5. Translated by James Strachey. New York: Norton, 1953.

———. 1905. "Three Essays on the Theory of Sexuality." In *Standard Edition of the Complete Psychological Works of Sigmund Freud*. Vol. 7. Translated by James Strachey, 123–245. New York: Norton, 1953.

———. 1911. "Psycho-Analytic Notes on an Autobiographical Account of a Case of Paranoia (*Dementia Paranoides*)." In *Standard Edition of the Complete Psychological Works of Sigmund Freud*. Vol. 12. Translated by James Strachey, 1–82. New York: Norton, 1958.

———. 1915. "[Drives] and Their Vicissitudes." In *Standard Edition of the Complete Psychological Works of Sigmund Freud*. Vol. 14. Translated by James Strachey, 111–140. New York: Norton, 1957.

———. 1923. "The Ego and the Id." In *Standard Edition of the Complete Psychological Works of Sigmund Freud*. Vol. 19. Translated by James Strachey, 1–66. New York: Norton, 1961.

———. 1925. "Negation." In *Standard Edition of the Complete Psychological Works of Sigmund Freud*. Vol. 19. Translated by James Strachey, 235–239. New York: Norton, 1961.

Harari, Roberto. 2004. *Lacan's Four Fundamental Concepts of Psychoanalysis*. New York: Other Press.

Jakobson, R. 1953. "Results of the Conference of Anthropologists and Linguists." In *Selected Writings II: Word and Language*, 554–567. Berlin: Mouton.

Lacan, Jacques. 1955–1956. *The Psychoses: The Seminar of Jacques Lacan*, Book III. Edited by Jacques-Alain Miller. Translated by Russell Grigg. New York: Norton, 1993.

———. 1956–1957. *The Object Relation: The Seminar of Jacques Lacan*, Book 4. Edited by Jacques-Alain Miller. Translated by A. R. Price. Cambridge UK: Polity, 2020.

———. 1962–1963. *Anxiety: The Seminar of Jacques Lacan*, Book X. Edited by Jacques-Alain Miller. Translated by A. R. Price. Cambridge, UK: Polity, 2014.

———. 1964. *The Four Fundamental Concepts of Psychoanalysis: The Seminar of Jacques Lacan*, Book XI. Edited by Jacques-Alain Miller. Translated by Alan Sheridan. New York, NY: Norton, 1977.

———. 2006. *Écrits: The First Complete Edition in English*. Translated by Bruce Fink, 722–725. New York: Norton, 2007.

Maleval, Jean-Claude. 2022. *La Différence autistique*. Paris: Presses Universitaires de Vincennes.

Meltzer, Donald. 1994. "Adhesive Identification." In *Sincerity and Other Works: Collected Papers of Donald Meltzer*. Edited by Alberto Hahn, 335–350. London: Karnac.

Ogden, Thomas H. 1989. "On the Concept of an Autistic-Contiguous Position. *International Journal of Psycho-Analysis* 70: 127–140.

Schilder, Paul. 1939. "The Treatment of Depersonalization." *Bulletin of the New York Academy of Medicine* 15 (4): 258–272.

Schreber, Daniel Paul. 1955. *Memoirs of My Nervous Illness*. Translated by Ida Macalpine and Richard A. Hunter. Edited by Ida Macalpine and Richard A. Hunter. New York: New York Review of Books.

Tustin, Frances. 1969. "Autistic Processes." *Journal of Child Psychotherapy* 2 (3): 23–39.

———. 1972. *Autism and Childhood Psychosis*. London: Karnac, 1995.

———. 1986. *Autistic Barriers in Neurotic Patients*. London: Karnac.

Vanheule, Stijn. 2011. *The Subject of Psychosis: A Lacanian Perspective*. New York: Springer.

Winnicott, D. 1945. "Primitive Emotional Development." *International Journal of Psycho-Analysis* 26: 137–143.

Chapter 12

# The Respiratory Drive

## Psychoanalysis's Ground Zero

*Jamieson Webster and Patricia Gherovici*

---

*The neglected respiratory drive is considered by U.S.-based psychoanalysts Jamieson Webster and Patricia Gherovici who undertake an invaluable psychoanalytic reading of respiration. They draw from a range of early psychoanalytic literature from Ferenzi, Freud, Winnicott, and more recently, Lacan, Marie Rhode, and Catherine Vanier to pose its biologistic nature as operating in support of the psychic function of separation, from the infant's gulp of air and first scream to the role of inhalation and exhalation in speaking and self-representation. Delving into a case of Winnicott with an asthmatic seven-month-old, they consider his observations of the role of anxiety and inhibition in the infant and its movement from helplessness to decisive motor force by identifying three distinct temporal waves in the case—being, having, not-having. They also draw from a case of autistic breathing by Rhode, and Vanier's work with premature infants. In Lacanian terms, the respiratory drive is erogenous and is a valuable site of psychic elaboration. They argue that psychoanalytic work with speech and its respiratory drive not only supports accessing the unconscious but can contribute to studies of the respiratory drive and more generally to the revitalisation of the psychoanalytic field.*

In this time of global health crisis and poor individual and environmental health, can we take a breather and ask ourselves if there is something that psychoanalytic thought can contribute specifically to the urgent issue of breathing? Breathing has always been tied by psychoanalysis to symptoms related to anxiety, to forms of panic-attacks such as hyperventilation or one of the most common psychosomatic symptoms, namely asthma, where the problem isn't the excessive intake of air but a kind of constriction that becomes a failure to exhale. Some consider asthma the psychosomatic symptom par excellence since, unlike stomach aches or headaches, the effect in the body is unambiguous and the reflex involved is absolutely palpable. These breathing symptoms are directly linked to feelings of fear and anxiety—you hold your breath and wait! The idea of breathing or not is embedded in many idiomatic expressions—"smother," "choke," "breathing room," "breathing easy," "breathing down my neck," "breath of fresh air," "in the same breath," "top of one's lungs," "catch your breath," "say something under your breath," "take my breath away," "breathless," "waste your breath," "breathe new life," and so on.

DOI: 10.4324/9781003300649-14

As one of the latest acquisitions in human evolutionary development (roughly three hundred and sixty million years ago), the lungs are one of the last organs to develop in utero, making them especially vulnerable. If every surface were unfolded and laid out, they are also, by some measures, the largest organ in the body (after the skin). Birth trauma, in this regard, is not only separation from the mother but also the struggle to breathe, having to take something foreign into the body. We are not only dependent on our caregivers; we are also dependent on air. Separation is a fact but it is also a fragile process and as with breathing, there are vulnerabilities, forms of resistance, ways of co-opting what seems, at least on the surface, as though it should just *happen*.

What kind of evolutionary trick is this? Well, the trick is also key to the development of language. It is not only breathing, but eating, and, more importantly, speaking (and *singing*) that make use of the mouth, nasal passages, airways, and diaphragmatic structure of the lungs. Very early, the baby must find a new kind of life rhythm to that of in utero, centering on sucking, breathing, and cooing as an oral counterpart to what is taken in from the world through looking, smelling, hearing, and touching. This sensorium swaths the infant in its first months of life. If psychoanalysis is about speaking—say anything, say everything—speech is dependent on respiration. We speak as we exhale—the longer the inhalation, the more words that can be uttered while breathing out. The deeper the breath, the louder the voice's projection. Breathing acts like a hidden navel, psychoanalysis's ground zero, the site of our separation from the mother, where we lose our words, maybe even a capacity for self-representation. Breathing is also the space where extreme anxiety, the mute body, and the scars of being born rear their head.

Leo Bersani takes the newborn's first autonomous gulp of air, the "exuberantly welcomed scream," as an inaugural assertion not just of "breathing independence" but of existence, of "being-in" the world:

> Having accomplished the at once biologically and symbolically necessary severance from the mother's breathing rhythm, she is on her own, depending on her own lungs to sustain the precarious individual life into which she just has fallen. Breathing is the tiny human's first experience of her body inescapable receptivity, a taking in which is inseparable from a letting out. Breathing initiates the dual rhythm of receptivity: absorption and expulsion. Repeated continuously and involuntarily throughout human life (we become aware of it only when it is momentarily blocked), it is the most fundamental model of the organic dualism intrinsic to all animal life.
>
> (2018, 85)

But this involuntary rhythm of exchange, shared with other living human beings, is subordinated to the regulation not of instinct but of the drive. Interestingly, it was recently reported that a female free diver beat the world record for holding her breath and descended to a depth of seventy-three meters (Adcock 2022). If one hundred percent oxygen is breathed, the world record for breath holding is twenty-four minutes and thirty-seven seconds (Suggitt 2021). What is fascinating is that the ability to do this cannot be related to physiology, though some people do have larger lungs or larger spleens (crucial for flooding the body with oxygen-rich blood cells). It is, in fact, a learned skill. These quasi-superhuman record-breaking feats suggest that we can tap into an evolutionary reflex by which, instead of triggering involuntary breath, we tap into a vestige of aquatic life from billions of years ago and slow the heart rate and metabolism and redirect blood to vital organs and bolster the lungs against underwater pressures. One has to push through a certain limit, not give in to panic, and allow the blood to desaturate itself of oxygen and begin a new process. In a sense, it is a real mastery of anxiety.

In psychoanalytic history, breathing is, of course, linked to the notion of birth trauma—the first breath being the somatic sign of separation from the mother. Here, one must return to the important arguments that took place between Freud, Ferenczi, and Rank about the origins of anxiety. For Rank, the breathing symptoms of asthma reenact the traumatic effect of parturition: "all neurotic disturbances in breathing (asthma), which repeat the feeling of suffocation, relate directly to the physical reproductions of the birth trauma" (1924, 51). Rank thought all anxiety was linked to the trauma of birth, whereas for Freud, birth and breathing was just one of many traumatic encounters that extended throughout psycho-sexual development. Freud did not want to privilege birth trauma, which he felt de-sexualized and over-generalized anxiety. But despite fighting with Rank, Freud acknowledged the importance of birth trauma as a question of the separation from the mother and the emergence into helplessness or *Hilflosigkeit*, which is present in the formation of inhibitions, symptoms, and anxiety:

> The innervations involved in the original state of anxiety probably had a meaning and purpose, in just the same way as the muscular movements which accompany a first hysterical attack. In order to understand a hysterical attack, all one has to do is to look for the situation in which the movements in question formed part of an appropriate and expedient action. Thus at birth it is probable that the *innervation*, in being directed to the respiratory organs, is preparing the way for the activity of the lungs, and, in accelerating the heartbeat, is helping to keep the blood free from toxic substances. Naturally, when the anxiety-state is reproduced later as an affect it will be lacking in any such expediency, just as are the repetitions of a hysterical attack. When the individual is placed in a new situation of danger it may well be quite inexpedient for him to respond with an anxiety-state (which is a reaction to an earlier danger) instead of initiating a reaction appropriate to the current danger.
>
> (1926, 134, italics, Webster and Gherovici)

Freud points out, however, that there is no mental content for the infant just being born. So how could the anxiety-state be a repeated memory? While birth may prepare us for anxiety, Freud argues that the later developments of a more cognitive child bring anxiety to a maximum, not birth itself. The feelings of danger and helplessness are what link anxiety *retroactively* to conditions of birth.

Ferenczi, always the off-beat mediator, tried to bridge Freud and Rank and made the trauma of breathing not the individual experience of the trauma of birth but a phylogenetic question of our emergence from the sea onto land where we were forced to learn to breathe and engage in the violent and impossible constraints of sexed reproduction. In his book, *Thalassa: A Theory of Genitality*, Ferenczi (1939) proposed that a series of evolutionary traumas repeat in our sexual development and are covered over by the fantasy of returning to the bliss of inter-uterine life during intercourse. The rapid breathing and heart palpitations of sexual excitement reproduce anxiety and link it not only to sexual pleasure but the fantasy of immortality in procreation. Genitality then is both catastrophe and mastery—linked to our most distant past, precivilization, and a projection of our future, in the immortality granted to us in returning to the womb in procreation in compensation for sexuation and death.

Interestingly, these arguments between Freud, Rank, and Ferenczi were central to Freud's writing of *Beyond the Pleasure Principle* (1920), where the idea of the death impulse became more central in his thinking. Ferenczi (1929), following *Thalassa* and greater experience of clinical work, wrote in his paper "The Unwelcome Child and His Death Instinct" about the explicit link between asthma and the death drive. Psychosomatic asthma is caused by what he calls "an aversion to life" or drive diffusion that manifested this self-destructive form. In his analyses, he picked up on these patients' unconscious awareness of signs of having been unwanted or unwelcome, namely an inter-generational transmission of their parent's death drive:

> The child has to be induced, by means of an immense expenditure of love, tenderness and care, to forgive his parents for having brought him into the world without any intention on his part; otherwise the destructive instincts begin to stir immediately. And this is not really surprising, since the infant is still much closer to individual non-being, and not divided from it by so much bitter experience as the adult. Slipping back into this non-being might therefore come much more easily to children. The 'life force' which rears itself against the difficulties of life has therefore not really any great innate strength, and becomes established only when tactful treatment and upbringing gradually give rise to progressive immunization against physical and psychical injuries
>
> (Ferenczi, 128)

The child felt unconsciously a danger to their own life from those that gave them life, which manifested in the form of asthmatic attacks and bodily dysregulation, and is unable to build up the life force to counter-act this push towards non-being. Ferenczi's subtle point is that loving a child is immunization against physical *and* psychic injury.

Winnicott (1941) comes to similar conclusions in "The Observation of Infants in a Set Situation" where he observes an infant's asthma at the point of hesitation in relation to oral gratification. Winnicott says the hesitation transformed into bronchial spasms must be related to anxiety from a form of primitive mental conflict. In the apprehensive fantasy, the impulse is controlled which leads to a control of breath. After observing a seven-month-old infant having an asthma attack, Winnicott writes,

> The breathing out might have been felt by the baby to be dangerous if linked to a dangerous idea-for instance, an idea of reaching *in* to take. To the infant, so closely in touch with his mother's body and the contents of the breast, which he actually takes, the idea of reaching in to the breast is by no means remote, and reaching in to the inside of mother's body could easily be associated in the baby's mind with not breathing.
>
> (1941, 241)

Asthma, according to Winnicott, is an involuntary control of expiration, a difficulty in letting go of one's breath, or, from another angle, an excessive holding of breath. It can only be a fantasy of imagined repercussions, he posits, that would stop the baby from surrendering to a natural impulse. When natural inclinations are brought to a halt unnecessarily, symptoms erupt. Fortunately, this kind of inhibition in infants, in contrast to that in adults, can be reversed quite quickly by allowing the wish to carry on in its merry way. Babies are so new to the world and are miraculously open to help.

In Winnicott's words, meeting the infant's desire for help was a "good-enough," "facilitating environment." His observations of the secure infant are fascinating. Three temporal moments transpire which all have a logical, rhythmic structure and one of them is like breathing. The composition is uncannily close to the three temporalities that Lacan described in "Logical Time" in the prisoner's dilemma from game theory (1945, 161–169).

First, according to Winnicott, the mother enters and walks across a large room with her baby to Winnicott, who is sitting at a table. She is asked to sit catty-corner across the table from him. The scene of arrival is important so that the mother, child, and doctor have a chance to see one another and make visual contact before settling in. Winnicott then places a shiny, right-angled tongue depressor (which he calls a spatula) on the table. He tells the mother to sit in such a way that if the baby should wish to take the object, it can—but she is instructed not to help or interfere and to contribute as little as possible to the situation. The classical setting with the couch, patient, speech, and analyst is here transformed into mother, baby, spatula, and doctor.

During what Winnicott calls stage one, the baby puts its hand out to the spatula, but realizes that the situation requires more thought. The baby grows still but not necessarily rigid—looking at the doctor or its mother with big eyes, or withdrawing from the situation and burying itself in the mother's chest. No reassurance is given since what is crucial is the spontaneous and gradual return of the child's interest in the seductive object (230–231). Like the moment of the child's glance, what dominates is a question about what this object, and this strange other, means for the baby. Who are you? Who am I? What is possible here?

This leads to the next stage, in which the hesitation conflicts with desire. The baby must become "brave enough to let his feelings develop," which will change the encounter quickly, an alteration evident first in the child's body. The baby's mouth becomes "flabby," its tongue "thick and soft," and it might even begin drooling. Stillness then gives way to movement with a decisive action. With the spatula finally in hand, the infant displays a sense of confidence, even power, giving rise to play—putting the spatula in its mouth, joyfully banging it on the table, offering it to its mother's mouth, or the doctor's, pretending to feed them like a baby (231).

One might imagine that this would be the final stage, and Winnicott himself says he thought so, too—that it took him some time to see there is an important final move. In stage three, the infant drops the spatula, perhaps by accident, but then plays with getting rid of it, which is thoroughly enjoyed. The infant may want to get down and mouth the object again on the floor but will eventually lose interest in the spatula, leave it behind, and turn its attention to the wider room (231–232). Leaving the scene of the object is a second act of bravery (247).

The infant must feel that what is left can be returned to, and yet this can never be guaranteed. If the moment for concluding an encounter is always the negotiation of an exit, for the baby this comes after the triumphant exploration of its satisfaction, whereas, in the prisoner's dilemma, it is about coming face to face with the inability to completely understand, or square the loss implied in leaving, but leaving nonetheless. Perhaps both types of third stage speak to a limit that encourages a renunciation of what is found, risking giving it up to look farther afield and step into an unknown future.

So what happened with the aforementioned asthmatic seven-month-old? Paralyzed in the time of hesitation, the baby may have felt too greedy, too wary of retribution, too great a threat of loss, or without hope for more satisfaction (1945, 234–237). According to Winnicott, basic anxieties must be run through and remodeled. This isn't about the perfect protection of parents that may, in fact, make one *more* neurotic; rather, the complexity of the infant's feelings is held by a good-enough caretaker until they can unfold in their own time, becoming more distinct desires. Could we say that the asthmatic infant is thrown back into its being, especially that of being a body, inhibited in the face of the object that he or she cannot take, play with, or feel untrammeled pleasure in relation to. Is this the first manifestation of inhibition?

The infant at stage two, on the other hand, creates an object, is seduced, plays at being seductive, turning subject into object, passive into active. In the game of feeding mother just as one is fed, the infant has a self-representation on the outside to test, perhaps a little like curating one's image on Instagram and looking to see how many people like it. Only after the glittering object is ready to hand can the infant explore not-having, losing it, dispensing with it—a breach that opens onto the wider world. This makes me think of when my son was able to give up an obsessive concern with the integrity of his Lego figures, which were finally, to my great relief, exploded all over the room, as if I could finally exhale and not hold my breath waiting for or dreading the reaction to loss.

So we have three distinct temporal waves—being, having, not-having. Beginning and end meet; being is close to not-having, but it is modified by the step of having-had. One might even say that being is finally transformed through an act of mourning, of loving and losing, and not a place of retreat, of losing oneself entirely, or sticking with the repetitive power of having. Traversing these three moments, Winnicott says, is a preparation for the advent of language.

These observations of Winnicott extend to other observations in child work, notably by another British psychoanalyst, Maria Rhode, who wrote about "Autistic Breathing." She lays out her thesis regarding breathing in autistic patients,

> In the womb, both nutrients and oxygen are supplied by the same organs, that is, by the placenta and the umbilical cord. With the cutting of the cord, breathing and eating become distinct processes. Indeed, although both are essential to survival, they may sometimes be in competition with each other, as for instance when a baby with a cold cannot suck because his breathing is interfered with. My impression in the two cases I shall be discussing has been that breathing has come to be used as an alternative to food, as a means of making oneself feel full that *is* always under one's own control and that is not felt to carry with it the dangers implied by the object relationships involved in eating.
>
> (Rhode 1994, 26)

Rhode's two severe cases seem to use breathing not as the sign of separation but as a denial of it. She says, following the work of Francis Tustin, that breath isn't even really an object but is closer to an autistic shape, a more auto-erotic, sensory, tranquilizing, object than for Tustin (2003) who focused on the catastrophe of separation.

A patient whom Rhode named Charles, who didn't speak until the age of twelve, would hyperventilate, use noisy breathing to seal himself off from others, and breathe in sync with rhythmic rocking or tapping as a means of self-soothing. Rhode surmised that this gave him a full feeling and seemed to arise at moments in which he felt the analyst's boundaries, and thus more out-of-control. Speaking to him about these feelings enabled him to loosen his grip on the autistic objects. In a later session, he punched himself in the stomach, winding himself, which she interpreted as Charles showing her how separation felt to him like suffocation (Rhode 1994, 26–31).

Another patient who came to treatment with Rhode at the age of four was obsessed with balloons, which Rhode thought of as breath made visible and kept within. The string on the balloon symbolized for her the umbilical cord, or tie, to the mother. In session, he would speak about hating a girl he thought was the analyst's daughter, and then would fill up his cheeks with air like big balloons. This obsession with balloons and air, through treatment, was eventually transformed into singing to himself, which allowed him to dare to speak his first words against this constancy of song (32–36). Rhode says this was an important turning point in the treatment, and she began to see his use of breath not as an obstacle or a form of sterility but in the image of God breathing new life into Adam (36).

Catherine Vanier (2015), in her book, *Premature Birth: The Baby, the Doctor and the Psychoanalyst*, asks why some babies survive and others do not in the neonatal intensive care unit (NICU) when medical pathology fails to explain why some succumb to sudden infant death syndrome or failure to thrive. She decided it was a psychoanalytic problem. Vanier points out that even as it became physiologically possible to save premature infants through new technologies, it took time for us to see them as having been born and needing to be treated accordingly. These infants were enclosed in boxes and hooked up to machines and feeding tubes, devoid of human contact. This made weaning the infants from these devices even more difficult. Furthermore, doctors, until about thirty years ago, thought that premature infants didn't feel pain, so they operated without anesthesia.

Protocols began to change fifteen years ago with the recognition of the importance of contact time between newborns and parents, although the explanations for the new procedures were purely behavioral and stopped short of addressing the infant as a subject, even as a nascent one. Vanier saw her work as a co-resuscitation, bringing the infant into life with the doctors, as well as bringing the parents to life for the child. She saw that parents, who were terrified that their infants might die at any moment, often wanted to abandon them to the care of doctors who couldn't themselves understand the implications of their power to keep alive, or not, the tiny infants. Someone was needed to gather up these forces.

The critical point was often in taking the infant off the ventilator: would they take up the task of breathing, or not? One story from Vanier is particularly fascinating. Together with the NICU staff, the care team noticed that one of the infants could be taken off the ventilator if the ventilator was left running so its sound was audible from the baby's incubator. If the sound stopped, the infant stopped breathing. It was as if the respiratory drive could exist if minimally propped up by the rhythmic noise of the whirring machine.

What could wean this baby off their attachment to the noise of a machine? Vanier speculated that it could be the voice of the mother—and she encouraged her to speak to her child often and showed the mother that the baby reacted strongly to the sound of her mother's voice. It was also important, Vanier insisted, that the mother speak the truth—her worries, her anger, her concern, her love, all of it; empty speech would not do. The infant was eventually able to make this vital transfer from one object to another—from machine to mother—which was the difference between life and death. We may be born, but we are not all carried to term.

Vanier is a student of Jacques Lacan, the psychoanalyst who proposed that the human subject is a "speaking-being." This is a being whose speech production depends on sounds created by moving air—air flows from the lungs to the mouth via the throat—which makes the vocal cords vibrate. For George Steiner, respiration and breath are indistinguishable, and they constitute the singular, unique mark of subjectivity:

> Speech, uttered or unspoken, is as intimate to the pulse of the [hu]man's being, is as much the love context of normal human existence, as it is breath. No [hu]

man can reduplicate perfectly, can substitute for, another [hu]man's breath. This, perhaps, is why πνεῦμα [pneuma] and πνοή, 'the breath which inspires, which blows us into being' and 'the word', are so closely meshed in theological and metaphysical speculations on the essence of the human person.

(1996, 203)

In "The Subversion of the Subject and the Dialectic of Desire in the Freudian Unconscious," a text presented by Lacan at a colloquium of philosophers, he mentions breathing in passing just after introducing the status of the object in psychoanalysis as an object that commemorates loss. Lacan observes that the erogenous zones in the body become sexualized by partial sexual drives and thus expands their importance beyond organic function (for example, the ingestion of food involves other organs besides the mouth). Erogenous zones appear as the result of a cut; they take advantage of a margin or borders of bodily orifices ("the lips, 'the enclosure of the teeth,' the rim of the anus, the penile groove, the vagina, and the slit formed by the eyelids, not to mention the hollow of the ear" (Lacan 1960, 692), but more importantly, Lacan notes that they are areas of exchange and connection (the mouth opens and foods comes in; the anal sphincters contract and relax to eliminate feces). This closing and opening follows the pulsating rhythm of partial drives that is also the rhythm of the unconscious. In this discussion, Lacan mentions, without further elaborating, "respiratory erogeneity," commenting that it "has been little studied, but it is obviously through spasms that it comes into play" (1960, 692). The spasm relates to another uncontrolled muscle movement—the orgasm—often listened to by children in the form of hearing the parent's rhythmic sexual breathing. Lacan also points out that to listen, one often holds one's breath.

The drive for Freud (1905) is the psychical representative of an intra-somatic stimuli in continuous flow. In "[Drives] and their Vicissitudes," Freud (1915) defines more clearly the drive as a border concept between the psychic and the somatic, as a psychic representative of stimuli coming from the body that reaches the spirit. It is worth mentioning the collection edited by the Argentinean psychoanalyst Alfredo Eidelsztein (2003), which is a compilation of theoretical and clinical texts that call on the psychoanalytic community to meditate on our condition as "respirators." The writers convincingly argue for the importance of further studies on the respiratory drive.

So, is the respiratory erogeneity a neglected zone in the unconscious libidinal economy? Or furthermore, since Lacan identifies four partial drives, could we talk about a fifth drive, the respiratory drive involved in breathing? What can we say about respiratory erogeneity and Freud's unrelenting habit of smoking even after developing mouth cancer, which connects the oral drive to a beyond? What is the object of the respiratory drive? Is it simply air? Air appears always mediated, the production of an exchange that is not necessarily with another human being but nevertheless is overdetermined by the specific conditions of life for speaking beings. In the case of asthma, air is in the audible manifestations created by the spasms that take the form of choking and wheezing.

The action involved in the respiratory drive is inspiration and exhalation. A cut in the erogenous zone is centered on the hollow of the lungs which is a point from where inhalation and exhalation comes and it can be replaced by a spasm whose reflexive form appears mostly as choking. Here we see that the respiratory drive is not regulated like an instinct; it is no longer "natural" but excessive, repetitive, and ultimately destructive (think of the death rattle, the crackling, terminal wet sound heard with each breath when someone is dying). Like the Freudian definition of the drive, the respiratory drive functions like a montage of discontinuous elements—pressure, end, object, and source (Freud 1915, 122).

It is fascinating that this neglected erogenous zone is also tied to the primal scene of psychoanalysis. How can we forget Freud's unrelenting habit of smoking even after he developed mouth cancer? In revisiting canonical case studies such as Dora, we might respecify anew her respiratory symptoms of childhood asthma, adolescent apnea, hysterical imitative cough, and her aversion to the smell of cigars. There is also Freud and Fleiss's obsession with the erectile tissue in the nose that could be stimulated by smells but which is also subject to its own periodicity and rhythms.

For Freud, when humans stood on their feet to walk and took distance from the ground, the olfactory dimension of experience diminished. In the origin of culture, standing up, away from the surface of the Earth, no longer with our noses close to its odors forced humans to undergo a biological "repression" of our ability to breathe in and smell. Evolution gave primacy to other senses. Perhaps Freud was wrong in this pessimistic assessment of a shrinking awe-inspiring world of smell and breath. The exploration of our smelly surroundings was not suppressed, but, quite on the contrary, the respiratory experience has been the most consistent way of addressing the link between body and soul/psyche.

Notions of life and breath and spirit and smell are intertwined in many cultures. *Spiritus* is literally "breath" and is the same word for "psyche"—making breath part of the compound word, psycho-analysis. From Aristotle to Hegel, from Heidegger to Derrida, there is a great tradition in philosophy of what we can call "pneumatics," an extensive exploration of this articulation of spirit as life force and breath. Maybe the current moment can be an inspiring one and make us rediscover and embrace breath in psychoanalysis. Language cuts out the body, carving out erogenous zones, extracting, as it were, the drives from their place of inscription. While making meaning emerge (some body parts become taboo) this distribution of meaning is the paradoxical consequence of a foundational lack of meaning.

Here we can blend current philosophical thought and psychoanalytic investigation. The philosopher Emanuele Coccia argues that everything in the living world is the articulation of breath. Living is breathing, "from perception to digestion, from thought to pleasure, from speech to locomotion. Everything is a repetition, intensification, and a variation of what takes place in breath" (2019, 55). According to Coccia, we are not inhabitants of the Earth but rather of the atmosphere, living in a constant exchange with an air-filled surrounding. The philosopher and psychoanalyst Luce Irigaray, in her "*From the Forgetting of Air* to *To Be Two*," asserts the focus on the forgetting of death by philosophy and psychoanalysis hides an even deeper forgetting, namely of air and breathing. Breathing, she says, signifies taking care of life, a renunciation of a dream of fusional proximity, infantile passivity, in the distance between us that air suggests. "Life is cultivated by life itself, in breathing. . . . It corresponds to the shaping of a life that is never simply mine even if the task of its fulfillment is my responsibility" (Irigaray 2001, 311).

In essence, breath can symptomatically express an aversion or a fear in relation to life or Eros (*prana*, the Sanskrit word for breath, means "life force" or "vital principle"). "Breathing problems" can betray the intergenerational transmission of the death drive via the superego. In its erogenous form, it manifests a sexual desire that cannot be expressed as such because it would imply a lethal over-proximity, an over-exposure to the excitement of the rhythmic breathing of the parents during the primal scene.

In 1978, the philosopher Jean-Louis Tristani, in *Le Stade du Respir*, argued that before desire there is breathing and turning our attention to the respiratory will revitalize both psychoanalysis and philosophy and update our theory of the unconscious and of enunciation. Freud would have agreed with the alignment of breathing and desire. In a love letter to his future wife, Martha, written on August 6, 1885, he aligns healthy breathing with desire: "When the breath comes short, interest narrows, the heart abandons all desire" (Freud 1960, 167). Around that time, Freud gave an example of what we may call respiratory erogeneity in a case of obsessional thinking about the body:

> A woman suffered from attacks [of] obsessional brooding and speculating . . . this obsession which ceased only when she was ill, and then gave way to hypochondriacal fears. The theme of her worry was always a part or function of her body; for example, respiration: "Why must I breathe? Suppose I didn't want to breathe?" etc.
>
> (1895, 78)

But, as Beckett observes in *Murphy*, suicide by apnea appears physiologically impossible (1957, 185). Nevertheless, from the first breath to the last, we catch traces of the death drive.

To conclude, in his book *Breathing* (2018), Franco "Bifo" Berardi suggests that the oppressive apocalyptic chaos of the late capitalist period brings up a question of breath as a need to reconnect to our unconscious and to its rhythms, which must be sought beyond the chaos and the ensuing narcissism (my survival) that are colonizing our experience of reality. In CPR, the mouth-to-mouth maneuvering is called "rescue breathing." The superegoic mandates whistling in our ears, as well as the recurrence of the primal scene, show a dimension of life that is going beyond the pleasure principle. We need "rescue breathing," to have less "hot air," which is to perform a move from the empty speech that conceals unconscious truth to reintroduce the theoretical challenges of a neglected respiratory drive and thus revitalize a theory of the unconscious that is gasping for air.

## References

Adcock, Bronwyn. 2022. "'I didn't even know this was humanly possible': the woman who can descend into the sea in one breath." *The Guardian*. See www.theguardian.com/society/2022/feb/06/i-didnt-even-know-this-was-humanly-possible-the-woman-who-can-descend-into-the-sea-on-one-breath.

Beckett, Samuel. 1957. *Murphy*. New York: Grove Press.

Berardi, Franco. 2018. *Breathing: Chaos and Poetry*. South Pasadena, CA: Semiotext(e)/Internations Series.

Bersani, Leo. 2018. *Receptivity*. Princeton, NJ: Princeton University Press.

Coccia, Emanuele. 2019. *The Life of Plants*. Cambridge, UK: Polity Press.

Eidelsztein, Alfredo. 2003. *La pulsión respiratoria*. Buenos Aires: Letra Viva.

Ferenczi, Sandor. 1929. "The Unwelcome Child and his Death-Instinct." *International Journal of Psycho-Analysis* 10: 125–129.

———. 1939. *Thalassa: A Theory of Genitality*. New York: Routledge, 1989.

Freud, Sigmund. 1895 [1894]. "Obsessions and Phobias." In *Standard Edition of the Complete Psychological Works of Sigmund Freud*. Vol. 3. Translated by James Strachey, 74–82. New York: Norton, 1955.

———. 1905. "Three Essays on the Theory of Sexuality." In *Standard Edition of the Complete Psychological Works of Sigmund Freud*. Vol. 7. Translated by James Strachey, 123–245. New York: Norton, 1953.

———. 1915. "[Drives] and Their Vicissitudes." In *Standard Edition of the Complete Psychological Works of Sigmund Freud*. Vol. 14. Translated by James Strachey, 111–140. New York: Norton, 1957.

———. 1920. "Beyond the Pleasure Principle." In *Standard Edition of the Complete Psychological Works of Sigmund Freud*. Vol. 18. Translated by James Strachey, 3–64. New York: Norton, 1955.

———. 1926. *Inhibitions, Symptoms and Anxiety*. The *Standard Edition of the Complete Psychological Works of Sigmund Freud*. Vol. 20. Translated by James Strachey, 75–176. New York: Norton, 1955.

———. 1960. *Letters of Sigmund Freud*. Edited and selected by Ernst Freud. New York: Basic Books.

Irigaray, Luce. 2001. "*From the Forgetting of Air* to *To Be Two*." In *Feminist Interpretations of Heidegger*. Edited by Nancy Holland and Patricia Huntington, 309–316. University Park, PA: Pennsylvania State University Press.

Lacan, Jacques. 1945. "Logical Time and the Assertion of Anticipated Certainty." In *Écrits: The First Complete Edition in English*. Translated by Bruce Fink, 161–175. New York: Norton, 2006.

———. 1960. "The Subversion of the Subject and the Dialectic of Desire in the Freudian Unconscious." In *Écrits: The First Complete Edition in English*. Translated by Bruce Fink, 671–702. New York: Norton, 2006.

Rank, Otto. 1924. "The Trauma of Birth in its Importance for Psychoanalytic Therapy." *Psychoanalytic Review* 11 (3): 241–245.

Rhode, Maria. 1994. "Autistic Breathing." *Journal of Child Psychotherapy* 20 (1): 25–41. http://doi.org/10.1080/00754179408256739.

Steiner, George. 1996. *Antigones*. New Heaven: Yale University Press.

Suggitt, Connie. 2021. "56-year-old Free Diver Holds Breath for Almost 25 Minutes Breaking Record." Guinness World Records. See www.guinnessworldrecords.com/news/2021/5/freediver-holds-breath-for-almost-25-minutes-breaking-record-660285.

Tristani, Jean-Louis. 1978. *Le Stade du Respir*. Paris: Editions de Minuit.

Tustin, Frances. 2003. *Autistic States in Children,* revised edition. New York: Routledge.

Vanier, Catherine. 2015. *Premature Birth: The Baby, the Doctor and the Psychoanalyst*. London: Karnac Books.

Winnicott, Donald. 1941. "The Observation of Infants in a Set Situation." *International Journal of Psycho-Analysis* 22: 229–249.

# Chapter 13

# And Yet It Moves[1]

*Bice Benvenuto*

---

*Psychoanalytic clinician and writer, Bice Benvenuto, founder of the Maison Verte-UK centre for children, distils the psychoanalytic drive from the biological conception of instinct via a number of vignettes from her work with children and adults. The disorder and chaos of drive activity, powerfully at work in the primary relationship between children and adults is revealed in cases characterized by closed disastrous circuits of entropy and emptiness, including that of anorexia, self-harm, manic-depression, substance abuse. With a metaphoric style of writing, Benvenuto draws from Lacan, Dolto, Klein, Landau, Tustin and literary sources. The gap between desire and satisfaction constitutes that ambiguity of life which is the motor of the coming into being of a subject. This is failing in the contemporary "golden caged" nuclear families, when the oedipal triangulation fails where no alternative structures are as yet emerging. Cloistered and autistic children and those suffocated by panic attacks can be supported by the interlocutory function of psychoanalysis as long as the psychoanalyst is willing to engage creatively with the "web" of technology and machines that children and young people increasingly rely on.*

The earth rotating on its axis and around the sun, life moving on the earth, children running, jumping, shouting, and crying. It moves, all seems to turn with a relative regularity, the regularity of physical laws and biological codes.

The silent breakdown of an English couple's marriage explodes during a prolonged stay in Naples. The husband dangerously distances himself from his wife, while she begins a journey in search of their love between the excavations of Pompeii, where she watches in terror the recovery of two lovers petrified by lava, or between the skulls of the Fontanelle cemetery where, surrounded by the local women invoking grace from the dead, she tries to mourn her love. But just when they decide to separate, they are swept away by a religious procession, by a crowd apparently alien to them in that moment. At the sight of his wife drifting away, dragged by the tranced crowd that flows like lava from all the pores of the square, and calling him, he too succumbs to the crowd, both on the verge of being overwhelmed by the loss of sense of this human flow and their own. In this panic, the couple tries to find a new anchorage, looking for each other yet again.[2]

(Benvenuto 2005)

[Little Agnes] was five days old when her mother, who had been breastfeeding her, was suddenly rushed to the hospital. . . . In the days that followed, the girl utterly refused nourishment or even the water that her father . . . offered with the bottle or the spoon. The pediatrician suggested to the father that he call me [the psychoanalyst Françoise Dolto]. . . . I simply told the worried father, "Go to the hospital and bring one of your wife's shirts with you. When you return home wrap the shirt around the girl so that she can smell her mother, then give her the bottle." She gulped down the milk from the bottle immediately. . . . What was newborn Agnes missing, deprived of her mother, that she needed in order to swallow?

(Dolto 1984)

Was it the thrill of her mother's fragrance that triggered Agnes's so called "instinct for nourishment"? If so, Agnes's refusal to feed would be a sign of having fallen out of the thrill of living, represented by mother's smell, and of drifting towards death. Galileo's heretic claim that the Earth moves around its star points to how the laws of gravity and the planets' spatial relations can also describe what moves our human relations. Desire, a central concept in psychoanalysis, which comes from the Latin *de-sidere*, coming from the stars and having lost them, is a parting movement from the stars from which our drives have cut their orbit, if even for only five days for Agnes!

Still, the regular repetitions of planetary movement can go bang and go into sudden disorder. In thermodynamics this is called entropy, which Freud used in tackling the concept of drive. Everything can drift away or be drawn by the force of gravity into new orbits, new planetary systems. Even when Agnes is offered satisfaction to her hunger, she does it only when driven, not by an instinct for nourishment, but by a reminder of what was the true source of her drive to feed which was being wrapped by the fragrance of her mother's bosom. Vital is the "eternal return" to the source. This orientates our position in space with a force that attracts without crashing. Collision or getting stuck to the star would be the end of the drive.

If the whiff of mother's smell was able to resuscitate Agnes's drive to live, in Rossellini's film, it was in the flowing lava of a human procession in Naples, which engulfed and threatened the English couple, that a call emerged. She is calling him and he cannot but reply to the call, to the memory of a marriage whose orbit was drowning in the lava of renounced adventures and the vicissitudes of their drives. The couple is swept adrift by the challenging encounter with a city that doesn't know or like any regularity, that lives dangerously between strife and uncanny accord with the volcano's expected eruptions, a readiness for death while fighting for life.

### "There Was an Embrace in Death" (Woolf 1925)

Rossellini turns the lava/procession scene into one of envelopment, like Agnes in her mother's shirt, in some sort of exquisite embrace—an archaic memory of a placental shirt or amniotic lava. Having had their marriage's tensions at near zero and which were about to meet their final extinction, the couple come to a point in which they call out for each other not to succumb to the disorder of the crowd's deadly embrace and try to grab on to the substance of their love: a voice, a sniff. These subtle as well as substantial airborne elements pave our paths towards others in an intricate maze of repetitions and disruptions.

We come into being along the loops of our drives, made out of our fantasies' productions of regular ellipses and defenses, which allow some pleasures and despair of enjoying others, when waiting, for example, for the mother who does not come but whose breast babies can hallucinate, invent, fantasize, and replace by their own fist. As a decentered Galilean planet, the subject is being made while waiting, crying, and playing with their star's whiffs and lights.

This loop brings home the pleasure of a possible friction with *(de)sidera*, an exciting tension that gets us moving or sucking again. Freud sticks to the unpleasurable quality of the tensions, while pleasure is comparable to a state of Nirvana, stillness, inertia. Freud goes back and forth in his elaborations of the concept of the drive, entangled in a game of reversals to sort out the ways of life and death. Isn't it evident, Freud insists, that when Eros attains its satisfaction after love making, one enters a temporary state of death of desire? Was there not death in that embrace?

Freud constantly reworked the death drive from his early work on the *Project* (1895) up to his work on Moses (1939), as if troubled by his theoretical hypotheses that the life drive is inconsistent because the death inevitably kills it. Like the killer in Dostoyevsky's *Crime and Punishment* (1867), Freud kept returning to the scene of the crime of striking life from the unconscious. In assessing the predominant pathologies of his time, neurosis and psychosis, Freud discovered there is no unconscious representative of death. It appeared only as a rhetorical instrument of the neurotic discourse at the turn of twentieth century, something like "no sex, please, or someone dear will be struck by death." Freud was cautious about his farfetched speculations which were resisted by his colleagues who regarded the concepts of life and death as belonging to physics and biology with no equivalence in the discourse of the unconscious. Yet Freud could not let go of the drives which jeopardize the principle that should dictate the driving force of mental life—the pleasure principle—as it allowed him to query why most of his patients went beyond domesticated pleasure in their lives, and if homeostasis is a reset of pleasure on the side of death.

Balzac (1831) described such a dilemma in his novel, *La Peau de Chagrin (The Wild Ass's Skin)*, in which the young libertine Raphaël, on the brink of suicide, comes across a magic wild ass's skin which satisfies every wildest wish, with the condition that each enjoyment will shrink the skin, which consumes itself until it comes to the end. When Raphaël decides to stop himself from pursuing life's pleasures to keep death at bay, it does not occur to him that by giving himself up to a state of stillness, he is giving himself up to Nirvana, the quintessential deadly pleasure. Therefore, all pleasures, whether due to a homeostasis of tensions or to their disordered turmoil, are driven towards their end. Freud, in *Beyond the Pleasure Principle*, says the death drive's "function is to assure that the organism shall follow its own path to death" (1920, 39).

Both Melanie Klein and Jacques Lacan welcomed the death drive, though in different ways. Klein takes up Freud's later Manichean revision of the two basic drives: the good cohesive sexual one turns inwards, while the evil deadly one becomes a drive of mastery and aggression towards the external world. Babies are born with a fragmented body, without a psychic cohesion, with a body inhabited by the death drive with fantasies of a sadistic and auto-destructive nature (Klein 1975a, 1975b). Françoise Dolto, by contrast, takes up Freud's early work on inertia which is not a force that wants to annihilate the object but is passive and is a renunciation of the fight for existence. Life, being active, requires aggressiveness, fighting external dangers, moving towards the other who calls, whereas death works as a mortification of the arousing activity of Eros. The death drive is on the side of Nirvana, deep sleep, ecstatic pleasure, even letting oneself be a possible object of annihilation at the hands of the other. We shall see how Dolto's less dichotomous reading of the drives is relevant to today's clinic.

## Symptoms in Search of an Author

Both Klein and Lacan agree, though for different reasons, that the satisfaction of the drives can only be of a partial and differential value. Their very driving factor is the difference between the pleasure demanded and what is achieved, and then it always pushes forward relentlessly because it is never completely satisfied. Lacan's modulations of desire and pleasure gave this Freudian approach new focus. The pleasure/unpleasure spectrum is diversified by different intensities of enjoyment which determine the length and speed of our driving forces. A loop or orbit maintains a safe distance for the unrestrained push from crushing into an attained jouissance of deadly incestuous embraces. Freud's neurotics were masters at keeping their drives zigzagging through the most idiosyncratic paths to circumvent this.

But is this still the case in the clinic of today? Self-harm, substance abuse, manic-depression, anorexia and, last but not least, autism, are all symptoms that the DSM lists as stripped of a psychical structure, while psychoanalysts are focusing on clinical structures stripped of their classical symptoms—we can think of asymptomatic psychosis which is trending so much nowadays. But these opposite visions highlight the same new phenomenon of disjunction between clinical structures and symptoms, the latter appearing in the absence of a clinical definition as well as an author, a subject who produces them.

Psychotherapists working with young adults have underlined the recurring phenomenon of the evacuation of time, a doing away with the necessary sequence to design a pathway for the drive to reach out towards its object. Lowenthal illustrates the cutting short of the construction of the drive's trajectory in favor of the quickest access to immediate gratification (Loewenthal 2020). The tables seem to have turned from our good old procrastinating neurotics to the quick fix lovers.

There is always a gap, however small, between our wish and the satisfaction afforded by the wished-for object. It is in this waiting time that we must invent strategies to tolerate such a frustration. When babies cry, as if demanding immediate gratification from their mother's objects of satisfaction—the breast, a cuddle, a clean nappy—they are also creating fantasies, transitional objects, and appeasements to partially meet their wished-for object, which, if only partial, represents the mother's sensory and sensual connection (Benvenuto 2017). In Agnes's case, the smell guaranteed the regular recurrence of the memory of an "original," however unfathomable, state of pleasure which makes feeding and existing a worthy endeavor.

Lacan describes how a lamella leaves the baby's body at the first wail of birth, at the first call, towards a lost thin layer of our very being. Therefore, rather than being fragmented, the newborn is already marked by the co-existence in utero with the mother whose placenta, even before her breast, is not simply a source of nourishment but the enveloping enchantment of her body, a body once so close to the baby's body as to be almost one with it, but not quite. And after birth, not quite two yet. This is undecided and will remain a founding ambiguity for life.

During pregnancy, there is a specific topology of linked bodies in which the mother is implicated at the level of her own "body's unconscious image," to use Dolto's (1984) fertile concept. The work of psychoanalysts Bracha Ettinger (2006) and Tamara Landau (2012) try to shake the veils off the complexities of pregnancy and the taboos concerning original incestuous intimacies. Working with children and parents, one realizes that intra-uterine life is not just biological development but is already the time and the space of an intense psychic activity, already implicating forms of jouissance, separation, and pain and mourning for all involved. That the tightest loops and symbolic connections are organized in the archaic is something that upsets some more orthodox colleagues. Is it not proper to psychoanalysis to make prehistory the history of the subject? Was it not a major scandal when Freud discovered children's sexuality and then later, the infant's schizo-paranoid fantasies by Melanie Klein?

Landau (2012) suggests that something happens at the end of the sixth month of pregnancy. The fetus can hear the father's external voice as well as the mother's not only internal voice, and it falls silent and doesn't move much. These are important moments of silence, already the experience of a distancing from these others—a meditative time of preparation for birth. During these important moments of apparent suspension, we can assume the making or not of primary symbolic integration.

With birth, the coordinates the senses acquired earlier are lost but the voices and the smell, which are found again outside, return the child to their earlier libido which now needs more complex loops to help them find their place in the family. A problem emerges when the agora, the family, remains closed in on itself and to others. It can easily degenerate to a loop-knot, a seducing as well as agoraphobic enclosure. Being cloistered reduces the drive to zero with no vicissitudes that would extend the loop around the object; the time of its circuit is stunted. Living does not always take its own time and it can burn itself out just like Balzac's skin of chagrin.

Something resembling a burnt-out drive is what characterizes the "golden cage" of the young, and also less young, of this new century (Benvenuto 2020). This is an era Lacan saw coming when, in his "Note on the Child," he suggests the child is the "symptom" of the family structure (1969, 7). He was concerned about the dangerous outcomes for children over-involved with one parent or in a situation in which triangulation with the other parent fails. They can become an object of abduction and "have the sole function of revealing the truth of this object" (1969, 8).

I don't think Lacan is referring solely to psychosis here but rather to the effects of changes in the family structure needing new internal dialectics. There are no longer extended family systems with their own multilayered hierarchy of voices and family histories; the family has caged itself in a nuclear amorphous unit with indistinct conformations. But being a-structured does not make it less oppressive. A patient of mine referred to his family as the "cauldron" and everything else is the "outside." It's a new form of symbiosis which differs from the classical mother/child symbiosis that is the core of psychosis due to a failure of primary relations. Mothers are not symbiotic by definition; on the contrary, from very early on, a complex foundational communication with the mother is crucial to processing otherness and interconnection with the other. The "cauldron child" is, therefore, not in a symbiosis with the mother but with the parentally enmeshed turmoil in which the child is an object of moral abuse in being reduced to a pawn between parents. The ego-ideal is evanescent, not embodied by a meaningful presence that orientates our emotional paths and their ethical configurations. A striking similarity with the Stockholm Syndrome is found in the child who tends to embrace the seemingly "good cause" of the more abusive and powerful parent (Parsloe 2020). In divorce disputes, the law finds itself dealing with the arbitrary law of a primal parent (whether mother or father), the idol who owns the children and is worshipped by them.

The emerging monadic family also reflects certain placental topological figures which contrast with the not-one-not-two-yet undecided status of the fetus. This is when the fetus is inside the placenta but with no points of contact with the rest of the mother or with external stimuli. The fetus, later the baby, is caged inside the mother but is in no contact with her. There is no call towards the child or by the child to others. The placenta encircles the fetus as the parents may later encircle the child while neutralizing the impact of their reciprocal presence. This does not account for an ordinary psychosis, today often diagnosed. When all cows look black at night, darkness may have obstructed our vision rather than foreclosed that of our analysands. True, there are blank, short-winded, and suicidal symptoms that do not seem to address an interlocutor, and apathy breaks into sudden panic rather than pathos breaking into anxiety. Nevertheless, rather than diagnosing contemporary mind-sets with old labels, we do well to check the potential of these cloistered people for being moved by and towards an interlocutor, even through a web. Once I managed to work with a videogame-addicted boy by playing on the PlayStation with him during sessions. He had just needed a human mediation between him and the all-encompassing machine.

## Towardness

Autism is our era's pathology, and it seems to foreshadow our contemporary ideal of a calculating and data processing mind that makes out the world for us. An awe of science, with high technology as its offspring, makes real fathers and mothers redundant as the privileged conveyors of family discourses through which we construct our erotic ties. Parents are at sea regarding their positions vis-à-vis their children, being themselves golden caged children. Claims of autism not being a pathology and on a par with LGBT is an index of the discourse of the time. The spectrum/specter of autism involves mainly children who cannot make or dispute claims and some psychoanalysts relegate the diagnosis to neuroscience, a treatment by CBT as well as brain re-education. By addressing the brain rather than the mind, we seem to become affected ourselves by a form of autistic "mindlessness."

The autistic mode of relation to both animate and inanimate objects is that they are ready for use and guarantors of an identical repetition of that use. Nothing has to change because their existence depends on the sameness of naked objects, stripped of their symbolic value. When autistic children spin strings, they seem to fix on an unmoved center of a speed that goes round and round rather than towards something. There is no state of towardness, no mental elaborations traversing the middle layers. The world adheres to the body, thus producing an atrophy of sense. As masters of technology and the art of immediate gratification (some of the giants of social media who are shaping today's social relations claim to be autistic), the young pursue a priority of numbers in the place of addressing or responding to a call. Unconscious elaborations and their effects of thought take time to obtain their gratification. Tustin, a well-known expert on autism, quotes the physicist Bohr when he once rebuked his son with "You are being logical, you are not thinking" (Tustin 1992).

Whether in a pathological way or on the way to a social normalization, the young who spend most of their time in their rooms in front of a screen, possibly on social welfare, and typically with one parent behind the scenes that feeds and is fed by their sheer presence, well represent the phobia of the agora and the preservation of the cloister of solipsism. Somebody else keeps the keys to the cloister/cage, but they are evanescent; they do not respond to the child's presence, the cage has a bounty after all! Washing hands, shielding with gadgets and screens, panic attacks when a date is coming up, and refusing food or vomiting it are maneuvers aimed at not encountering otherness, at keeping it at a safe distance. The relational conflict is avoided rather than worked over. Compulsion to act or refusing to act is antagonistic to an unconscious production of sense and has little to do with the ideational brooding of long-winded neurotics, or the complex paranoid constructions of psychotics, both hyper-producers of sense. Cutting your own numb flesh or injecting it with a substance seems necessary to feel you at least own it rather than being owned by an all-enveloping otherness.

## Panic Attacks

Unlike phobics who choose an object to represent their anxiety, panic is without objects; it reveals raw unbound anxiety. The panic attack has no elaboration, it is a cry, an emergency signal for something unnamable which feels like death, the heart goes mad, breathing almost stops.

Claude was troubled by hypochondria, a persistent psoriasis, sexual and social phobia, and panic attacks. At first, he described his wealthy father as a good person whose demands he adhered to without discussion despite the fact that he was a tyrant who was violent with his children. His mother also submitted to this sort of primal father. With sex, he has never gone beyond some occasional erections with masseuses just to obey the only advice father gave him: "Show it to girls. They like it."

One night before leaving for a holiday with friends, he rang me at 2:00 a.m. in the grip of a panic attack. He was proud he had called me rather than his mother, as if a dislocation had been taking place from surrendering to panic in his mother's arms to the rough cast of avoiding the panic as a possible emancipation from a psoriasis/father wrapping his skin. This time, panic was addressing me in my role of agent provocateur who demanded his enjoyment outside of what he called the family "cauldron," while he begged me not to expect obedience. While driving back home from holiday, Claude narrowly missed a self-provoked serious car accident. He was very shaken by the evidence that whenever his own drive emerges, it needs to be severed and near-death gains the upper hand.

"By the way," Neil said to his analyst whom I supervise, "I betray my wife from time to time." When he was made aware of a connection between his extra-marital relations and his panic, he was surprised but took it on as an explanation: "So we decided they cause me anxiety." But as he was leaving his session, he had a panic attack there and then, at the analyst's door. He could not see the reason why he panicked and, in fact, his betrayals of his wife did not cause him any anxiety. He had recently stopped taking medical drugs and there were restructuring works in his house. Between the loss of his short-circuited relation to the object drug and the long and laborious making of a bigger house, he could "use" his panic to address a call to the analyst. The panic emerges where there is a drive-less space, a hole in psychical connections. However, speechless and short of meaningful reasons, the symptom of "panic" can enter the conversation with the analyst, just as Claude made an emergency night call to me rather than being meat stewed in the family's cauldron. To his horror, his dreams started to feature dismembered bodies hidden in plastic bags or in the boot of his father's car.

Starting to set up their own drives' circuits, whether at the threshold of the analyst's room or with night calls, can be dramatic. It is like tightrope walking on the side of near miss suicidal accidents, the horizon of the extreme escape from the cluster/cloister. This is very different from death as an ideational threat that keeps the obsessional away from incestuous desires and is also different from the successful suicide of the melancholic. One has to bear the tightrope walking between the God Cronus who devours his children and cloisters erected out of microchips and digital screens with no smell.

When Neil is separating from the authority of medical drugs and from his lovers, he tries to stick to an analyst he perceives as giving orders: "We decided: no betrayals." Without drugs and betrayals, he collapses at the analyst's door crying for help. Finally, he was asking for something, but at what risk! For the cloistered drive to find the source of a possible call, it needs interlocutors, a polyphony of voices countering the monadic incestuous triangle. When a conversational drive has been set off, it may happen that an internal voice takes shape with a less dramatic turn. Neil imagined an inside non-psychotic voice speaking in the dialect of his analyst's place of origin which makes comments on all his actions in a comical way. Claude too is much amused by an imagined voice which speaks in the dialect of his own city, with a lewd humor that is liberatingly swearing. At other times, the voice speaks in his father's family language to give him orders to which Claude replies with laughter without obeying. The sellotaped super-ego can be distanced through a voice which speaks vulgar non-sense, a reassuring, clowning act that can be laughed at instead of panicking without knowing why. But the price of such attempts at unsticking painlessly, with laughter, can be paid for with a panic attack, addressed hopefully to their analysts. The clinic of symptoms without an author who construct their drive, without a plot or a scene, is a rollercoaster against death.

Because death is not a drive, but the drive's death.

## Notes

1 Galileo Galilei, after recanting his heliocentric claim, is said to have exclaimed, "*Eppur se move*" ["And yet it moves"] (Baretti 1757).
2 Roberto Rossellini's 1954 film, *Journey to Italy*.

## References

Balzac, Honore de. 1831. *La Peau de Chagrin*. Oxford: Oxford University Press, 2012.
Baretti, Giuseppe. 1757. *The Italian Library*. London: A. Millar in the Strand.
Benvenuto, Bice. 2005. *Della Villa dei Misteri o dei Riti della Psicoanalisi*. Napoli: Liguori.
———. 2017. "Dolto, Klein and Lacan in a Polylogue or The Agora Effect in the Maison Verte." In *Lacanian Psychoanalysis with Babies, Children, and Adolescents: Further Notes on the Child*. Edited by Carol Owens and Stephanie Farrelly-Quinn. London: Karnac.
———. 2020. "The Golden Cage." *European Journal of Psychotherapy and Counselling* 22: 3–4, 255–267. http://doi.org/10.1080/13642537.2020.1814832.
Dolto, Francoise. 1984. *L'image inconsciente du corps*. Paris: Seuil.

———. 2024. *The Body's Unconscious Image*. Translated by Sharmini Bailly. London: Routledge.
Dostoevsky, Fyodor. 1867. *Crime and Punishment*. London: Penguin Classics, 2003.
Ettinger, Bracha. 2006. *The Matrixial Borderspace*. Minneapolis: University of Minnesota Press.
Freud, Sigmund. 1895. "Project for a Scientific Psychology." In *Standard Edition of the Complete Psychological Works of Sigmund Freud*. Vol. 1. Translated by James Strachey, 281–397. New York: Norton, 1953.
———. 1920. "Beyond the Pleasure Principle." In *Standard Edition of the Complete Psychological Works of Sigmund Freud*. Vol. 18. Translated by James Strachey, 3–64. New York: Norton, 1955.
———. 1939. "Moses and Monotheism." In *Standard Edition of the Complete Psychological Works of Sigmund Freud*. Vol. 23. Translated by James Strachey, 6–137. New York: Norton, 1953.
Klein, Melanie. 1975a. *Love, Guilt and Reparation and Other Works, 1921–1945*. London: Hogarth Press and The Institute of Psychoanalysis.
———. 1975b. *Envy and Gratitude and Other Works, 1946–1963*. London: Hogarth Press and The Institute of Psychoanalysis.
Lacan, Jacques. 1969. "Note on the Child." *Analysis* 2 (1990): 7–8.
Landau, Tamara. 2012. *Les funambules de l'oubli*. Paris: Imago.
Loewenthal, Del. 2020. "Toxic Young Adulthood: Therapy and Therapeutic Ethos." *European Journal of Psychotherapy & Counselling* 22 (3–4): 165–172. http://doi.org/10.1080/13642537.2020.1820136.
Parsloe, S. 2020. "The Narratives of Parental Alienation." *European Journal of Psychotherapy and Counselling* 22 (3–4): 192–207. http://doi.org/10.1080/13642537.2020.1814374.
Tustin, Frances. 1992. *Autistic States in Children*. London: Routledge.
Woolf, Virginia. 1925. *Mrs. Dalloway*. London: Hogarth Press.

## *Film*

*Journey to Italy*. 1954. Directed by Roberto Rossellini.

Chapter 14

# The Look and the Drive

*Dan Collins*

---

*Dan Collins proposes the "look" as a better translation than the "gaze" for* le regard *and sets out a case for distinguishing the psychoanalytic look from the Sartrean look and the action of looking. "Look" implies an experienced passivity that is lost in the concept of the gaze which implies a more active form, that of gazing at or being gazed upon. The role of object a in the visual field, as stain, is important in elucidating the look as the empty place/thing that looks at the subject. The famous "sardine can" vignette from Lacan's eleventh seminar is refreshingly explored as an example of Lacan's own subjectification to the look. The screening roles of the Other and of fantasy are unpacked as is the question of why Lacan took up the look in the first place. All this is linked to Lacan's developing conception of the real as deeply embedded in the symbolic but also what goes beyond the structuring automaton of the symbolic and opens out importantly to the* tuché *of surprise and chance.*

---

The first difficulty is one of translation. When he translated Lacan's Seminar 11, *The Four Fundamental Concepts of Psychoanalysis*, Alan Sheridan chose to translate Lacan's French noun *le regard* as "the gaze." This is not entirely wrong. The related French verb *regarder* can mean "to gaze," but more generally *le regard* and *regarder* are, respectively, simply "look" as a noun and "to look" as a verb. If a French speaker wanted to specify gazing as opposed to other kinds of looking, he or she would have to add an adverb, as in *regarder fixement*, "to look fixedly." We might say "stare," but *gaze* implies something beyond *stare*. One can stare blankly or dumbly, while a gaze implies intent, something of desire, which is the point.

Why, then, is "the gaze" a problematic translation? Well, first of all, Lacan borrows his term from Jean-Paul Sartre, and an English translation of Sartre's term *regard* as "look" had already been established for some twenty years when Sheridan took up his work of translating Lacan. So his translation of *le regard* as "the gaze" introduced a second term where there really should be just one. Lacan rectifies and supplements Sartre's theory of the look, but he's referring to the same concept. Further, because the English term *gaze* is so specific, it restricts the meaning of what Lacan referred to as *le regard*. And finally, *the gaze* is one of those Lacanian term that has caught on, first in film theory and then in popular usage, and now it is put to many non-Lacanian uses, such as "the male gaze," for example. So arguably, translating *le regard* simply as "the look" returns the word to its more neutral and properly Lacanian denotation.

Lacan is, of course, aware of Sartre's use of the term, and he refers to it in his seminars prior to Seminar 11. But it is only in Seminar 10 that he begins to develop the concept rigorously, if only tentatively. Lacan is concerned with the concept of desire, and so he wants to consider the category of space, since desire implies space: desire implies a distance between the subject and object *a*, the cause of desire. Object *a* is "eluded," Lacan says, "somewhere other than where it sustains desire" (1962–1963, 252). The elusion of object *a*, he goes on, "is nowhere more tangible than at the level of the function of the eye" (Lacan 1962–1963, 252), and that is why fantasy privileges the visual.

Object *a*, as cause of desire, then, is distanced from the subject, this distance being the condition of desire. But what Lacan calls the elusion of object *a* presents a problem. Object *a* doesn't simply appear in the visual field as an object of desire. The objects of our desire are those that we want one after another after another as manifestations of object *a*, but it is object *a* as lack that keeps desire active. It is the real object of desire behind, as we could say rather clumsily, our imaged objects of desire. What is the nature of the elusion of object *a*? Essentially, the field of visual space appears to us as "homogeneous" (1962–1963, 252), as Lacan says. And this is true. We look around our visual field and everything appears continuous. Object *a*, as real, appears nowhere in this homogeneous imaged field.

What follows in the pages of Seminar 10 that we are reading is a condensed and difficult argument. Lacan takes up the question of the body in space, and the passage can be read as referring both to our own bodies and to those bodies—that is, objects—that we perceive. If the visual field appears to the subject to be continuous, it is first of all because the subject is subtracted from it. The subject is the point from which the visual field is seen. The subject is punctiform and does not perceive the point from which he or she sees as a gap in the field. On the other hand, in the visual field that we see, we construct objects on the basis of what Lacan calls the $i(a)$, the image of the other. This is the image that we first encounter in the mirror stage. It's the image of unity and wholeness that we take on as the basis of our ego, but also—and this is a point that's often missed in the "Mirror Stage" essay—as the basis of all our objects. Thus in the visual field, we identify objects and identify with them. Lacan draws the conclusion: "through the form if $i(a)$, my image, my presence in the [field of] Other has no remainder" (1962–1963, 253). And he also says that since the image is "inalienable," it "can in no way be the *a*" (Lacan 1962–1963, 253).

There may be an objection here. Didn't I just say that the object *a* is the real object of desire behind the imaged objects that we imagine will bring us satisfaction? Doesn't that imply a remainder? Doesn't that imply a split between the object as it appears and object *a*? Perhaps, but to understand it that way would reintroduce a kind of Kantianism, a mere split between appearance and being, between phenomena and noumena. The objects that we select in the visual field are, as I said, ones that we identify and identify with. They may be lures for our desire, but that is precisely because we select and construct them. In some sense, we put them there. That is why they have no remainder.

Does object *a*, then, have any manifestation in the visual field at all? In answer to this question, Lacan introduces a surprising innovation. He says,

> To reveal what is mere appearance in the satisfying character of the form as such . . . to see what is mere illusion being torn away, all it takes is for a stain to be brought into the visual field and you can see where the point of desire is truly tethered.
>
> (Lacan 1962–1963, 253)

The example of this stain that Lacan chooses is the beauty mark. Imagine a beautiful woman. She may be desirable and desired, but it is the beauty mark that fascinates, Lacan says, even more than the look of the partner (1962–1963, 253). The woman may be "my type" in the sense that I just discussed: I have constructed her on the basis of my fantasy, which she matches more or less well. She may have a pleasing form. I may find in her everything that I find visually desirable. But the stain alerts us that it is something other than the woman that attracts. The stain is thus the manifestation of object *a* in the visual field. It is not object *a*, but it is, as Lacan says, "where the point of desire is truly tethered." Thus the *a*, as manifested by the stain, is also punctiform. It is a point. And Lacan adds here the crucial argument. The subject is transfixed by the stain, fascinated by it. The stain indicates the point from which the subject is looked at. Lacan says, "the beauty spot [looks at] me" (1962–1963, 253).

This is the essential point in Lacan's argument on the look. I look out on the visual field, but I am also looked at. I construct the objects in my world, but I am also constructed by the look that takes me in. This is a difficult point conceptually, but it is familiar experientially. We all worry about how others perceive us. We all "dress to impress" and modulate our appearance and gestures to correspond to what the Other expects of us. In psychology, this is simply known as the spotlight effect (Gilovich et al. 2000). We all move through the world with an awareness of how we are seen, as if a spotlight were on us. We experience this effect when we are embarrassed or "found out," or when we are "seen for who we really are." The stain—something out of place in our homogenous picture of the world—makes us aware, if even only momentarily, that we are looked at. And correspondingly, when are aware that we are looked at, we become the stain in the picture—selected, picked out, out of place.

To illustrate this point, Lacan, in Seminar 11, tells a funny story. It's an autobiographical story told with self-effacing humor, but the point of the story is that Lacan was not, in fact, effaced! Lacan was a young man in his twenties. He says, "being a young intellectual, I wanted desperately to get away, see something different, throw myself into something practical, something physical, in the country, say, or at the sea" (Lacan 1964, 95). So he travels to Brittany and goes out on a fishing boat with the poor, working-class fishermen who worked there. We must picture

Lacan, the sophisticated young Parisian, out on a boat with men who were struggling to make a living. He may be dressed in his fine Parisian clothes—he doesn't tell us—or what's perhaps worse, he may have bought clothes like theirs to wear as a kind of costume. A fisherman named Petit-Jean points out to Lacan a sardine can floating on the water and glinting in the sun, and he says to Lacan, "*You see that can? Do you see it? Well, it doesn't see you!*" (1964, 95).

Lacan says that Petit-Jean found this very funny. He himself found it "less so" (Lacan 1964, 95). Why?

> To begin with, if what Petit-Jean said to me, namely, that the can did not see me, had any meaning, it was because in a sense, it was looking at me, all the same. It was looking at me at the level of the point of light, the point at which everything that looks at me is situated—and I am not speaking metaphorically.
>
> (Lacan 1964, 95)

The floating sardine can does look at Lacan. The world looks at us, a fact that we are usually able to ignore, given the fullness of our own vision, but it looks at us all the same. In another passage in Seminar 11, Lacan makes this clear: "The world is all-seeing, but it is not exhibitionistic—it does not provoke our gaze. When it begins to provoke it, the feeling of strangeness begins too" (1964, 75). This is one of the most difficult things for readers of the seminar to appreciate. We associate looking with our own look. We look at the world from our vantage point, and Lacan uses the term *look* this way. But more importantly, he situates the look outside. It is the look that looks at us. If the sardine can "sees" Lacan, that is when his "feeling of strangeness begins." In truth, Lacan must have looked ridiculous and completely out of place on that boat, and the moment Petit-Jean points out the sardine can to him, he feels it. He is the stain in the picture. If a beauty mark or sardine can make us aware that we are looked at, then we become the stain in the world's picture. Lacan sums all this up:

> I am not simply that punctiform being located at the geometral point from which the perspective is grasped. No doubt, in the depths of my eye, the picture is painted. The picture, certainly, is in my eye. But I am in the picture.
>
> (1964, 96)

Unfortunately, Sheridan makes a mistake of translation here that is famous among Lacanians. He translates "But I am *not* in the picture" (96, my emphasis). He must have read the "But" as a contrast to the previous sentence, "The picture, certainly, is in my eye," and assumed that the "not" was mistakenly left out of the French text. Instead, the "But" is intended not to negate the previous sentence but to counter expectations. Lacan's second sentence, then, has the sense of "But I am *also* in a picture."

All of this has been preliminary. We now must consider Lacan's complicated argument on the look. Why does this argument arise? At the point he's reached in Seminar 11, he's been considering repetition, which is, according to him, one of the four fundamental concepts of psychoanalysis. Chapter four in the seminar is

"Of the Network of Signifiers," and he identifies repetition as certain preferential returns in the play of the signifier. For each subject, the synchronic signifying network is established in such a way that certain signifying combinations recur. Lacan wants to link this with Aristotle's term *automaton*. Lacan makes this quite clear:

> If the subject is the subject of the signifier—determined by it—one may imagine the synchronic network as it appears in the diachrony of preferential effects. This is not a question, you understand, of unpredictable statistical effects—it is the very structure of the network that implies the returns. . . . [T]his is the figure that Aristotle's *automaton* assumes for us.
>
> (1964, 67)

The signifying system works, we could say, automatically. As the saying goes, "Wherever you go, there you are," and there you are because you've brought your signifying network with you. There's another variation of this saying: "If during the day you happen to meet an asshole, then that person's an asshole. If you meet nothing but assholes all day long, then you're the asshole."

We're talking about a kind of structuralism here, a determination of the subject by the signifying network. But Lacan wants to go beyond what we can call, by a kind of shorthand, Lévi-Straussian structuralism. He wants to account for the real so that psychoanalysis isn't reduced to a kind of idealism (Lacan 1964, 53). If we only encounter what the signifying network determines that we encounter, what, in short, our minds determine, then we would be trapped in a kind of Berkeleyan idealism. Lévi-Strauss at least places the determining network of signifiers outside of the subject. But I would add another point: if, according to the function of the signifying network, the same combinations of signifiers keep returning, how would we even know that it is repetition at work? We'd just think that we live in a world of assholes. It's only when the real intrudes, through a kind of encounter, that it occurs to us that we may be the asshole.

Lacan is not in favor of a blind structuralism that leaves no room for the real. And so he invokes Aristotle's other term, *tuché*. There are many translations that try to make clear Aristotle's distinction between *tuché* and *automaton*, but I'll give pair of translations that may not be the best but that, I hope, makes the distinction plain. *Automaton* is destiny. We each have a destiny that is determined by the signifying network that determines us as subjects. But *tuché* is fate. It is the chance encounter. It is the encounter with the real. We may be destined to such-and-such an outcome, that's *automaton*. But then fate intervenes. In the most recent translation of Aristotle, by Irwin and Fine, *automaton* is translated by *chance*, and *tuché* by *luck*. We can consider the example of a slot machine. On each pull of the lever, the result is left to chance, but the signifying system of the machine is such that 7–7–7 is going to come up a certain number of times—and then you win, a stroke of fate. It's like that when someone plays the lottery. For the person who wins, it's *tuché*, a life-changing event, fate. But down at the lottery office, it's the most bureaucratic functioning of *automaton*. Someone was bound to win. It's just the way the system is set up.

192  Dan Collins

In the fifth chapter of Seminar 11, Lacan starts developing the notion of *tuché*, and he lays his cards on the table right away: "The function of the *tuché*, of the real encounter . . . first presented itself in the history of psycho-analysis in [the] form . . . of the trauma" (1964, 55). This remark is telling. Trauma cannot be assimilated into the signifying network, that's why it's traumatic. Trauma is the emergence of the real. In this chapter, chapter five, before he even starts talking about the look, Lacan refers to "The place of the real, which stretches from the trauma to the phantasy—in so far as the phantasy is never anything more than [a] screen" (1964, 60). This remark will make no sense to us until we examine Lacan's diagrams of the look. When we do, we'll find that he refers to this place of the real quite literally.

Lacan wants to establish the encounter with the real in the field of visual perception. He takes four chapters to do so. This lengthy digression apparently came as a surprise to him. After spending just one seminar session on the look—the first of the four—he begins the next one by saying, "I did not realize at the time that I would be developing the subject of the gaze to such an extent. I was diverted into doing so by the way in which I presented the concept of repetition in Freud" (Lacan 1964, 79). This is the answer to our question, why does Lacan take up the look? If we meet assholes all day long, then of course that fact is determined by our signifying network. Wherever we go, there they are. We see how closely *tuché* and *automaton* are linked. If we just blindly go through our day, we never take account of those chance encounters that bring us into contact with others. We simply assimilate them into our signifying network. For us, everyone's an asshole. That's how we're set up. But every once in a while, we may get a look from someone that strikes us and breaks through the screen that we impose on the world. That look is like the beauty mark or stain. We suddenly sense that in the picture of the world that the other makes, the other who looks at us, we're the asshole. We're literally the stain in the picture. It's an encounter with the real that breaks through the *automaton* of our everyday life.

How does Lacan summarize all this in diagrams? The first two diagrams that Lacan presents us with at the beginning of chapter eight are these (1964, 91):

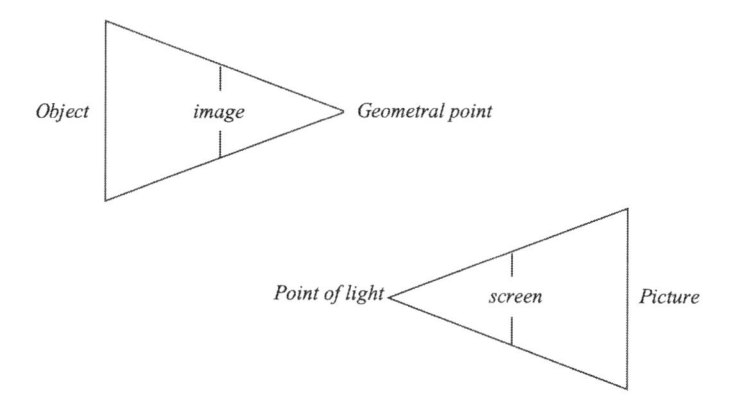

*Figure 14.1* Lacan's optical diagrams of the look.

And here we can see illustrated many of the points that we've been covering in Lacan's text. In the upper diagram, there is an object in the real. We are at the geometral point of the perceiving subject, and before our eyes hangs the image of the object. In the lower diagram, there's the point of light, like the sardine can glinting in the sun, that makes a picture of us. We are in the picture. But as we don't usually perceive ourselves as seen, that reality is usually screened off from us. What's clear in Lacan's commentary on these diagrams is that he offers them to us in order to critique them. They present the philosophical approach to vision. We can see in the upper diagram, for instance, the classical philosophical split between an object and its appearance. And the lower diagram represents only those situations when we are, in fact, in the spotlight, just as we shield our eyes from the sun so as to regain our vision. Lacan summarizes his critique this way: "The whole trick . . . of the classic dialectic around perception, derives from the fact that it deals with geometral vision, that is to say, with vision in so far as it is situated in a space that is not in its essence the visual" (1964, 94). In other words, the classical theory of vision is embedded in a pregiven objective space and not the space of a subject who is implicated in vision. Everything in this classical model could be reconstructed with points of light and cameras with no need of any subject whatsoever.

What is Lacan's answer to this critique? He says immediately in chapter eight, before he introduces a diagram of it in chapter nine, that "the two triangles . . . must be placed one upon the other. What you have here is the . . . interlacing . . . which structures the whole of this domain" (Lacan 1964, 94–95). Why would this address the problem? Even in the classical model, we would suspect that the two triangles are superimposable. The answer is that the field we are dealing with is not that of a geometral pregiven space, but the subjective space of the subject in its interaction with the Other. It's the psychoanalytic subject of desire that determines the visual field. This insight does not negate the classical conception which has been of such great use in the fields of optics and perspective art but rather supplements it by showing precisely how the subject is implicated in it.

In chapter nine, Lacan does indeed give the interlaced diagram that he promised (1964, 106).

And since we see in three dimensions, it might be helpful to redraw this diagram as a three-dimensional model.

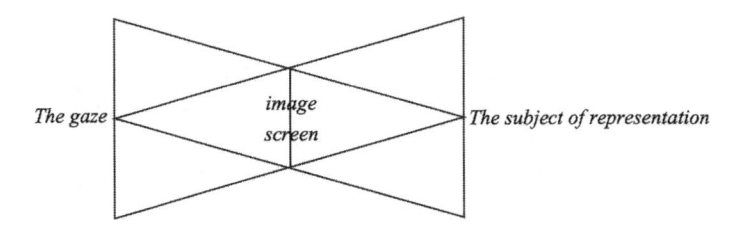

*Figure 14.2* The optical diagrams superimposed.

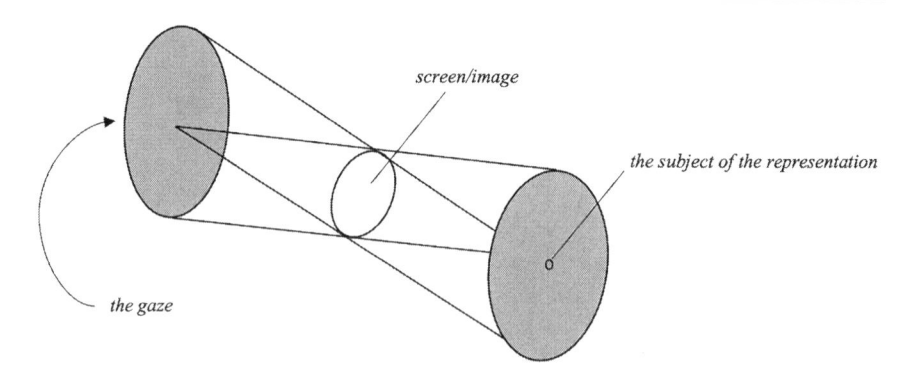

*Figure 14.3* The optical diagrams superimposed pictured in three dimensions.

Here the point that was designated as the object in the earlier geometral diagram from chapter eight is properly relabeled as "the gaze." It is no longer, so to speak, "objective." The subject is implicated and even determined by the look that looks at him or her. The point Lacan is making is a difficult one but it crucial to understanding the scopic drive as drive. Lacan approaches this point in an earlier chapter when he takes up the fort/da game of Freud's grandson. He refers to the reel that the little boy throws out of the crib and then pulls back:

> This reel is not the mother reduced to a little ball by some magical game . . . it is a small part of the subject that detaches itself from him while still remaining his. . . . If it is true that the signifier is the first mark of the subject, how can we fail to recognize here . . . that it is in the object to which the opposition is applied in act, the reel, that we must designate the subject. To this object we will later give the name that it bears in the Lacanian algebra—the *petit a*.
> 
> (Lacan 1964, 62)

The look is being anticipated here, and we could in fact say that this argument is the whole reason why Lacan takes up the look so thoroughly even though he did not anticipate doing so. For it occurs to him that the look is one of the avatars of object *a*. He'll summarize his argument when he introduces the look:

> The gaze is presented to us only in the form of a strange contingency, symbolic of what we find on the horizon, as the thrust of our experience, namely, the lack that constitutes castration anxiety.
> 
> The eye and the gaze—this is for us the split in which the drive is manifested at the level of the scopic field.
> 
> (Lacan 1964, 72–73)

What Lacan has realized is that the look, while it retains its status as the look in the field of the Other, is also the look of the subject, detached, like the little reel, and indeed like the castrated phallus. In fact, this passage is a milestone on the path that Lacan takes in reconceptualizing the object of castration not as the phallus, as -j, but as object *a*. Both forms of the object will continue to exist in Lacan's work, but more and more, the functions of the castrated phallus will be assigned to object *a*.

What, then, of the disk in the center of our diagram which is now both screen, when viewed from one side, and image, when viewed from the other? The image indeed comes from the field of the Other. It is our image of the world as we look upon it. But the image is not a neutral, objective presentation as it was in the classical theory of vision. We construct it. We look at the world, we could say, with an eye of desire. And what of the screen? The screen is our image of the world that shields us from the look, and we've already alluded to the ways in which this happens. We present ourselves. We appear as the Other wants us to appear. We want to fit in to the picture that the Other makes of us. Lacan wanted to experience the real life of fishermen, so he thought that he could just join them, insert himself into their space—perhaps, as I suggested, even wearing a workingman's costume. He thought he fit in. That was his screen by which he attempted to elude the look of Other. His screen fell when Petit-Jean made his wry joke and Lacan realized that he was ridiculously out of place. He became the stain in the picture. This doesn't always happen. In one passage, Lacan comments:

> The split between gaze and vision will enable us, you will see, to add the scopic drive to the list of the drives. If we know how to read it, we shall see that Freud already places this drive to the fore in . . . "Instincts and their Vicissitudes" . . . and shows that it is not homologous with the others. Indeed, it is this drive that most completely eludes the term castration.
>
> (1964, 78)

If the scopic drive eludes castration so successfully, it is because most of the time, the screen functions.

The screen projects into the world our ego-ideal, that is, how we want to be seen by the Other. And like the ego-ideal, it is closely linked to the superego. We *conform* to what the Other wants to see in us. But the screen is also linked to the ideal ego, that is, how we see ourselves and how we take satisfaction in that image. Yet again, it is linked to the objects of satisfaction that we see in the world. We do not perceive the essential lack of object *a*. Instead we present ourselves with imagined objects of satisfaction. Lacan comments on the unreality of our view of the world and offers a diagram (1964, 108).

He says, "in its relation to desire, reality appears only as marginal" (Lacan 1964, 108). We can see this graphically depicted in our three-dimensional diagram. In fact, this small diagram of the two circles is generated, we could say, by placing ourselves at the subject end of the intersecting-triangles diagram and looking at it straight on from the subject's side. In relation to the field of reality at the far end of the intersecting-triangles diagram, the smaller circle of the screen in the center only partially screens the visual field, but the screen of our desire is strong enough to marginalize reality.

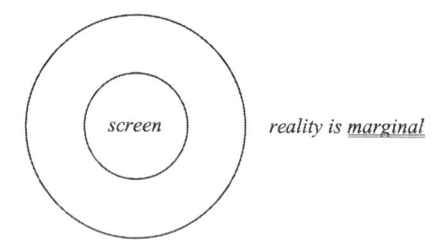

*Figure 14.4* Lacan's diagram of the screen and marginal reality.

We can also add that the screen is a fantasy screen. We've already looked at the passage in which Lacan refers to "The place of the real, which stretches from the trauma to the phantasy—in so far as the phantasy is never anything more than [a] screen" (1964, 60). Our view of the world is a fantasmatic one. We see the world as offering us opportunities for satisfaction. Reality is marginalized by our desirous eye. Meanwhile the fantasy screens the traumatic lack, the object *a*, as a look that sees through our idealized screen image of ourselves and reveals us to be the stain in the world's picture.

The idea of the fantasy screen helps us to understand a passage that comes some 180 pages later. At the end of the seminar, Lacan refers to traversing the fantasy (Lacan 1964, 273). Again, this is an unfortunate translation on Sheridan's part. The French verb *traverser* has as one of its meanings "to go through," while the cognate English verb *to traverse* has the primary sense of "to go across." *Traverser*, then, should be translated simply as "going through" the fantasy. But what does it mean to go through the fantasy and to come out the other side? Lacan indicates that this is a criterion for the end of analysis. The analysis is over when the subject has gone through the fantasy. I think we can take this as a literal reference to the diagram.

In analysis, the subject literally breaks through his or her fantasmatic reality screen to confront lack. This process sounds traumatic, and it often is. Analysis is not easy. But the result is giving up of demand, both the illusory, fantasmatic objects of satisfaction that we demand and the demands of the Other. The result, Lacan says in the same sentence, is that we are able to *live the drive* (1964, 273). This may sound utopian, but couldn't we give a very prosaic example? Imagine an obsessional who has always struggled to live according to his father's impossible demands and covertly to rebel against them, which is the same thing. He's struggled to live up to the way in which his father sees him, and he is ashamed when he doesn't, and of course he never can. He sees himself both as his father's son and as an abject failure. Wouldn't breaking through this fantasmatic reality and confronting the reality—that his father is not the imposing figure that he imagined him to be, but rather an angry, bitter shell of a man who imposed his own fantasies on his son—be a kind of liberation? Wouldn't the son then be free to live his life, his drive? We can certainly imagine such a case.

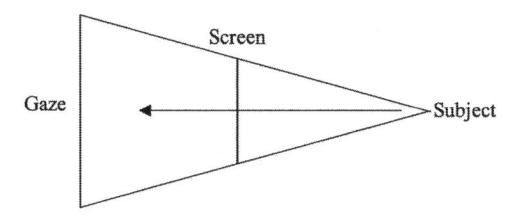

*Figure 14.5* Going through the fantasy screen.

Or we could take a literary example: Nathaniel Hawthorne's (1835) story "Wakefield." It's about a happily married man who one day leaves his house and secretly takes an apartment opposite. For twenty years he remains absent, observing his house across the street until one day he simply returns and rejoins his life and his wife. This story seems to me to be one of those presentiments of psychoanalysis that sometimes turn up in nineteenth-century literature. Wakefield seems to me to be a man who wants to step out of the picture and see what his life is like from the outside, from the point of view of the gaze. Of course, this is impossible, and the story doesn't even suggest that Wakefield gains anything from it. But isn't this what each of us does in analysis? Don't we step outside of our lives, for at least a part of each day, and try to look at our lives from the outside? The difference between us and Wakefield is that we have a partner, the analyst, who takes on the whole burden of being our screen—by a rigorous method of refusing to be it. Eventually, if we're successful, the screen falls, or rather we go through it, as the diagram depicts. We confront our lack and, free from oppressive demand, we live the drive.

## References

Gilovich, Thomas, Victoria Husted Medvec, and Kenneth Savitsky. 2000. "The Spotlight Effect in Social Judgement: An Egocentric Bias in Estimates of the Salience of One's Own Actions and Appearance." *Journal of Personality and Social Psychology* 78 (2): 211–222.

Hawthorne, Nathaniel. 1835. "Wakefield." In *Nathaniel Hawthorne's Tales*, 2nd edition. Edited by James McIntosh, 96–103. New York: Norton, 2013.

Lacan, Jacques. 1962–1963. *Anxiety: The Seminar of Jacques Lacan*, Book X. Edited by Jacques-Alain Miller. Translated by A. R. Price. Malden, MA: Polity, 2014.

———. 1964. *The Four Fundamental Concepts of Psychoanalysis: The Seminar of Jacques Lacan*, Book XI. Edited by Jacques-Alain Miller. Translated by Alan Sheridan. New York, NY: Norton, 1977.

# Chapter 15

# The Voice and Its Drive

*Eve Watson*

*To the canonical list of drive objects, the breast, feces, the phallus—for him, avatars of object* a—*Lacan added the look and the voice. Of these, the voice has been the least theorized, a situation that Watson goes a long way towards rectifying. The first thing to note is that while the voice is undoubtedly related to speech, it "falls outside of vocalization." It is the "non-aural aspect of the speaking voice." The infant first experiences the aural world as a "hubbub," Watson notes, which includes the voice of the Other. But when the infant first makes itself heard with a cry, its own voice too is an audible hubbub, the remainder of which evades meaning. The challenge for the subject is to in-corps-orate the voice, to embody it. Watson concludes with several clinical observations that illustrate the voice—and the theoretical challenge of giving it body—in practice.*

During a session, my analysand hiccupped loudly and continuously. This was repeated in many sessions over subsequent weeks. With the hiccups, something loud and inescapable entered the clinical room. The hiccups, corporeally actualized "mishaps," in so far as they were involuntary and unintended, made it impossible for her to speak. They were spellbinding, and while seeming to have a positive quality in their presence and intrusiveness, the hiccups could not be pinned down to any meaning or signification, nor could they be distinguished as a series having any kind of pattern or rhythm.

The presence of these hiccups contrasted starkly to the absence of signifiers. While it might be tempting to view the hiccupping fits solely as resistance to the fundamental rule of free association, the context surrounding them allowed for an additional interpretation. This analysand had been undergoing analysis for some years and much had changed in her life, love, and work. The hiccups were not bits and pieces of unnamed desire but manifestations of the invocatory drive and its remainder, the object-voice. This aphonic voice embodies a zero-point of representation and is indexed by its very non-articulation. The hiccupping convulsions of the diaphragm, fitting for this analysand who enjoyed a personal hobby requiring special breathing, expressed a pure point of origin beyond history and meaning. Having exhausted the field of phonematic meaning, the drive's asymbolic language, lalangue, was being ventilated as spasmodic hiccup and breath. This real voice resonated only when speaking was impossible and, in this case, no longer of interest.

The voice as object *a* is included by Lacan in the field of separable objects—lamella, breast, feces, phallus, gaze—that cause desire and are the drive's remainders. While declaring the significance of the objects *a* in so far as they are "the inaugural point of the unconscious structure" (1964–1965, 132), Lacan in fact says little about the voice in contrast to the other objects. The gaze is developed in *The Four Fundamental Concepts of Psychoanalysis* (1964) and elsewhere, with the exception of the voice, the objects *a* are scrupulously disarticulated from conceptions of developmental determinism and are posed in terms of their structural consequences (Lacan 1961–1962, 1962–1963, 1964, 1964–1965). It is, however, possible to trace the significance of the voice in comments extractable from Lacan's tenth and eleventh seminars and earlier in his seminar on psychosis. As well, the voice can be understood more generally in the later Lacan as the centralization of speech effects and the resituation of the register of the real in relation to the symbolic and imaginary registers. This resituating was posed by Lacan as a knot in which the three registers of the symbolic, the imaginary, and the real are interlinked in a Borromean-type knotting which is held together by a linguistic unit such as a signifier or a *sinthome*.

The middle and later periods of Lacan's work are characterized by an emphasis on anxiety and jouissance which emanate in speech and are highly determinative but, as affects of the real, are non-representable. The voice, while indubitably linked to speech, is that aspect of speech that falls outside of vocalization and, as the invocatory object *a*, is what in speech is resistant, as all objects *a*, to any "phonemization" (Lacan 1962–1963, 249). While often manifesting as strange aspects of speech, the voice is "a-phonic" (Miller 2007, 139) and is precisely what cannot be said. In this vein, Mladen Dolar describes the voice as the missing link that brings the body and language together but without actually having a phonological presence itself, and, as a non-heterogenous remainder of the operation of signifier, its unintelligible presence is the aphonic support of the structural logic of the signifier (2006, 36). The voice, along with the gaze, is described by Lacan as "the closest to the experience of the unconscious" (1964, 104), which puts it in intimate connection with the drive and the constitution of the subject (Vincegeurra 2010, 41). Let's assess this in light of the voice as object, the role of the Other in the invocatory drive, and implications for analytic practice.

## The Voice and the Other

In his anxiety seminar, Lacan meanders through a detailed description of the ear and the functions of the cochlea, timpani, and vestibuli of the auditory canal to arrive at his essential point about its workings: it is the function of the void of the acoustic tube that allows sound to resonate and be heard (1962–1963, 274–275).

The "making contact" of the phatic and the social dimension of speech embraced by linguists does not, he claims, go far enough. Rather, the act of speaking which involves the Other also involves something *ex nihilo*, a void of the Other incorporated as an otherness that is central to the speaking voice (275). How may we conceive of this void of the Other? Lacan proffers Theodor's Reik's analysis of the sacred Jewish wind instrument, the shofar, which is sounded on the special feast days of Rosh Hashanah and Yom Kippur. He notes its deeply moving auricular effects, which, according to Lacan, illustrate the function of the object-voice as something that "exceeds the level of the occultation of anxiety in the desire linked to the Other" (1962–1963, 245). He criticizes Reik's analysis of the shofar, which Reik concluded imitated the sound of God (1946, 301–305), for emphasizing the shofar's sounds as meaningful representation (Lacan 1962–1963, 246). For Lacan, the shofar is a manifestation of the voice insofar as the voice is not music (276), and it is unrepresentable because the voice of Yahweh is akin to an unassimilable thunderous "roar" (250).

The Other's voice first addresses the baby as unintelligible din through ears which "are the only orifice that cannot be closed" (Lacan 1964, 195). The world in thus imposed as an indistinct perceptum, and all means of communication are entirely on the side of the Other (1962–1963, 272). There is a silent jouissance that resounds in the voice-din which is described by Vinceguerra as "hubbub" (2010, 41). This din becomes a remainder when the baby becomes established in the network of language and field of intentionality. This remainder comprises both the part-object voice, which is the non-aural aspect of the speaking voice, as well as being one of the remainder-components of the "real" which underpin the symbolic field. These drive remainder-components include the gaze, breast, turd, and phallus, in addition to the voice.

A first step is the baby's cry to the Other, which is a vocal sounding of suffering and discomfort and a ventilation of primal anxiety. In responding to the baby's cry, the Other offers a space that hollows out the anguishing immediacy of the voice-din and the real, absolute Other. Henceforth anxiety is linked to the "lack of lack," when there is no possibility of lack and when, as Lacan puts it, the mother is on the baby's back all of the time (1962–1963, 53–54). Moreover, the Other's voice that intones without meaning is experienced as an imperative that calls for obedience and conviction and it "takes the form of command" (1962–1963, 276). In his fifth seminar, Lacan (1957–1958) describes this early superego as signifying the first vague articulations of need and frustration. This recalls an even earlier delineation of the superego in Lacan's first seminar where in addition to being consonant with the register of the law, it has a "senseless, blind character, of pure imperatives and pure tyranny" that is identified with a ferocious figure linked to the primitive traumas of the child (1953–1954, 102). Articulation initially is an absolute commandment prior to any question of "*Che vuoi?*" ("What do you want from me?")

This is the wending of the baby's cry as it passes to articulated speech by way of demand. Demand takes several levels. There is demand directed to the Other as a real object capable of giving satisfaction, and demand directed to the Other as symbolic object which gives or refuses and is present and absent (1957–1958, 473). Demand is, in effect, directly linked to the early modulating effects of presence and absence by which the voice is made separable as a partial object. As a drive object, it is "the otherness of what is said" (Lacan 1962–63, 275) and is what comes before meaning. The voice is, as Leader puts it, "that part of the cry which wasn't absorbed in the network of meanings" (2005, 136), and as lalangue, it is the aphonic meaningless support of the signifier. The voice in this sense, and for my hiccupping analysand, encapsulates an impossible relation to what cannot be present except as a kind of a disruptive presence that ruptures full presence and is an obstacle to self-presence (Dolar 2006, 42). It momentarily appears in dreams and in those hypnogogic moments before falling asleep and before fully awakening when there is an inner voice that insists. But the words can never be recalled upon waking as they have slipped away and are never to be refound (Lacan 1962–1963, 276; Leader 2005). The voice that haunts language resounds for the subject who is left waiting to hear from the Other. It is also the basis of the elementary phenomenon that is auditory delusion and "hearing voices."

Ultimately, the responsive exchanges between baby and the Other introduce intonation and intentionality, which brings into play the signifier and an appeal to the Other whose answer determines the question that subsequently emerges. This is the significance of the fort/da game played by Freud's grandson, Ernst (Freud 1920), whose "play" modulated the Other into a sequence of presences and absences with the differentiating use of the signifiers "*fort*" and "*da*." The meaninglessness of the mother's material absence, but aphonic proximity, was regulated by the toddler's playful and clever articulations which introduced a play of signifiers that cut into his anxiety and modulated it with a rhythmic sequence of "there" and "gone."

## The Incorporation of the Voice

How does the voice that is on the side of the Other come to be on the side of the subject who has a voice and speaks? Lacan specifies that the voice, as otherness in what is said, is a void that must be "incorporated" (1962–1963, 277). It must be "in-corps-orated," and, as with the gaze, to which it is closely related, the voice has both an inner and outer quality. It seems to substantialize personality insofar as each person has a singular voice while it also retains an alien aspect. One way of thinking about this alien aspect is that it retains an otherness and defies meaning and relatability. This is demonstrated when the voice is detached from ourselves and appears to have a strange otherness which can be heard, for example, when we hear our voices played back and when we hear ourselves being mimicked. This idea can be traced to the Project for a Scientific Psychology, where Freud writes of the child's scream as directing attention to the object whereby "the information of one's own scream serves to characterize the object" (Freud 1895, 366). This shows how the voice is initially outside, and it is only when the object-voice becomes linked to a body, in this case, that of the speaker, that they can appropriate it to themselves as their own screaming voice. Instances of transitivism of babies show

how one howling baby causes another to cry, as the cry has not yet been incorporated and assimilated to a particular body. A cinematic paradigm for the unlocatable indiscernible voice is exemplified in the mother's voice in the film *Psycho* (1960) and the indistinguishability of body, the son's or mother's, from which it emanates (Dolar 2006, 66).

The unseen and unknown source of the voice is also indicated in certain non-alignments of bodies and voices. The expression "You don't look as I expected" often emphasizes the look as the thing which doesn't match up, but what is being emphasized is a voice cannot be pinned down to a certain body. The voice which comes from inside the body mundanely falls short or misses the encounter with its bodily envelope. There are also those strange eerie moments when screen images and sound do not match up, and it is why the most powerful and authoritative voices are those detached from bodies. In cinematic terms, we can think of Hal from *2001: A Space Odyssey*, the wizard in the *Wizard of Oz*, and the disembodied voice of the Great Dictator from the film of the same name. The crank caller is all the more terrifying and threatening because the voice is disconnected from a known body, and when they are unmasked, they are often insipid desperate creatures who are disappointingly and banally attached to a particular body (Dolar 2006; Watson 2015).

In terms of the structural causation of the subject, the voice as partial object is a leftover of the operation of the signifying chain and a remainder of the infant's interaction with the Other through which acoustic productions are given meaning. This is when the infant's cry is interpreted by the Other, and a foundation for meaning is established. The voice the child tries to respond to initially presents a puzzling causality, and it is difficult to disentangle from the gaze as the gaze is superimposed by the voice of the Other in the mirror-stage in its assent of the child's assumption of the image. This means that both the gaze and the voice appear in the gap as objects that the subject can never quite match (Dolar 2006, 67). Freud's (1900) dream of Irma's injection is a good example of this and shows the void that is constitutive of the voice as a partial object. In his dream, Freud looks into Irma's silent accusing mouth, and this causes him to become disturbed and speak nonsense. The void of the mouth represents the nothing from whence psychoanalysis came: the trauma of Emma Eckstein's surgery with Fleiss, Freud's failure as a doctor, and his "lost" career as the anesthesiologist. The voice is thus an effect without *a* cause. Freud's interrogation of Irma's gaping non-articulating mouth indicates that what he is aiming at is making himself addressed by an Other who will finally recognize and prize him.

The addressee function goes back even before the subject's birth to when they were spoken into existence and signifiers were organized in a discourse about them (Vanier 2000, 27). The addressee function is also taken up by Leader and is linked to the infant who is not equipped to make sense of being addressed by the adult's interpellations which are initially enigmatic. While the infant can defend against interacting with the Other by some kind of intervention—the main one being to refuse what the adult wants, such as refusing to eat—it cannot defend against or refuse the experience of being addressed. This experience of being addressed from the outside, which is also a feature of the gaze, can be experienced as invasive and threatening (Leader 2005, 141). Usually, Leader argues, the infant goes on to process this experience by linking it to a structure, which in its earliest form is crib speech, which functions as a kind of early incorporation procedure that tempers anxiety, and later in the dialogue that children generate with themselves, which mediates the experience of being addressed (143). It is this phenomenon of the child that Lacan notes in his anxiety seminar (1962–1963, 273), who monologues before going to sleep. Of course, this is not a monologue, as the Other is already in play, and it is the Other whom the child addresses.

Let's take the case of the paranoid young woman which Lacan discussed in his psychosis seminar, with features of auditory delusion. In a case conference with Lacan present, the woman spoke of the persecution and victimization upon hearing an insulting word "sow" said to her by a neighbor, a man she knew. In reply to Lacan's questioning, she revealed that immediately prior to hearing this insult, she had said to him "I've just been to the butcher's." It transpired the man was in a circuit of people known to the patient and functioned as one in a series of little others, counterparts of the patient herself, and the big Other, as a reference point which would have contextualized the encounter and made it less antagonizing, was excluded (1955–1956, 52). The reference to a butcher's was a reference to a pig, and the insult is the woman's own message that reflected her relationship with her mother, one in which she feared being cut up like a piece of meat (52). The word "sow" was a signifier without a signified and in its voice-like quality carried an alien "inhuman" kernel that could not be taken up and absorbed by the signifier. In not functioning as a signifier that links to another signifier and conveying meaning effects by way of metaphorization, the word "sow" was inaccessible to any metaphorical effects of the signifying chain; it stood alone, as a "real" signifier that indexed the presence of the Other as real and threatening.

## The Analyst and the Voice

In the analytic procedure, the fundamental rule is the method in which the patient presents his or her associations in the presence of the analyst. To facilitate this, the analyst is required not so much to keep her mouth shut but to give voice to the silence in the midst of the signification she builds or allows to be built. This means that as a function of the Other, the analyst is neither a person nor a subject nor consciousness but, as Le Gaufey puts it, the Peircean "someone" required to turn signifiers into signs (2007, 106). This is the basis of the analyst's position as an empty place that "causes" the analysand's speech. This follows the principle that speech and symptoms are linked just as speech and the unconscious are linked, and by speaking, something can be changed that is not necessarily of the order of speech. As Soler notes, by situating speech on the side of the Other, the listener decides what they have heard, and the message becomes more precise, although the subject sometimes doesn't like the message the Other hears in the subject's statements (1996, 48).

Through her silence, the analyst becomes the embodiment or semblance of the object cause of desire. This is not the master's voice or the voice of the superego but the impossible voice to which the analysand, who is invoked to speak whatever comes to mind, is called upon to interrupt and silence the silence. But in being called upon to respond, as mentioned earlier, what comes to feature for the analysand is a demand to be addressed, which is what lies behind the desire to be heard. In analysis, as Miller notes, this translates into

> I am waiting for the Other's voice, the one that will tell me what I have to expect, what will become of me and what has already become of my being unspeakable. And that is precisely what makes me attached to the Other: it is the voice in the field of the Other that makes me attached to the Other.
>
> (145)

But in order for the analysand to constitute him- or herself in relation to the Other, this involves resonating in a void which is the emptiness of the Other. This is the work of approaching lack as emanating on the side of the analysand and the Other and working through its significance. In other words, what is it the analysand does not have or cannot be? What can the Other not do or provide? By incorporating lack as doubled (on the side of the subject and the Other) in its structuration of the analysand's choices, acts, and symptoms, a different choice, act, or symptom opens up as possible. In his or her interventions, the analyst proffers this lack that emerges in the analysand's signifying articulations, in particular in the moments when the signifier breaks down. Let us consider this lack in the context of the voice in the case of Emmy von N.

Freud's patient, a hysteric with a range of classic conversion symptoms, literally put herself into Freud's hands after years of suffering from neurotic illness after the death of her husband. In setting aside the pressure and hypnotic techniques and simply listening, thanks to Frau Emmy's exasperated instruction, Freud noted in particular one symptom: in addition to a facial tic and a stammer, Emmy frequently interrupted her remarks with a strange clacking sound when she was frightened. Emmy linked this peculiar phenomenon to the time "when she was sitting by the bedside of her youngest daughter who was very ill, and had wanted to keep absolutely quiet" (1895, 54). The case history revealed that Emmy rejected her newborn daughter after her husband died, as she blamed her daughter for distracting her from her husband's illness prior to his death. She told Freud that her daughter had subsequently been "very queer for a long time," screamed all the time, did not sleep, and had developmental impairments until the age of four, although as Freud pointed out, she had developed normally since then (1895, 60–61). Emmy's relationship with her daughter was highly ambivalent and caused her intense feelings of guilt.

It is tempting to consider the strange clack as an affective representation of helplessness in the face of Freud's rather dogmatic and overbearing approach, but a close examination of the case indicates that Emmy's phonic peculiarities emerged at points of high anxiety and constituted a verbal link to the traumatic core of her history. The clacking is a rendering of the imaginary relationship between daughter and mother, a relation that at its core is characterized by a lack of unifying sound, a real element. The mother's mourning of her husband's death and subsequent depression—which was a loss to the child and involved the loss of the child to the mother—was encapsulated in the sonorous kernel of the voice, represented by the clacking. It could be said to indicate, in its imprecision as to whom it belongs, the daughter's blotting out of the mother's voice through her screaming in those months after Herr von N. died and the demand made of the mother to be quiet so she, the daughter, could be well. The clack may also represent Emmy's clacking around her already dead husband, and therefore it represents desire (Watson 2015, 168).

The clack, on the one hand, emanated from the mother in her confrontation with both her dead husband and her screaming child. But, on the other hand, the clack represented the excess of the Other and can be linked to the child who occupied the same room as her parents and was present the morning that Herr von N. collapsed and died. It is also possible that the clack refers to the maternal superego and its embryonic introjected preobject identifications and love of the mother. Emmy personified the addressee function inasmuch as she was powerless to close her ears to Freud's voice which guided and also admonished and fussed, but it also pointed to an intermediary space between mother and child and its clacking object, a remnant of enjoyment not encapsulated by the paternal metaphor (168). The clack points to what is beyond Freud's voice as speech and for Emmy, a point of alterity containing bits and pieces of unsignifiable jouissance, desire for a dead husband, and an enjoyment beyond her child, perhaps feminine (169).

## Concluding Remarks

The voice is present in the non-alignment of bodies and voices. Crank callers such as those in *Scream* (1996) and *Phone Booth* (2002) are all the more terrifying and threatening because the voice is disconnected from a known body. The film *Contact* (1997) offers a good illustration of the voice in action. The principal character, Ellie, an astronomer obsessed with searching for extra-terrestrial life, finally hears a sign of the alien life she has been searching for since she was orphaned at the age of nine. She hears an alien "call" in a pounding aphonic noise that emanates in her headset, picked up by an array of powerful radio telescopes. It is assumed this noise is "intentional," and it is decoded as a mathematical schema for space travel. On board a ship made from the schema, Ellie falls into a void where she is visited by her dead father and experiences strange sensorial encounters and a permeable boundary between self and Other. While there is no evidence that she found any answers in her quest, it is possible to say she discovered a question. Ellie's obsession with listening for a sign of alien life was an escape hatch from the ungrievable loss of her father, which found a "voice" which addressed her. In her fall from the known world (of the world of signifier and meaning), her encounter with the Other as a spectral ghost-father cut into her unassimilated loss so it could be remade it into the emptiness of lack. He will never return. This recognition freed her, as indicated in the film's conclusion, to pursue love with someone other than her father.

The "timelessness" of Ellie's travel indicates its psychical aspect, and while it is tempting to read her fall as an analogy for the fall of the ego and the course of a psychoanalysis—a quest to find answers that produces a question to which the patient produces a livable answer—the film offers considerations of the voice. Ellie's earnest and aesthetically pleasing voice contrasts with the pure alterity of the alien noise and highlights the asymmetry between the voice as bearer of vocalization and the voice as excess. This is indicated, for example, in psychosis when the voice is not properly absorbed into the signifier, and rudiments of the voice, congruent with what Lacan calls the unassimilated "continuous current of the signifier" (1955–1956, 294), can be experienced as disturbances such as hissing, whispering, noises, or buzzing. The installation of a signifier and the metaphorization of the Other's desire humanizes the Other by delimiting it within a linguistic structure of meaning. This is subjectively structured by fantasy, which organizes within a psychically organized desiring relation the drive's partial objects, including the auditory object. What psychosis demonstrates in auditory delusion is the exteriority of the auditory object, highlighting its non-relational aspect, which in neurosis has been incorporated so that it is internalized as well as externalized. While the drives, silent and constant, quietly pursue their aim of mute enjoyment, the invocatory drive can be heard from time to time in its aim of being addressed.

## References

Dolar, Mladen. 2006. *A Voice and Nothing More*. Cambridge, MA: MIT Press.
Freud, Sigmund. 1893–1895. "Studies on Hysteria." In *Standard Edition of the Complete Psychological Works of Sigmund Freud*. Vol. 2. Translated by James Strachey, 48–105. New York: Norton, 1955.
———. 1895. "Project for a Scientific Psychology." In *Standard Edition of the Complete Psychological Works of Sigmund Freud*. Vol. 3. Translated by James Strachey, 295–397. New York: Norton, 1962.
———. 1900. "The Interpretation of Dreams." In *Standard Edition of the Complete Psychological Works of Sigmund Freud*. Vols. 4 and 5. Translated by James Strachey. New York: Norton, 1953.
———. 1920. "Beyond the Pleasure Principle." In *Standard Edition of the Complete Works of Sigmund Freud*. Vol. 20. Translated by James Strachey, 1–64. New York: Norton, 1955.
Lacan, Jacques. 1952–1953. *Freud's Papers on Technique: The Seminar of Jacques Lacan*, Book I. Translated by John Forrester. New York: Norton, 1988.
———. 1955–1956. *The Psychoses: The Seminar of Jacques Lacan*, Book III. Translated by Russell Grigg. New York: Norton, 1993.
———. 1957–1958. *Formations of the Unconscious: The Seminar of Jacques Lacan*, Book V. Translated by Russell Grigg. Cambridge, UK: Polity, 2017.
———. 1961–1962. *Identification: The Seminar of Jacques Lacan*, Book IX. Translated by Cormac Gallagher. See www.lacaninireland.com/web/wp-content/uploads/2010/06/Seminar-IX-Amended-Iby-MCL-7.NOV_.20111.pdf.
———. 1962–1963. *Anxiety: The Seminar of Jacques Lacan*, Book X. Translated by Adrian Price. Cambridge, UK: Polity Press, 2014.

———. 1964. *The Four Fundamental Concepts of Psychoanalysis: The Seminar of Jacques Lacan*, Book XI. Translated by Alan Sheridan. New York: Norton, 1977.

———. 1964–1965. *Crucial Problems for Psychoanalysis: The Seminar of Jacques Lacan*, Book XII. Translated by Cormac Gallagher. See www.lacaninireland.com/web/wp-content/uploads/2010/06/12-Crucial-problems-for-psychoanalysis.pdf.

Le Gaufey, Guy. 2007. "Is the Analyst a Clinician?" *Journal of the Centre for Freudian Analysis and Research* 17: 94–107.

Leader, Darian. 2005. "Psychoanalysis and the Voice." *Journal of the Centre for Freudian Analysis and Research* 16: 131–151.

Miller, Jacques-Alain. 2007. "Jacques Lacan and the Voice." In *The Later Lacan*. Edited by Véronique Voruz and Bogdan Wolf, 137–146. Albany, NY: State University of New York Press.

Reik. Theodor. 1946. *The Psychological Problems of Religion, Ritual: Psychoanalytic Studies*. New York: Farrar, Straus and Company, 1981.

Soler, Colette. 1996. "The Symbolic Order (II)." In *Reading Seminars I and II: Lacan's Return to Freud*. Edited by Richard Feldstein, Bruce Fink, and Maire Jaanus, 47–55. Albany, NY: State University of New York Press.

Vanier, Alain. 2000. *Lacan*. London: Other Press.

Vincegeurra, Rose-Paule. 2010. "The Object Voice." In *Psychoanalytic Notebooks 20: Object a & the Semblant*, 40–49.

Watson, Eve. 2015. "The Voice and the Analyst's Ear." *Lacunae: International Journal for Lacanian Psychoanalysis* 10: 159–171.

## Film

*2001: A Space Odyssey*. Directed by Stanley Kubrick.
*Contact*. 1997. Directed by R. Zemeckis.
*Phone Booth*. 2002. Directed by Joel Schumacher.
*Psycho*. 1960. Directed by Alfred Hitchcock.
*Scream*. 1996. Directed by Wes Craven.
*The Great Dictator*. 1940. Directed by Charlie Chapin.
*The Wizard of Oz*. 1939. Directed by Victor Fleming.

Chapter 16

# On Self-Relating Negativity
## The Lacanian Death Drive

*Derek Hook*

*Perhaps no topic in psychoanalytic theory is as fraught as the death drive. Some one hundred years after Freud's formulation of the concept, there's consensus without agreement: everyone grants that the death drive is of crucial importance, but the psychoanalytic community cannot settle upon its definitive meaning. Derek Hook enters into this conceptual morass with an attempt to clarify the meaning of the death drive through a close reading of Žižek, among others. Part of the confusion, is that the death drive has been considered a positive entity rather than an "active nothing." How that nothing is active occupies Hook for much of this paper. Most simply, Hook emphasizes that much of our uncertainty about the drive results from our confusing it with desire. The death drive, as Hook importantly puts it, is a concept that allows us to clearly see their difference.*

The work of Slavoj Žižek contains perhaps the most philosophically ambitious elaboration of the Lacanian death drive. My agenda in this chapter is at once expository and synthesizing: I offer, via Žižek, a map connecting various Lacanian conceptualizations of the death drive. I begin by highlighting a series of fallacious assumptions pertaining to this concept before moving on to explain two apparently inconsistent ideas: symbolic mortification and undead life. A question which emerges from Žižek's descriptions helps unify the discussion: is death drive essentially a type of excess (a libidinal surplus) or a radical form of negativity (an ontological impasse)?

### What Death Drive Is Not

For Žižek, four ideas should be opposed when approaching the notion of the death drive, namely death drive as: 1) instinct, 2) cosmic principle (Thanatos), 3) Nirvana-like release, 4) suicidality. Consider the following:

> [W]e have to abstract Freud's biologism: "death drive" is not a biological fact but a notion indicating that the human psychic apparatus is subordinated to a blind automatism of repetition beyond pleasure-seeking, self-preservation. . . . [The] "death drive" [is the] dimension of radical negativity. . . . [It is a] radical

antagonism through which man cuts his umbilical cord with nature, with animal homeostasis.

(Žižek 1989, 4–5)

Žižek here alludes to Lacan's (1955) early insistence that death drive should be understood as a form of repetition, indeed, as *repetition automatism*, a fact which accords with Lacan's assertion that repetition is an inherent feature of the unconscious. Lacan (1955) credits Freud for having intuited that repetition is fundamentally symbolic in nature and that it is *determining of* as opposed to *determined by* human subjects. This over-riding form of agency is beyond (human/biological) life in the sense that it is the result of the automatism of symbolic-linguistic structures. Death drive is hence not biological. We might note here—anticipating a theme to come—that death drive in Lacan typically involves death in form (mortifications of the symbolic) rather than in content (issues of mortality, organic demise).

There is an additional argument here concerning how death drive transcends the merely biological/natural. Death drive, argues Žižek, is an imbalance or antagonism which enables—*compels*—the subject to transcend the domain of the instinctual/natural. It is the means by which we pass from animal to properly human sexuality: "death drive is the transcendental form which makes [human] sexuality proper out of animal instincts" (2010, 305). The death drive then is both the aberration of instinct, the reason the human animal is fundamentally *de-natured* and never merely the subject of evolutionary adaptation and that which enables the transition between nature and culture.

Adjusting "Freud's own misleading formulations," Žižek insists that death drive be understood not as a conflict between two opposed forces, but as "the inherent self-blockage of the drive" (2010, 305). Žižek draws on the work of Jonathan Lear (2000)—who advances his own critique of the Freudian death drive—to argue that the conceptualization of Eros and Thanatos as opposing forces is "a pseudo-explanation generated by [Freud's] . . . inability to properly conceptualize the dimension 'beyond the pleasure principle'" (2014, 122). The fact that the mental apparatus regularly disrupts its own functioning is not reason enough to posit a broader, overarching teleological principle. Freud, says Lear (2000), claims to be discovering a new life force, when in fact he is covering over a trauma in psychoanalytic theory itself. The assertion of Thanatos as a cosmic principle and the reconceptualization of libido as Eros are attempts to sublimate a more traumatic realization: the ontological inconsistency of the mind. Lear hence proves an unexpected ally in the Lacanian project of de-substantializing the death drive. Freud, for Lear, was mistaken in postulating the death drive to account for the breakdowns in the operations of the pleasure principle. More particularly, in respect of the idea of a compulsion to repeat, Lear (2000) asks:

Why . . . consider the compulsion to repeat a compulsion *to* repeat? . . . [T]o talk of a compulsion *to* repeat is to suggest that the aim or the point of the compulsion is to produce a repetition. . . . [I]t is implicitly to import a teleological assumption. . . . On the contrary, there is a more austere hypothesis that better fits the evidence: that the mind has a tendency to disrupt itself, that these disruptions are not *for* anything—they are devoid of purpose.

(77)

Rather than assume the existence of a type of quasi-ontological force (or cosmic principle) that insists on repetition, Lear suggests that there are simply occasions when the mind malfunctions. One might allow then the possibility of the mind as a "self-disrupting organism" existing "in conditions of excess" (Lear 2000, 112), without requiring any over-arching principle by way of explanation. Impasses and failures in psychical functioning, do not, in other words, need to be accounted for in terms of the imposition of an external "demonic" force; such breakdowns may be inherent to psychical functioning as such. While there are, of course, important differences in the arguments advanced by the two philosophers—Žižek *does* wish to retain the death drive as an explanatory principle, whereas Lear does not—their arguments harmonize in refuting the "positivization" of the death drive seen as a substantial or stand-alone entity. The Lacanian death drive can thus be approached as an (ontological) gap enlarged until it seems to be a thing itself, a type of content. Or, to echo terms introduced previously: the death drive does not, in Lacan, exist *as content* but rather as the *form* of ontological incompletion.

Back then to the topic of Thanatos. Lear and Žižek concur: what is labeled Thanatos can simply be viewed as the inner inconsistency of the psychic apparatus:

> "death drive" is not an opposing force with regard to libido, but a constitutive gap which distinguishes the drive from instinct . . . [guaranteeing that the drive is] always derailed, caught in a loop of repetition, marked by an impossible excess . . . Eros and Thanatos are not two opposing drives. . . . [T]here is only one drive, the libido, striving for enjoyment, and the "death drive" is the curved space of its formal structure.
>
> (Žižek 2010, 305)

We should not think death drive as a substantial entity; it is, by contrast, a type of negative inherence, a constitutive gap. We might ask, though: is death drive a psychical force (libidinal surplus) or a type of negativity? At times, Žižek emphasizes the *psychical* nature of the death drive as *a drive* characterized as an excess. Yet he is also wary of reading the death drive exclusively within psychological parameters and is intent on operationalizing the concept philosophically as a type of ontological absence or failure (constitutive gap, radical negativity). The oscillation between these two characterizations is often striking:

> [For] Lacan . . . to properly grasp what Freud was aiming at with the death drive (the . . . libidinal stance of the human individual for self-sabotaging . . .), is to

read it against the background of negativity, a gap as fundamental to human subjectivity.... Psychoanalysis in this way is no longer just a psychiatric science; it's a kind of mental and philosophical theory of the utmost radical dimensions of human beings.

(Žižek 2013)

Death drive here is at once agency *and* absence, psychical attribute *and* excess of negativity. How then are we to bridge these seemingly incompatible descriptions? A related question: is the death drive primarily of the subject, or does it simply refer to a type of ontological impasse?

Before attempting to answer these questions, let us note why, for Žižek, death drive is not the "Nirvana principle." Death drive, he insists, is not the striving to escape the cycle of life or to "achieve the ultimate equilibrium, the release from tensions" (1999a, 190). For Freud, death drive is not merely "a decadent reactive formation—a secondary self-denial of the originally assertive will to power" but is instead "the innermost radical possibility of a human being" (1999a, 190). We should read the concept *against* "the usual inscription of psychoanalysis into the naturalistic deterministic framework" (Žižek and Daly 2004, 135) and grasp death drive as a type of *life in excess of life*. Lacan likewise insists that death drive "is not . . . a perversion of instinct but rather a desperate affirmation of life that is the purest form . . . of the death instinct" (1953, 263). Žižek elaborates:

> The Freudian death drive has nothing whatsoever to do with the craving for self-annihilation, for the return to the inorganic absence of any life-tension; it is, on the contrary, the very opposite of dying—a name for the 'undead' eternal life itself.... The paradox of ... "death drive" is ... that it is Freud's name for its very opposite, for the way immortality appears within psychoanalysis, for an uncanny excess of life ... an "undead" urge which persists beyond the (biological) cycle of life and death.... [H]uman life is never "just life": humans are not simply alive, they are possessed by the strange drive to enjoy life in excess, passionately attached to a surplus which sticks out and derails the ordinary run of things.
>
> (Žižek 2006b, 62)

There is much emphasis here on death drive as a psychical excess, a libidinal force. This contrasts with descriptions in foregoing extracts, where Žižek stresses how the asubstantial death drive is akin to nothing so much as a form of self-relating negativity. Leaving this apparent contradiction to one side, we can ask what Žižek has in mind here in his reference to immortality, to death drive as "the indestructible life that insists beyond death" (1999b, 211).

When Žižek speaks of "an excess of obscene life . . . a pressure, a compulsion which persists beyond death" (2006b, 182) he is invoking the notion of jouissance. While in many of Žižek's philosophical elaborations of death drive the notions of libido and jouissance fall by the wayside, there are moments when they are foregrounded:

> Dis-attachment is ... death drive at its purest, the gesture of ontological "derailment" which throws the order of Being "out of joint," the gesture of disinvestment, of "contraction"/withdrawal from being immersed in the world. ... [T]his negative tendency to disruption is none other than *libido* itself: what throws a (future) subject "out of joint" is none other than the traumatic encounter with *jouissance*.
>
> (2000, 289)

This description is followed by an equation: "drive equals *jouissance* since *jouissance* is ... 'pleasure in pain,' that is, a perverted pleasure provided by the very painful experience of repeatedly missing one's goal" (2000, 297). Lacan (1969–1970) himself insists that "the path towards death is nothing other than what is called *jouissance*" (18). Nonetheless, one understands Žižek's reticence to invoke libido and jouissance: stressing the link between jouissance and death drive risks implying that jouissance is the *cause* of the death drive, that death drive is *epiphenomenal* rather than—such is Žižek's implication—a "meta-causative" force. Although Žižek often fails to stress this connection, it is vital, in bridging philosophical and clinical domains, to highlight that the death drive necessarily entails jouissance. Doing so goes some way to accounting for the repetitive—and indeed *compulsive*—quality of death drive phenomena that are so central to Freud, and it stresses the intimate relation between that which is excessive, traumatic, and the sexual.

In pointing out a possible inconsistency in Žižek's (and Lacan's) descriptions of death drive, we point to a bifurcation with Lacanian theory itself. It starts to become apparent that, for Lacan, there are two related theorizations—or modes—of death drive. Rather than seeking to pre-emptively resolve this apparent incompatibility (death drive as libidinal surplus or ontological impasse), let us deepen the apparent disparity by foregrounding the factor of symbolic mortification.

## Undead Life and Symbolic Mortification

Lacan often insists that death drive is a function of the symbolic order. For example: "If everything that is immanent ... in the chain of natural events may be considered as subject to the ... death drive, it is only because there is a signifying chain" (Lacan 1959–1960, 212). If we take this emphasis on symbolic mortification to its logical conclusion, we confront:

> the possibility of ... the radical annihilation of the symbolic texture through which ... so-called reality is constituted. The very existence of the symbolic order implies a possibility of its radical effacement, of "symbolic death"—not the death of the ... "real object" in its symbol, but the obliteration of the signifying network itself.
>
> (Žižek 1989, 132)

Žižek offers a related clarification which assists us also in respect of the problem of understanding death drive primarily as type of libidinal substance:

> The trap to be avoided . . . is that of conceiving this pure life drive as a substantial entity subsisting prior to its being captured in the Symbolic network: this "optical illusion" renders invisible that it is the very mediation of the Symbolic order that transforms the organic "instinct" into an unquenchable longing. . . . [T]his "pure life" beyond death . . . is it not the *product* of symbolization, so that symbolization itself engenders the surplus that escapes it?
>
> (2006a, 145)

In short, the appearance of an outside of the symbolic (a "pure life" of the death drive, for example) must itself be viewed as produced via instances of signification. These foregoing conceptualizations helpfully prioritize the role of the signifier and the symbolic in making a higher order of death possible. And yet, is Žižek not going too far here? This prioritization of the signifier seems to risk demoting the libidinal dimension to a strictly secondary role, even so in the processes of "radical effacement" which are clearly infused with jouissance. Recall Freud's (1924) "even the subject's destruction of himself cannot take place without libidinal satisfaction" (170). Then again, Žižek's previous reference to an optical illusion is instructive insofar as it suggests that there are two adjacent theories of death drive. Our task now is to clarify the difference between these two related theorizations and consider how they might work in conjunction.

We should insist then that death drive often presents exactly as an excessive libidinal force, as a type of "unholy" animation which exceeds the parameters of that which is life-sustaining or pleasurable. In such circumstances we confront a deathly or "undead" life (of jouissance/libido) animated by the denatured, circuit of the drive. Yet, in addition to this there is also the state of symbolic mortification, of being rendered *dead while alive*. What is required then is a reconfiguration of how *both* life and death are to be understood:

> Life is the horrible palpitation of the . . . "undead" drive which persists beyond ordinary death; death is the symbolic order itself, the structure which, as a parasite, colonizes the living entity. What defines the death drive in Lacan is this double gap: not the simple opposition between life and death, but the split of life itself into "normal" life and horrifying 'undead' life, and the split of the dead into "ordinary" dead and the "undead" Machine.
>
> (Žižek 2008, 112)

We can thus distinguish between *the phenomena of "undead" life* (the libidinal animation of jouissance), on the one hand, and the condition of being *made dead while still alive* (the function of symbolic mortification), on the other:

> For a human being to be "dead while alive" is to be colonized by the "dead" symbolic order; to be "alive while dead" is to give body to the remainder of

Life-Substance.... [W]e are dealing ... [here with] the split between ... the "dead" symbolic order which mortifies the body and the non-symbolic Life-Substance *of jouissance*.

(2008, 112)

The notion of the death drive applies then to two apparently discontinuous spheres: that of symbolic mortification (death in or via the symbolic order) and that in which the obscene stuff of enjoyment overruns the self-preservative imperatives of the organism (a type of *deathly—or "undead"—life*). This goes some way to addressing our earlier concerns in respect of how Žižek invoked the death drive simultaneously as excessive libidinal "substance" (jouissance) and as form of negativity (the mortification imposed by the symbolic). The dual location of the death drive is also thus illuminated, that is, the fact that the death drive is both (as libidinal force) *of* the subject and psychical as such, yet also of the broader ontological realm more generally.

## Failure, Jouissance, Drive, Subject

We have covered much ground since the beginning of this chapter. Yet at least two issues remain. We have seen, first, how the Lacanian death drive may be taken as negative inherence, a type of "active nothing" or, more precisely, an instance of "the self-disruption of substance ... its inner malfunctioning" (Johnston 2008, 189). This theorization, elegant as it may be, seems to fall short in accounting for the *agency*—indeed, the self-sabotaging quality—so frequently attributed to the death drive. Second, we have seen that the death drive is tantamount to a type of "supra-agency," both in the sense that it is capable of over-riding other forms of agency (such as the pleasure/reality principle) and in the sense that as a transcendental form it eludes a natural/biological order of causality. The death drive could thus be said to be "meta-causative." What then causes—or acts as the origin of—the drive? The most direct means of unlocking these two inter-related dilemmas—of the agency and the causative capability of the drive—involves the idea of the drive's own inner impossibility. It requires, more to the point, engaging the death drive *as drive*.

To appreciate the specificity of the concept of the drive, we need, first, to distinguish drive from desire:

[D]esire concerns the gap that forever separates it from its object, it is about the lacking object; drive, by contrast takes the lack itself as object, finding a satisfaction in the circular movement of missing satisfaction itself.

(Žižek 2014, 372–373)

Two points should immediately be stressed here: first, drive is object-less, and, second, it entails satisfaction (jouissance) at its own failure (an important fact apropos the self-sabotaging aspect of death drive.) Žižek frequently revisits this distinction in ways that stress the inherent deathliness of the drive:

[The] movement called "drive" is not driven by the "impossible" quest for the lost object; *it is a push to directly enact the "loss"—the gap, cut, distance—itself*. . . .

> [D]rive is not an infinite longing ... which gets fixated onto a partial object; "drive" IS this fixation itself in which resides the "deathly" dimension of every drive.
> (Žižek 2009, 229)

So, in the case of desire, there is invariably something of the (lacking) object at play, an object that the subject wishes—via a series of metonymic displacements—to reclaim. Drive, by contrast, is the libidinal stuckness that occurs *en route* to the ostensible object of desire, which, in the final analysis, is dispensable. It is in the action of the drive that a *denatured* element appears: "We become 'humans,'" states Žižek, "when we get caught into a closed, self-propelling loop of repeating the same gesture and finding satisfaction in it" (2008, 63). The specifically human dimension arises "when a mere by-product is elevated into an autonomous aim.... [M]an perceives as a direct goal what for the animal has no intrinsic value" (Žižek 2008, 61).

This libidinal factor—that is, the compulsion to enjoy—helps us understand something about both the force (the agency) and the self-thwarting quality of the death drive. What had seemed an inconsistency regarding the exact nature of the death drive (i.e., libidinal surplus or ontological negativity) is now easier to grasp. These two factors must be understood in tandem. They are necessarily interwoven in the sense that a given failure itself becomes libidinized, a source of jouissance. Žižek recalls here the fort/da game, noting that something here has gone wrong: the child's mother is absent, and symbolization is the (failed) means of restitution through which the loss is both enacted and repetitively "enjoyed" (Žižek and Daly 2004).

How though to grasp the causative power, and more than that, the origin, of the death drive? Well, we can argue that the drive does not need an origin, certainly not in the sense of an originating object or activity or process beyond the sphere of its own activity. All that drive requires is a *failure*—particularly of a minimally traumatic sort—that then becomes gratifyingly rearticulated, *enjoyed*. It is in this way that we should read Žižek's (2010) description of the death drive as *self-relating negativity*, that is, via the role of a type of mediating *jouissance*. In his description of the logical prehistory of the drive, Žižek notes:

> [D]rives are ... not simply happy self-enclosed circular movements that generate pleasure; their circular movement is a repeated failure, a repeated attempt to encircle some central void.... [T]he drive is not a primordial fact.... [W]hat logically precedes the drive is the ontological failure—the thwarted movement towards a goal, some form of radical ontological negativity—and the basic operation of the drive is to find enjoyment in the very failure to reach full enjoyment.
> (2014, 206)

It is easier now to understand how the drive is at once asubjective ("acephalous") and yet, via the impetus of the enjoyment it incurs, also a mediator between the not-yet-subject and the subject (or, the *instinctual* and the properly *human*). Fink develops just such an argument in insisting that "the drives involved in compulsive repetition of the traumatic ... seek to insert the subject in some way, to bring the subject into being where formerly there had been no subject" (2014, 62). Of the multiple paradoxes that we have encountered in this overview of Lacan's rearticulation of the death drive, this is perhaps both the most challenging and also the most crucial: the idea that the death drive is the "self-relating negativity," that is, the libidinally gratifying act of failure, which opens up the possibility of the subject.

## References

Fink, Bruce. 2014. *Against Understanding: Commentary and Critique in a Lacanian Key*. New York & London: Routledge.

Freud, Sigmund. 1924. "The Economic Problem of Masochism." In *Standard Edition of the Complete Psychological Works of Sigmund Freud*. Vol. 19. Translated by James Strachey, 159–170. New York: Norton, 1961.

Johnston, Adrian. 2008. *Žižek's Ontology*. Evanston, IL: Northwestern University Press.

Lacan, Jacques. 1953. "The Function and Field of Speech and Language in Psychoanalysis." In *Écrits the First Complete Edition in English*. Translated by Bruce Fink, 197–268. New York: Norton, 2006.

———. 1955. "Seminar on 'The Purloined Letter.'" In *Écrits the First Complete Edition in English*. Translated by Bruce Fink, 6–48. New York: Norton, 2006.

———. 1959–1960. *The Ethics of Psychoanalysis: The Seminar of Jacques Lacan*, Book VII. Edited by Jacques-Alain Miller. Translated by Dennis Porter. London: Norton, 1992

———. 1969–1970. *The Other Side of Psychoanalysis: The Seminar of Jacques Lacan*, Book XVII. Edited by Jacques-Alain Miller. Translated by Russell Grigg. New York: Norton, 2007.

Lear, Jonathan. 2000. *Happiness, Death, and the Remainder of Life*. Cambridge, MA: Harvard University Press.

Žižek, Slavoj. 1989. *The Sublime Object of Ideology*. London: Verso.

———. 1999a. "There is No Sexual Relationship." In *The Žižek Reader*. Edited by Elizabeth Wright and Edmond Wright, 174–205. London: Blackwell.

———. 1999b. "Death and the Maiden." In *The Žižek Reader*. Edited by Elizabeth Wright and Edmond Wright, 206–221. London: Blackwell.

———. 2000. *The Ticklish Subject: The Absent Centre of Political Ontology*. London: Verso.

———. 2006a. "A Hair of the Dog that Bit You." In *Interrogating the Real*. Edited by Rex Butler and Scott Stephens, 126–154. London: Continuum.

———. 2006b. *The Parallax View*. Cambridge, MA: MIT Press.

———. 2008. *The Plague of Fantasies*. London: Verso.

———. 2009. "An Answer to Two Questions." In *Adrian Johnston, Badiou, Žižek, and Political Transformations*, 174–230. Evanston, IL: Northwestern University Press.

———. 2010. *Living in the End Times*. London: Verso.

———. 2013. "Lacan as Philosopher." http://darkecologies.com/2013/05/04/slavoj-zizek-on-lacan-as-philosopher.

———. 2014. *Absolute Recoil: Toward a New Foundation for Dialectical Materialism*. London: Verso.

Žižek, Slavoj and Glyn Daly. 2004. *Conversations with Žižek*. Cambridge: Polity.

Part III

# The Drive in the Clinic, Culture, and Art

Chapter 17

# Beyond the Breach

Drive in the Case of a Traumatic Neurosis

*Kristen Hennessy*

---

*Kristen Hennessy is an analyst who works primarily with children in the foster system in rural Pennsylvania. Here she presents a case from her practice as an occasion to consider the partial drives and specifically the partial drives in a case of traumatic neurosis. The case illustrates well how the drives are governed by language as the perpetrator of sexual abuse on the child in question obscured his deeds by using an alternate set of words and phrases to name his activities. The obfuscating language and the enforced secrecy of the abuse forced the child to behave in "inappropriate" ways in social settings, in fact satisfying the partial drives in a manner that classical psychoanalysis calls "acting out." Also apparent in the case are how the child's body was overwritten by the abuse that she suffered. Hennessy's treatment of her young patient involves a kind of rewriting of the child's drive.*

## Introduction

This chapter explores the partial drives through a case of traumatic neurosis. In this case, in which names and other identifying details have been changed, a child survivor of commercial sexual exploitation presents with an extraordinarily troubled relationship to her body and to the partial drives. The child's difficulty managing the partial drives endangers her wellbeing, and we see the child create ways to manage the partial drives as the case unfolds, first through play, and then through language. Names and other identifying details have been changed to protect confidentiality. Through the case of Elizabeth, we are able to explore the partial drives within the context of traumatic neurosis.

## History

Elizabeth lived with her biological parents, Jerry and Brenda, until she was two years old, when the parents divorced and Jerry successfully petitioned the courts for custody of the little girl, citing the mother's intellectual disability and the poor conditions of her home. Jerry quickly began to groom and then sexually abuse the child. He trafficked her, selling her to other pedophiles for specific periods of time. In an effort to conceal the abuse, he used linguistic tricks in which he taught the child incorrect signifiers for acts of abuse. For example, he referred to incidents in which he penetrated her with his fingers as "playing" and he referred to events in which he sold her to other for sexual abuse as "tea parties." He concealed the abuse through these linguistic tricks but also through his reference to the law. He told the child that they were both breaking the law and showed her child pornography that culminated in the arrest of both adult and child. Furthermore, he arranged for the child to be raped at a "tea party" by a man dressed as a police officer. Elizabeth's life with her father was structured around the abuse and sale of the child.

Jerry presented the child to the world as a mentally ill and medically fragile child, often carrying her around town, like a doll rather than a child, despite her perfectly adequate capacity to walk on her own. When Elizabeth was five years old, he enrolled her in kindergarten in a program for children with mental illness. There, the child signaled to that which could not be said: she stripped, masturbated, and sucked suggestively on markers, sometimes attacking adults who came close. Finally, when the child was seven years old, an exasperated teacher asked the naked, masturbating child, "Elizabeth, where did you learn this?" Elizabeth whispered, "Daddy!" before kicking the teacher in the genitals and running out of the school. Her actions were finally understood as an attempt to speak. The teacher contacted the authorities, Elizabeth entered foster care, and we began our work the next day.

The chaos of her life did not end for quite some time. Elizabeth was initially placed with a couple that believed that they were infertile, and she was to be the baby they could not have, a difficult position for any child. When, a year into Elizabeth's placement, the foster mother became unexpectedly pregnant, they requested that Elizabeth move, and she lost those caregivers as well. With her first foster family, she functioned as a placeholder rather than a subject.

Elizabeth's next set of foster parents thought that Elizabeth's significant symptoms were the result of what they termed a "lack of discipline," which they intended to provide. They terrorized the child further, subjecting her to extreme forms of physical punishment, and she was removed from their care when their "discipline" resulted in the child sustaining a concussion. This concussion was in dialogue with the treatment—the family was not consistently taking her to her sessions, and Elizabeth protested this, ultimately getting into an argument in the car when they took her to church instead of to my office. It was during this altercation that she was seriously injured. In this home, the theme of inaccurate or misleading signifiers continued. In the family of origin, the father simply gave inaccurate words. In this foster family, the child was given signifiers that seemed to capture something of what the parents believed about what they were doing, while concealing their violence. For example, her foster father used the signifiers of "teaching" and "Biblical parenting" to refer to acts such as submerging the child in ice water and shoving dirty clothing in the child's mouth as punishment. Her biological father taught her inaccurate signifiers, and this foster family provided her with misleading signifiers to describe her experiences in their care.

After the concussion, Elizabeth was placed with the family that ultimately adopted her. She was one of several foster and adoptive children in a home with parents who believed that they were called by God to foster and adopt. This was the first home in which she was not the only child, and this seemed to take some of the pressure off of the child—there was a status of "child" that she could occupy, alongside other children. Indeed, at her adoption, she wore a shirt with the family's last name and the number eight on it—she was the eighth child to be adopted by the family. For a child singled out for abuse, being one of eight was a relief.

## Treatment: Establishing a Protective Barrier

> *Protection* against stimuli is an almost more important function for the living organism than *reception* of stimuli. The protective shield is supplied with its own store of energy and must above all endeavor to preserve the special modes of transformation of energy operating in it against the effects threatened by the enormous energies at work in the external world—effects which tend towards a leveling out of them and hence towards destruction.
>
> (Freud 1920, 27, italics Freud)

Seven-year-old Elizabeth presented as a terrified and highly dissociative child who did not even recognize me or my office from session to session. I noticed a pattern of four presentations, which she revealed corresponded to four versions of her name (Elizabeth, Liz, Beth, and Eliza). In one type of session, she rocked silently, seemingly in a trance. In the next, she behaved seductively, strutting around the office and offering to make me "feel good." In the third, she hid inside the tent, peeking out and then suddenly retreating. In a fourth type of session, she behaved as a feral cat, crawling around the office and yowling and hissing at me. I asked her at the end of each session if she would like to return, and she consistently agreed, even in her cat form, meowing and nodding. She was far from able to articulate a demand for treatment, but I offered her what agency I could, attempting to communicate to this terrified child that I saw her as a subject.

When we started our work, the thirty-five-pound eight-year-old was not eating, drinking, or defecating. Elizabeth was at risk of medical hospitalization. Her body and its orifices and needs posed an unmanageable problem. Her inability to manage the partial drives placed her in medical danger.

After a month of regular sessions, the child did something different: Elizabeth urinated on the tent and crawled inside. This was a kind of primitive claiming, a symbolic means of creating an interior and exterior. She went inside the tent for every session thereafter for several months. Elizabeth's fluctuations in presentation continued, but she consistently requested food from inside the tent, either by saying "hungry!" or, as the cat, meowing urgently and gesturing to her mouth and belly. I brought a large selection of play food, naming each food. She said "yes" or nodded assent to some, which I placed in front of the tent. Elizabeth waited until I backed away before reaching out and pulling the food inside. With the food inside, she pretended to gobble some up with elaborate demonstrations of pleasure, while making loud disgusted sounds and violently ejecting other food back out of the tent. I highlighted her agency, and made comments such as, "You can say yes, and you can say no" and "You decide what comes in." In the case of the profoundly abused child, the erogenous zones are not yet mediated via speech as much as they have been mediated through brute force. The capacity to choose became necessary for her to respond to the demands of adults in her life—including the demand for the child to survive.

The child verbalized her hunger, and then made decisions at two levels—first, which foods went into her tent, and second, which foods entered her body. I was careful to respect the sanctity of her tent, and never touched or opened the flaps myself. In doing so, the child was playing both about hunger and its satisfaction, but also about the boundaries of her body. There was an interior and exterior to her body and she had some control over what enters and exits. She began to eat outside of sessions, carrying around a lunchbox out of which she accepted some foods and rejected others. She began to defecate more regularly as well, although, as we will see, her relationship to bowel movements remained troubled for years to come.

Elizabeth accomplished what she had set out to do with the tent. She wrapped herself tightly within the cloth of the tent, wiggled free before presenting herself in a heap at my feet, delivering herself. She crawled around the office, babbled in baby talk, then whispered: "Bad people coming! Save me!" Elizabeth delivered herself into a world where there were bad people against which she had a chance of protection. Having moved beyond the tent, she began to appeal to an Other. The child needed to experience having a body before she could come to request protection for that body. The tent allowed her to have an interior and exterior, to begin to experience herself as having a body that begins and that ends. This marked the transition to a new phase of her treatment. In this initial phase, Elizabeth was focused on creating a "protective crust" of the sort that Freud speaks of in *Beyond the Pleasure Principle* (Freud 1920, 168–169).

## Translation

Next, she began to focus more directly on the problem of her father, using a stuffed dog in the process. Just as she had multiple names for herself, she had different names for her father, each representing a different aspect of her thoughts about him. She wrote Daddy Dog love letters and begged for forgiveness for telling on him, spanked Naughty Daddy, and alternately mocked the incarcerated Jail Bird and hatched elaborate plans to free him. This took on a different tenor as she began to talk to me about the fights in her head between Elizabeth, Liz, Beth, and Eliza. I encouraged her to elaborate as fully as possible the stance of each. Over time, I could prompt elaboration by saying, "But Liz thinks," and later I could just say "But on the other hand." She began to recall each session consistently, called herself Elizabeth, and stopped talking about voices. She settled on one name for her father: Mean Daddy. This name seemed to be an integration of sorts—a daddy who is mean, representing both the "mean" and "daddy" aspects of her father.

Alongside this, Elizabeth began the project of symbolizing her experiences of abuse. She often developed a conversion symptom right at the start of a session and spent her time putting the experience into words with the symptom resolving throughout the session. For example, Elizabeth developed paralysis that resolved when she gave an in-depth account of being held at gunpoint or felt pain in her toe that resolved when she articulated an experience of a man ripping out her toenail. This was difficult work, but it led to significant reduction in intrusive phenomena. This work not only involved the difficult work of putting the real into speech, it involved a process of translation. Through speech, the real drained from her body.

Elizabeth came to understand that she had been taught incorrect signifiers for certain signifieds. "Playing a game" only euphemistically, at best, refers to a sexual act. She not only lacked the signifiers that could communicate her experiences to others, but she was also unaware that they did not link to a shared signified. When, at five years old, she fearfully told a child protective services caseworker that her daddy plays games with her and takes her to tea parties, she was genuinely confused that the case worker smiled and said that sounds like fun. The child needed to learn new signifiers, signifiers that referenced shared signifieds. She needed to learn signifiers to become able to communicate her experiences, words for the parts of her body, words for sexual acts.

As the child learned more signifiers and became aware that some of the signifiers in her lexicon have very different signifieds than those she had been taught, the child embarked on a project of translation. She slid between her two languages—the private language of her family and a shared language. There may be a way that each family has a private language that gets unpacked in the course of an analysis, but this is certainly unique in the degree to which the private language worked to intentionally avoid shared meanings. She also developed a third way of speaking, a way that seemed to bridge the two. In this category, she used the signifiers taught to her by her father while also acknowledging, through her intonation, that she knew that this was a kind of a code, and not shared references. If she said, "We *played a game*," I was to understand that she was referring to an incident of sexual abuse, but if she said, "We played a game," I was to understand that they had played a game, such as checkers. Over time, she was less satisfied with this as an answer, and began to put the translation process into words itself, using both the words taught by her father, as well as the new signifiers she had learned. For example, she might say: "He took me to a *tea party*, you know, a hotel where men were there to rape me."

## Dreams and History

As she dealt with her painful history, Elizabeth was quite capable of free association, but she struggled to see manifestations of the unconscious as something in which she, Elizabeth, was implicated. For example, regarding a transference dream, she asked me, "Why would you do that?" as though this was an event, not a dream. She needed repeated prompts to remind her that it was a dream that *she* had, not something I did. In other words, she struggled to see her dreams as coming from her mind, as fantasies of which she was the author, instead reacting as though these events occurred in the world. This highlights a key point in the treatment of traumatic neurosis: the threat is experienced as coming from without rather than from within.

> And secondly, a particular way is adopted of dealing with any internal excitations that produce too great an increase of unpleasure: there is a tendency to treat them as though they were acting, not from the inside, but from the outside, so that it may be possible to bring the shield against stimuli into operation as a means of defence against them.
>
> (Freud 1920, 33)

Elizabeth needed to symbolize the external threat such that she could speak about fantasy and desire. She needed to learn to differentiate between what comes from the outside, versus what comes from within.

Early in her treatment, she had the types of dreams one would expect in traumatic neurosis: she dreamt about the traumas she experienced, in order to avoid being caught unaware this time around. It was only as the treatment progressed that she began to have dreams about other things. Perhaps this is where her case begins to go beyond Freud's *Beyond the Pleasure Principle*—when the focus shifts away from the breach of the protective crust and she begins to speak about her own desire. Perhaps the process of symbolization patched the breach or allowed the protective crust to reform. This is, perhaps, what occurs in later stages of treatment of traumatic neurosis. The analysand whose symptoms formed around such a breach does not become a different kind of neurotic, and yet, the focus is no longer on the breach, but on the drive.

One such moment of transition is as follows: Elizabeth was angry with her mother and caseworker for leaving her out of an outing, and she was angry with me because I did not receive an email from her mother that Elizabeth wanted to speak with me in time to arrange for an extra session. This was a situation in which Elizabeth had a hand—she would typically call me herself about such matters.

The next day, Elizabeth reported the following dream. "You and I were in your office with Stacy" (her caseworker). "I don't know why Stacy was there, that makes no sense. One of the guys from the *parties* was there, one of the rapists, I don't know his name. And all of a sudden, you and Stacy were gone. Well, not gone. You were, shall we say, *ashes*." Elizabeth struggled to speak more: "Uh, that makes no sense—it wouldn't really happen," and she began to cry.

> After a while, I said, "Well, lots of dreams are wishes."
> She replied suspiciously. "Yeah, I know."
> "And Stacy and I were piles of ashes?"

She replied suspiciously, "So what?"

I said, "You were pretty angry with us yesterday—"

Elizabeth began to laugh. "Well, let's just say that the man from the party killed you. That's why you were ashes, you were dead. The man had help. It was me. Well, it's more like I killed you and he helped. I said that I was a doctor, and you were here for surgery. I told you that you would fall asleep, and we would do surgery, or, shall I say, *surgery*, until you die. Or almost die. Then you wake up and want to know what's happening and I tell you that nothing's wrong, we're just doing a little surgery." We spent quite some time following her associations, the details of which carried much significance.

With this dream, Elizabeth engaged in translation of her own. She referred to violent stabbing as *surgery*, clearly aware (and enjoying) that calling this violence *surgery* was to engage in deception, to prevent me from having the ability to escape her violence. She was no longer the passive recipient of this kind of struggle—she was the deceiver, not the deceived. There was also a new capacity for play and metaphor—in talking of the dream, she became aware that the torture and murder of the dream is but a dream. There is finally space in her case for metaphor. Unlike in her history, no one has to die. It was just a dream.

This points to the significance of the dream. The dream is no longer a typical nightmare of traumatic neurosis in which the wish is to not be caught unprepared for the shock of the trauma:

> We may assume, rather, that dreams are helping to carry out another task, which must be accomplished before the dominance of the pleasure principle can even begin. These dreams are endeavouring to master the stimulus retrospectively, by developing the anxiety whose omission was the cause of the traumatic neurosis.
> (Freud 1920, 32)

Despite the similarity in the content, this dream showed a transition from passivity to activity in a manner that was reminiscent of the infamous fort/da game: "As the child passes over from the passivity of the experience to the activity of the game, he hands on the disagreeable experiences to one of his playmates and in this way revenges himself on a substitute" (Freud 1920, 17). The initial recounting of the dream involved Elizabeth responding to the violence of someone else, but the retelling takes us to her own aggressive urges.

The dream calls to mind the fort/da game on other levels as well. Elizabeth was working to master the trauma of her mother and caseworker leaving her for a period of time. She was playing about the capacity to make them go permanently, and to be in physical control of adults in her current life, master of their presence and absence. Her own agency was in question. Perhaps most significantly, the dream lodged a complaint against adults in her present life, not her history. In cases of foster care and adoption, there is often a moment where the symptom shifts from that which addresses the family of origin alone to that which addresses the foster or adoptive family either alone or as a kind of combined symptom that manages to address both family systems.

## Returning to Life

Elizabeth began to want to engage in the world, campaigning for permission to participate in sports and clubs. Outside of sessions, Elizabeth focused on learning more about the world and what it offers, learning a bit more about what she liked and disliked. There were ways that this called to mind her experiences in the tent. At this point, Elizabeth said "yes" to trying certain activities and "no" to others, and engaged enthusiastically with some while rejecting others. She became more aware of her own interests. Some of these interests, such as painting, allowed her to express herself in new ways.

The gaze was prominent at this point of the case. Elizabeth was unaware that people could see her when she was in a trance state, and she sometimes engaged in behaviors that were highly socially inappropriate. Elizabeth was reported by teachers to be masturbating in class, sometimes while still actively participating in the class. When we spoke about this, she told me that she did not realize that she could be seen by others—that her own vision got hazy when she thought about sexual matters and that she did not realize that her teachers could see what she was doing. This realization was mortifying to Elizabeth, and she stopped masturbating at school.

Her fantasy life was quite active. In particular, she repeatedly fantasized that she was pregnant and in labor, attended to by a mixture of people from the child protective services world, her clinical team, and her family. The idea of giving birth made her feel aroused, and this arousal was associated to the pain of sexual assault, something she could make sense of through the process of labor. She spoke a lot about the idea of being cared for and of feeling a painful sexual feeling. Despite imagining that others could not see her during times when she felt sexual, this fantasy involved all of these people witnessing her painful aroused state.

## Not Choosing/Not Going

Elizabeth had solved several problems connected to the partial drives via her process of saying "yes" and "no" to various foods and experiences. Her bowel symptoms took longer to resolve. Analysts working with children with abuse histories involving anal penetration should be aware that medical assessment and intervention may be warranted alongside analytic treatment. In Elizabeth's case, anal stenosis, a condition caused by scarring of the anus, required medical intervention. Years after medical treatment, Elizabeth had times when she became physically ill, vomiting, with intense stomach pain alongside painful constipation. Elizabeth ultimately revealed that, at these times, she had stopped taking her medications to treat her bowel issues. This was initially puzzling to her, but she noticed that she tended to do this when she was facing a decision she did not wish to make.

For example, Elizabeth was asked by a group of girls and boys to go to a movie. She wanted to go, but the situation felt a bit like a group date, and she felt uncertain if she was ready for something like this. She told her friends that she would go but then stopped taking the medication that allows her to have regular bowel movements. I noted to her that she *chose* not to go ("go" here meaning both having a bowel movement and attending the social event) by not taking her medication. She said that it felt to her that she did want to go but that she also did not and that it felt to her that she was finding a way out of making a choice. "If I get sick, I can't go, but it's not me saying that I don't want to go." By not taking her medication, she made it such that she could no longer go. In doing so, she also caused herself to bloat, and experience pain (and pleasure) and was in the position of being ill and attended to (at least by her adoptive mother) while she expelled something from her body, much like the aforementioned pregnancy fantasy. Of course, she knew that was, indeed, full of shit. At this point, sessions focus on her own unconscious acts.

## Discussion

This case focuses on the partial drives in the context of a traumatic neurosis. Elizabeth came to treatment with a case of severe traumatic neurosis, with a crisis of the partial drives that connected to the ways in which demand was not mediated through language but rather inflicted upon the body of the child quite directly and brutally. At the start of her analysis, the child focused on establishing a metaphorical protective crust that had never been given a chance to form, allowing the child to experience a kind of protection from external threat. This case shows us the operation of the drive in a child whose metaphorical protective crust did not yet have a chance to form.

We see that the first task to treatment was to develop a protective barrier, an inner and an outer, that could allow the child to exist. Without this protective crust, she is so overwhelmed by the partial drives that her very survival is at risk. Her case teaches us that the subject requires a protective barrier in order to begin to regulate the drives themselves and reminds us that a child's very survival can depend on this capacity. Of course, this protective crust is symbolic and yet is nevertheless vital to her capacity to manage the partial drives sufficiently for the child to survive.

In the second phase of treatment, Elizabeth set about symbolizing her experiences, with a focus on the real and horrifying events of her young life. Although she continued to deal with the partial drives in this second phase of treatment, she was primarily focused on what was inflicted upon her body by others.

It was not until the later phase of her analysis that she was able to recognize and work with her own fantasy life, where Elizabeth was able to truly work with the partial drives in direct contact with her desire. Of course, this is too simplistic, and she moved between these three stances repeatedly throughout the treatment.

Elizabeth's case also highlights the importance of diagnosis: Elizabeth's case is one of traumatic neurosis, with the overarching question of the Other regarding the Other's role in the breach of the protective barrier. This is important because the analysand with traumatic neurosis is at risk for being read either as a hysteric—given the strong similarities in presentation, this is not a surprise—or as a psychotic. Both types of misrecognition can limit what the treatment can accomplish and can focus treatment at the wrong register.

Furthermore, this case serves as a reminder that the analyst is looking for the child to work with the unconscious material, *not* to place blame on the child for the abuse the child suffered. One would hope that this would go without saying, but there continues to be a subset of analysts who forget that children do not create the circumstances of their lives, who continue to believe that children cause adults to rape them. Children are sexual, and their sexuality does not cause abuse. We ought not ask analysands: "How did you create COVID-19, racism, or the hurricane that flooded your home?" Instead, we ask analysands *what they did* with those experiences in their lives, how they interacted with those events, and where their subjective stake landed in response. The child does not choose their circumstances, but the child has freedom—and responsibility—in the way that they respond. This is, in fact, the path to the cure.

Because the child's troubled relationship to the drive was so focused on this protective crust, both the literal sanctity of her body and its right to avoid violating penetration, the child needed a space to develop a self and then to learn to speak not only of the horrors that come from without, but the thoughts and wishes that belong to the child. Restoring a sense of inner and outer was crucial to allowing the child to ultimately work with her fantasy.

## Reference

Freud, Sigmund. 1920. "Beyond the Pleasure Principle." In *Standard Edition of the Complete Psychological Works of Sigmund Freud*. Vol. 18. Translated by James Strachey, 3–64. New York: Norton, 1955.

Chapter 18

# Where the Image Falls
## The Drive of the Living Body in Analysis

*Kate Briggs*

---

*Kate Briggs, an Australian analyst, here details two cases. What's striking about her paper is that it emphasizes the drive as following the itinerary of the signifier. Crucial statements heard by the subject govern the drive and become part of the subject's drive vocabulary. Quoting Jacques-Alain Miller, Briggs notes that the speech of the subject is an attempt to "master and efface" the drive and its satisfactions. Especially to be applauded here is Briggs's observation that attention to the drive is what distinguishes psychoanalysis from psychotherapy. Her careful analysis allows Briggs to bring to the forefront the body and its jouissance in both of her cases. This essay stands as an important contribution to the clinic of psychoanalysis, an attempt to delineate what is at stake beyond the therapeutic calming of unruly drives. What's at stake is their satisfaction.*

What are we afraid of? Of our body. This is what the curious phenomenon that I spent a whole year on in my Seminar, which I called *Anxiety*, shows.
In our body, precisely, anxiety is situated somewhere other than fear. It is the feeling that arises from the presentiment that comes to reduce us to our bodies. It is the feeling that arises from the presentiment that we are being reduced to our body. It is quite curious that the debility of the *parlêtre* had led him so far as to grasp that anxiety is not the fear of anything that the body could provide the motivation for. It is the fear of fear.
—Jacques Lacan, "The Third"

The concept of the *parlêtre* hinges—this is what I am putting forward—on the originary equivalence between unconscious and drive.
—Jacques-Alain Miller, "*Habeas Corpus*"

During the time of the COVID-19 pandemic, people said that the body was more present than ever, and regardless of the viruses we carry, is it not jouissance that determines whether we are at home or not with our complaints? In the clinic, when encountering the pains and paralyses of hysterics, Freud was struck by the evident construction of the hysteric's body along the lines of ideas and words rather than anatomy (Lacan 1964b, 12). The contemporary clinic witnesses the too much of the body affected by a drive without limit, particularly evident in eating disorders and addictions. But which body? The living body is not symbolic or imaginary. It is a body affected by jouissance and repetition and as such prevails in every symptom, for "there is no jouissance without a body" (Miller 2017, 98), and the symptom is an event of the body providing satisfaction of the drive: "The body affected by jouissance is neither imaginary not symbolic, but a living one" (Miller 2001, 22–23). Lacan spoke of the drives as effects of speech echoing in the body, as headless, without a subject, noting that they separate the subject and desire (1964a). Yet they can also function to circumscribe and hollow out an edge or rim that taken into signification can help knot signifier and the body in a consistency for the speaking being whose body is marked by language. By way of clinical vignettes, this chapter considers the living body brought into the session and seeks to illustrate how, as a treatment of jouissance, psychoanalysis affects the body by drawing attention to the subject of the drive. For the "vital point, the point of emergence of . . . [the] speaking being, is this disturbed relation to our bodies that is called jouissance" (Lacan 1971–1972, 31–32).

The body is impossible for each of us in particular ways, being at the confluence of excitation, sexual difference, reproduction, ageing, life, and death. In some respects, it functions as a hole in the symbolic: the impossible real marked there in the very material life that sustains us. The disjunction between the subject and the body is amplified in forms of addiction and cutting where to have a body that one abuses in response to the Other's demand is a sign of the impossibility of separating from it—the lacerated body of protest, a sign that "one cannot subtract one's body" from the Other (Miller 2001). To make the body the site of impossibility through addiction—an engineering of the drive—is to demonstrate the insistence of demand taken to a further reach of impulse, a circuit into which the subject of speech might break. To consider how the unconscious might graft itself onto the real body of the drive (Lacan 1975–1976), let's take two vignettes.

Gina, an African American woman married with three children and stable employment, contacts me after hearing me speak. Her complaint is the way she disappears, waiting to be seen and suffering from the sense no one "told her how to be a person"; she wants to find a discourse for the film-making practice she abandoned.

After cutting the session one morning as she complained of having no time that day and of people at work not recognizing all that she does, she recounts in the next session how she felt angry with me, thought of not coming back or coming back to say she would not return, then registered that this is what she does and drove to work without anxiety for the first time. A first step in her analysis was to register the repetition in her sense of being excluded, the jouissance that repeats in feeling herself abandoned, just as she was as a child to a mother who would disappear and not respond. Gina registers the repetition she orchestrates in feeling excluded by an Other whom she sees as non-responsive. This is why she left art school: despite evident interest shown in supporting her career, a particular lecturer had failed to respond to her graduate show. Bringing attention to her demand, how its force stops her from speaking and from asking, introduces a space to which she responds. To register that her mother may not have been able was a first move in locating the suffering of being one who is not seen.

Her mother, who may be "on the spectrum," had struggled to feed and to respond to her daughter, who at one point was said to be starving. Not finding a place in her mother's mind from which as a child she might receive signifiers to latch on to and respond to, left a vacancy that echoes in her complaint of being empty as an adolescent, unable to speak for herself. To clothe the real of that vacancy by way of the image is something inscribed in her work. It is also there in the complaint that her father only took her to cheap clothing stores when as an adolescent she wanted something else, to be fashionable, to be noticed. He nonetheless provided consistency, and in tandem with her mother's lack of interest, his words would mark her symptom. From the lineage of absence—mother's milk, touch, gaze, and words to tell her "who I am"—the gaze as object is distilled while crossed by his comments about what a young woman should do. She and her father were close, and he had said she shouldn't give in to what boys want, not outside marriage nor outside love; she needed to be the one who said "no."

She comments on the look of disgust from people in the supermarket when they see her body as a sign of lack of care, saying that she doesn't want to be seen as someone who can't control herself, but "that's what they see." The drive, the gaze, and judgment form a circuit on and around the abandoned body, the body as a vehicle of sedation. Gina describes learning to "pig out" with a friend from school whose mother, extremely overweight, was close to her friend, just as she wished to be with her own mother. The taste, she says, is secondary to the sensation of swallowing, pushing it down or away: it has to be quick so there is no time to feel anything else. What preceded this induction to bingeing was a sexual experience in adolescence for which she was unprepared: she "didn't know there was a hole there." Despite the trauma of this time "when she didn't have it in her to say 'no,'" she kept this boyfriend for a number of years, valuing his attention while otherwise feeling adrift in a silent suffering of shame. Having felt passed around as a child when her father was working and her mother was not there, she describes her late teens and early twenties as promiscuous, until she married.

In one session, Gina casually mentions she has not been overeating for several weeks, and she has decided it was enough. Having found a place and words to describe the moment where she disappears, she gives up what had been a ritual of consumption. Noting the too much of the object that was never enough, and how this operates in her despair, her relation to her body shifts. Previously, she said, after a session that provoked "some insight" she would plan to pig out that night. Now, she says, she hasn't "done it" for weeks, "this thing that excludes me from everything else."

We might note here a jouissance of the body that initially passes via identification and perhaps for that reason is more easily left behind. Unpacking her adolescent trauma shows that her father's words about being a good girl marked her with shame. At the time, she felt she'd betrayed him, had lost an ideal reflection in his eyes even though or perhaps because he did not know. The ideal she was aiming for as a way of feeling worthy had fallen and was barred, outlawing satisfaction.

Gina brings to the session images of her work, where she had used a camera to capture the gaze of the subject and viewer alike: the split second of recognition, framing the body that speaks to the real of the drive. Of the image that works, she says, "you know it when you see it" and to see the effect on the Other, to see the Other stopped by the image, is "compelling." The image has an impact via the gaze, as an object, that organizes an enjoyment of the body. Other work involves framing the body—her own and later her parents, and this is not incidental—to mark out being excluded by a primal scene.

Body phenomena in ordinary psychoses often point to a body that does not exist, where the surface image of the body is lacking. The subject might complain of not having an existence, of "wanting to live as a dress," or might use tattoos and piercings to try and "staple his or her body" to him- or herself (Stevens 2021). This however is a case of neurosis—where the subject searches for what she is not in the Other. A hole exists in the symbolic, and the body image is negated rather than not formed.

While jouissance is the substance of the living body and is on the side of the Thing, desire comes from and calls out to the Other, asking for an identification: "tell me who I am." As Miller notes, "Desire as desire to be is a desire of recognition in as much as only recognition can confer being upon it" (2011). The silence of the drive comes to enact its work on the body of this subject in the place where identification by way of recognition stalled via the maternal Other. As Lacan said, "Discourse begins from the fact that there is a gaping hole there. . . . When it comes down to it the partner is reduced to a *one*, not just any one, but the one who bore you" (1971, 25–26). Faced with not being seen or heard in the vacancy of her mother's response, Gina attributes to this mother the cause of her sense of non-existing, overlooking that something about femininity cannot be found or represented in the image. The consistency of her father's words about being the good girl who refuses had an impact upon her, giving her over later to the silence of a drive to consume without restraint. Miller (2011) notes how, contrary to desire, which is want-to-be, that which exists was approached by Freud through the drive, and Lacan named it jouissance (Miller 2001).

Freud defined the oral and anal as objects around which the drive turns; Lacan adds the voice and gaze. The drive takes shape as a montage, an apparatus of the body as it sets out from the source of an erogenous zone and returns upon the body; it marks out and might organize the body in this movement. The trajectory or aim of the drive moves out from the rim, around the object *a*, and returns on the rim in an action of hollowing that satisfies the goal of the drive. In returning to the rim, it marks out an object in the form of a semblance. In overconsumption it is as if the drive isn't able to stop, can't abandon the object and return to the body.

We can see Gina's work in shaking loose the identifications (of being not good, unseen) tied to jouissance, linking instead to the unconscious in a way that provokes desire. Her use of the rim of the mouth and throat in swallowing, described in the session, was marked in some of her earlier photographic works. These works circumscribed her body and its jouissance with, for example, an image of a mouth stuffed with hair, an inedible remainder. The object *a* as a stopper for the want-to-be of desire marks out the rim of the mouth, captured in an image. Something can fall from the body, but what to do with it? The camera is used in constructing a space between herself and an Other, between one body and an Other, by way of the gaze object and the image. Thus documenting the space between herself as a subject and her body as an Other, sessions are spent circling and hollowing out this space of lack with words. While the pathos of wanting others to understand without having to tell them what she thinks or feels—that is, without giving up some jouissance by using speech—overwhelms and makes her weep, there is a visible shift.

Returning to the fear arising from the presentiment of being reduced to our body, let us consider the situation of Martin, a forty-year-old functioning alcoholic of Italian descent, who recounts the droning sound of his mother and grandmother complaining about his father and himself on Sunday afternoons over coffee and cake throughout his childhood. The grandson of an authoritarian fascist on his mother's side, his deceased grandfather had regarded him with disdain. Martin comments on "how strong the drive runs" on his mother's side of the family. These afternoons were marked by the moment his mother or grandmother would let him "go for it" like a dog unleashed, a switch would flip and allow him to enjoy the cake. He notes the Pavlovian effect, how their words affected his body: they would, he said, release the drive by saying "now you can go for it." Their enjoyment was in seeing how their words affected his body. "I was never given an opportunity to learn how to regulate," he says.

It isn't clear whether he has a body outside the consistency provided by his substance use. From the mirror stage where the construction of the ego is synonymous with the body or body ego, a place for the imaginary as a field of feeling opens up with regard to others. Martin appears empty of feeling. There is a vacancy noted by his child, who says, "Dad, we are both a bit autistic." This is a question as to the status of his ego.

His girlfriends complain about his lack of emotional intimacy, and what they want in this regard perplexes him. I ask him where he goes in the moments of disengagement they complain of, and he says, "a neutral space where nothing is happening." Is it the real of the drive presenting in these speechless moments of stupor where the absence of signifiers makes itself felt (Declercq 2002, 103)? Addiction provides a means of administering jouissance, bypassing the symbolic Other and the dialectic of desire. Substances are used to give consistency to a body that is otherwise circumscribed by fear. In these moments his body operates not from desire but as an automaton of the drive determined by the maternal imperative. He uses alcohol to reach another "droning" state, as a way both to come closer to the body of the Other and to block out the anxiety of being reduced to a body controlled by words of the Other, reduced to an object in the gaze of the mother and her parents.

Over the years, his interest in transgression seemed to fade. His drug use and drinking lessened, and his anxiety diminished until recent encounters with a woman who pushes him back to jouissance. Beginning this new sexual relationship, he notes that he is "driven by access to the female body" and comments on his "psychotic tendency to take things literally." One day he announces that his "body is in turmoil" with body events provoked by this encounter: he sees the image of one woman superimposed on another, and on high alert, cannot sleep. While disrupting any "marriage between jouissance and the Little Willy" (Lacan, qtd. in Wright 2017, 79), there is a question of whether he can hold something together without drinking. This is marked by "an irrational thought" that maybe drinking less is straining his body parts. While he seeks out jouissance in order to fulfill the maternal imperative ("go for it") and have something happen in the place otherwise marked by a troubling vacancy, this leads to moments of encounter where his body is invaded by jouissance.

The image of a woman doesn't seem to operate as a cause of desire for him; rather the substance of his body gives him a jouissance in front of the woman/women. Fearing the effect of being reduced to an object body via the gaze and words of the maternal family, we could say that something doesn't function in the clothing of this object by the image, $i(a)$.

In the "Seminar on the Names-of-the-Father," Lacan commented on what is at stake in

> the scoptophilic drive, in which the subject encounters the world as a spectacle that he possesses. He is thus victim of a lure, through which what issues forth from him and confronts him is not the true *petit a*, but its complement, the specular image: *i(a)*. His image, that is, what appears to have fallen from him.
>
> (1974, 86)

Martin said he knew a previous relationship was over when his girlfriend saw him looking at her body and said something like "don't look" in a way that made him feel like an "old pervert." A nightmare had followed in which the terrifying gaze of the maternal grandfather appears as his own in an *unheimlich* way. This, Lacan notes, happens when

> through some accident more or less fomented by the Other, that image of himself within the Other appears to the subject as shorn of recourse. Here the entire chain in which the subject is held captive by the scopophilic drive comes undone. The return to the most basal mode anxiety is there ... registered ... in the relation of the subject to the *petit a*.
>
> (1974, 86)

When Martin senses he is not registered or received by an Other, anxiety seizes him as his image falls, as if his body ceases to be, and he seeks out an instrumental jouissance to reassure himself of a consistency where there is none. The image of the gaze that he sees in the dream is what he works with, though the object is not extracted and located in the field of the Other. It is rather the jouissance of the Other by which his body itself is reduced to an object while droning is a bodily experience, a stand-in for proximity to the Woman that makes his body exist.

Vacancy and the "neutral space where nothing is happening" are perhaps a version of the "unspeakable nakedness" that, Lacan writes, "insinuates itself into the place of" Lol V. Stein's body in the novel by Marguerite Duras, where "everything stops" as emptiness emerges from the specular image, $i(a)$ (1965, 125).

Éric Laurent, in a lecture on drug addiction and alcoholism given in 1996, commented that a prelude to analytic treatment might occur by means of imaginary identification with the statement "I am an alcoholic," yet it is a matter of turning this statement "I am an alcoholic" into a question regarding the subject's being so as to explore the identifications leading to it, to develop an interest in the unconscious, to "search in the unconscious for signs of this possible identification" (134) and the signifiers involved in marking the body's jouissance. The first thing drug addiction teaches us, he says, is that the object in question is not a substance but a semblance:

> It is precisely in drug addiction that we can find the most strongly sustained effort to incarnate the object of jouissance in an object of the world. It is precisely here that it may be verified that the object is semblance and that on the horizon, the true object of jouissance . . . is death.
> (Laurent 1996, 138)

Laurent adds that every

> object is a semblance precisely because it is a semblance of the core of absence; that which may be called death in the Freudian tradition. So the second thing drug addiction teaches psychoanalysis is . . . the fundamental link between all these toxic substances and man's fascination with feminine jouissance.
> (Laurent 1996, 138)

How then to slip something of this jouissance into the letter, both to isolate what is incurable and facilitate knotting a consistency? As an acoustic engineer, Martin worked with the aural object before focusing on another form of writing in online accounting. As Miller notes in 2016, the object $a$ "lies at the heart of the drive" and possesses some

> properties of the signifier. Notably, it presents through units. It is countable and numerable, and therefore is already a jouissance. If it is *surplus jouissance*, it's a surplus jouissance that is already shading off of jouissance, a modeling of jouissance on the model of the signifier.
> (2017, 100)

This, it would seem, is a way forward.

Analysis of the drive not only distinguishes psychoanalysis from psychotherapy, it constitutes, "the clinical weight" of each case, as Lacan says in his eleventh seminar (1964b, 162). Miller explicates how Lacan's earlier efforts to write the drive by identifying it with the signifying chain gave way to an emphasis on "the object *a* which he turned into his major invention" (2017, 100). The principle of Lacan's graph of desire consisted, Miller says,

> in identifying the drive with the signifying chain on the upper level of the graph.... This is a way of writing the drive as though it were nothing but a signifying chain, as though it had the same structure as the signifying chain.
>
> (2017, 100)

Stepping aside from downgrading the object *a* by seeing it only as a "sham" or false semblant in Seminar 20 allows this reversal, he says, to come about. In early work such as the Rome discourse of 1953, Lacan sought to conceptually separate the unconscious and the drives, in a binary division whereby the drives, drive satisfaction, and jouissance were seen as imaginary with "the symbolic intervening through speech only to master and efface" (Miller 2017, 99). This division gives way with the emphasis on the body as the instrument through which the speaking being speaks, where we see that from the "beginning of the signifying chain there is *jouis-sens*. The fort/da pair brings about an effect of meaning and allows for a production of jouissance," showing how the child accedes "to his '*parlêtre* by nature'" (Miller 2017, 100).

As Miller notes in his Commentary on Lacan's paper on the drive, what "needs to be determined is whether the institution of another relationship between the subject and identification can translate into another relationship between the subject and the drive" (1994, 424–425). Where castration as a lack of jouissance is not quite registered, substitution signals a signification of jouissance, which can occur without recourse to the Oedipal standard. The symptom is written with the body through the incidence of the letter.

By detaching the signifiers connected to the subject's jouissance, these marks of the subject's singularity, unveil "the function of the object, the roots of one's jouissance, beyond meaning" (Marret-Maleval 2020, 66). Without spaces in the body or between the body of one and the Other, the body is in trouble. We have seen the jouissance of the drive seeks to protect the subject from an anxious encounter, while operating in distinct ways in each of these cases.

A particular feature of the contemporary clinic is the presentation of vacancy. We have seen its manifestation in these two vignettes in different ways, though presenting in each case with regard to the imaginary clothing of the object, with the subject reduced or not registered via maternal speech or gaze. Evident in the imaginary, in the field of meaning and intersubjective relations, vacancy as a presentation of the real is distinct from absence marked in the symbolic with regard to presence. We might attribute this to a lack of symbolic registration on the one hand and mark its effects on the other. In this clinic of vacancy, if we can call it that, the work of construction comes to the fore. For "Being is signifying articulation with meaning and it is therefore a question of reading the letter in order to catch the body" (Stevens 2021).

## References

Declercq, Frédéric. 2002. "The Real of the Body in Lacanian Theory." *Analysis* 11: 99–114.

Lacan, Jacques. 1964a. "On Freud's '*Trieb*' and the Psychoanalyst's Desire." In *Écrits: The First Complete Edition in English*. Translated by Bruce Fink, 722–725. New York: Norton. 2006.

———. 1964b. *The Four Fundamental Concepts of Psycho-Analysis: The Seminar of Jacques Lacan*, Book XI. Edited by Jacques-Alain Miller. Translated by Alan Sheridan. New York: Norton, 1977.

———. 1965. "Homage to Marguerite Duras, on *Le ravissment de Lol V Stein*." In *Marguerite Duras by Marguerite Duras*. Translated by Edith Cohen and Peter Connor, 122–129. San Francisco: City Lights Books, 1987.

———. 1971. "On a Function That Is Not to Be Written—The Seminar of Jacques Lacan, Book XVIII, Chapter VI." Translated by Philip Dravers. *Hurly Burly* 9 (2013): 15–28, 25–26.

———. 1971–1972. *. . . or worse: The Seminar of Jacques Lacan*, Book XIX. Edited by Jacques-Alain Miller. Translated by A. R. Price. Cambridge: Polity, 2018.

———. 1974. *Television: A Challenge to the Psychoanalytic Establishment*. Translated by Denis Hollier, Rosalind Kraus, and Annette Michelson. New York: Norton, 1990.

———. 1975–1976. *The Sinthome: The Seminar of Jacques Lacan, Book XXIII*. Edited by Jacques-Alain Miller. Translated by A. R. Price. Cambridge: Polity, 2016.

Laurent, Éric. 1996. "From Saying to Doing in the Clinic of Drug Addiction and Alcoholism." *Almanac of Psychoanalysis* n.d.: 129–140.

Marret-Maleval, Sophie. 2020. "Purloined Letters." Translated by Arunava Banerjee. *Psychoanalytical Notebooks* 35: 9–125.

Miller, Jacques-Alain. 1994. "Commentary on Lacan's Text." In *Reading Seminars I and II: Lacan's Return to Freud*. Edited by Bruce Fink, Richard Feldstein, and Maire Jaanus, 422–427. Albany: State University of New York Press, 1996.

———. 2001. "Lacanian Biology and the Event of the Body." *Lacanian Ink* 18: 6–29.

———. 2011. "Being is Desire." Translated by Samya Seth. *Symptom* 18 (Fall 2019). lacan.com.

———. 2017. "*Habeas Corpus*." Translated by A. R. Price. *The Lacanian Review* 3: 94–100.

Stevens, Alexandre. 2021. "The Body Marked by Language." [Orientation text for the NLS Congress, Bodily Effects of Language, May 2021]. www.nlscongress2021.com/.

Wright, Colin. 2017. "'When the Fun Stops, Stop': Betting on Psychoanalysis in the Era of Segregation." *The Lacanian Review* 3 (Spring): 77–86.

Chapter 19

# The Liminal and the (Oral) Drive

Neurotic Tensions and Neo-Liberal Recuperations

*Carol Owens and Stephanie Swales*

---

*In this chapter, Carol Owens and Stephanie Swales explore liminality as a crucial concept in drive theory and argue that approaching the role and function of the drive requires considering the proxies for satisfaction afforded by late capitalism and contemporary culture. Capitalism's ceaseless injunction to enjoy, along with post-modern ideals and accompanying technologies and the requirement of interminable reinvention that never satisfy, means subjects are caught in an ideology of ceaseless liminality and consumption. This unceasing consumption results in disturbances of the oral drive indicated in the cultural proliferation of the culinary field and an explosion of eating disorders. Drawing with precision from Freud's case of Emmy von N., they propose that liminality is not only a site of psychic disorder locatable in disordered bodies and pathological eating/non-eating but that eating disorders are an attempt to offer a solution to the drive's encounter with the liminal.*

---

Drawing on conceptualizations of the liminal from research at the intersections of anthropology and the social sciences and integrating these with Lacanian psychoanalytic theory, we will propose that bodies come to act as sites of liminality and we will consider how that happens. As such, they set in motion the crafting of identities, regulatory practices, and methodologies at certain crucial points in the experiences of subjective transition and abjection. We come at this idea in two ways. First, we suggest a critique of the neo-liberalist promotion of the ideal of endlessly deferred becoming at the level of identity. We argue that this ideological apparatus of capitalism engages the speaking being in a series of transactions where an abundance of proxies for drive satisfaction are offered in exchange for ceaseless libidinal investment. Our second route brings us to a reconsideration of the acquisition of certain practices which may be viewed as solutions arrived at by the *parlêtre* (speaking-being) in her/his response to the irruption of drive and its relation to jouissance.

### But First, the Liminal

The liminal was originally conceptualized by Arnold van Gennep (1909) in his book *The Rites of Passage* to designate a transition from one social state to another and to identify patterns and forms associated with phases of transition. In his conceptualization, the "liminal phase" corresponded to a period during which a subject experiences ambiguity and inherent uncertainty with regard to identity. British anthropologist Victor Turner is credited with promoting the significance and relevance of van Gennep's work and the elaboration of the notion and implications of liminality. Turner (1969) was interested in exploring how an individual's experience and personality are shaped by liminality. In his work, Turner argued that individuals sometimes voluntarily enter a state of liminality by engaging in performative acts or by adopting behaviors unrestrained by the mundane classifications of every-day life. Turner's use of the phrase "betwixt and between" (95) captures the subject's liminal position in terms of conventional and everyday structures. We are particularly interested in the ways that the liminal concept has been taken up by recent theorists of culture and critical psychology, most notably Bjorn Thomasson (2014) and Paul Stenner et al. (2017).

What each draws attention to is the "experience" of the liminal. Thomasson emphasizes that liminality per se explains nothing; rather, liminality is a happening, and human beings react to liminal experiences in different ways (2014, 7). Liminality then is not a state of existence to be celebrated or glorified or wished for but instead duly and carefully problematized. This is so, he argues, because in a period such as ours which adopts a celebratory attitude towards anything that presents novelty and constant innovation, the notion of the liminal can be taken up as a positive expression of what Homi Bhabha in 1994 termed "cultural hybridity," an aspect of what Zygmunt Bauman (2000) described as "liquid modernity." Thomasson argues that liminality is a powerful tool of analysis used to explore different problems at the intersections of the anthropological and the political whereby *the formative and transformative* significance of liminal experiences can be studied. Considered in this manner, we are interested in how the analysis of liminal situations or encounters may indicate the ways that technologies of the self, in the Foucauldian sense, can be used to shape identities and institutions. Stenner's work on the liminal emphasizes the liminal experience as happening during occasions of significant transition, passage, or disruption. According to Stenner, we experience liminality when the forms of process (socio-psycho-organico-physical) that usually sustain, enable, and compose our lives are for some reason disrupted, transformed, or even suspended (2017, 14). Liminal experiences obtain a double function: they untie the ties that bind a given person into a given psycho-social position or place and they form new connections.

Coming at these uses of the concept of the liminal with our own Lacanian psychoanalytic lens raises a couple of issues for us in the first instance:

1. anthropological instances of the liminal as a phase or observable stage in the human life span raise the liminal to the status of experience but reify the notion of the liminal as a discrete object of study, as a phase or stage of existence;
2. critical theorists' conceptualizations of liminal experiences as essential responses to disruption at the level of identity and psycho-social position mobilizes a reflexive and ideologically accountable use of the concept but largely ignores that those experiences can only be articulated and experienced through

bodies that are speaking bodies, marked by the signifier, and caught in the circuit of the drives.

From our point of view, the speaking being is a being in time and has no other recourse except to that of a traumatic encounter with *tuché* as limit. As opposed to the automaton whereby the subject is determined by the chain of signifiers, the *tuché* is a causality marked by the drive, by the failures of the law and of meaning. The *tuché* as limit could be called the real as that which resists symbolization—death as a limit is an example—but other experiences of the liminal, the time between times, or between states of existence, take place within and between the registers of human experience, relying upon the signifier for their articulation with the symbolic economy within which each speaking being dwells.

## Liminal Beings: Biting off More Than They Can Chew?

In support of Thomasson and Stenner's emphases upon the experiences of the liminal and the trend towards the idealization of the liminal in our culture of liquid modernity, we are moved to introduce the term "liminal being" as a problematic new psycho-social position. Within this position, which is tied to the super-egoic injunctions of late capitalism to enjoy and to be unique, one is always becoming, never arriving. We argue that post-modern liminal creatures have a correlative new ego ideal, indexed upon the *destination* of a ceaseless reinvention, and the possibility of an endless source of existential guilt for never succeeding, never arriving there. One place where we can observe this performativity of the liminal is in contemporary practices associated with eating—food production, consumption, commodification, and preparation—together with their fetishistic variations under capitalism (e.g., nutritional "supplements" advertised as making the body complete). Here, the promotion of competing ideals under neo-liberalism fostering the endless consumption of objects in the quest for identity production crafts an interminable range of proxy possibilities for drive satisfaction and at the same time perpetuates an ideology of ceaseless or permanent liminality.

The food industry is a big business, and eating practices under modernity have become established as the signs and traits of the civilized subject with respect to social position. The post-modern turn according to which every consumer can be a producer, every lay-cook a culinary master in their own home, every home-baker an Instagram star with thousands of followers examining their sourdough experiments, exemplifies how post-modern ideals and their accompanying technologies are used to shape identities and practices. Via the logic of Lacan's discourse of the capitalist (1972), both as consumers and producers, speaking beings today are paradoxically more disturbed by the oral drive even as they consumptively reach toward $S_1$ after $S_1$—toward this or that culinary delight or new sourdough technique—that promises to satisfy and sooth the ravages of the drive. The home-baker Instagram star can both be a dispenser of S1s and herself—or her "brand"—operate as an $S_1$.

In his *Birth of Biopolitics* seminar, Michel Foucault (1979) described how neo-liberal doctrine was swiftly becoming widely established in Western societies, pointing to the creation of "homo economicus"; whereas in liberalism we had "a man who exchanges" (194), in neoliberalism we have a man who competes (12), and this extends from his economic activity to his social relations and identity. As ideology, it is produced from the experience of buying and selling goods which is then extended to other social spheres, forming an image of the daily life and typical subjects of a society. Neoliberalism subjugates not through governance but by operating on the desires and jouissance of homo economicus.

Homo economicus is "an entrepreneur of himself" (226), reducing the status of the *parlêtre* to its economic activity, to its status as consumer or producer. From marriage to higher education to eating a slice of pizza, any action carried out by homo economicus to increase its ability to achieve pleasure or earn money is an investment. In claiming that the neoliberal subject is an entrepreneur of the self, Foucault pointed out that what had been the self's relatively immutable feature—the body—has now become transformative through technologies. We can think here of contemporary practices of transforming the body: Lasik, plastic surgery, "cool sculpt," as well as the following of diets such as the Paleo diet, Slim Fast, Nutrisystem, flexitarian, Eco Atkins, Supercharged Hormone, and so on. When taken up by someone driven by the superegoic dictate of ceaseless liminality, just one of these social-capital-increasing practices is not enough. Here, where the liminal creature intersects with the ideal of the homo entrepreneur there is an unending attempt to acquire more and to improve the self.

The ideal of entrepreneurship is to be self-directed and self-employed, to make lots of money (of course), and often to be on the cutting edge of the tastes of consumers—perhaps even creating something consumers did not even know they craved. On both the side of the consumer and that of the entrepreneur, the invention and reinvention of products corresponds to the new superegoic imperative of perpetual doing and perpetual becoming that is "you doing you." Inevitably, with entrepreneurs such as Elon Musk being promoted in the social imaginary, complaints of anxiety and depression abound in the psychoanalytic clinic, along with an endless source of guilt for never "making it big." The demands to "enjoy yourself" and to succeed economically rest on an adulation of the image of the Other. On the other side of the coin are clinical complaints of falling short, which often manifest in attempts to bolster the ego or control the drives, through, for example, the unending quests to have more willpower, to become healthy, and so on.

We focus briefly now on a particular type of entrepreneur that we see as emblematic of the performativity of the liminal in modes of consumption, production, preparation, and commodification. The celebrity chef, as Mihalis Mentinis points out in his book, *The Psychopolitics of Food*, is at once a romantic figure of culinary artistic genius and, at the same time, the entrepreneurial ideal. Those who have achieved celebrity chef status have seemingly managed, as culinary artists, to have become uniquely themselves while achieving success and wealth in the same effort. "The 'magic' of cooking," says Mentinis, "intersects with discourses on the 'discovery of the true self' and 'self-actualization'; it is about the 'cooking' of the self so as to bring out its tastes and flavors" (2016, 15). The celebrity chef thus serves a function of transmission of the neoliberal injunctions to "be happy," to "enjoy," and to "be yourself"—which are all propagated at the level of the oral drive in our relationship to food. What's more, these days celebrity chefs are increasingly those who are always cooking up something more inventive than the next guy.

However, unlike other celebrity entrepreneurs such as Warren Buffett, the celebrity chef is intimately involved in the process of the food's production with her or his own hands. This seems to make the celebrity chef an unalienated worker, one that, according to Mentinis, is united organically with his or her product of work (2016, 14). In our view, the idea that the celebrity chef or anyone, for that matter, can de-alienate the worker from the product is a fantasy. Nevertheless, it is a fantasy which has a certain kind of effectiveness as it allows the liminal creature to imagine an end to the ceaseless striving for success and authenticity while at the same time paradoxically inspiring more efforts to cook inventively, to achieve a career as YouTuber doing what one already loves, and so on. In essence, this constitutes a doomed project of attempting to bring the drives under conscious control, involving a fantasy of the ego's ability to incorporate the drives into itself.

## Emmy, Oh Emmy, Why Did You Throw Your Pudding Away?

Another place where the liminal functions as suspended identity is in the permanent "betwixt and between" of the anorexic, the bulimic, and the orthorexic, where the noun functions not as identity but rather as a sign for the Other that the subject's desire is halted in flux. In psychiatry terms such as anorexia nervosa qua diagnosis are used once the presence of a number of pathological characteristics are observably present. Lacanian psychoanalysis, on the other hand, considers how these and other terms are adopted or adduced (but also refused) by the speaking being, who suffers in certain ways from permutations of the oral drive and the detours of the signifier. The speaking being may introduce themselves as "bulimic," as "anorexic," as "binge-eating," and so on, but the analyst may hear these terms as signifiers denoting that the subject's desire has become stuck, but stuck in a place of non-sticking, in a liminal space, that is. (However, even in this space, and perhaps especially because the liminal is so pressing, the identity captured by the adoption of the clinical term may prove useful in an otherwise transitory and transitional space and time.) If, along with Stenner et al., we consider that liminal experiences arise as responses to psychical disruption, interruption, and transition at the level of identity and to the destitution or disarray that accompanies an exit from a psychosocial position, we can think anew about the function of eating disordered symptoms and their signification for the desire of the speaking being.

As such we turn now to our second pathway of examination of the liminal and the drive. Here, in a move reminiscent of Durkheim's analysis of suicide, we are going to see how the liminal is another way of thinking about the existential dramas of the speaking being whose identity had held an important psychical function for them but it either has been torn away or the very position in which that identity functioned no longer exists.

As psychoanalysts, we observe that when the insignias of identity as constitutive of a "centered" self no longer hold, the speaking being may become temporarily or permanently derailed; we may see this in the experience of any lived pregnancy, marriage, separation, or bereavement, as examples of the most ordinary but typical disruptions to our notions of self-hood, identity, and subjectivity. In these experiences, our typical manner of drive satisfactions in the way we miss the object are subverted, and the beyond of the pleasure principle is painfully experienced. We may also see how encounters with the signifier of the lack in the Other may halt the *parlêtre* in a variety of traumatic episodes which set in motion an experience of the liminal. We can most often see this is in the clinical work with children and adolescents working through the traumata of change, loss, parental separation, or gender and sexuality troubles at the level of identity. As such, in our clinical work, we can come to consider how severely disordered speaking bodies come to act as sites of liminality; we use this term conscientiously, taking for granted that the liminalized body is one which is already dis-ordered, as in a state of disarray and disruption. What we see as ultimately disordered is desire, that which Lacan identifies as the drone of human existence, the motor of the fantasmatic relation with the Other. And this experience may then set in motion the attempt at recrafting an identity, making use of signifiers which are borrowed or imitated (we can think here of hysterical anorexic identification as a signifying operation by which the subject can temporarily tether themselves to the other, or anchor themselves in the Other). But we can also think of regulatory practices of eating and dieting which, together with techniques and crafts for bringing the body to order, provide practical and sometimes very effective responses to experiences of subjective transition and abjection. On the one hand, pro-ana and pro-mia blogs and websites inform and promote ways of eating/non-eating which allow the subject to ally with the other via the hysterical method of identification so nominated by Freud and later developed by Lacan (Freud 1923; Lacan 1958). On the other hand, seemingly banal practices of Paleo, Slimming World, Weightwatchers, and so on also allow for the mobilization of identification through crafting an eating practice founded on the notion of a community. In both cases, the subject forms a link with the Other or with others by way of the drive, just as in both cases the subject can find something which offers stillness in a time of extreme flux and liminality.

Let us review a very old case of Freud's (1893–1995), practically prepsychoanalytic, as a case study of a liminal being. We join Fanny Moser—Frau Emmy Von N.—for her session at lunchtime in the sanatorium with Freud. As he entered the room, he caught her in the act of throwing her dessert out through the window. It turned out that this was something she had been doing daily, and he further discovered that she regularly left about half of every meal on her plate. She told Freud that she was not in the habit of eating more and that she had the same constitution as her late father, who was also a "small eater." In addition, she only liked to drink "thick" fluids like milk, coffee, or cocoa, whereas water or minerals ruined her digestion. Freud straightaway responded to this very new material in the same way as many medical and mental health practitioners do today: even though she didn't strike him as "noticeably thin," he nonetheless thought it a good idea to recommend for her to drink more and to increase her food intake (Freud 1893–1995, 81).

On his next visit to her, he instructed her to drink alkaline water and forbade her from disposing of her pudding. Conceding to Freud's orders, she nonetheless warned him that it would turn out badly (81). When Freud found her the next time having eaten all of her food helpings and having drunk water, she was in a profoundly depressed state and complained of violent gastric pains. Things went downhill after this for both Emmy and Freud: she threatened to starve herself to rectify her digestion, he threatened to have her removed from the sanitorium if she didn't accept his theory that her gastric pain was due to [her] fear (82). At the end of this time period, Freud found her docile, submissive, and willing to accept his theory (but only because Freud told her so!). After putting her under hypnosis later that day, Freud finally asked her about her eating habits. An account of Emmy's eating and drinking particulars emerges at this point which indicates four key moments where a disruption at the level of subjectivity can be seen to launch Emmy into a liminal experience. In an attempt to shore up the disorder of this experience, Emmy adjusts her consumption of food and water or, as we could term it, crafts a regulated practice of eating in such a way as to allow her to move forward.

The first moment occurs when she is a child. Asked to eat her meat at dinnertime, Emmy refused, and her mother demanded that Emmy eat the meat two hours later after it had been left standing there, congealed, cold, and with the fat set hard on the plate. Her disgust upon recollecting this punishment remained current in her everyday experience of eating, since regardless of what was on the menu she saw "the plates before me with the cold meat and fat on them" (82).

The next part of the story is a memory of when she was in her early twenties following the death of her mother, and she was living with her brother who was an officer who had "that horrible disease" (82). Emmy knew that it was contagious, and she was terrified of picking up his knife and fork by mistake at the dinner table. Again, at this point in her telling of the story, she was visibly disturbed, and Freud said she shuddered. She went on to say that in spite of this fear, she ate her meals with him so that no one would find out that he was ill.

Soon after that, she recalled how she nursed her other brother, a consumptive, whose spittoon accompanied him to the dinner table and whose illness, coughing up phlegm, and so on, necessitated frequent spitting across the plates into the open spittoon (more shuddering). This made Emmy feel sick to her stomach, but she couldn't show it, she said, for fear of hurting his feelings. And when she sat down to eat, in her mind's eye she saw those spittoons on the table, and they still made her feel sick.

Finally, she recalled that when she was seventeen, she had gone with her family to Munich where they had all contracted a gastric virus due to drinking the water. The others had improved following medical attention, but her condition had persisted and had not even gotten better after drinking "mineral" water. She remembered thinking that *it wouldn't be of any use* even though "the doctor" had prescribed it.

Freud made short shrift of these eating symptoms—banishing them under hypnosis—and was delighted to report in the case history that the therapeutic effect under hypnosis was immediate and lasting, as she went on to eat and drink without "making any difficulty" (83). In his discussion of the case as a whole, Freud comments:

> She ate so little because she did not like the taste, and she could not enjoy the taste because the act of eating had from the earliest times been connected with memories of disgust whose sum of affect had never been to any degree diminished; and it is impossible to eat with disgust and pleasure at the same time.... Her old-established disgust at mealtimes had persisted undiminished because she was obliged constantly to suppress it, instead of getting rid of it by reaction. (89)

Certainly, we can see Freud's understanding of Emmy's anorexia as a hysterical symptom or, more precisely, what he would go on to develop as such.

We revisit Emmy's anorexic solutions here because they also seem to us to offer a valuable clue to thinking about the acquisition of certain eating habits at a time when desire/appetite is disordered, what we have been introducing here as the inauguration of the liminal experience in relation to the demand of the Other.

What we know from Lisa Appignanesi and John Forrester's (1992) detailed research on the background of Freud's case histories is that Emmy's entire childhood was seasoned with death. Her mother had fourteen children, of which only four (including Emmy) survived to adulthood, and Emmy would have experienced six of these deaths during the course of her own childhood and adolescence. When she was nineteen, Emmy found her mother dead. Hers is an existence marked by death and disease, giving rise to a recurring liminal state during which her desire is the only thing that lends stability to her existence. What makes the material Emmy gives to Freud even more interesting is the account of her anorexia which begins by her refusal of her mother's initial demand to eat meat by swallowing down the less appetizing version with the meat fat set hard. We thought it would be interesting to subject this symptom to Lacanian psychoanalytic scrutiny in relation to the signifier.

The German *Kummerspeck* is a compound noun consisting of two words. The first is *der Kummer*, which refers to emotional pains like concern, worry, sorrow, or anxiety. The second is *der Speck*, which can either mean "bacon" or "fat." Most translations of *Kummerspeck* render it as something like "grief fat" or "sorrow fat." So, what Emmy swallows down is a kind of suffering that has a name, *grief-fat*. This is a possible naming of the response of a little girl to a constant state of bereavement and sorrow, significantly a state of affairs in which her mother is the epicenter. Perhaps then the order of the material she gives to Freud from swallowing down the grief fat of her mother's, to swallowing down a whole host of other disgusting meals following her mother's death, can be considered afresh in this light.

The most affectively charged state in Emmy's case is not, as Freud thought, the disgust of the hysteric but rather the absence of limit between life, sickness, and death. Emmy installs an oral solution in order to delimit the liminal arising out of the *tuché* of her existence. This is a solution which Freud undoes under hypnosis, despite her having found it to be helpful to her for almost twenty years. Freud sees the presence of anorexia and responds with a demand for her to eat; we can see now with this attention to the signifier that Emmy's experience of the liminal inaugurated a shift in her desire/appetite such that refusal/delimitation and an identification with her father, whom she called a "small eater," functioned in certain important psychical ways. We may wonder if this late father also liked to refuse something of Emmy's mother and found a way to stage this refusal in his just eating a little of what he was offered. What seems clear is that what Emmy eats and drinks is conditioned by her own attempt to preserve a space for desire, a space that quite literally ends up as "half a plate." We can say that Emmy eats half a plate of food and half a plate of nothing. Having nothing, eating nothing, as Lacan realized, are ways to preserve desire in the encounter with the demand of the Other (1964, 104).

Eating disorders are very often attempts at an oral solution to the problematic of experiences of the liminal. As such attempts aim at ways to preserve a space for one's own desire, we find problematic the use of diagnostic labels because they try to fix the speaking being's identity and therefore result in wresting away the agency involved in any passage from one subjective position to another. Put differently, the speaking being's experiences of the labor of becoming are foreshortened in favor of an identificatory destination imposed upon them. Such an identity qua diagnosis operates according to a set of signs (for example, BMI, bone density loss, etc.) read from the body of the *parlêtre*, which could also be described as the attempt to solve or re-solve the tensions or paradoxes of the drive's encounter with the liminal. Missing this paradox risks condemning the *parlêtre* to endlessly circulate within a system of signs rather than finding, as with Emmy's "half a plate," a singular solution to the suffering of the drive's encounter with the liminal.

## References

Appignanesi, Lisa and John Forrester. 1992. *Freud's Women*. London: Phoenix.
Bauman, Zigmunt. 2000. *Liquid Modernity*. Cambridge: Polity.
Bhabha, Homi. 1994. *The Location of Culture*. London: Routledge.
Freud, Sigmund. 1893–1895. "Studies on Hysteria." In *Standard Edition of the Complete Psychological Works of Sigmund Freud*. Vol. 3. Translated by James Strachey. New York: Norton, 1953.
———. 1923. "The Ego and the Id." In *Standard Edition of the Complete Psychological Works of Sigmund Freud*. Vol. 19. Translated by James Strachey, 7–64. New York: Norton, 1953.
Foucault, Michel. 1979. *The Birth of Biopolitics. Lectures at the College de France 1978–1979*. London: Palgrave Macmillan.
Lacan, Jacques. 1958. "The Direction of the Treatment and the Principles of its Power." In *Écrits. The Complete Edition in English*. Translated by B. Fink. New York and London: Norton, 2006.
———. 1964. *The Four Fundamental Concepts of Psycho-Analysis: The Seminar of Jacques Lacan*, Book XI. Edited by Jacques-Alain Miller. Translated by Alan Sheridan. New York: Norton, 1977.
———. 1972. "Discours de Jacques Lacan à l'université de Milan." *Lacan in Italia* 32–55.
Mentinis, Mihalis. 2016. *The Psychopolitics of Food: Culinary Rites of Passage in the Neoliberal Age*. London: Routledge.
Stenner, Paul, Monica Greco, and Johanna Motzkau. 2017. "Introduction to the Special Issue on Liminal Hotspots." *Theory and Psychology* 2 (27): 141–146.
Thomasson, Bjørn. 2014. *Liminality and the Modern: Living Through the In-Between*. London: Ashgate.
Turner, Victor. 1969. "Liminality and Communitas." In *The Ritual Process: Structure and Anti-Structure*, 94–130. Chicago: Aldine Publishing.
Van Gennep, Arnold. 1909. *Les Rites of Passage*. Paris: A. et J. Picard.

# Chapter 20

# The Drive as Montage

## Freud, Lacan, Moths, and Poetry

*Annie G. Rogers*

---

*The psychoanalyst, writer, and artist Annie Rogers draws inspiration from the interweaving of the mysterious worlds of moths and poetry to give an account of the drive as both discontinuous and metaphorical. These contradictory characteristics of the drive are playfully rendered and offer the reader a deeply creative approach to the drive that resounds in its writing in the existential crisis of the 2020 COVID-19 pandemic. Annie's extraordinary prints and the work of their creation set out the death-bearing aspect of moths that connects to our unbound excessive, potentially deadly drive in so far as we live by the death drive and carry death in our most intimate relations and ardent desires. Dreams, montage, and assemblage are themes that underpin a Lacanian field of drive, the implications of which are essential to the psychoanalytic act of listening.*

## Introduction

To explore the drive as a montage, I turn to original prints of moths and lines of poetry that grew out of a daily practice of writing and drawing—alongside my practice as an analyst—over a period of four months. Turning to Freud and Lacan, the online Oxford English Dictionary, and the South African printmaker William Kentridge, in the context of my project, I construct the working of the drive as a metaphoric process (bridging discontinuous elements to convey something otherwise impossible) and as metonymic in its path (illustrated through images presented as a series with linkages among them). The moth prints and poetry, made together during the ongoing COVID pandemic, retain their references to this particular historic moment.

Why moths? To moths, light is both irresistibly attractive—and potentially deadly.

## One: Drawn to the Light

1626. Francis Bacon *Sylua Syluarum* §696, The Moath breedeth upon Cloth; . . . It delighteth to be about the Flame of a Candle (OED, "moth" 2a).

In the summer and autumn of 2020, during the pandemic, I found myself drawing moths. Why were they were calling out to me? I did not know.

*Figure 20.1* Drawn to Light, Annie G. Rogers

This writing on the drive grew out of my daily practice of drawing and writing lines of poetry to accompany the drawings. My drawing of moths became a monotype with an overlay of darkness. Moths navigate by traverse orientation, staying on course over long distances by the light of the moon. The lights of our world have disoriented them, and, more than that, light pollution has contributed to their thinning numbers.

I wrote on September 17: "Ready to go to that unmistakable destiny, is it a thrill emptied of fear? How radiant the moths become before immolation."

The lines I wrote do not pertain to moths but to the human subject, the subject of the drive, particularly the death drive.

Freud conceived of the death drive (*Todestrieb*) as following a compulsion to repeat and in fundamental opposition to the life drive, or Eros. But he also claimed that the life drive and the death drive never exist in their pure states. The death drive pushes the subject "beyond the pleasure principle" (1920)—outside of stasis and pleasure into bodily dysregulation, whose next limit is death.

Lacan argued that "Every drive is virtually a death drive" (1964b, 719). Every drive goes beyond the pleasure principle, involves the subject in repetition, and produces an excess of jouissance in which enjoyment is experienced as suffering.

The unbound drive is excessive, potentially deadly. As human beings, far from following the instincts of moths, we live by the death drive, ourselves carriers of death in our most intimate relations and ardent desires.

To be drawn to the light is to veer toward death. And, even if we conceive the light as "enlightenment" and ourselves as knowing what we are doing and saying, the effects of our acts are, in fact, deadly.

## Two: Time and Its Guest

> 1885. *Cent. Mag.* Dec. 258/1 Bee-time and moth-time, add the amount; White heat and honey, who keeps the count? (OED, "moth time")

When I first drew this image of two bees on August 26, 2020, I did not expect moths to appear in the dark corners. I did not anticipate them, nor did I later recognize them, even after pulling the print, but thought instead that the bees were moths! Although the unconscious does not keep time, the drive counts in a strange way: forwards, backwards, in loops and reversals, erasing, repeating, turning this way and that, endlessly. And what is counting but some attempt to order disorder?

If, as Freud proposed, the unconscious is timeless, how is it possible that the temporality of the drives is governed by repetitions and reversals, loops of time? Freud is eloquent on the versatility of the drives: "Reversal of an [drive] into its opposite revolves around two processes: a change from activity to passivity, and a reversal of its content" (1915, 127). The objects of the drive may be displaced, given up, turned into something else, and reversed. If the unconscious is timeless, it is also intent in a periodicity of what is at play in the drive and does so through a strange counting. At one time, this is at play, then that, then whoops, the "that" erased, the "this" repeats, then "that" insists yet again.

The artist William Kentridge, leaning into repetition in his studio practice, writes in his book *Six Drawing Lessons*:

> I find and repeat the list four or five times in different notebooks. . . . Each time I expect the list to be different; each time to my surprise, it is the same, or almost

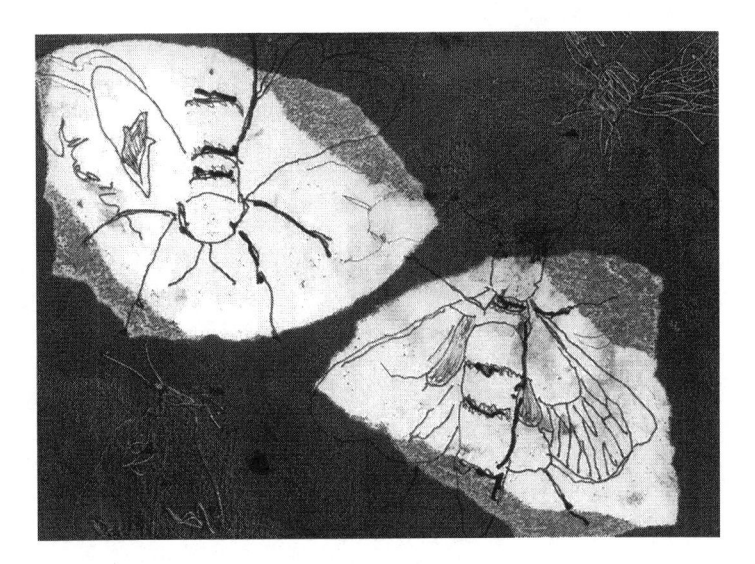

*Figure 20.2* Bee-Time and Moth-Time, Annie G. Rogers

the same. But in the reordering, the slight shift, the word that is illegible, we make some new crack, a new element enters the list, makes a space for itself—and this is the guest we have been waiting for.

(117)

What is happening with time here? Lacan characterized the unconscious in terms of a temporal movement of opening and closing (1964a, 143, 199). He also abandoned any linear notion of time in the formation of the subject and in the experience of analysis. The unconscious functions in retroaction, and in anticipation. This *après-coup* moment of return does not return our histories, but resignifies them, re-marking time. Likewise, the time of anticipation follows the future perfect tense, an expected future that does not arrive; in our haste, something else that escapes us, does arrive. This reminds me of Kentridge's "guest."

And what of the drive? Let us recall that "the letter" for Lacan underpins the entire structure of language and the symbolic, but it has no meaning in itself; it is of the real and is also of the body and its drives. Another way to think of the letter is that it is the guest of language circulating through signifiers to form the body itself. The letter is the guest of the drive.

### Three: Marks and Traces

> 1950. T. S. Eliot *Cocktail Party* i. i. 42 There's no memory you can wrap in camphor but the moths will get in.
>
> (OED, "moth" 4a)

These two prints, made on the same day, entailed brushing graphite powder on drafting vellum, pushing the powder around with my fingers and drawing a few lines in graphite pencil before turning the vellum upside down on a plate rolled with transparent extender to transfer the graphite image in reverse. Then the plate went through an etching press. The second print is the ghost, which appears to dissolve. I made the prints from two drawings on August 17, 2020, accompanied by my note: "A surface becomes a dusted wing." In the process of printing, marks of the drawing became traces.

In 1925, Freud composed a little essay, "Note on a Magic Notepad," in which he developed an elaborate metaphor for the disappearance of memories and the remains or traces of them in the unconscious:

> It does not strike me as excessively audacious to equate the covering sheet consisting of celluloid and waxed paper with the system of Pcpt.-Cs. and its stimulus barrier, and the wax slab with the unconscious behind it, the visible appearance of the writing and its disappearance with the flashing and fading of consciousness in perception.
>
> (1925, 104–105)

The Drive as Montage 251

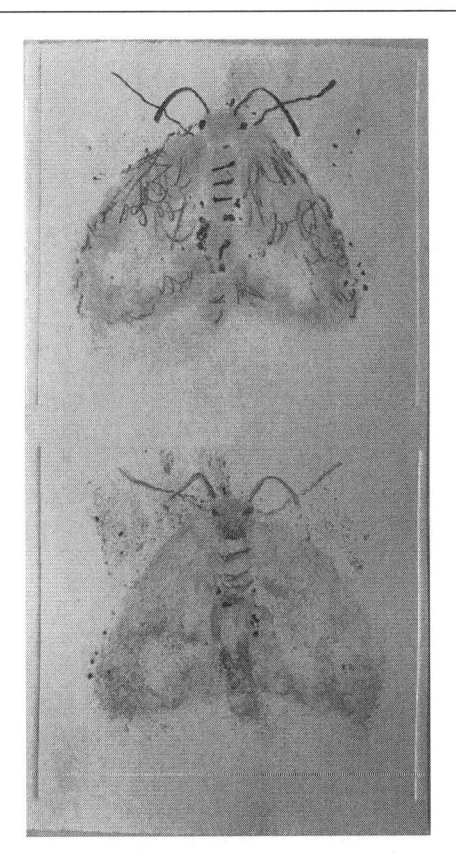

*Figure 20.3* Moth and Ghost, Annie G. Rogers

The wax slab contains all the marks, but they have become lost to us, unreadable, a palimpsest of memories that have vanished. Writing anything new entails clearing the sheet, making a space for new notes through a process of erasure. How does the drive inscribe and erase memory? What of the drive can we read in unconscious marks and traces? And how? Lacan too writes of marks, memories, history, and traces.

The unconscious is a chapter of my history that is marked by a blank or occupied by a lie: it is the censored chapter. But the truth can be refound; most often it has already been written elsewhere:

- in monuments: this is my body, in other words, the hysterical core of neurosis in which the hysterical symptom manifests the structure of a language, and is deciphered like an inscription which, once recovered, can be destroyed without serious loss;
- in archival documents too: these are my childhood memories, just as impenetrable as such documents are when I do not know their provenance;

- in semantic evolution: this corresponds to the stock of words and acceptations of my own particular vocabulary, as it does to my style of life and my character;
- in traditions, too, and even in the legends which, in a heroicized form, convey my history;
- and lastly, in its traces that are inevitably preserved in the distortions necessitated by the insertion of the adulterated chapter into the chapters surrounding it, and whose meaning will be reestablished by my exegesis.

(Lacan 1953, 50–51)

The drive inscribes the body, marks us in ways that can only be deciphered to a point—where memories become impenetrable and traces become distorted by elements inserted as "the adulterated chapter," which can only be read through the subject's own exegesis.

We are inscribed with the dust of vanished memories and distorted readings.
We are the moth-eaten clothes of the drive.

## Four: A Necessary Stupidity

1921. W. de la Mare. *Veil & Other Poems*. Soundless the moth-flit.

(OED, "moth-flit")

After a week of drawing moths in flight, in arcs and trajectories, getting off the ground like small planes, I drew this moth and was immediately struck by its

*Figure 20.4* Still Moth, Annie G. Rogers

stillness. "Moths waken you," I wrote on September 22; "Stilled, they wait for you." But what was I doing during these months? What were they wakening me for, and waiting for what from me?

"A necessary stupidity," a phrase William Kentridge repeats in interviews, writings, and lectures, is the heart of his practice in the studio. "I am a great believer that stupidity gives the work its impulse," he said in an interview for the *Harvard Magazine* (2012). He described walking about, playing with materials, filming himself and watching himself, playing with projections, animations, texts, his etching press, with an air of extraordinary stupidity about what will come of any of these moments. I have come to trust this stupidity in myself, too.

Freud wrote of his famous case, the Wolf Man, "Soon a missing blank between the two incidents, as regards both time and content, came into his memory" (1918 [1914], 265). To arrive at such a moment, both the patient and the analyst must enter a space of stupidity, of not knowing and of waiting. This stupidity—not knowing, is it crucial to the drive, drive as desire? It waits. It wakens, reawakens, and you do not know what it is that is driving you, or where it is taking you.

In a chapter from his eleventh seminar titled, "The Freudian Unconscious and Ours," Lacan caught something of the stupidity of the unconscious in its vacillation: "Discontinuity, then, is the essential form in which the unconscious first appears to us as a phenomenon—discontinuity, in which something is manifested as a vacillation" (1964a, 25). The drive working in the body is stupid with respect to what we can say of it, its circuits through and around the body, opening, vacillating, closing, seeking its object at its very source.

Silence has its say; stillness and waiting, not knowing, gaps that form a void. The unconscious opens, vacillates, closes. Signifiers chain, circle the unsayable, the unknowable, session after session, year after year, and, in the end, what?

A necessary stupidity—when all that deciphering ends, there is impossibility, and you must learn what to do with your symptom, how to live with a distinctive signature of impossibility, a kind of necessary stupidity.

My moth in its stillness wakens me to this necessary stupidity.

## Five: The Dream, the Navel, the Real

> 1965. J. Caird *Murder Reflected* iii. 31 I just wanted to ask if you'd be free to come mothing with me this evening ... (OED, "moth," v. 2).

"Moth" may be used as a verb, with its variant "mothing"—hunting moths.

I drew this large moth on September 1 and printed it two days later. I'd wakened from a dream: I saw an infant in a hospital, supine in an ICU, unconscious. Yet the infant was able to observe a beautiful, large moth flying above her. I wrote, "What is it to mark and re-mark a moth?"

We waken from a dream, and assure ourselves it wasn't real, yet the dream lingers and insists that we search for a meaning. But why, when we write down the dream as faithfully as possible, does it become so *un*readable?

*Figure 20.5* Moth, Beside Itself, Annie G. Rogers

Our dreams, Freud argued, are triggered by an excess of drive energy in the body that cannot be spoken. The dream constructs the drive as it seeks images and words for experiences that we cannot access. Freud noted that dreams embrace impossible contradictions, cobble together vastly different times and places, use word play such as puns and idioms, and include nonsense elements. If we are to read our dreams, we must go through associations to each element, finding the "dream thoughts" that formed the dream we remember (Freud 1900).

Even so, the drive will leave us with a conundrum, the impenetrable "navel" of the dream, where the elements of the dream revolve around the unknown.

For Lacan, the dream uses signifiers to give its distinctive form. The subject of the unconscious, speaking the dream and her/his associations, appears in a flash—through surprising linkages between signifiers. The analyst, listening, underlines words, phrases, even phonemes.

When we receive our own "message" coming back to us in some *surprising or new form*, it comes from the *Es*—what Freud called the *id*—the "it," which we cannot know directly. When this happens, if only for a split second—the unconscious opens and gives us a glimpse of a world that is utterly Other to us.

There is something about a dream that eludes us, something beyond speech, which Lacan called "the real."

That real of the dream left in its wake, a moth, moving out its own body in flight. Was that flight into death itself, or into life, a life signed already by the death drive? Signed from the start, from my origins?

> We traverse the difficult space between 'I dreampt' and 'there came to me in a dream.' We are projectors and receivers of that which is in us, which we do not know.
> (Kentridge 2014, 20)

I am "mothing" my dreams during this pandemic. I am the moth, hunted and haunted by signifiers from the unknown.

## Six: Drive as Montage

> Acronym MOTH, the initial letters of *Memorable Order of Tin Hats*, the name of an organization founded in Durban, Natal, in 1927 by Charles Evenden.
> (OED, moth, n. 3)

When I assembled these collage pieces on October 30, I did not recognize that the various fields alongside the moths resembled the intricate marks of moth wing veins I'd been drawing for months.

Moths Other Than Hoped.
Mythic Other Too Harrowing.
M Oth(er) . . .
M. O. T. H.

Collage or montage? A depiction of edges and relations, or an assemblage utterly beyond recognition.

Freud conceived of the drive as a montage built of discontinuous elements: pressure, end, object, and source. It seeks an object irretrievably lost and thus impossible. Drives are not instincts, which follow a biological logic, nor are they primordial. Human beings experience the drives bodily, and yet the drives are inextricably caught in language and culture. Freud argued that the drives were mobile in the body and polymorphous with respect to sexuality (any part of the body can be eroticized). For Freud the pressure of the drive never ceases and, in fact, can and does go too far, into death itself.

The unbound drive.

Lacan returned to Freud's idea of the drive as montage. He added new elements and articulations to the drive, conceptualizing the drive as a constellation of lost partial objects: breast, feces, gaze, and voice, working together as a montage.

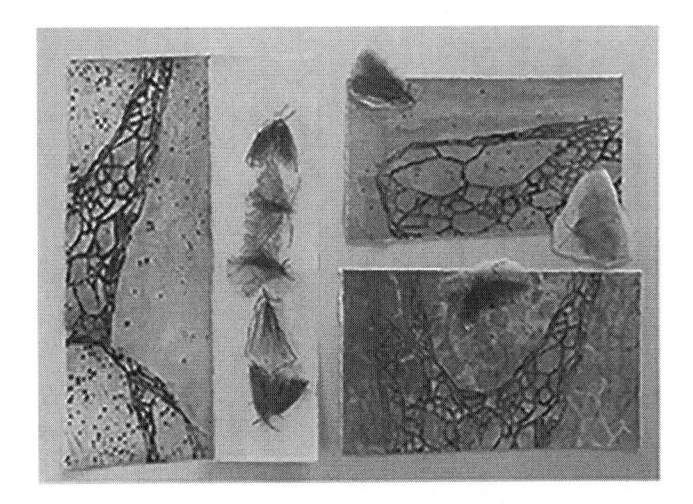

*Figure 20.6* Moth Collage in Progress, Annie G. Rogers

In his *Anxiety* seminar, Lacan (1962–1963) linked the drive with the object cause of desire, as object *a*, itself a montage, a residual of language, yet unnamable. For Lacan every drive partakes of death, veering toward a destructive excess without limit.

The drive makes a path in our bodies that marks us; as it circles an impossible object, it signs our life and our death.

An impossible object, already lost, makes a montage of drive elements and makes the experience of drive bearable.

What else could I possibly say? Nothing. Mothing much more.

"I am only an artist; my job is to make drawings not to make sense" (Kentridge, 41).

I am only an analyst; my job is to listen, not to make sense.

## EPILOGUE

"Moths—in a Time of Pandemic"

Wherever moths land
    A surface becomes a dusted wing

                  Resembles a worn carpet moss and peaches
                        Its body a crude tunnel

One has come to rest on the rough ceiling
    Its sugar-sprinkled wings stilled

                    Introduce any changes slowly
                        So as not to startle the moth

It is injurious to move them
    No matter how gently

                    Like white peonies blooming by the porch
                        Moths give off a certain light

In the early hour cosmology
    A large moth summonses
    A smaller one

                    We know nothing of their multitudes-
                        Of wings washing the dark.

I do not know myself dreaming
    And moths forget me as I sleep.

                    Folding myself toward sleep
                        Nothing suits me, I am a suit of nothing.

I put on my wings like a great coat
    Soft, floating at night.

**Annie G. Rogers**

## References

Freud, Sigmund. 1900. "The Interpretation of Dreams." In *Standard Edition of the Complete Psychological Works of Sigmund Freud*. Vols. 4 and 5. Translated by James Strachey. New York: Norton, 1955.

———. 1918 [1914]. "From the History of an Infantile Neurosis [The Wolfman]." In *The "Wolfman" and Other Cases*, 203–320. New York: Penguin Books, 2002.

———. 1915. "[Drives] and Their Vicissitudes." In *Standard Edition of the Complete Psychological Works of Sigmund Freud*. Vol. 14. Translated by James Strachey, 111–140. New York: Norton, 1957.

———. 1920. "Beyond the Pleasure Principle." In *Standard Edition of the Complete Psychological Works of Sigmund Freud*. Vol. 18. Translated by James Strachey, 3–64. New York: Norton, 1955.

———. 1925. "Note on the 'Magic Notepad." *The Penguin Freud Reader*. Edited by Adam Phillips. London & New York: Penguin Books, 2006.

Kentridge, William. 2014. *Six Drawing Lessons*. Cambridge, MA: Harvard University Press.

Lacan, Jacques. 1953. "The Function and Field of Speech and Language in Psychoanalysis." In *Écrits: A Selection*. Translated by Bruce Fink, 31–106. New York: W. W. Norton & Company, 2004.

———. 1962–1963. *Anxiety: The Seminar of Jacques Lacan*, Book X. Edited by Jacques-Alain Miller. Translated by Adrian Price. Cambridge: Polity Press. 2014.

———. 1964a. *The Four Fundamental Concepts of Psychoanalysis: The Seminar of Jacques Lacan*, Book XI. Edited by Jacques-Alain Miller. Translated by Alan Sheridan. New York, NY: Norton, 1977.

———. 1964b. "The Position of the Unconscious." In *Écrits: The First Complete Edition in English*. Translated by Bruce Fink, 703–721. New York: Norton, 2006.

Lenfield, S. L. 2012. *Harvard Magazine*. See harvardmagazine.com/2012/03/william-kentridge-in-praise-of-shadows.

# Index

abuse, sexual abuse 217, 221
acting out 126
addiction, drug use, alcoholism 227, 228, 231–233
affirmation (*Bejahung*) 133, 136
alienation 29–30, 109, 132
analytic treatment 62, 94, 141, 151, 224, 232
anxiety 11, 92, 100, 112, 128, 156, 163–166, 180–182, 192, 197–200, 202, 223, 227, 228, 231, 232, 239, 243, 253
art, artwork 93, 181, 191, 228
autism 110, 155, 157, 159, 160, 178, 180, 181
autoerotic, autoerotism 14, 91, 111, 112, 132, 133
*automaton,* automatism 23, 32, 143, 144, 147, 188–190, 206, 231, 237

*Beyond the Pleasure Principle* (Freud) 1, 6, 15–21, 32, 33, 53–65, 67–75, 90–91, 128, 129, 139, 142, 165, 173, 177, 207, 220, 222, 246
binary, binarism 30, 72, 104, 108, 156, 234
biological determinism 3, 80, 84, 87
biology, biological processes 9, 15, 20, 21, 48, 67, 69, 73, 80, 84, 85, 99, 101, 115, 119, 177
bisexuality 57, 84–86
body 8–9, 12, 13, 18, 22, 31, 55, 57, 61, 62, 82, 83, 87, 93, 101, 103–110, 112, 115, 123, 128, 130–132, 140, 143–145, 151–154, 157, 159, 163, 164, 166–168, 170–173, 177–179, 181, 186, 197, 199–200, 203, 211, 217, 219–221, 225, 226, 227–234, 238, 239, 241, 244, 248–254

breast 101, 104, 105–107, 110, 111, 118–119, 123, 132, 152, 153, 166, 175, 176, 178, 179, 196, 198, 253

castration 21, 25, 27, 138, 145–146, 192–193, 234
childhood 22–23, 90, 110, 111, 113, 171, 243, 249
*Civilization and its Discontents* (Freud) 20, 32, 34, 36, 37, 56
constancy, principle of 60, 102, 142, 169
consumption 101, 238–239, 242
COVID-19 106, 112, 128, 225, 227, 245
cut of the signifier 16, 152, 199
cutting (symptom) 181, 228

demand 7–9, 22–28, 53, 57, 63, 82, 90, 92, 107, 113, 123, 125, 135, 147, 181, 194, 195, 198, 201, 202, 219, 225, 228, 239, 242–244
depersonalization 159
desire 1, 4, 24, 28, 30, 35, 63, 82, 92, 99, 112, 124–125, 131, 132, 134, 136, 147, 148, 167–168, 170, 178, 182, 185–187, 191, 193, 196–197, 201–204, 222, 225, 230–233, 240–241, 243–244, 251, 253
development 1, 3, 5, 21–22, 102, 129, 134, 163, 165, 179, 196
diagnosis 180–181, 225, 240, 244
discourse 23, 31, 129, 177, 180, 200, 238
displacement 100, 141, 212
displeasure 91, 118, 132
dream, dreams, dreaming 105, 172, 182, 200, 221–223, 251–252
drive, aim of the (*Ziel*) 9, 47, 93, 105, 117, 119, 120, 124, 140, 230
drive, anal 9, 21, 102, 104, 111, 112, 152–155

drive, as myth 82, 92, 99, 122, 133, 140
drive, circuit 106–108, 112, 113, 121, 141, 182, 237, 251
drive, death (in Freud) 19–20, 32–34, 36–37, 59–65, 67–75, 90–92, 94, 134, 139–141, 146–148, 177–178, 206–213, 245, 246, 252
drive, death (in Lacan) 34, 37, 62–64, 75, 91–92, 94, 109, 129–131, 136, 206–213, 246, 252, 254
drive, death (*Thanatos*) 1, 18, 20, 71, 90, 206–213
drive, dermic 151–161
drive, enjoyment 110, 123, 178, 182, 203–204, 246
drive, genital 9, 21, 91, 103, 122, 165
drive, goal of the 126, 230
drive, grasping (*Grieftrieb*) 106
drive, invocatory 99, 102, 104, 111, 152, 154, 155, 196–197, 204
drive, life (*Eros*) 1, 18, 20, 33, 71, 72, 90–91, 134, 172, 177, 178, 207, 245
drive, object of the (*Objekt*) 9, 12–15, 19, 24, 27–28, 33–34, 94, 101, 104, 117–121, 125, 131–134, 136, 140, 167–171, 177–182, 185–187, 192–194, 196–200, 204, 251, 253–254
drive, oral 107, 112, 118, 119, 153, 154, 171, 238, 239, 240
drive, partial 16, 57, 62, 103, 121, 122, 132, 151, 152, 171, 217, 219, 224, 225
drive, polymorphic 253
drive, pressure of the (*Drang*) 8, 34, 102, 117, 139, 253
drive, respiratory 163–173
drive, scopic, scopophilic 12–13, 102, 104, 107–108, 152, 154, 155, 192–193
drive, sexual (libido) 1, 9, 11, 17, 19, 22, 24, 26, 32–34, 36, 45, 53, 57–61, 63–65, 81, 82, 90, 91, 115, 122, 131, 132, 134, 140, 143, 152, 170, 179, 208–210
drive, silent, mute 3, 38, 164, 204
drive, source of the (*Quelle*) 9–10, 22, 103, 119, 121, 140, 142, 145
"Drives and their Vicissitudes" (Freud) 1, 6–15, 18, 45, 48, 50, 51, 84, 102, 108, 110, 112, 117, 120–122, 132–134, 139, 141, 171, 176
drives, ego 14–17, 20, 33–37, 58
DSM 84, 178

eating disorders 227, 240, 244
ego 53, 58, 62, 73, 74, 75, 132–134, 151, 154, 159, 160, 203
*Ego and the Id, The* (Freud) 61, 65, 74, 151
ego ideal 134, 136, 238
ego psychology 36, 77, 82–86
elusion 185, 186
Emmy von N. (case) 202–203, 240–244
entropy 74, 176
enunciation 123, 124, 147, 173
erogenous zones (rim structures) 22, 101, 119, 152, 170–172, 219, 230
ethics, psychoanalytic ethics 15, 36, 87
exhibitionism 12–13, 108, 111, 122

fantasy, fantasm, fundamental fantasy 23–28, 55–59, 61–65, 71, 99, 102, 125, 132, 134, 140, 146, 148, 165–166, 185, 187, 194, 204, 222, 224–226, 239–241
fate 29, 78, 82, 142, 152, 189
father 26, 194, 203, 231, 241, 243
Fellini, Federico 136
fetus 179–180
film 35, 119, 203
fixation 29, 104, 122, 152, 155, 161, 212
foreclosure 64, 160
fort/da 60, 61, 72, 91, 142, 192, 199, 213, 223, 234
frustration 105, 145, 147, 148, 178, 198
fundamental concept (*Grundbegriff*) 51, 129, 140

gaze, look 13, 111, 132, 185–195, 196–200, 225, 229–232, 253
German language 6, 28, 43–52, 90, 243
*Group Psychology and the Analysis of the Ego* (Freud) 128, 134, 136

hate 12, 14–15, 132–133
helplessness (*Hilfosigkeit*) 112, 133, 165, 202
homeostasis 177
homosexuality 77, 79, 81, 83–87
hunger 7, 101–102, 176
hysteria, hysterics, hysterical 58, 119, 165, 171, 241, 243, 250

id 53, 62, 74, 75, 124
identification 23, 35, 108, 132, 136, 159, 229, 230, 232, 234, 241, 243
imaginary 28–29, 31, 58, 134, 144–146, 197, 202, 227, 231, 232, 234, 239

instinct (*Instinckt*) 1–2, 6, 14, 34, 47–49, 51, 57, 59, 80–84, 86, 90, 93, 99–102, 109, 130, 152, 164, 171, 176, 206–210, 246, 253

Jakobson, Roman 158
jouissance of the body 91, 109, 180–181, 229–231, 232, 229
jouissance, feminine 233
jouissance, of speech 25–26, 197–487, 234
jouissance, of the Other 26, 110, 131, 232
jouissance, phallic 57, 126
jouissance, sexual 57, 64, 141, 212
jouissance, surplus 123, 206, 233

Klein, Melanie 177–179
knotting 130, 146, 197, 233

lalangue 131, 141, 196, 198
language 9, 25–27, 29, 32, 92–94, 99, 105, 108, 117, 121–124, 129–131, 135, 141–144, 147, 164, 168, 172, 183, 196–199, 248–249, 253
law 4, 136, 180, 198, 217, 237
lay analysis, lay analysts 77–87
letter 233, 234, 248
libido, libidinal *see* "drive (sexual)"
literature 86, 195
look *see* gaze (look)
love 12, 14–15, 17, 19, 24, 35, 37, 121, 131–137, 166, 170, 173, 175, 177, 196, 203

masochism 12, 73, 108
metaphor 9–10, 25, 124, 131, 203, 223, 249
metonymy, metonymic 9, 25, 158, 212, 245
Miller, Jacques-Alain 22, 64, 117, 122–124, 201, 230, 233–234
mirror image, specular image, *i*(*a*) 35, 92, 186, 200, 231, 232
Moebius strip 140
mother 24, 26, 30, 91, 101, 106, 110–111, 113, 122–123, 132, 163–170, 175, 176, 178–182, 192, 198, 199, 201–203, 228–231, 242–244
motivation 1, 3, 23–24, 28, 84, 100, 115–116

*Nachträglichkeit see* "retroaction"
Name-of-the-Father 30, 64, 232
narcissism 19–20, 34–37, 58–59, 132–136, 173
natural order 21–22, 115–120, 130

negation (*Verneinung*) 121, 133, 188, 190
negativity 206–213
neologisms 156
neurosis, neurotic 16–18, 36, 57–60, 62, 64, 65, 126, 164, 168, 177, 178, 181, 202, 217–226, 230, 236–244, 249
Nirvana principle 60, 141, 177, 178, 206, 208

object *a* (*objet a*) 125, 131, 132, 140, 141, 148, 185–187, 192–194, 196, 197, 230, 233, 253
object relations 111
object, partial 198, 200, 204, 253
obsessional neurosis 22, 169, 173, 194
"On Narcissism" (Freud) 58–59, 132, 173
Other, big Other 18–27, 32, 36, 57, 67, 77, 90, 100, 116, 129, 138, 144, 151, 164, 175, 185, 196, 201, 207, 217, 227, 237, 249

philosophy 20, 28–29, 86, 172–173, 190, 206
plasticity, mental 100–101, 102, 104, 107
pleasure 90–91, 93, 104, 118–119, 131–133, 153, 154, 165, 168, 172–173, 176–178, 224, 238, 242, 246
pleasure principle 15–21, 54–61, 63, 64, 67–75, 128, 129, 142, 148, 153, 165, 173, 177, 207, 240, 246
poetry, poetic 73, 86, 93, 94, 104, 245
primary process 18, 74, 75, 151
privation 146
psychiatry 240
psychosis 64, 65, 144, 155–157, 159, 160, 177–180, 197, 200, 203, 204
psychotherapy 233
punctuation 128, 134–137, 146, 155–161

real 2, 14–15, 54–56, 58, 65, 108, 128–134, 146, 186, 189–190, 198, 201, 202, 228, 231, 237, 248, 251–252
reality principle 16, 18, 55, 59, 63, 140, 145, 212
reflexivity 122, 171, 237
repetition, repetition compulsion 16–19, 60, 61, 67, 73–75, 139, 181, 207, 209, 213, 245
representation, mental 2, 4–6, 9, 10, 28, 71, 115, 123, 143, 166, 168, 197
repression 11, 16, 29–30, 37, 57, 64, 102, 119, 120, 130, 141, 172
retroaction, deferred action (*Nachträglichkeit*) 21, 121, 122, 165, 248

sadism 12–13, 32, 108, 122
Saussure, Ferdinand de 121, 155, 160
Schema, graphs 29, 82, 102, 107, 203
schizophrenia 58, 158
Schreber, Daniel Paul 156
Science and Truth (Lacan) 43
secondary process 18, 73, 74
semblance 201, 230, 233
Seminar, Lacan's Seminar 1 (*Freud's Papers on Technique*) 62; Seminar 2 (*The Ego in Freud's Theory*) 61, 62, 82, 189; Seminar 3 (*Psychosis*) 156; Seminar 4 (*Object Relations*) 5; Seminar 5 (*Formations of the Unconscious*) 27, 48; Seminar 6 (*Desire*) 147; Seminar 7 (*Ethics*) 47, 124; Seminar 8 (*Transference*) 135; Seminar 10 (*Anxiety*) 152, 185, 186; Seminar 11 (*Four Fundamental Concepts*) 3, 14, 31, 38, 46, 61, 62, 82, 99, 107, 109, 110, 116, 118, 121, 123, 143, 185, 187–189; Seminar 14 (*Logic of Fantasy*) 125, 126; Seminar 17 (*The Other Side of Psychoanalysis*) 214; Seminar 18 (*On a Discourse*) 230; Seminar 19 (*. . . or worse*) 235; Seminar 20 (*Encore*) 122, 233; Seminar 23 (*Sinthome*) 197
separation 29, 30, 33, 92, 109, 125, 132, 134, 163–165, 169, 179, 240
sexuality, human 57, 81, 84, 86, 90, 207
sexuation, sexual difference 131, 165
signifier, cut of the 130, 192, 201
signifier(s) 23–30, 74, 82, 104, 107–108, 121, 130, 143, 145, 147, 157–161, 172, 189, 192, 211, 218, 220, 221, 228, 231, 233, 237, 240, 241, 243, 248, 251, 252
skin (*see also* "drive, dermic") 151–161
speaking-being (*parlêtre*) 129–131, 136, 170, 227, 234, 236, 239, 240, 244
specular image, *i(a) see* "mirror image"
speech 29, 91–93, 104, 107, 111, 115–126, 129, 131, 156, 164, 167, 170, 197–198, 200, 201, 219, 230
subject 11–17, 22–30, 32, 34–36, 43–45, 53, 58, 64, 91–93, 102, 104, 108–112, 121–125, 129–134, 136, 138–148, 151–157, 168, 170, 178–179, 185–194, 197, 199–202, 204, 206–213, 218, 219, 225, 226, 227–230, 232, 234, 236, 238, 240–247, 250, 252
sublimation 10, 117, 120, 124, 130, 141
suicide 138, 139, 240
symbolic 6, 6, 14, 22–23, 28, 54–56, 58, 61, 65, 75, 131, 134, 141, 179, 181, 206, 207, 210–212, 219, 225, 227, 228, 230, 231, 234, 237, 248
symbolization 60, 74, 133, 210, 213, 222, 237
symptom 62, 91, 100, 117–119, 131, 163–165, 167, 180, 182, 201–202, 218, 220, 222–224, 227, 229, 234, 243, 249, 251

technology, technological devices 169, 180, 181, 237–239
Thing, the (*das Ding*) 64, 230
*Three Essays on the Theory of Sexuality* (Freud) 57, 80, 90
transference 16, 17, 60, 73, 99–100, 121, 123, 125, 135–136, 144, 147, 221
translation, translating 38, 43–48, 50–52, 93, 116–119, 121, 124, 131, 185, 188, 189, 194, 220–221, 243
trauma, traumatic 16–18, 24, 67, 72–75, 92, 129, 163–165, 189, 194, 200, 237, 240
*Trieb* 1, 6, 28, 37, 43–52, 90, 99, 124, 130, 131
*tuche* 143, 189–190, 237, 243
Twain, Mark 44, 49

unconscious 4, 11, 18, 29–30, 37, 54–58, 61, 62, 64, 65, 70, 73–75, 81, 86, 93, 94, 99, 108, 109, 116, 121–122, 129–131, 136, 139–143, 145, 147, 148, 166, 170, 171, 173, 177, 179, 181, 196, 197, 201, 206, 221, 225, 227, 228, 230, 232, 234, 246–249, 251–252

voice, (*see also* "drive, invocatory") 122, 132, 170, 179, 182, 183, 196–204, 230, 253
voyeurism 108, 111, 122

Winnicott, Donald 106, 111, 166–168

Žižek, Slavoj 206–213

9781032292496